Contents

Component 1 Section A

Component 1 Section B

Component 2 Section A

Component 2 Section B

Tables of Legislation

Acts

Bills

Statutory instruments

Conventions and Treaties

EU Law

Table of cases

xxi

Introduction

This book has been written and designed for the new OCR Law specifications introduced for first teaching in September 2017.

OCR A Level Law for Year 1/AS covers the content for required for OCR AS Law for first examination in 2018. To view the full specifications, and examples of assessment material for OCR AS or OCR A Level Law, please visit OCR's website: www.ocr.org.uk.

How to use this book

Each chapter has a range of features that have been designed to present the course content in a clear and accessible way, to give you confidence and to support you in your revision and assessment preparation.

Learning objectives

Each chapter starts with a list of what is to be studied and how these relate to the specification.

Key terms

Key terms, in bold in the text, are defined.

Key case

Description of a case and a comment on the point of law it illustrates.

Tips

These are suggestions to help clarify what you should aim to learn.

Extension tasks

These include challenging activities for students striving for higher grades.

Look online

These weblinks will help you with further research and reading on the internet.

News story

Real events relating to specific areas of law are covered.

Summary

These boxes contain summaries of what you have learned in each section.

Activities

Activities appear throughout the book and have been designed to help you apply your knowledge and develop your understanding of various topics.

Practice questions

These are questions to help you get used to the type of questions you may encounter in the exam.

Book coverage of specification content

AS Level	A Level	Coverage
H015/01 (AS) H415/01 (A Level) The legal system and criminal law		
Section A: The legal system		
Introduction to the nature of law	**Introduction to the nature of law**	
Law and rules: the difference between enforceable legal rules and principles and other rules and norms of behaviour	Law and rules: the difference between enforceable legal rules and principles and other rules and norms of behaviour	Book 1, Chapter 1.1
The connections between law, morality and justice	The connections between law, morality and justice	Book 1, Chapter 1.2
The differences between civil and criminal law	The differences between civil and criminal law	Book 1, Chapter 1.3
An overview of the development of English law: custom, common law, equity, statute law	An overview of the development of English law: custom, common law, equity, statute law	Book 1, Chapter 2.1
An overview of common law and civil law legal systems	An overview of common law and civil law legal systems	Book 1, Chapter 2.2
The rule of law: definition and importance	The rule of law: definition and importance	Book 1, Chapter 2.3
Civil courts and other forms of dispute resolution	**Civil courts and other forms of dispute resolution**	
County Court and High Court: jurisdictions, pre-trial procedures, the three tracks	County Court and High Court: jurisdictions, pre-trial procedures, the three tracks	Book 1, Chapter 3.1–3.5
Appeals and appellate courts	Appeals and appellate courts	Book 1, Chapter 3.6
Tribunals and Alternative Dispute Resolution	Tribunals and Alternative Dispute Resolution	Book 1, Chapter 4.1–4.3
Online courts and Online Dispute Resolution	Online courts and Online Dispute Resolution	Book 1, Chapter 4.3.4
Evaluation of the civil courts and other forms of dispute resolution	Evaluation of the civil courts and other forms of dispute resolution	Book 1, Chapter 3.7, 4.2–4.4
Criminal courts and lay people	**Criminal courts and lay people**	
Criminal process: Jurisdiction of the Magistrates' Court and the Crown Court, including classification of offences and pre-trial procedures	Criminal process: Jurisdiction of the Magistrates' Court and the Crown Court, including classification of offences and pre-trial procedures	Book 1, Chapter 5.1–5.4
Appeals and appellate courts	Appeals and appellate courts	Book 1, Chapter 5.5–5.7
Sentencing and court powers: aims, factors and types of sentences	Sentencing and court powers: aims, factors and types of sentences	Book 1, Chapter 6
Lay magistrates and juries: qualifications, selection, appointment and their role in criminal cases	Lay magistrates and juries: qualifications, selection, appointment and their role in criminal cases	Book 1, Chapters 7 (lay magistrates), 8 (juries)
Evaluation of the different types of sentences and of using lay people in criminal cases	Evaluation of the different types of sentences and of using lay people in criminal cases	Book 1, Chapter 6.3 and 6.4 (sentences), 7.7 (magistrates), 8.5 (juries)
Legal personnel	**Legal personnel**	
Barristers, solicitors and legal executives: qualifications, training, work and the regulation of legal professions	Barristers, solicitors and legal executives: qualifications, training, work and the regulation of legal professions	Book 1, Chapter 9.1–9.7

AS Level	A Level	Coverage
Changes and trends in legal services, including the impact of technology and globalisation	Changes and trends in legal services, including the impact of technology and globalisation	Book 1, Chapter 9.9
The judiciary: qualifications, selection and appointment, training, role, retirement and removal	The judiciary: qualifications, selection and appointment, training, role, retirement and removal	Book 1, Chapter 10.1–10.5
The separation of powers and the independence of the judiciary	The separation of powers and the independence of the judiciary	Book 1, Chapter 10.7, 10.8
Evaluation of the legal professions and the judiciary	Evaluation of the legal professions and the judiciary	Book 1, Chapter 9.2.2, 9.3.2, 9.8 (legal professions), Chapter 10.6, 10.7, 10.9.7 (judiciary)
Access to justice	**Access to justice**	
Government funding for civil and criminal cases	Government funding for civil and criminal cases	Book 1, Chapter 11.1–11.5
Private funding, conditional fees and other advice agencies	Private funding, conditional fees and other advice agencies	Book 1, Chapter 11.6–11.7
Evaluation of access to justice	Evaluation of access to justice	Book 1, Chapter 11.8
Section B: Criminal law		
Rules	**Rules**	
An outline of the rules of criminal law	An outline of the rules of criminal law	Book 1, Chapter 12
General elements of criminal liability	**General elements of criminal liability**	
Actus reus: conduct and consequence crimes; voluntary acts and omissions; involuntariness; causation	*Actus reus*: conduct and consequence crimes; voluntary acts and omissions; involuntariness; causation	Book 1, Chapter 13
Mens rea: fault; intention and subjective recklessness; negligence and strict liability; transferred malice; coincidence of *actus reus* and *mens rea*	*Mens rea*: fault; intention and subjective recklessness; negligence and strict liability; transferred malice; coincidence of *actus reus* and *mens rea*	Book 1, Chapter 14
Non-fatal offences against the person	**Non-fatal offences against the person**	
Common assault: assault and battery under s 39 Criminal Justice Act 1988	Common assault: assault and battery under s 39 Criminal Justice Act 1988	Book 1, Chapter 15.1
Assault occasioning actual bodily harm, wounding and grievous bodily harm under s 47, s 20, s 18 Offences Against the Person Act 1861	Assault occasioning actual bodily harm, wounding and grievous bodily harm under s 47, s 20, s 18 Offences Against the Person Act 1861	Book 1, Chapter 15.2–15.4
Critical evaluation of non-fatal offences against the person, including ideas for reform	Critical evaluation of offences against the person, including ideas for reform (offences against property and defences – covered in Book 2)	Book 1, Chapter 15.5

H015/02 (AS) H415/02 (A Level) Law making and the law of tort

Section A: Law making		
Parliamentary law making	**Parliamentary law making**	
Influences on Parliament: political, public opinion, media, pressure groups and lobbyists	Influences on Parliament: political, public opinion, media, pressure groups and lobbyists	Book 1, Chapter 16.2
Legislative process – Green and White Papers, different types of Bill, legislative stages in the House of Commons and the House of Lords, and the role of the Crown	Legislative process – Green and White Papers, different types of Bill, legislative stages in the House of Commons and the House of Lords, and the role of the Crown	Book 1, Chapter 16.4
Advantages and disadvantages of influences on law making	Advantages and disadvantages of influences on law making	Book 1, Chapter 16.3
Advantages and disadvantages of the legislative process	Advantages and disadvantages of the legislative process	Book 1, Chapter 16.5

AS Level	A Level	Coverage
Delegated legislation	**Delegated legislation**	
Types of delegated legislation: Orders in Council, statutory instruments and by-laws	Types of delegated legislation: Orders in Council, statutory instruments and by-laws	Book 1, Chapter 17.1
Controls on delegated legislation by Parliament and the courts, and their effectiveness	Controls on delegated legislation by Parliament and the courts, and their effectiveness	Book 1, Chapter 17.2
Reasons for the use of delegated legislation	Reasons for the use of delegated legislation	Book 1, Chapter 17.3
Advantages and disadvantages of delegated legislation	Advantages and disadvantages of delegated legislation	Book 1, Chapter 17.4
Statutory interpretation	**Statutory interpretation**	
Rules of statutory interpretation – the literal rule, the golden rule, the mischief rule	Rules of statutory interpretation – the literal rule, the golden rule, the mischief rule	Book 1, Chapter 18.2
The purposive approach	The purposive approach	Book 1, Chapter 18.3
Aids to interpretation: rules of language, intrinsic and extrinsic aids	Aids to interpretation: rules of language, intrinsic and extrinsic aids	Book 1, Chapter 18.4, 18.5
Impact of European Union Law and the Human Rights Act 1998 on statutory interpretation	Impact of European Union Law and the Human Rights Act 1998 on statutory interpretation	Book 1, Chapter 18.6, 18.7
Advantages and disadvantages of the different approaches and aids to statutory interpretation	Advantages and disadvantages of the different approaches and aids to statutory interpretation	Book 1, Chapter 18.5 (aids), 18.4 (approaches)
Judicial precedent	**Judicial precedent**	
The Doctrine of Precedent including *stare decisis*, *ratio decidendi* and *obiter dicta*	The Doctrine of Precedent including *stare decisis*, *ratio decidendi* and *obiter dicta*	Book 1, Chapter 19.1–19.2
The hierarchy of the courts including the Supreme Court	The hierarchy of the courts including the Supreme Court	Book 1, Chapter 19.3–19.5
Binding, persuasive and original precedent; overruling; reversing; distinguishing	Binding, persuasive and original precedent; overruling; reversing; distinguishing	Book 1, Chapter 19.6–19.7
Advantages and disadvantages of precedent	Advantages and disadvantages of precedent	Book 1, Chapter 19.9
Law making: law reform	**Law making: law reform**	
Law reform including the Law Commission	Law reform including the Law Commission	Book 1, Chapter 20.1–20.2
Advantages and disadvantages of law reform bodies	Advantages and disadvantages of law reform bodies	Book 1, Chapter 20.3, 20.4.1, 20.5.1
European Union law	**European Union law**	
Institutions of the European Union	Institutions of the European Union	Book 1, Chapter 21.2, 21.3
Sources of European Union law	Sources of European Union law	Book 1, Chapter 21.4
Impact of European Union law on the law of England and Wales	Impact of European Union law on the law of England and Wales	Book 1, Chapter 21.5
Section B: The law of tort		
Rules	**Rules and theory**	
An outline of the rules of the law of tort	An outline of the rules of the law of tort	Book 1, Chapter 22.1
	An overview of the theory of the law of tort	Book 1, Chapter 22.2
Liability in negligence	**Liability in negligence**	
Liability in negligence for injury to people and damage to property: The duty of care – *Donoghue v Stevenson* (1932) and the neighbour principle, and *Caparo* test	Liability in negligence for injury to people and damage to property: The duty of care – *Donoghue v Stevenson* (1932) and the neighbour principle, and *Caparo* test	Book 1, Chapter 23.1–23.2

AS Level	A Level	Coverage
Breach of duty: the objective standard of care and the reasonable man; risk factors	Breach of duty: the objective standard of care and the reasonable man; risk factors	Book 1, Chapter 23.3
Damage: factual causation and the 'but for' test; legal causation	Damage: factual causation and the 'but for' test; legal causation	Book 1, Chapter 23.4
	Defences	
	Contributory negligence	Book 1, Chapter 23.7.1
	Volenti non fit injuria	Book 1, Chapter 23.7.2
Occupiers' liability	Occupiers' liability	
Liability in respect of lawful visitors (Occupiers' Liability Act 1957)	Liability in respect of lawful visitors (Occupiers' Liability Act 1957)	Book 1, Chapter 24.3
Liability in respect of trespassers (Occupiers' Liability Act 1984)	Liability in respect of trespassers (Occupiers' Liability Act 1984)	Book 1, Chapter 24.4
	Defences	
	Contributory negligence	Book 1, Chapter 24.3.5, 24.4.3
	Volenti non fit injuria	Book 1, Chapter 24.3.5, 24.4.3
Remedies	Remedies	
Compensatory damages	Compensatory damages	Book 1, Chapter 25.1
Mitigation of loss	Mitigation of loss	Book 1, Chapter 25.2
	Injunctions	Book 1, Chapter 25.3
Evaluation	Evaluation	
Critical evaluation of liability in negligence including ideas for reform	Critical evaluation of liability in negligence including ideas for reform	Book 1, Chapter 23.6
Critical evaluation of liability in occupiers' liability, including ideas for reform	Critical evaluation of liability in occupiers' liability, including ideas for reform	Book 1, Chapter 24.5

Preface

This book and the follow on Book 2 are written for the OCR Specification for A Level Law. All the topics for AS Law for the English legal system, criminal law and the law of tort are included in this book. The order of topics follows that of OCR's AS specification. There is also a chart setting out the coverage and where to find the related material in this book.

As well as the factual material on the topics, evaluation is included for all areas where it is required by OCR's specification.

The text is broken up into manageable 'bites' and throughout the text we have used features which have proved popular in previous texts for A and AS Level Law. These include key facts charts, case charts, highlighting cases and diagrams.

Activities for students are also included. These are based on a variety of material such as newspaper and internet articles, research material and cases. There are also application tasks for students to practice applying the law to given scenarios.

The law is as we believe it to be on 1 March 2017.

Jacqueline Martin
Nick Price

Component 1

SECTION A

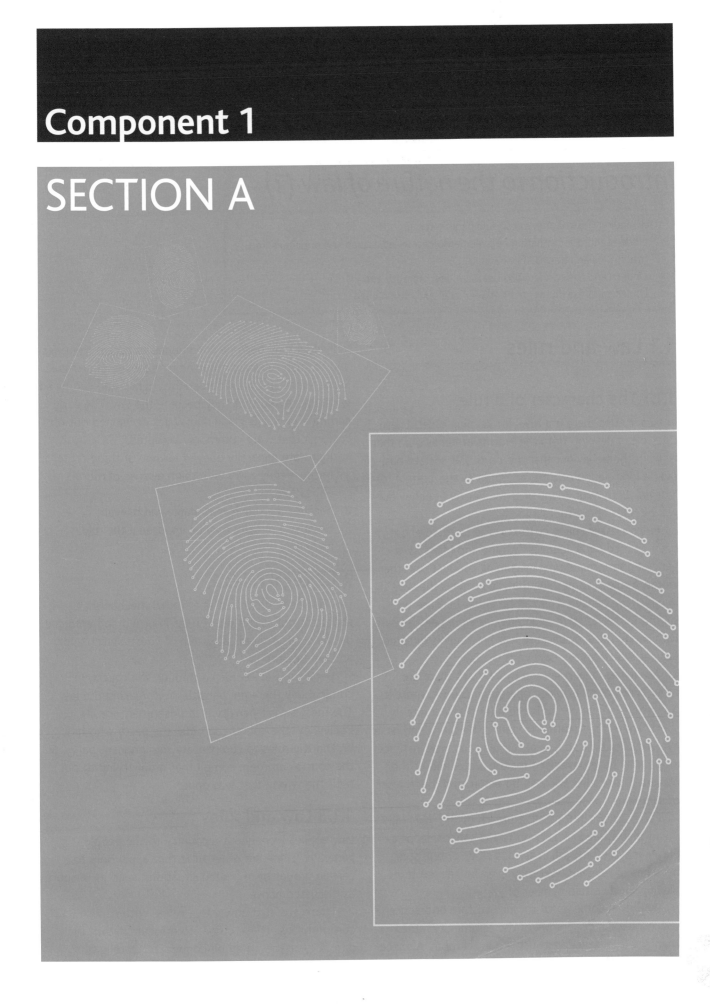

Chapter 1

Introduction to the nature of law (1)

After reading this chapter you should be able to:
- Understand the distinction between enforceable legal rules and principles and other rules and norms of behaviour
- Understand the connections between law, morality and justice
- Understand the differences between civil and criminal law

1.1 Law and rules

1.1.1 The character of a rule

In all societies there are rules for keeping order. These rules often develop from the 'norms of behaviour': that is, from the behaviour that the particular society has, over a long period of time, accepted as the 'correct' or 'normal' behaviour. Many of these norms of behaviour will be rules about morality.

Rules exist in many contexts. The term 'rule' has been defined by academics Twining and Miers as 'a general norm, mandating or guiding conduct'. In other words, a rule is something that determines the way in which we behave. This can be either because we submit ourselves to it voluntarily, as would be the case with moral rules, or because it is enforceable in some way, as would be the case with the law.

As well as legal rules and moral rules there are other types of rules which operate in specific contexts. A classic example of this is the rules that operate in sport. These rules started to define the sport, and have evolved over time to ensure fair play. In some instances a rule may have developed for the protection of the players. These rules will also be enforced through a set of sanctions.

For example, in football, a breach of the rules may mean that a free kick is given to the other side, or a player may be sent off. In serious cases or repeated breaches of rules a player may even be banned from playing for a certain number of games.

Rules that come about through custom or practice will involve the disapproval of the community rather than any legal sanction if such a rule is broken. Also the individual may become conditioned to accept the rules and so such rules are enforced by a feeling of self-guilt. Some such rules may 'harden into rights' and can be so widely accepted that they become the law. The early common law of England and Wales developed out of customs that were commonly accepted.

Rules are generally obeyed for one of three reasons:
1 because they carry with them a sense of moral obligation
2 because the rule is reasonable and relevant
3 because a penalty may be imposed if the rule is broken.

1.1.2 Legal rules

Law has been described as a formal mechanism of social control. It is a set of rules imposed and enforced by the state. There is a system of courts which apply and enforce the law.

Legal rules are enforced through the courts. In criminal law there are penalties for breaking the law. The most severe penalty is imprisonment for life. In civil law the courts can order the party who has broken the rules to compensate the innocent party, or the courts can make some other order trying to put right the wrong that was done.

1.1.3 Law and rules

Law applies throughout a country to the people generally. There are other rules that apply only to certain groups or in limited situations, such as in sport as discussed above.

There are also unwritten 'rules' within communities. These come from local custom or practice, or they may be connected to religious beliefs. They enforce what is regarded by the community as the norm for behaviour. If you break such rules, others in the community may disapprove of your behaviour, but there is no legal sanction to force you to comply or to punish you if you refuse to do so. Such normative values are often connected with sexual behaviour and the concept of morality. The relationship of law and morality is explored in the next section of this chapter.

1.1.4 Norms of behaviour

Norms are values, customs and traditions which represent individuals' basic knowledge of what others do and think that they should do. Norms exist as collective representations of acceptable group conduct as well as individual perceptions of particular group conduct. They evolve slowly through time.

Norms may be based on religious ideas: the Bible teachings provide a code for Christian communities and the teachings in the Koran for Muslims.

The law of a country will usually reflect the moral values accepted by the majority of the country, but the law is unlikely to be exactly the same as the common religious moral code. One example is adultery: this is against the moral code for both Christians and Muslims but is not considered a crime in Christian countries; however, in some Muslim countries (though not all) it is against the criminal law.

Law	Norms of behaviour
Can change instantly	Develop over time
Must be obeyed	Ought to be obeyed
Are enforced by the courts	Are enforced by disapproval of the community
Are obligatory and apply to everyone	Are voluntary and apply only to those who accept them

Figure 1.1 Differences between norms of behaviour and law

1.2 The connections between law, morality and justice

1.2.1 Law and morality

The moral values of communities lay down a framework for how people should behave. Concepts of morality differ from culture to culture, although most will outlaw extreme behaviour such as murder.

The moral standards of a community are recognised as having a profound influence on the development of law, but in complex societies, morality and law are never likely to be co-extensive. Major breaches of a moral code (such as murder and robbery) will also be against the law, but in other matters there may not be consensus.

In England and Wales there has been a move away from religious belief and the way that the law has developed reflects this. Abortion was legalised in 1967, yet many people still believe it is morally wrong. A limited form of euthanasia has been accepted as legal with the ruling in *Airedale NHS Trust v Bland* (1993), where it was ruled that medical staff could withdraw life-support systems from a patient who could breathe unaided, but who was in a persistent vegetative state. This ruling meant that they could withdraw the feeding tubes of the patient, despite the fact that this would inevitably cause him to die. Again, many groups believe that this is immoral as it denies the sanctity of human life.

Extension activity ✔

In *Re A (conjoined twins)* (2000) the Court of Appeal had to decide whether doctors should operate to separate conjoined twins when it was certain that the operation would kill one twin as she could not exist without being linked to her twin.

1 Search on the internet for a report of this case. Try **www.bailii.org** and look under the England and Wales reports and search using the case citation (reference) of [2000] EWCA (Civ) 254.
2 Discuss:
 a whether this sort of decision should be made by judges
 b whether you think that, knowing one child would die, it was right for the operation to go ahead.

Right to die

This is another area where law and morality can be in conflict. In medical cases, doctors and nurses should act in the best interests of the patient. This may be in conflict with the patient's wishes. Where a patient is mentally capable of deciding what treatment they wish to receive, then the medical staff must act in line with those wishes. A good example of this conflict is the case of *Re B (Adult: Refusal of Medical Treatment* (2002).

Key case

Re B (Adult: Refusal of Medical Treatment) (2002)

Ms B was a 43-year-old woman, who was paralysed from the neck down. She needed a ventilator to breathe. There was no prospect of her recovering. She made numerous requests for her ventilator to be switched off, knowing that it would inevitably lead to her death. The doctors refused to do this, so she applied to the High Court for a declaration that she had the necessary capacity to refuse treatment and that her ventilator should be removed.

The court held that she was competent to decide on her medical treatment and that any continued treatment would be unlawful.

The judge in the case pointed out that the fact that a patient's wishes go against the medical team's values and their beliefs about what is in the patient's interests is not a valid justification for refusing the patient's request.

If the team in charge of the patient is unwilling to act on the patient's request, they must find someone who will.

Differences between law and morality

There are also differences between law and morality in the way the two develop and the sanctions imposed. The following is a suggested list of such differences.

1 Morality cannot be deliberately changed; it evolves slowly and changes according to the will of the people. Law can be altered deliberately by legislation: this means that behaviour which was against the law can be 'decriminalised' overnight. Equally, behaviour which was lawful can be declared unlawful.

2 Morality is voluntary with consequences, but generally carries no official sanction (though some religions may 'excommunicate'); morality relies for its effectiveness on the individual's sense of shame or guilt. Law makes certain behaviour obligatory with legal sanctions to enforce it.

3 Breaches of morality are not usually subject to formal adjudication; breaches of law will be ruled on by a formal legal system.

1.2.2 Law and justice

It is often said that the law provides justice, yet this is not always so. Justice is probably the ultimate goal towards which the law should strive, but it is unlikely that law will ever produce 'justice' in every case.

First there is the problem of what is meant by 'justice'. The difficulty of defining justice was commented on by Lord Wright, a judge in the House of Lords in the mid-twentieth century, who said:

> the guiding principle of a judge in deciding cases is to do justice; that is justice according to the law, but still justice. I have not found any satisfactory definition of justice ... what is just in a particular case is what appears just to the just man, in the same way as what is reasonable appears to be reasonable to the reasonable man.

In some situations people's concept of what is justice may not be the same. Justice can be seen as applying the rules in the same way to all people, but even this may lead to perceived injustices – indeed rigid application of rules may actually produce injustice.

This can be seen in the case of *London & North Eastern Railway Co. v Berriman* (1946).

Key case

London & North Eastern Railway Co. v Berriman (1946)

Mr Berriman (V) was a railway worker who was killed while doing maintenance work, oiling points on a railway line. Regulations said that a look-out person should be provided for those working on the railway line 'for the purposes of relaying or repairing'.

Mrs Berriman claimed compensation for her husband's death, but her claim was rejected because he had not been 'relaying or repairing' the line.

This illustrates that following the exact wording of laws can lead to an injustice. It was correct that Berriman was not 'relaying or repairing', but most people would agree that applying the law in this way was not justice. You will come across this case again in Chapter 18 on statutory interpretation.

In the law of tort, an example of where many people thought that justice had not been done by the law were the cases which arose out of the Hillsborough Football Stadium disaster in 1989. Families of the victims tried to claim for psychiatric injuries they had suffered as a result of the death of their loved ones in the disaster. Judges in *Alcock v Chief Constable of South Yorkshire* (1992) rejected such claims on the basis of public policy.

1.2.3 Morality and justice

People's ideas of what justice is may be founded on their religious beliefs and the moral code they follow. In this way there is an overlap between morality and justice. However, many people with no religious views will still have a sense of justice. This may come from the law that operates in their country or it may come from a wide view of what is just.

From the sections above it is clear that the three concepts of law, morality and justice are quite distinct. There is, however, a large overlap between law and morality, law and justice and also between morality and justice. This idea of the overlapping of the three is illustrated in diagram form in Figure 1.2.

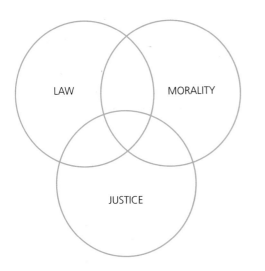

Figure 1.2 Diagram of the relationship of law, morality and justice

1.3 Civil law and criminal law

In the English legal system criminal and civil law are quite separate. The purpose of the law is different and the cases are dealt with in different courts.

1.3.1 Civil law

Civil law is about private disputes between individuals and/or businesses. There are several different types of civil law. Some important ones are:

- law of tort
- contract law
- human rights
- family law
- employment law
- company law.

If you are doing OCR AS Law you will study areas of the law of tort. These are covered in Chapters 23–26 of this book. If you are doing OCR A Level Law you will study both law of tort and law of contract or human rights. The further areas of the law of tort, criminal law and the areas of contract law and human rights that you need for A Level are covered in Book 2.

Law of tort

Consider the following situations:

a A child passenger in a car is injured in a collision (the tort of negligence).

b A family complains that their health is being affected by the noise and dust from a factory which has just been built near their house (the tort of nuisance).

c A woman is injured by faulty machinery at work (the tort of negligence, but may also involve occupiers' liability and/or employer's duty under health and safety regulations).

All these cases come under the law of tort. A tort occurs where the civil law holds that, even though there is no contract between them, one person owes a legal responsibility of some kind to another person, and there has been a breach of that responsibility. If there is a breach of this responsibility, then the person affected can make a claim under the law of tort. If successful the court can award damages – that is, a sum of money to compensate the person.

Where there is a situation which is continuing (such as in (b) above), it is also possible for the court to award an injunction. This is an order to the defendant to do or to stop doing something.

There are many different types of tort, and the above examples demonstrate only some of them. Many cases arise from road traffic crashes, since drivers owe a duty of care to anyone who might be injured by their negligent driving.

Law of contract

Look at the following situations:

a A family complains that their package holiday did not match what was promised by the tour operator and that they were put into a lower-grade hotel than the one they had paid for.

b A woman has bought a new car and discovers the engine is faulty.

c A man who bought a new car on hire purchase has failed to pay the instalments due to the hire-purchase company.

All these situations come under the law of contract. There are, of course, many other situations in which contracts can be involved. A contract is where the parties have made an agreement and each side has put something into the agreement. In (a) the tour operator provided the holiday and the family paid for that holiday. In (b) a garage had sold the car to the woman and she had paid for it. In (c) the hire-purchase company had provided the money for the man to have the car, while the man promised to pay back that money in instalments to the company.

If one party to the contract has not kept their side of the bargain, then the other party can bring a claim against them.

Human rights law

Consider the following situations:

a A man is arrested and held in a police station for longer than the law allows.

b At the trial of a woman in the Crown Court, one of the jurors is a police officer. This officer knows (and has worked with) one of the police who gives important evidence in the case.

c The eight-year-old child of a well-known author is photographed by a journalist as he goes to school. The journalist does not have permission to take the child's photo. The photo is then published in a newspaper.

All these situations involve breaches of human rights. In (a) there is a breach of Article 5 of the European Convention on human rights – the right to liberty. In (b) there is a breach of Article 6(1) of the Convention – the right to a fair trial. In (c) there is a breach of Article 8 of the Convention – the right to respect for private life. These rights will be upheld in the English courts. There is also a right to take the case to the European Court of Human Rights.

Compensation can be awarded where there is a breach of human rights. It is also possible for other remedies to be given, such as an injunction to prevent the future publication of photographs.

1.3.2 Criminal law

Criminal law sets out the types of behaviour which are forbidden at risk of punishment. A person who commits a crime is said to have offended against the state, and so the state has the right to prosecute them. This is so even though there is often an individual victim of a crime as well. For example, if a defendant commits the crime of burglary by breaking into a house and stealing, the state prosecutes the defendant for that burglary. The criminal courts have the right to punish those who break the criminal law. So, at the end of the case where the defendant is found guilty,

that defendant will be sentenced. The courts have a wide range of sentences that they can use. These include sending the defendant to prison, making a community order or fining the defendant.

Any individual victim of the crime will not necessarily be given any compensation though, where possible, the courts will order the offender to pay the victim compensation, as well as passing a sentence on him.

1.3.3 Differences between civil and criminal law

There are many differences between civil cases and criminal cases. The newspaper articles below show some of these differences. There are other differences as well and it is important to understand fully the distinctions between civil and criminal cases.

Purpose of the law

Civil law upholds the rights of individuals and the courts can order compensation in an effort at putting the parties in the position they would have been in if there had not been any breach of the civil law.

Criminal law is aimed at trying to maintain law and order. So, when a person is found guilty of an offence, that offender will be punished. There are also the aims of trying to protect society and trying to deter criminal behaviour, and these are the justifications for sending offenders to prison.

Person starting the case

In civil cases the person starting the case is the individual or business which has suffered as a result of the breach of civil law.

Criminal cases are taken on behalf of the state, and so there is a Crown Prosecution Service responsible for conducting most cases. The person starting the case is given a different name in civil and criminal cases. In civil cases they are called the claimant, while in criminal cases they are referred to as the prosecutor.

Key terms

Claimant – the legal term for a person or organisation starting a civil claim in the courts.

Prosecutor – the legal term for the person or organisation bringing a criminal charge against a defendant.

Courts

The cases take place in different courts. In general, civil cases are heard in the High Court or the County Court.

The High Court deals with more serious cases while the County Court deals with cases of lower value. Family cases, however, take place in the Family Court.

In both the High Court and the County Court a judge will try the case.

Criminal cases will be tried in either the Magistrates' Courts or the Crown Court. The Magistrates' Courts deal with less serious offences and the case is tried by a panel of lay magistrates or by a single legally qualified District Judge. Serious offences are tried in the Crown Court. The case is tried by a judge sitting with a jury. The judge decides points of law and the jury decides the verdict of 'guilty' or 'not guilty'.

Standard of proof

Criminal cases must be proved 'beyond reasonable doubt'. This is a very high standard of proof, and is necessary since a conviction could result in the defendant serving a long prison sentence.

Civil cases have to be proved 'on the balance of probabilities'. This is a much lower standard of proof, where the judge decides who is most likely to be right. This difference in the standard of proof means that it is possible for a defendant who has been acquitted in a criminal case to be found liable in a civil case based on the same facts. Such situations are rare, but have sometimes occurred.

Outcome of case

A defendant in a civil case is found 'liable' or 'not liable'. A defendant in a criminal case is found 'guilty' or 'not guilty'. Another way of stating this in criminal cases is to say that the defendant is 'convicted' or 'acquitted'.

At the end of a criminal case a defendant found guilty of an offence may be punished. The courts

have various sentences available depending on the seriousness of the offence.

At the end of a civil case, anyone found liable will be ordered to put right the matter as far as possible. This is usually done by an award of money in compensation, known as damages, though the court can make other orders such as an injunction.

	Civil cases	Criminal cases
Purpose of the law	To uphold the rights of individuals	To maintain law and order: to protect society
Person starting the case	The individual whose rights have been affected	Usually the state through the Crown Prosecution Service
Legal name for that person	Claimant	Prosecutor
Courts hearing cases	County Court High Court	Magistrates' Court Crown Court
Standard of proof	The balance of probabilities	Beyond reasonable doubt
Person/s making the decision	Judge	Magistrates in Magistrates' Court A judge and jury in Crown Court
Decision	Liable or not liable	Guilty (convicted) or not guilty (acquitted)
Powers of the court	Usually an award of damages (compensation) Other remedies are also possible e.g. injunctions	Prison, community order, fine

Figure 1.3 Differences between criminal and civil cases

Activity

Read the newspaper article below and decide whether it is about a civil or a criminal case. Explain what specific points or words led to your decision.

Rip-off plumber danced jig of joy in OAP's garden after overcharging her £6,000

A rogue plumber was spotted dancing a jig outside a frail pensioner's house after he conned her out of nearly £8,000, a court heard.

Dodgy tradesman Russell Lane, 38, made no attempt to hide his joy after shamelessly ripping off Patricia Binks, 72, who had called for help after suffering a blocked drain.

But yesterday he was counting the cost of his dishonesty after the company he worked for was fined £15,000 in fines and costs.

Lane was also found guilty of fraud and is due to be sentenced in March. Bournemouth Crown Court heard Mrs Binks contacted Plumbers 24/7 Ltd after finding the number in Yellow Pages.

Lane, who was with a second unnamed man, produced paperwork he ordered Mrs Binks to sign. It had no prices on and the men told her that if she didn't sign they wouldn't be able to carry out the work.

The men worked on the drains for five hours – then handed Mrs Binks a bill for £7,800. They produced a card machine and ordered her to pay the full amount immediately.

... Officials called in an expert to examine the work who found Lane overcharged Mrs Binks by £6,000.

The jury agreed the price charged by Lane was so significantly above a reasonable charge that the demand to pay that amount could only have been made dishonestly.

Source: Adapted from an article by David Pilditch, in the *Daily Express* online, 21 January 2016

Summary

- Law and rules
  - A rule is something that determines the way in which we behave.
  - Rules often develop from the 'norms of behaviour'.
  - Law is a formal mechanism of social control and legal rules are enforced by the state.
  - Norms of behaviour are enforced by the attitudes of the community and by personal guilt.

- Connections between law, morality and justice
  - Law of a country will usually reflect the moral values.
  - Major breaches of a moral code will also usually be against the law.
  - Justice is the ultimate goal towards which the law should strive.

- Rigid application of laws may actually produce injustice.
- People's ideas of what is justice may be founded in their religious beliefs.

- Civil and criminal law
  - Civil law governs private disputes between individuals and/or businesses.
  - Criminal law sets out the types of behaviour which are forbidden at risk of punishment.
  - Civil cases are heard in the County Court and the High Court.
  - Criminal cases are heard in the Magistrates' Court and the Crown Court.
  - The standard of proof for criminal cases is 'beyond reasonable doubt': the standard of proof for civil cases is the 'balance of probabilities'.

Chapter 2

Introduction to the nature of law (2)

After reading this chapter you should be able to:
- Have a basic understanding of the development of English law, including custom, common law, equity and statute law
- Understand the differences between common law and civil law systems
- Understand the definition and importance of the rule of law

2.1 Development of law

The law has developed through various sources of law including custom, common law, equity and statute law.

2.1.1 Custom

A custom is a rule of behaviour which develops in a community without being deliberately invented. Historically customs are believed to have been very important in that they were, effectively, the basis of our common law (see below). It is thought that following the Norman Conquest, judges were appointed by the king to travel around the land making decisions in the king's name. The judges based at least some of their decisions on the common customs. This idea caused Lord Justice Coke in the seventeenth century to describe these customs as being 'one of the main triangles of the laws of England'. Custom is a historical source and is unlikely to create new law today.

2.1.2 Development of the common law

Clearly the legal system in England and Wales could not rely only on customs. Even in Anglo-Saxon times there were local courts which decided disputes, but it was not until after the Norman Conquest in 1066 that a more organised system of courts emerged. This was because the Norman kings realised that control of the country would be easier if they controlled, among other things, the legal system. The first Norman king, William the Conqueror, set up the Curia Regis (the King's Court) and appointed his own judges. The nobles who had a dispute were encouraged to apply to have the king (or his judges) decide the matter.

The King's Bench was founded in 1215

As well as this central court, the judges were sent to major towns to decide any important cases. This meant that judges travelled from London all round the country that was under the control of the king. In the time of Henry II (1154–89) these tours became more regular and Henry divided up the country into 'circuits' or areas for the judges to visit. Initially the judges

9

would use the local customs or the old Anglo-Saxon laws to decide cases, but over a period of time it is believed that the judges on their return to Westminster in London would discuss the laws or customs they had used, and the decisions they had made, with each other. Gradually, the judges selected the best customs and these were then used by all the judges throughout the country. This had the effect that the law became uniform or 'common' through the whole country, and it is from here that the phrase 'common law' seems to have developed.

Common law is the basis of our law today: it is unwritten law that developed from customs and judicial decisions. The phrase 'common law' is still used to distinguish laws that have been developed by judicial decisions from laws that have been created by statute or other legislation. For example, murder is a common law crime while theft is a statutory crime. This means that murder has never been defined in any Act of Parliament, but theft is defined by the Theft Act 1968.

The judges can still create new law today. However, they can only do this when a relevant case comes before them. And then they can only rule on the point in that case. This then becomes the law for future cases. Judges cannot make wide-ranging changes to the law. This can only be done by statute law.

2.1.3 Equity

Historically this was an important source of law and it still plays a part today, with many of our legal concepts having developed from equitable principles. The word 'equity' has a meaning of 'fairness', and this is the basis on which it operates, when adding to our law.

Equity developed because of problems in the common law. Only certain types of case were recognised. The law was also very technical; if there was an error in the formalities the person making the claim would lose the case.

Another major problem was the fact that the only remedy the common law courts could give was 'damages' – that is an order that the defendant pay a sum of money to the claimant by way of compensation. In some cases this would not be the best method of putting matters right between the parties. For example, in a case of trespass to land, where perhaps the defendant had built on his neighbour's land, the building would still be there and the claimant would have lost the use of that part of his land. In such a situation the claimant would probably prefer to have the building removed, rather than be given money in compensation.

People who could not obtain justice in the common law courts appealed directly to the king. Most of these cases were referred to the King's Chancellor, who was both a lawyer and a priest, and who became known as the keeper of the king's conscience. This was because the Chancellor based his decisions on principles of natural justice and fairness, making a decision on what seemed 'right' in the particular case rather than on the strict following of previous precedents. He was also prepared to look beyond legal documents, which were considered legally binding by the common law courts, and to take account of what the parties had intended to do.

To ensure that the decisions were 'fair' the Chancellor used new procedures such as subpoenas, which ordered a witness to attend court or risk imprisonment for refusing to obey the Chancellor's order. He also developed new remedies which were able to compensate claimants more fully than the common law remedy of damages. The main equitable remedies were: injunctions; specific performance; rescission; and rectification. These are all still used today.

Conflict between equity and common law

The two systems of common law and equity operated quite separately, so it was not surprising that this overlapping of the two systems led to conflict between them. One of the main problems was that the common law courts would make an order in favour of one party and the Court of Chancery an order in favour of the other party. The conflict was finally resolved in the *Earl of Oxford's case* (1615) when the king ruled that equity should prevail; in other words, the decision made in the Chancery court was the one which must be followed by the parties. This ruling made the position of equity stronger and the same rule was subsequently included in s 25 of the Judicature Act 1873.

2.1.4 Statute law

An Act of Parliament is law that has been passed by both Houses of Parliament and received Royal Assent. Law can be changed by an Act of Parliament or new law can be created. This is useful for new situations or inventions such as computer technology. Parliament has created new offences involving computer hacking. It has also created new rules in respect of 'designer babies' and what is allowed in the Human Fertilisation and Embryology Act 2008.

Statute law can bring together all the existing law in one area in a single Act of Parliament. This was done in the Consumer Rights Act 2015.

Statute law can create, change or revoke any law. It is useful for make wide-sweeping changes to the law.

The process for enacting a new Act of Parliament is explained in Chapter 16.

However, the judges still play an important role as they may have to interpret the meaning of words in a statute if they are not clear.

This problem of statutory interpretation is dealt with in Chapter 18.

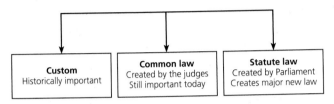

Figure 2.1 Historical development of sources of law

2.2 Common law and civil law legal systems

Today there is a major difference in how legal systems in various countries operate. The systems are broadly divided into common law systems and civil law systems.

In countries with a common law system, decisions by the judges are considered law and have the same force of law as statutes. In countries with a civil law system, there is a written code of laws and courts follow the principles in the code. Decisions by the judges have less importance.

> **Key term**
>
> **Civil law system** – this is based on a written code and aims to cover all possibilities with broad principles. Decisions of judges can be considered but are not binding.
> **Common law system** – this is largely unwritten and relies on decisions of the judges. All lower courts are bound by decisions of judges in the higher courts.

2.2.1 Civil law systems

History

The idea of having a written code for law goes back thousands of years. The first known written laws date from about 3000BC in the Middle East where they were cut into clay or stone. One of the earliest detailed codes is from Hammurabi in Babylon in about 1700BC. This contained nearly 300 sections but did not cover the whole law of Babylon.

The first full code is from Rome where over the period 100BC to AD300 Roman lawyers published hundreds of law books. This amount of material became unmanageable and in the sixth century, Emperor Justinian reduced it to three volumes (about a million words!). This was intended as a complete and consistent code. There was to be no law except what was in them.

Shortly after this the Roman Empire collapsed, but Justinian's laws were still used especially in the Holy Roman Empire under the rule of Charlemagne and his successors. It was therefore natural that, when universities began in West Europe in the eleventh and twelfth centuries, the law studied was the code of Justinian.

This had a lasting effect on the legal systems in Western Europe, with the exception of England, as Western European countries still use civil code-based systems of law today. From the eighteenth century onwards individual European countries began to replace Justinian's code by new codes of law, so that each country now has its own code.

Civil law systems today

Civil law systems today rely on a written code. However, in modern complex society, it is also usual to have supplementary laws.

Codes are not lightly altered. In particular judges cannot overrule a principle set out in the code. They can only reason from the general principles in the code. Lawyers will base their arguments on the broad principles of the code.

Although the code is unlikely to be altered, the interpretation of it may change with changing social and economic conditions. This has been obvious with the French Napoleonic code which dates from 1804. So there is some possibility of change in the law.

The courts do not follow decisions in previous cases. Such decisions may be considered but are not binding, unlike common law systems and, in recent times decisions in cases have become more important.

One of the original ideas of having a code was that it would make the law accessible to ordinary citizens. However, as society has become more complex this aim has proved impracticable. Most codes are now too detailed and too technical for ordinary people to be able to consult and understand easily.

2.2.2 Common law systems

History

As already stated in sections 2.1.1 and 2.1.2, English law was developed from custom and the decisions from the judges. This led to a very different system from the civil law code-based system. English law does not have a written set of laws. Much of the law is left to be developed by the judges.

From the thirteenth century onward most criminal and civil cases were tried by jury and it was understood that issues of fact were decided by the jury. This meant that the judges and lawyers had to work out what the law was so that the issues of fact could be put to the jury. This separation of law and fact never became part of civil law systems. But it also accounts for the fact that common law systems rely more on oral presentation of cases and face-to-face argument on points of law in court.

The English took their common law system to the areas of the world that they colonised. This includes countries such as Australia, Canada, India and Malaysia. All these countries have common law systems.

Common law systems today

In a common law system of law there is unlikely to be any written code, although some countries may have a partial code. There will be some written law: in England this is through Acts of Parliament.

Decisions of the judges are important and lawyers will argue cases by basing their arguments on past decisions. Decisions of the higher courts are binding under the doctrine of judicial precedent.

Unlike a civil law system, a common law system does not use broad principles. The law is built up by individual case decisions on the point raised in the particular case. However, in recent times there have been efforts to make the law less piecemeal and more rational. The work of the Law Commission in reform of the law has included some codification of the law. In addition, the use of the purposive approach in statutory interpretation (see Chapter 18) has encouraged looking at broad principles.

See Chapter 20 for more information on the Law Commission.

2.2.3 Systems operating today

England and Wales use a common law system. So too do many of the countries which were colonised by the British in earlier centuries, even though such countries have been independent countries for a long time. They include the United States of America, Canada and Australia.

European countries use civil law systems. Other countries, such as Brazil and Argentina, which were originally colonised by European countries also use civil law systems.

The map below shows the legal systems used around the world.

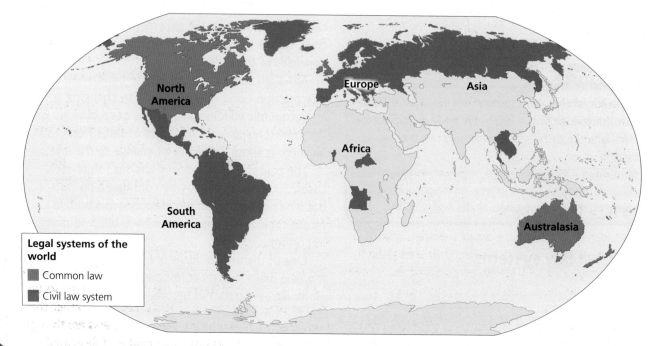

Legal systems of the world
- Common law
- Civil law system

Figure 2.2 Map of legal systems around the world

Civil law systems	Common law systems
Relies on a written code	The law is largely unwritten and relies on decisions of the judges
Code aims to cover all possibilities with broad principles	Law is argued from case to case on specific points
Decisions of judges can be considered but are not binding	Decisions of judges in the higher courts are binding
In modern times case law has become more important	In modern times codification of law by the Law Commission and the use of the purposive approach in statutory interpretation has encouraged broad principles

Figure 2.3 Comparison of common law and civil law systems

2.3 Concept of the rule of law

The 'rule of law' is a symbolic idea. It can be defined in different ways. However, the main principles are:
- all people are subject to and accountable to law that is fairly applied and enforced; and
- the process by which the laws of the country are enacted, administered and enforced must be fair.

The rule of law is a safeguard against dictatorship. It supports democracy. This is because the government and its officials are accountable under the law. Also authority is distributed in a manner that ensures that no single organ of government can exercise power in an unchecked way.

Tony Honoré, an academic lawyer, points out that the rule of law exists when a government's powers are limited by law and citizens have a core of rights that the government is bound to uphold.

These rights include:
- no person shall be sanctioned except in accordance with the law: this is in both civil and criminal cases
- there is equality before the law: there must be no discrimination on any grounds
- there must be fairness and clarity of the law.

2.3.1 Academic views

Many academics have written about the rule of law. The best-known explanation of the 'rule of law' was given by Professor Dicey in the nineteenth century, but there have been other writers with different views on the topic.

Dicey thought that the rule of law was an important feature that distinguished English law from law in other countries in Europe. He held that there were three elements that created the rule of law.

These were:
- an absence of arbitrary power on the part of the state
- equality before the law
- supremacy of ordinary law.

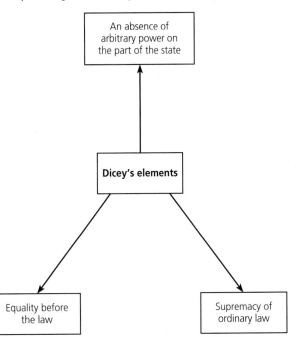

Figure 2.4 Dicey's elements in the rule of law

An absence of arbitrary power of the state

The state's power must be controlled by the law. The law must set limits on what the state can or cannot do. In the English legal system actions of, and decisions by, government ministers can be challenged in court by judicial review. One of the main aims of the rule of law is to avoid the state having wide discretionary powers. Dicey recognised that discretion can be exercised in an arbitrary way and this should be avoided to comply with the rule of law.

Everyone must be equal before the law

No person must be above the law. It does not matter how rich or powerful a person is, the law must deal with him in the same way as it would anyone else. Another side of this part of the rule of law is that those who carry out functions of state must be accountable under the law for their actions.

The law must be supreme

This is particularly true in the law of England and Wales in the time of Dicey, as many of the main developments up to that time were through judicial decisions rather than being created by Parliament. Today most laws are through legislation, that is Acts of Parliament and delegated legislation, though judicial decisions do still create law.

2.3.2 Problems with Dicey's views

A major problem with Dicey's view of the rule of law is that it conflicts with another fundamental principle, that of parliamentary supremacy. This concept holds that an Act of Parliament can overrule any other law. The concept also holds that no other body has the right to override or set aside an Act of Parliament.

So under the rule of law there should be no arbitrary power on the part of the state, yet under parliamentary supremacy Parliament has the right to make any law it wishes and these can include granting arbitrary powers to the state.

Also, statutes passed by Parliament cannot be challenged through judicial review. This is different from some other countries where the legislative body is subject to the rule of law, so that laws passed by them can be challenged in the courts.

Another problem is that equality before the law in Dicey's theory refers to formal equality. It disregards the differences between people in terms of wealth, power and connections. Real equality can only be achieved if there are mechanisms in place to address these differences. For example, the cost of taking legal cases to court is very high. In order to allow the poorest in society to be able to enforce their rights and so be equal under the law, it is necessary to have some form of state help in financing their case.

Dicey's view of the rule of law is based on abstract ideas. This makes it difficult to apply in real-life situations.

2.3.3 Other views

Von Hayek, an academic economist, who also wrote on the inter-dependence of economics and institutions, agreed with Dicey that the key component of the rule of law is the absence of any arbitrary power on the part of the state. However, von Hayek thought that the rule of law had become weaker. His reason for this was that, provided actions of the state were authorised by legislation, any act in accordance with this legislation was lawful. He also pointed out that the modern state is directly involved in regulating economic activity and this is in conflict with the rule of law.

Another academic, Joseph Raz, a professor of law at Oxford in the late twentieth century and early twenty-first century, recognised that the rule of law was a way of controlling discretion rather than preventing it completely. He saw the rule of law as of negative value, acting to minimise the danger of the use of discretionary power in an arbitrary way. He thought that the key point which emerged from the rule of law was that the law must be capable of guiding the individual's behaviour.

He set out a number of principles which come from this wider idea. Some of these are:

- There should be clear rules and procedures for making laws.
- The independence of the judiciary must be guaranteed.
- The principles of natural justice should be observed; these require an open and fair hearing with all parties being given the opportunity to put their case.
- The courts should have the power to review the way in which the other principles are implemented to ensure that they are being operated as demanded by the rule of law.

Within our legal system there have been changes in the twenty-first century which support these principles. A major example is the Constitutional Reform Act 2005 which recognised the rule of law and the importance of the independence of the judiciary. Section 1 of that Act states:

This Act does not adversely affect –

a the existing constitutional principle of the rule of law; or

b the Lord Chancellor's existing constitutional role in relation to that principle

While s 3(1) states:

The Lord Chancellor, other Ministers of the Crown and all with responsibility for matters relating to the judiciary or otherwise to the administration of justice must uphold the continued independence of the judiciary.

For more on the independence of the judiciary see Chapter 19.

These safeguards in the Constitutional Reform Act 2005 show the importance that is attached to the rule of law.

Look online

Look up the Constitutional Reform Act 2005 on **www.legislation.gov.uk**. What other changes were introduced by the Act?

Dicey	von Hayek	Raz
Absence of arbitrary power on the part of the state	Absence of arbitrary power on the part of the state	Clear rules and procedures for making laws
Equality before the law	Rule of law weakened by an increasingly interventionist state	Judicial independence must be guaranteed
Supremacy of ordinary law	Modern state is directly involved in regulating economic activity in conflict with the rule of law	Principles of natural justice should be observed
		Courts should have the power to review the way in which the other principles are implemented

Figure 2.5 Comparing views of the rule of law

Lord Bingham's views

Lord Bingham, who had held the post of Lord Chief Justice and then become Senior Law Lord in the House of Lords, gave a lecture in 2006 at the Centre for Public Law on the rule of law.

In this lecture, '*The Rule of Law*' he pointed out that although the Constitutional Reform Act 2005 specifically states that it 'does not adversely affect the existing constitutional principle of the rule of law', the Act does not define the rule of law.

Lord Bingham put forward a definition, the essence of which was that:

> all persons and authorities within the State, whether public or private, should be bound by and entitled to the benefit of laws.

He went on to consider points which were essential in the rule of law. These included:

- the law must be accessible and, so far as possible, intelligible, clear and predictable
- questions of legal right and liability should be resolved by the application of law
- the laws of the land should apply equally to all, save to the extent that objective differences justify differentiation
- the law must afford adequate protection of fundamental human rights
- means must be provided for resolving, without prohibitive cost or inordinate delay, civil disputes which the parties are themselves unable to resolve

- ministers and public officers must exercise power conferred on them reasonably and in good faith
- adjudicative procedures provided by the State should be fair.

2.3.4 The rule of law and law making

The rule of law is very important when it comes to law making. The process by which laws are made must be open and fair.

In the English legislative system, Acts of Parliament have to be passed by both Houses of Parliament. In practice the government of the day usually has a majority in the House of Commons. So most proposed new laws will be passed by the House of Commons, although there will be debate on all contentious issues which can lead to changes being made.

The House of Lords exercises a check on the law-making process as all new laws have also to be passed by them. One area where the House of Lords has consistently voted against change in the law has been in relation to allowing trial in the Crown Court without a jury.

The government can also make regulations through statutory instruments (delegated legislation). As these regulations do not always have to be considered by Parliament as a whole, there are several checks on this method of law making. First, Parliament must pass an Act granting power to make regulations. Then Parliament also has various powers to scrutinise and check the regulations. Finally, the regulations can be challenged in the courts through the process of judicial review to make sure that they have not gone beyond the powers granted by Parliament.

See Chapter 17 at section 17.2 for more information on control of delegated legislation.

2.3.5 The rule of law and the legal system

The way in which the legal system works is also covered by the rule of law. One of the most important points is that every defendant in a criminal case must have a fair trial. Trial by jury is seen as an important factor in maintaining fairness and protecting citizens' rights.

Another very important point is that no person can be imprisoned without a trial. In countries where the rule of law is disregarded, people, often opponents of the government, are likely to be detained without a trial.

Civil justice system

The rule of law is also important in the civil justice system. Ordinary people need to be able to resolve their disputes effectively through the civil justice system. This means that the system should be free from discrimination. It must also be free from corruption and not improperly influenced by public officials. Our system is trusted and recognised for being impartial.

The civil justice system should be accessible and affordable. This point is open to debate as there have been major cuts to public funding of cases in the past 20 or so years. At the same time the costs of taking civil cases to court has increased. People of modest means are unlikely to be able to afford to take a case to court. However, there has been an increase in alternative ways of resolving civil disputes which are much cheaper to use.

See Chapter 4 for details on Alternative Dispute Resolution.

The rule of law and substantive law

Substantive means the law in the different areas of law. There is the substantive law of criminal law which sets out the definitions of the various criminal offences. There is the substantive law of tort which sets out what rights and responsibilities people owe to each other in everyday life. The substantive law of contract lays down the rules on such issues as when a contract is formed, what events may make that contract void or voidable and what will breach a contract. The substantive law of human rights sets out the various rights that individuals are entitled to expect.

Whatever the area of substantive law it is important that the rules recognise that people have key rights and that the laws are not oppressive.

Criminal law

Many criminal laws are aimed at protecting people such as murder, manslaughter and non-fatal offences against the person. Other offences are aimed at protecting property, such as theft, burglary or criminal damage. Other offences can be aimed at preventing disruptive behaviour and protecting public order. There are also regulatory offences aimed at such issues as preventing pollution, ensuring that food sold in shops is fit for human consumption and a wide range of driving offences aimed at safety on the roads.

For all offences the law has to be clear and the prosecution has to prove that the defendant has committed the offence. All offences also have a stated maximum penalty and the courts cannot impose a

higher penalty. In fact in nearly all cases the penalty imposed will be much lower than the maximum allowed.

Law of tort

Many torts are aimed at protecting people and their property and give the right to claim compensation for damage caused by breaches of the law. Unlike criminal law, where the prosecution is nearly always brought by the state, it is the person affected by the tort who claims. For example, if one person drives negligently and knocks down a pedestrian, that pedestrian has the right to claim compensation for his injuries.

One of the problems is that public funding for making claims in tort through the courts is no longer available. This means that although everyone has the right to claim, so there appears to be equality before the law, in fact financial problems can make it difficult for many people to claim. 'No win, no fee' agreements can be used to fund such cases, but there are still problems.

See Chapter 11, section 11.3.2 for more on legal aid.

Contract law

Contract law recognises that, in most cases, people should be free to make what agreements they wish. However, it does recognise that consumers may have very little choice when making contracts with businesses and that there is not really equality between the parties. In order to bring about greater equality, contract law provides some rights for consumers.

The Sale of Goods Act 1979 is one such example as it creates an implied term that items bought must be of satisfactory quality and fit for their normal purpose. In this way contract law supports real equality in the law. Another example is the Consumer Protection Act 1987 which gives consumers much wider rights where they are injured or their property is damaged by faulty goods. The Act allows any consumer to claim, not just the buyer of the goods. So where an item is bought as a present for another person, that person can claim if there is a fault in the goods which causes him injury.

Also the Consumer Rights Act 2015 has further increased the protection consumers have when making a contract with a business. This now includes rights where the contract is for the supply of digital content. This is also an example of the law being created to keep up with changes in technology.

Human rights law

Human rights law supports the rule of law in many ways. For example, all rights must be applied without discrimination. The European Convention on Human Rights sets out the right to liberty. This right should only be taken away where it is in accordance with the law, such as imprisoning someone who has been found guilty of murder. The Convention also states that there is a right to a fair trial. This Convention was made part of our law by the Human Rights Act 1998.

So the rule of law is central to any legal claim.

Tip 💬

When discussing the rule of law, use examples from the different areas of law.

Summary 📝

- Development of English law
  - The earliest source of law was custom.
  - The common law was developed from custom and the decisions of the judges.
  - Equity developed to fill in the gaps in the common law.
  - Today most law is made by Acts of Parliament.
  - Judges still have a role in the interpretation of statutes.

- Common law and civil law systems
  - Common law systems are based on decisions of the judges.
  - Civil law systems are based on a code of laws.
  - The reason for the use of different systems is historical, with Western European countries using a civil law system and England (and areas to which England took its system) using a common law system.

- The rule of law
  - The rule of law is important in a democratic country.
  - All people are subject to and accountable to law that is fairly applied and enforced.
  - There is equality before the law.
  - Dicey held that there were three elements that created the rule of law:
    - an absence of arbitrary power on the part of the state
    - equality before the law
    - supremacy of ordinary law.
  - FA von Hayek stated: 'Stripped of all technicalities the Rule of Law means that the government in all its actions is bound by rules fixed and announced in advance.'
  - Joseph Raz recognised that the rule of law was a way of controlling discretion rather than preventing it completely.
  - Lord Bingham held that the key feature of the rule of law was that all persons and authorities should be bound by and entitled to the benefit of laws.
  - The process by which laws are made must be open and fair.
  - Both criminal and civil justice systems must be fair.
  - The rule of law is an important element in all areas of substantive law.

Chapter 3

Civil courts

After reading this chapter you should be able to:
● Have a basic understanding of the County Court and High Court, their jurisdictions and pre-trial procedures
● Understand the track system used in the courts
● Have an understanding of the appeal system and appellate courts
● Evaluate the civil courts

3.1 Civil cases

As already stressed in Chapter 1, it is important to understand the differences between civil cases and criminal cases. A basic definition for **civil claims** is to say that these arise when an individual or a business believes that their rights have been infringed in some way. Some of the main areas of civil law are contract law, law of tort, family law, employment law and company law.

> **Key term** 🔑
>
> Civil claims – claims made in the civil courts when an individual or a business believes that their rights have been infringed in some way.

As well as dealing with different areas of law, the types of dispute that can arise within these areas are equally varied. A company may be claiming that money is owed to it (contract law); this type of claim may be for a few pounds or for several million. An individual may be claiming compensation for injuries suffered in an accident (the tort of negligence), while in another tort case the claim might not be for money but for another remedy such as an injunction to prevent someone from building on disputed land. Other types of court orders include the winding up of a company which cannot pay its debts or a decree of divorce for a marriage that has failed. The list is almost endless.

When a dispute occurs, it is normal to try to resolve it by negotiating with the other person/business or by trying another method of dispute resolution.

The Royal Courts of Justice

See Chapter 4 for details on other methods of dispute resolution.

The two courts in which civil cases are dealt with are:
● the County Court
● the High Court.

The types of cases they deal with are explained below.

3.2 Civil courts

3.2.1 County Court

There are about 200 County Courts, although the current government is planning to close about 50 of these. The County Court can try nearly all civil cases. The main areas of jurisdiction are:
● all contract and tort claims
● all cases for the recovery of land
● disputes over equitable matters such as trusts up to a value of £350,000.

Cases in the County Court are heard by a Circuit Judge or a District Judge. On very rare occasions it is possible for the judge to sit with a jury of eight. This will only happen for defamation cases or for the torts of malicious prosecution or false imprisonment.

3.2.2 High Court

The High Court is based in London but also has judges sitting in several towns and cities throughout England and Wales. It has the jurisdiction (power) to hear any civil case and has three divisions, each of which specialises in hearing certain types of case. These divisions are the Queen's Bench Division, the Chancery Division and the Family Division.

Queen's Bench Division

This is the biggest of the three divisions. It deals with contract and tort cases where the amount claimed is over £100,000, though it can hear smaller claims where there is an important point of law.

Cases are normally tried by a single judge, but there is a right to jury trial for fraud, libel, slander, malicious prosecution and false imprisonment cases. A jury is very rarely used. If a jury is used, there will be 12 members.

There is also an Administrative Court in the Queen's Bench Division. This court supervises the lawfulness of the conduct of national and local government, of inferior courts and tribunals, and of other public bodies through judicial review.

Chancery Division

The main business of this division involves disputes concerned with such matters as:
- insolvency, both for companies and individuals
- the enforcement of mortgages
- disputes relating to trust property
- copyright and patents
- intellectual property matters
- contested probate actions.

There is also a special Companies Court in the division which deals mainly with winding up companies.

Cases are heard by a single judge. Juries are never used in the Chancery Division.

Family Division

This division hears family cases where there is a dispute about which country's laws should apply and all international cases concerning family matters under the Hague Convention. In addition, it can hear cases which can be dealt with by the Family Court. Cases are heard by a single judge.

The Crime and Courts Act 2013 created a new separate Family Court. The majority of family matters previously dealt with in the Family Division are now dealt with by the Family Court. The Family Division can also deal with these cases, but is unlikely to unless the case is difficult or important.

3.3 Pre-trial procedures

Most people making a claim do not want to start a court case unless they have to. They will first of all try to negotiate an agreed settlement with the person who caused their injuries or damaged their property. Using a method other than going to court is known as Alternative Dispute Resolution (ADR). The vast majority of cases are settled and do not go to court.

3.3.1 Pre-action protocols

Parties are encouraged to give information to each other, in an attempt to prevent the need for so many court cases to be started. So before a claim is issued, especially in personal injury cases, a pre-action 'protocol' has to be followed. This is a list of things to be done and if the parties do not follow the procedure and give the required information to the other party, they may be liable for certain costs if they then make a court claim.

3.3.2 Which court to use

If the other person denies liability or refuses to use ADR, then the only way to get compensation for the injuries will be to start a court case.

The court to be used will depend on the amount that is being claimed. There are different limits depending on whether the claim is for personal injuries or for damage to property.

If the amount claimed is £100,000 or less the case must be started in the County Court. Where the claim is for less than £10,000 it is a small claim and will be dealt with on the small claims track. The exception is for personal injury cases – where the claim is for £50,000 or less, the case must be started in the County Court, and for less than £1,000 it is a small claim.

If the claim is for more than the above amounts (that is over £50,000 for personal injuries or over £100,000 for other claims), a claimant can choose whether to start the case in the County Court or the High Court. These limits are shown in Figure 3.1.

Claim	The court to start claim in
Claim for £100,000 or less Personal injury case claim for £50,000 or less	County Court County Court
Claim for over £100,000 Personal injury case claim for over £50,000	High Court or County Court High Court or County Court

Figure 3.1 Which court to start a claim in

3.3.3 Issuing a claim

If someone is using the County Court, then they can choose to issue the claim in any of the 200 or so County Courts in the country. If they are using the High Court, then they can go to one of the 20 District Registries or the main court in London. They need a claim form called 'N1' (see Figure 3.2). The court office will give notes explaining how to fill in the form. Alternatively people can make a money claim online.

The claim has to be filed at a court office and a fee will be charged for issuing the claim. This fee varies according to how much the claim is for. At the beginning of 2017, the fee for a claim of up to £300 was £35. The more the claim is for the higher the fee. At the top end of the scale the fee is £10,000 for claims of £200,000 or more.

Look online

Look up court forms such as N1 on the website **https://hmctsformfinder.justice.gov.uk**

Also use that website to find guidance on starting cases in the County Court.

3.3.4 Defending a claim

When the defendant receives the claim form there are several routes which can be taken. The defendant may admit the claim and pay the full amount. Where this happens the case ends. The claimant has achieved what he wanted.

In other cases the defendant may dispute the claim. If the defendant wishes to defend the claim, he must send either an acknowledgement of service (Form N9) or a defence to the court within 14 days of receiving the claim.

If the defendant does not do either of these things, then the claimant can ask the court to make an order that the defendant pays the money and costs claimed.

Once a claim is defended the court will allocate the case to the most suitable 'track' or way of dealing with the case.

3.4 The three tracks

The decision on which track should be used is made by the District Judge in the County Court or the Master (a procedural judge) in the High Court. To help the judge consider to which track a claim should be allocated, both parties are sent an allocation questionnaire.

There are three tracks and these are:

1 The small claims track – for disputes under £10,000, except for personal injury cases where the limit is at the time of writing £1,000. NOTE there are proposals to increase this limit to £5,000.
2 The fast track – for straightforward disputes of £10,000 to £25,000.
3 The multi-track – for cases over £25,000 or for complex cases under this amount.

If it is thought necessary, especially where there is a complex point of law involved, the judge can allocate a case to a track that normally deals with claims of a higher value. Alternatively, if the parties agree, the judge can allocate a case to a lower value track.

3.4.1 Small claims

These cases are usually heard in private, but they can be heard in an ordinary court. The procedure allows the District Judge to be flexible in the way he hears the case. District Judges are given training in how to handle small claims cases, so that they will take an active part in the proceedings, asking questions and making sure that both parties explain all their important points. The parties are encouraged to represent themselves and they cannot claim the cost of using a lawyer from the other side, even if they win the case.

3.4.2 Fast track cases

In fast track cases the court will set down a very strict timetable for the pre-trial matters. This is aimed at preventing one or both sides from wasting time and running up unnecessary costs.

Once a case is set down for hearing, the aim is to have the case heard within 30 weeks, but in practice the wait is likely to be nearer 50 weeks. The actual trial will usually be heard by a Circuit Judge and take place in open court with a more formal procedure than for small claims. In order to speed up the trial itself, the hearing will be limited to a maximum of one day and the number of expert witnesses restricted, with usually only one expert being allowed.

Claim Form

You may be able to issue your claim online which may save time and money. Go to www.moneyclaim.gov.uk to find out more.

In the	
Fee Account no.	
Help with Fees - **Ref no.** (if applicable)	H W F – ☐☐☐ – ☐☐☐

	For court use only
Claim no.	
Issue date	

Claimant(s) name(s) and address(es) including postcode

SEAL

Defendant(s) name and address(es) including postcode

Brief details of claim

Value

You must indicate your preferred County Court Hearing Centre for hearings here *(see notes for guidance)*

Defendant's name and address for service including postcode

	£
Amount claimed	
Court fee	
Legal representative's costs	
Total amount	

For further details of the courts www.gov.uk/find-court-tribunal.
When corresponding with the Court, please address forms or letters to the Manager and always quote the claim number.

N1 Claim form (CPR Part 7) (06.16)   © Crown Copyright 2016

Figure 3.2a Form NI (front)

Does, or will, your claim include any issues under the Human Rights Act 1998? ☐ Yes ☐ No

Particulars of Claim (attached)(to follow)

Statement of Truth
*(I believe)(The Claimant believes) that the facts stated in these particulars of claim are true.
* I am duly authorised by the claimant to sign this statement

Full name _____

Name of claimant's legal representative's firm _____

signed _____ position or office held _____
      *(Claimant)(Litigation friend)   (if signing on behalf of firm or company)
      (Claimant's legal representative)   *delete as appropriate

Claimant's or claimant's legal representative's address to which documents or payments should be sent if different from overleaf including (if appropriate) details of DX, fax or e-mail.

▶ Print form ▶ Reset form

Figure 3.2b Form NI (continued)

3.4.3 Multi-track cases

Each case is heard by a judge who will also be expected to 'manage' the case from the moment it is allocated to the multi-track route. This includes:

- identifying the issues at an early stage
- encouraging the parties to use Alternative Dispute Resolution if this is appropriate
- dealing with any procedural steps without the need for the parties to attend court
- fixing timetables by which the different stages of the case must be completed.

Case management is aimed at keeping the costs of the case as low as possible and making sure that it is heard reasonably quickly.

Activity ❓

Advise the people in the following situations:

1. Anika has bought a television set with a built-in DVD player costing £370 from a local electrical superstore. The DVD player has never worked properly, but the store has refused to replace it or to refund the purchase price to Anika. She wishes to claim against the store. Advise her as to which court to start the case in and how she should go about this. Also explain to her the way in which the case will be dealt with if the store defends it and there is a court hearing.

2. Samuel has been badly injured at work and alleges that the injuries were the result of his employer's failure to take proper safety precautions. He has been advised that his claim is likely to be worth £300,000. Advise him as to which court or courts could hear his case.

3. Sadiq has had an extension to his house built. It cost £50,000. Two months after the extension was finished it was found that the work had been defective and there was a serious problem with damp. It cost £12,000 to put the problems right. Advise him as to which court he should start the case in.

3.5 Reform of the civil courts

The present system of civil justice started in 1999 and is based on the reforms recommended by Lord Woolf. He stated that a civil justice system should:

- be just in the results it delivers
- be fair in the way it treats litigants
- offer appropriate procedures at a reasonable cost

- deal with cases at a reasonable speed
- be understandable to those who use it.

Lord Woolf found that virtually none of these points was being achieved in the civil courts, and criticised the system for being unequal, expensive, slow, uncertain and complicated. His reforms brought in the three-track system and gave judges more responsibility for managing cases.

The reforms also led to the simplifying of documents and procedures and having a single set of rules governing proceedings in both the High Court and the County Court. Lord Woolf also wanted more use of information technology and greater use of Alternative Dispute Resolution.

3.5.1 The effect of the Woolf reforms

The main improvements to civil cases have been that the culture of litigation has changed for the better, so that there is more co-operation between the parties' lawyers. There have also been improvements in the delays between issuing a claim and the court hearing, but these are not as great as had been hoped. For example, there is still a wait of at least one year between issuing a fast track claim or multi-track claim and the trial of the case in court.

However, there are still many problems with the civil justice system. The main problems are:

- Alternative Dispute Resolution is not used enough
- costs of cases have continued to increase – in particular, costs in fast track cases are often far greater than the amount claimed
- the courts are still under-resourced – in particular the IT systems are very limited.

3.5.2 Further reforms

Since the Woolf Reforms, the civil case system has been reviewed and some more changes made. The financial limits for small claims and fast track cases have been increased to avoid expensive trials for lower value claims. The level of £1,000 for personal injuries claims is likely to increase to £5,000.

The Civil Procedure Rules have been amended to emphasise that the courts 'deal with cases justly and at a proportionate cost'. The winning party can only claim back costs where they are proportionate to the value of the claim.

The latest Review was by Lord Briggs in 2016. He put forward several proposals. Two main ones are:

1. that there should be an out-of-hours private mediation service in the County Court and
2. that an online court should be set up.

Online court

Lord Briggs has proposed that there should be an online court. In his interim report he said: 'There is a clear and pressing need to create an online court for claims of up to £25,000.'

He believes this court would give litigants effective access to justice without having to incur the disproportionate cost of using lawyers.

Courts hearing civil cases	County Court High Court
Three-track system	Up to £10,000 (£1,000 for personal injury cases) – small track £10,000 to £25,000 – fast track Over £25,000 – multi-track
Starting a court case	Parties should try to resolve case (can use ADR) To start case must file Form N1 If case is defended, it will be allocated to most suitable track
Reform of civil justice system	1999 Lord Woolf's reforms Brought in the three-track system, encouraged use of ADR, simplified terminology and tried to improve waiting times **Post-Woolf reforms** Emphasis on proportionate costs in cases Increase in value the small claims and fast track cases can deal with **Lords Briggs proposals for the future** Private mediation service in the County Court Setting up of an online court

Figure 3.3 Civil courts

Tip

Make sure you understand the different courts that hear civil cases and the three-track system. These are the basis of the whole system.

3.6 Appeal routes in civil cases

Once a decision has been made in either the County Court or the High Court, there is always the possibility of appealing against that decision. There are different appeal routes from the County Court and the High Court. In addition, the value of the claim and the level of judge who heard the case affect which appeal route should be used.

3.6.1 Appeals from the County Court

For all claims the appeal route depends on the level of judge hearing the case. This means that:
- if the case was heard by a District Judge, then the appeal is to a Circuit Judge in the same County Court
- if the case was heard by a Circuit Judge, then the appeal is to a High Court Judge.

Second appeals

There is the possibility of a second or further appeal. This appeal will always be to the Court of Appeal (Civil Division). However, such further appeals are only allowed in exceptional cases as set out in s 55 of the Access to Justice Act 1999 which states:

no appeal may be made to the Court of Appeal ... unless the Court of Appeal considers that–

a the appeal would raise an important point of principle or practice, or

b there is some other compelling reason for the Court of Appeal to hear it.

These appeal routes are shown in Figure 3.4.

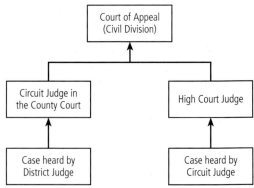

Figure 3.4 Appeal routes from the County Court

3.6.2 Appeals from the High Court

From a decision in the High Court the appeal usually goes to the Court of Appeal (Civil Division).

In rare cases there may be a 'leapfrog' appeal direct to the Supreme Court. Since 2015, such an appeal must involve an issue which is of national importance or raise issues of sufficient importance to warrant the leapfrog. In addition the Supreme Court has to give permission to appeal.

Further appeals

From a decision of the Court of Appeal there is a further appeal to the Supreme Court but only if the Supreme Court or Court of Appeal gives permission to appeal.

These appeal routes are shown in Figure 3.5.

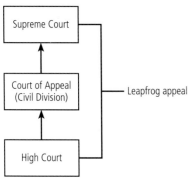

Figure 3.5 Appeal routes from the High Court

3.7 Evaluation of using the civil courts

3.7.1 Advantages of using the courts

The main advantages of using the courts to resolve a dispute are:

1   The process is fair in that everyone is treated alike. The judge is impartial.
2   The trial is conducted by a legal expert with the decision being made by a judge who is an experienced and qualified lawyer.
3   Enforcement of the court's decision is easier as any decision made by a court can be enforced through the courts.
4   There is an appeal process with specific appeal routes from decisions made in the courts, so, if the claimant is not happy with the decision, it is usually possible to appeal against it.
5   It may be possible to get legal aid, although legal aid for civil cases has been considerably reduced.

There are still a few types of case where it is available in the courts (see Chapter 11, section 11.3.2). Legal aid is not usually available in tribunals or other methods of dispute resolution.

Key term

Legal aid – government help in funding a case.

3.7.2 Disadvantages of using the courts

The main problems in using the civil courts are:

1   Cost – the costs of taking a case to court are often more than the amount claimed. In the High Court, the cost can be hundreds of thousands of pounds. For smaller claims, the costs are often more than the amount claimed.
2   Delay – there are many preliminary stages to go through that add to the length of a case. Even after the case is set down for hearing at court there is still a long wait – usually about one year for larger claims before the case is heard in court. The total of all this can mean that some cases are not finished for years.
3   Complicated process – there may be compulsory steps to be taken before a case is started in court. For example, for some types of case, the parties must use set pre-action protocols and give the other party certain information. When a case is started in court, there are forms to be filled in and set procedures to follow. These are all set out in the Civil Procedure Rules. All of this makes it complicated for an ordinary person to take a case without legal advice and help.
4   Uncertainty – there is no guarantee of winning a case. The person losing a case may have to pay the other side's costs. This makes it difficult to know how much a case is going to cost in advance. Delays in cases can also add to uncertainty and cost.

Summary

- Civil cases are heard in the County Court or the High Court.
- Claims are started by filing a claim form N1, setting out what is claimed and why.
- If a case is defended it is allocated to one of three tracks:
  - small claims
  - fast track
  - multi-track.
- The Woolf reforms:
  - brought in the three-track system
  - gave judges more responsibility for managing cases
  - simplified documents and procedures
  - created a single set of rules.
- Future proposals for reform include:
  - a mediation service to be available in the County Court
  - an online court.
- Appeals from the County Court:
  - Appeal from a decision by a District Judge is heard by a Circuit Judge.
  - Appeal from a decision by a Circuit Judge is heard by a High Court Judge.
- Appeals from the High Court:
  - normally go to the Court of Appeal (Civil Division)
  - 'leapfrog' appeal straight to the Supreme Court is possible where there is an issue of national importance or the case raises issues of sufficient importance.
- Advantages of using the courts are:
  - fair process
  - judge is a legal expert
  - easier to enforce decision
  - appeal system available
  - legal aid available for some cases.
- Disadvantages of using the courts are:
  - cost
  - delay
  - complicated
  - uncertain.

Chapter 4

Tribunals and Alternative Dispute Resolution

After reading this chapter you should be able to:
- Have an outline understanding of the tribunal structure
- Understand the role of Alternative Dispute Resolution
- Understand the role of online courts and Online Dispute Resolution
- Evaluate all forms of dispute resolution

4.1 Tribunals

Tribunals operate alongside the court system and have become an important part of the legal system. Many tribunals were created in the second half of the twentieth century, with the development of the welfare state. They were created in order to give people a method of enforcing their entitlement to certain social rights. However, unlike Alternative Dispute Resolution where the parties decide not to use the courts, the parties in tribunal cases cannot go to court to resolve their dispute. The tribunal must be used instead of court proceedings.

Key term

Tribunals – forums used instead of a court for deciding certain types of disputes. They are less formal than courts.

4.1.1 Role of tribunals

Tribunals enforce rights which have been granted through social and welfare legislation. There are many different rights, such as:
- the right to a mobility allowance for those who are too disabled to walk more than a very short distance
- the right to a payment if one is made redundant from work
- the right not to be discriminated against because of one's sex, race, age or disability
- the right of immigrants to have a claim for political asylum heard.

4.1.2 Organisation of tribunals

Tribunals were set up as the welfare state developed, so new developments resulted in the creation of a new tribunal. This led to more than 70 different types of tribunal. Each tribunal was separate and the various tribunals used different procedures. This made the system confused and complicated.

The whole system was reformed by the Tribunals, Courts and Enforcement Act 2007. This created a unified structure for tribunals, with a First-tier Tribunal to hear cases at first instance and an Upper Tribunal to hear appeals.

First-tier Tribunal

The First-tier Tribunal deals with about 600,000 cases each year and has nearly 200 judges and 3,600 lay members. It operates in seven Chambers (divisions). These are:
- Social Entitlement Chamber – this covers a wide range of matters such as Child Support, Criminal Injuries Compensation and Gender Recognition
- Health, Education and Social Care Chamber – this includes the former Mental Health Review Tribunal which dealt with appeals against the continued detention of those in mental hospitals – this Chamber also deals with Special Educational Needs issues
- War Pensions and Armed Forces Compensation Chamber
- General Regulatory Chamber
- Taxation Chamber
- Land, Property and Housing Chamber
- Asylum and Immigration Chamber.

As well as these, there is one tribunal which still operates separately from the First-tier Tribunal. This is the Employment Tribunal which hears claims for such matters as unfair dismissal, redundancy and discrimination.

Upper Tribunal

The Upper Tribunal is divided into four Chambers (divisions). These are:

- Administrative Appeals Chamber, which hears appeals from Social Entitlement Chamber, Health, Education and Social Care Chamber and War Pensions and Armed Forces Compensation Chamber
- Tax and Chancery Chamber
- Lands Chamber
- Asylum and Immigration Chamber.

From the Upper Tribunal there is a further possible appeal route to the Court of Appeal and from here a final appeal to the Supreme Court.

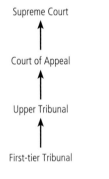

Supreme Court

↑

Court of Appeal

↑

Upper Tribunal

↑

First-tier Tribunal

Figure 4.1 Appeal route in tribunal cases

4.1.3 Composition of tribunals

Cases in the First-tier Tribunal are heard by a tribunal judge. Also, for some types of case, two non-lawyers will sit with the judge to make the decision. These people will have expertise in the particular field of the tribunal. For example, the two non-lawyers in a hearing about a claim to mobility allowance would be medically qualified, while there would be surveyors sitting on the Lands Tribunal. In Employment Tribunals one person will usually be from an employers' organisation and the other from an employees' organisation. This gives them a very clear understanding of employment issues.

4.1.4 Procedure in tribunals

Both sides must be given an opportunity to put their case. In some tribunals, especially Employment and Asylum Tribunals, this will be done in a formal way with witnesses giving evidence on oath and being cross-examined. Other tribunals will operate in a less formal way.

Funding for representation is only available in a few tribunals, so most applicants will not have a lawyer, but will present their own case. The exception is in Employment Tribunal cases, where employees often have representation provided by their Trade Union.

Where an applicant is putting his own case, then the tribunal judge must try to make sure that the applicant puts the case fully.

The decision of the tribunal is binding.

4.2 Evaluation of tribunals

4.2.1 Advantages of tribunals

Tribunals were set up to prevent the overloading of the courts with the extra cases that social and welfare rights claims generate and also to be a specialist venue for such cases.

For the applicant in tribunal cases, the advantages are that such cases are dealt with:

- more cheaply
- more quickly
- more informally
- by experts in the area.

Cheapness

As applicants are encouraged to represent themselves and not use lawyers, tribunal hearings do not normally involve the costs associated with court hearings. It is also rare for an order for costs to be made by a tribunal, so that an applicant need not fear a large bill if he loses the case.

Quick hearings

Most tribunal hearings are very short and can be dealt with in one day.

Informality

The hearing is more informal than in court. Parties are encouraged to present their own case. In addition, most cases are heard in private.

Expertise

In some tribunals two non-lawyers sit to hear the case with the tribunal judge. These members of the panel are experts in the type of case being heard. This gives them good knowledge and understanding of the issue in dispute.

First-tier Tribunal	• Operates in seven Chambers (divisions) • Deals with about 300,000 cases a year NB Employment Tribunal operates separately
Upper Tribunal	• Operates in four Chambers (divisions) • Hears appeals from the First-tier Tribunal • There is a further appeal to the Court of Appeal
Panel	• Case may be heard by a tribunal judge OR • By a tribunal judge sitting with two lay members who have expertise in the area
Advantages	• Cheaper than courts • Quicker than courts • More informal than courts • Use of experts
Disadvantages	• Legal aid only available in a few cases • More formal than ADR • There can be delay

Figure 4.2 Tribunals

4.2.2 Disadvantages of tribunals

Although there are a number of advantages there are also some disadvantages:
- lack of funding
- more formal
- delay.

Lack of funding

Legal aid funding is not available for most tribunals, which may put an applicant at a disadvantage if the other side (often an employer or government department) uses a lawyer. Legal aid is available for cases where fundamental human rights are involved, such as in cases about whether an asylum seeker has the right to remain in the United Kingdom or whether a patient should remain in a secure mental hospital.

More formal than ADR

A tribunal hearing is more formal than using ADR. The place is unfamiliar and the procedure can be confusing for individuals presenting their own case. Where applicants are not represented the judge is expected to take an inquisitorial role and help to establish the points that the applicant wishes to make. But this ideal is not always achieved.

Delay

Although the intention is that cases are dealt with quickly, the number of cases dealt with by tribunals means that there can be delays in getting a hearing. The use of non-lawyer members on the panel can add to this problem as they sit part-time, usually one day a

fortnight. If a case is complex lasting several days this can lead to proceedings being spread over a number of weeks or even months.

4.3 Alternative Dispute Resolution (ADR)

Using the courts to resolve disputes can be costly, in terms of both money and time. It can also be traumatic for the individuals involved and may not lead to the most satisfactory outcome for the case. An additional problem is that court proceedings are usually open to the public and the press, so there is nothing to stop the details of the case being published in local or national newspapers. It is not surprising, therefore, that more and more people and businesses are seeking other methods of resolving their disputes. Alternative methods are referred to as 'ADR', which stands for 'Alternative Dispute Resolution', and includes any method of resolving a dispute without resorting to using the courts. There are many different methods which can be used, ranging from very informal negotiations between the parties, to a comparatively formal commercial arbitration hearing.

Each method of ADR is examined and evaluated below.

4.3.1 Negotiation

Anyone who has a dispute with another person can always try to resolve it by negotiating directly with them. **Negotiation** has the advantage of being completely private, and is also the quickest and cheapest method of settling a dispute. If the parties cannot come to an agreement, they may decide to take the step of instructing solicitors, and those solicitors will usually try to negotiate a settlement.

In fact, even when court proceedings have been commenced, the lawyers for the parties will often continue to negotiate on behalf of their clients, and this is reflected in the high number of cases which are settled out of court. Once lawyers are involved, there will be a cost element – clearly, the longer negotiations go on, the higher the costs will be.

One of the worrying aspects is the number of cases that drag on for years, only to end in an agreed settlement literally 'at the door of the court' on the morning that the trial is due to start. It is this situation that ADR tries to avoid.

Evaluation of negotiation

All methods of ADR have advantages and disadvantages. Negotiation is the method with the most advantages and the fewest disadvantages.

Advantages of using negotiation

1 It can be conducted by the parties themselves. There is no need to use lawyers or other people in the process.
2 Negotiation can be used at any point in the dispute from the beginning right up to the start of a court hearing.
3 It is the cheapest method of resolving a dispute, particularly where the parties do the negotiation themselves.
4 A negotiated resolution can include agreement about future business deals. This can also be done in mediation and conciliation but cannot be done where the court makes the decision.

Disadvantages of using negotiation

1 It may not be successful, so that other ADR or court proceedings have to be used.
2 It is not suitable where the parties are very antagonistic towards each other as they will not be prepared to 'co-operate' in finding a resolution.
3 If there are repeated unsuccessful attempts at negotiation, it may prolong the whole issue.

4.3.2 Mediation

This is where a neutral mediator helps the parties to reach a compromise solution. The role of a mediator is to consult with each party and see how much common ground there is between them. He will explore the position with each party, looking at their needs and carrying offers to and fro, while keeping confidentiality.

A mediator will not usually tell the parties his own views of the merits of the dispute; it is part of the job to act as a 'facilitator', so that an agreement is reached by the parties. However, a mediator can be asked for an opinion of the merits, and in this case the mediation becomes more of an evaluation exercise, which again aims at ending the dispute.

Mediation is only suitable if there is some hope that the parties can co-operate. Companies who are used to negotiating contracts with each other are most likely to benefit from this approach.

Mediation is also important in family cases. Parties in a family case must normally show that they have attended a Mediation Information and Assessment Meeting (MIAM) before starting any court proceedings in a family case. There are exceptions, such as where there has been domestic violence, where they do not need to attend a MIAM.

Mediation can also take different forms, and the parties will choose the exact method they want. The important point in mediation is that the parties are in control: they make the decisions.

Mediation services

There are a growing number of commercial mediation services. One of the main ones for business disputes is the Centre for Effective Dispute Resolution (CEDR) which was set up in London in 1991. It has many important companies as members, including almost all of the big London law firms. In 2016 CEDR reported in its audit of mediation services that over the previous 12 months 10,000 commercial mediations had taken place through various mediation services. These mediations involved £10.5 billion worth of commercial claims. They also estimated that using mediation to resolve these disputes had saved £2.8 billion in management time, relationships, productivity and legal fees.

There are also mediation services aimed at resolving smaller disputes, for example, those between neighbours. An example of such a service is the West Sussex Mediation Service which offers mediation for disputes between neighbours to resolve disagreements arising from such matters as noise, car-parking, dogs or boundary fence disputes. The West Sussex Mediation Service also offers mediation for workplace disputes and for family disputes.

Other mediation services may offer mediation just for family issues. For example Kent Family Mediation Service offers mediation for family-based disputes on property, finances and children.

Look online

Search online for mediation services. You may be able to find a local service in your area. Look to see what types of disputes they deal with and what the mediation service will cost.

4.3.3 Conciliation

Conciliation is similar to mediation in that a neutral third party helps to resolve the dispute, but the main difference is that the conciliator will usually play a more pro-active role.

The conciliator discusses the issues with both parties in order to help them to reach a better understanding of each other's position. He will also be expected to suggest grounds for compromise, and the possible basis for a settlement. However, the conciliator has no authority to seek evidence or call witnesses.

In industrial disputes the Advisory Conciliation and Arbitration Service (ACAS) can give an impartial opinion on the legal position.

As with mediation, conciliation does not necessarily lead to a resolution, and it may be necessary to continue with a court action. In this both mediation and conciliation differ from arbitration where the arbitrator will make a decision that is final and binding on the parties.

Evaluation of mediation and conciliation

Advantages of mediation and conciliation

1. For both mediation and conciliation the parties are in control and can withdraw from the process at any point. Also a compromise cannot be reached without the agreement of both parties.
2. The decision need not be a strictly legal one sticking to the letter of the law: it is more likely to be based on commercial common sense and compromise.
3. This also makes it easier for companies to continue to do business with each other in the future, and it may include agreements about the conduct of future business between the parties. This is something that cannot happen if the court gives judgment, as the court is only concerned with the present dispute.
4. Mediation and conciliation avoid the adversarial conflict of the court room and the winner/loser result of court proceedings. It has been said that with mediation, everyone wins.

A high number of cases are resolved through mediation and conciliation. The Centre for Dispute Resolution claims that over 80 per cent of cases in which it is asked to act are settled. It has also been found that even if the actual mediation session did not resolve the dispute, the parties were more likely to settle the case without going to court than in non-mediated cases. There is also the possibility that the issues may at least have been clarified, and so any court hearing will be shorter than if mediation had not been attempted.

Disadvantages of mediation and conciliation

1. The main disadvantage of using mediation or conciliation is that there is no guarantee the matter will be resolved, and it will then be necessary to go to court after the failed attempt at mediation. In such situations there is additional cost and delay to resolution.

2 Successful mediation and conciliation requires a skilled mediator or conciliator with 'natural talent, honed skills and accumulated experience'. If these qualities are not present, mediation can become a bullying exercise in which the weaker party may be forced into a settlement. This was recognised by one mediator who said:

> Leaning on people is the only way that you will get a settlement. If you lean on two halves of a see-saw it is usually the weaker half that will break and that is where you should apply your effort.

This is even more likely to happen in conciliation where the conciliator plays an active role in suggesting grounds for compromise or settlement.

3 Amounts paid in mediated settlements are often lower than the amounts agreed in other settlements, and considerably lower than amounts awarded by the courts.

4.3.4 Arbitration

The word 'arbitration' is used to cover two quite different processes. The first is where the courts use a more informal procedure to hear cases. The second meaning of the word 'arbitration' is where the parties agree to submit their claims to private arbitration; this is the type of arbitration that is relevant to Alternative Dispute Resolution, as it is another way of resolving a dispute without the need for a court case.

Private arbitration is now governed by the Arbitration Act 1996, and s 1 of that Act sets out the principles behind it. This says that:

a the object of arbitration is to obtain the fair resolution of disputes by an impartial tribunal without unnecessary delay or expense;

b the parties should be free to agree how their disputes are resolved, subject only to such safeguards as are necessary in the public interest.

So, arbitration is the voluntary submission by the parties, of their dispute, to the judgment of some person other than a judge. Such an agreement will usually be in writing, and indeed the Arbitration Act 1996 applies only to written arbitration agreements. The precise way in which the arbitration is carried out is left almost entirely to the parties' agreement.

The agreement to arbitrate

The agreement to go to arbitration can be made by the parties at any time. It can be before a dispute

arises or when the dispute becomes apparent. Many commercial contracts include what is called a *Scott v Avery* clause, which is a clause where the parties in their original contract agree that in the event of a dispute arising between them, they will have that dispute settled by arbitration. Figure 4.3 shows a *Scott v Avery* clause in the author's contract for writing this book.

Dispute resolution

Any dispute or question which may arise under or in connection with this Agreement, or the legal relationships established by it, shall be referred to the arbitration scheme operated by the UK Publishers' Association from time to time.

Figure 4.3 Arbitration clause from author's contract

Where there is an arbitration agreement in a contract, the Arbitration Act 1996 states that the court will normally refuse to deal with any dispute; the matter must go to arbitration as agreed by the parties. However, the rules are different for consumer claims where the dispute is for an amount which can be dealt with in the small claims track. In such circumstances the consumer may choose whether to abide by the agreement to go to private arbitration, or to insist that the case be heard in the small claims track.

An agreement to go to arbitration can also be made after the dispute arises. Arbitration is becoming increasingly popular in commercial cases.

The arbitrator

Section 15 of the Arbitration Act 1996 states that the parties are free to agree on the number of arbitrators, so that a panel of two or three may be used or there may be a sole arbitrator. If the parties cannot agree on a number then the Act provides that only one arbitrator should be appointed. The Act also says that the parties are free to agree on the procedure for appointing an arbitrator. In fact most agreements to go to arbitration will either name an arbitrator or provide a method of choosing one, and in commercial contracts it is often provided that the president of the appropriate trade organisation will appoint the arbitrator.

There is also the Institute of Arbitrators which provides trained arbitrators for major disputes. In many cases the arbitrator will be someone who has expertise in the particular field involved in the dispute, but if the dispute involves a point of law, the parties may decide to appoint a lawyer. If there is no agreement on who or how to appoint, then, as a last resort, the court can be asked to appoint an appropriate arbitrator.

The arbitration hearing

The actual procedure is left to the agreement of the parties in each case, so that there are many forms of hearing. In some cases the parties may opt for a 'paper' arbitration, where the two sides put all the points they wish to raise into writing and submit this, together with any relevant documents, to the arbitrator. He will then read all the documents, and make his decision. Alternatively, the parties may send all these documents to the arbitrator, but before he makes his decision both parties will attend a hearing at which they make oral submissions to the arbitrator to support their case. Where necessary, witnesses can be called to give evidence. If witnesses are asked to give evidence orally then this will not normally be given on oath, that is the person will not have to swear to tell the truth. However, if the parties wish, then the witness can be asked to give evidence on oath and the whole procedure will be very formal. If witnesses are called to give evidence, the Arbitration Act 1996 allows for the use of court procedures to ensure the attendance of those witnesses.

The date, time and place of the arbitration hearing are all matters for the parties to decide in consultation with the arbitrator. This gives a great degree of flexibility to the proceedings; the parties can choose what is most convenient for all the people concerned.

The award

The decision made by the arbitrator is called an 'award' and is binding on the parties. It can even be enforced through the courts if necessary. The decision is usually final, though it can be challenged in the courts on the grounds of serious irregularity in the proceedings or on a point of law (s 68 of the Arbitration Act 1996).

Evaluation of arbitration

Advantages of arbitration

There are several advantages which largely arise from the fact that the parties have the freedom to make their own arbitration agreement, and decide exactly how formal or informal they wish it to be. The main advantages are as follows:

1. The parties may choose their own arbitrator, and can therefore decide whether the matter is best dealt with by a technical expert, a lawyer or a professional arbitrator.
2. If there is a question of quality this can be decided by an expert in the particular field, saving the expense of calling expert witnesses and the time that would be used in explaining all the technicalities to a judge.
3. The hearing time and place can be arranged to suit both parties.
4. The actual procedure used is flexible and the parties can choose that which is most suited to the situation; this will usually result in a more informal and relaxed hearing than in court.
5. The matter is dealt with in private and there will be no publicity.
6. The dispute will be resolved more quickly than through a court hearing.
7. Arbitration proceedings are usually much cheaper than going to court.
8. The award is normally final and can be enforced through the courts.

Disadvantages of arbitration

There are some disadvantages of arbitration, especially where the parties are not on an equal footing as regards their ability to present their case. This is because legal aid is not available for arbitration and this may disadvantage an individual in a case against a business; if the case had gone to court, a person on a low income would have qualified for legal aid and so had the benefit of a lawyer to present his case. The other main disadvantages are as follows:

1. An unexpected legal point may arise in the case which is not suitable for decision by a non-lawyer arbitrator.
2. If a professional arbitrator is used, his fees may be expensive.
3. It will also be expensive if the parties opt for a formal hearing, with witnesses giving evidence and lawyers representing both sides.
4. The rights of appeal are limited.
5. The delays for commercial and international arbitration may be nearly as great as those in the courts if a professional arbitrator and lawyers are used.

These problems of delay and expense have meant that arbitration has, to some extent, lost its popularity with companies as a method of dispute resolution. More and more businesses are turning to the alternatives offered by centres such as the Centre for Dispute Resolution or, in the case of international disputes, choosing to have the matter resolved in another country.

Prior to 1996, the law on arbitration had become complex, and the Arbitration Act 1996 was an attempt to improve the process. In general it can be said that certain types of dispute are suitable for arbitration, particularly commercial disagreements between two businesses where the parties have little hope of finding sufficient common ground to make mediation a realistic prospect, providing there is no major point of law involved.

4.3.5 Online Dispute Resolution (ODR)

The development of computers and the internet has led to Online Dispute Resolution services. There are a number of well-known sources that offer ODR for specific types of dispute. These include eBay for disputes arising from purchases on eBay, Resolver that aims at consumer problems and the Financial Ombudsman Service for disputes between consumers and financial service providers.

eBay

eBay at **www.ebay.co.uk** resolves a remarkable 60 million disagreements globally among traders on eBay every year using ODR. If there is a dispute over a transaction on eBay, for example non-payment by a buyer or a complaint by a buyer that items delivered did not match their description, the parties are initially encouraged to resolve the matter themselves by online negotiation. To help them do this, there is clearly structured, practical advice on how to avoid misunderstandings and reach a resolution. Guidance is also given on the standards by which eBay assesses the merit of complaints.

If the dispute cannot be resolved by negotiation, then eBay offers a resolution service in which the parties enter a discussion area to present their argument. Then a member of eBay's staff determines a binding outcome under its Money Back Guarantee. This e-adjudication process is fast with strict time limits.

Resolver

Another service is provided by Resolver at **www.resolver. co.uk**. Resolver is a UK-based online facility that helps consumers raise complaints with suppliers and retailers. This works in a very different way to the eBay site.

The Resolver site contains the email contacts of the complaint departments of over 2,000 major organisations. A consumer with a complaint is given online assistance in drafting the complaint. This is done through a form-filling exercise and helped by the provision of standard phrases. The complaint is then emailed directly to the complaint department of the relevant business. The businesses are urged to respond to the Resolver email address so that the exchange of messages can be stored on the consumer's case file that is then maintained on the site.

The service presently covers energy, telecoms, transport, loan companies, restaurants, high street shops, solicitors, and many more sectors. Resolver provides a platform through which parties can discuss their differences in a structured way. Users are alerted by email to any responses. The service is free of charge, both to consumers and to the organisations to whom they are complaining.

Financial Ombudsman Service

Another type of ODR service is offered by Financial Ombudsman Service at **www.financial-ombudsman.org. uk**. This service was established by statute in 2000 as the mandatory ADR body in the financial services sector. Its function is to resolve disputes between consumers and UK-based financial businesses quickly and with minimum formality.

It works on the principle that a dispute is usually best resolved at the earliest possible stage and that most problems can be resolved without needing a formal determination by an ombudsman. Where a complaint is referred to the service, the process is geared towards early and informal resolution.

The Service's case-handlers ('adjudicators') attempt to facilitate an amicable resolution to the dispute between the two parties, usually resulting in adjudicators writing to parties with their view on what the fair and reasonable outcome should be.

If both parties agree (which usually happens in around 90 per cent of cases), the dispute is resolved. If either party disagrees then they can ask for the case to be referred to an ombudsman for final, binding, determination.

An ombudsman's determinations can be accepted or rejected by a consumer, but if a consumer accepts the decision then it is binding. The Financial Ombudsman Service resolves about half a million disputes a year.

Other online services

There are also an increasing number of websites offering ODR. Most of these are aimed at disputes between businesses and are international, e.g. **www.onlinemediators.com** and **www.mediate.com**.

Evaluation of ODR

Advantages of ODR

1 The main advantage of ODR is that people can do it from their own home. With the ever increasing use of computers the majority of people are used to doing things online. Many sites also help the user by giving prompts and choices so that the issues are explained clearly.

2 For some sites, it is free. Even where there is a charge it is likely to be a set amount and known at the beginning of the process. There are no hidden costs. There is also no need to use lawyers, so saving these costs.

3 Where the dispute involves people in different countries, ODR is a very convenient way of resolving a dispute. No one has to travel and the saving of costs is considerable. For the many businesses that now operate worldwide, ODR is an important development in dispute resolution.

Disadvantages of ODR

1 ODR is only suitable for certain types of dispute. It is particularly useful where the issue is about a contract, as with eBay where all the disputes are related to contracts made to buy and sell on eBay. It is not so suitable where the issues arise from an event such as a car accident. In such cases it is often necessary to decide who is telling the truth and face-to-face questioning is more effective.

2 It is also necessary that the parties accept the decision; otherwise it may still be necessary to start court proceedings.

4.3.6 Online court

In 2016 it was proposed that there should be an online court. It is hoped this court will be in operation by 2020.

There would be three stages to the process:

Stage 1 A largely automated, interactive online process for the identification of the issues and the provision of documentary evidence.

Stage 2 Conciliation and case management carried out by case managers.

Stage 3 If the case is not resolved by Stage 2, then there would be resolution by a judge. For this the online court would use documents on screen, telephone video or face-to-face meetings according to the needs of each case.

The intention is that cases would be dealt with more quickly and at lower cost. The hope is that the online court will be in operation by 2020.

This proposal by Lord Briggs followed the publication of a report, 'Online Dispute Resolution for Low Value Claims', by the online dispute advisory group of the Civil Justice Council. They focused on the challenge of providing a court-based dispute resolution service for low value claims that would be:

- affordable – for all citizens, regardless of their means;
- accessible – especially for citizens with physical disabilities, for whom attendance in court is difficult if not impossible;
- intelligible – to the non-lawyer, so that citizens can feel comfortable in representing themselves and will be at no disadvantage in doing so;
- appropriate – for the internet generation and for an increasingly online society in which so much activity is conducted electronically;
- speedy – so that the period of uncertainty of an unresolved problem is minimized;
- consistent – providing some degree of predictability in its decisions;
- trustworthy – a forum in whose honesty and reliability users can have confidence;
- focused – so that judges are called upon to resolve disputes that genuinely require their experience and knowledge; ...
- proportionate – which means that the costs of pursuing a claim are sensible by reference to the amount at issue;
- fair – affording an opportunity for citizens to present their cases to an impartial expert, delivering outcomes that parties feel are just; ...
- final – so that court users can get on with their lives.

The group thought that the present court system fails on many of these points and that an online court would allow far more people access to justice. However, it did point out that online procedures will not be appropriate for all cases. It would work very well for paper-based disputes but would not work so well where the issue is which side is telling the truth about an incident, as might occur in a negligence case.

Method	How it works	Comments
Negotiation	Parties themselves	Quickest and cheapest
Mediation	Parties with the help of neutral third party	Suitable if parties can co-operate Parties are in control
Conciliation	Parties with the help of neutral third party who plays an active role in suggesting a solution	Suitable if parties are prepared to listen to the conciliator's suggestions Weaker party may be 'bullied'
Online Dispute Resolution	Various internet sites available – some for specific types of dispute, others general mediation services	Easy access
Arbitration	Parties agree to let a third party make a binding decision	Decision can be enforced through the courts More expensive than other forms of ADR
Litigation	Parties go to court to decide the dispute	Expensive Long delays

Figure 4.4 Methods of dispute resolution

4.4 Evaluating the difference between using the courts and ADR

Using ADR is usually much cheaper than going to court. For small local disputes the parties are unlikely to use lawyers so saving legal fees. In commercial mediations lawyers may be involved but CEDR's audit in 2016 shows that even so very large savings are made by using arbitration.

Another advantage of most forms of ADR is that the parties are in control. In negotiation and mediation, the parties can choose to stop at any time. An agreement will only be reached if both sides accept it.

The fact that the parties come to an agreement has another advantage; it means they will be able to go on doing business with each other. Court proceedings are more adversarial, and will end with one party winning and one party losing. This is likely to make the parties very bitter about the dispute.

Tip

Remember that tribunals and ADR are separate topics. Don't confuse them.

Summary

- Tribunals enforce rights granted by social and welfare legislation.
- Cases are heard in the First-tier Tribunal by a tribunal judge sitting alone or with two lay members.
- There is a right of appeal to the Upper Tribunal.
- Compared to going to court, tribunals:
  - are cheaper
  - are quicker
  - are more informal
  - use experts in the area.
- Disadvantages of using tribunals are:
  - lack of legal aid for applicants
  - more formal than ADR
  - delay in complex cases.
- Alternative Dispute Resolution (ADR) aims to resolve a dispute without the need to go to court.

- Negotiation is where the parties or their lawyers negotiate directly to see if they can find a resolution.
- Mediation is where an independent mediator helps the parties to reach a compromise solution.
- Mediation services are often used by businesses where they have a dispute with another business.
- Conciliation is where an independent conciliator plays a more active role in helping the parties to reach a compromise solution.
- Online Dispute Resolution is becoming increasingly available.
- Arbitration is where an independent arbitrator decides the case.
- Arbitration is more expensive than other forms of ADR.
- ADR is cheap, flexible and can allow the parties to remain on good terms

Chapter 5

Criminal courts

After reading this chapter you should be able to:
- Understand the classification of offences and which offences are tried in which court
- Understand pre-trial procedure
- Understand the jurisdiction of the Magistrates' Court
- Understand the jurisdiction of the Crown Court
- Understand the appeal system from both the Magistrates' Court and the Crown Court

5.1 Classification of offences

The type of offence will make a difference as to where the case will be tried and who will try it. For trial purposes criminal offences are divided into three categories. These are:
- summary offences
- triable-either-way offences
- indictable offences.

5.1.1 Summary offences

Summary offences are the least serious offences. They are always tried in the Magistrates' Court. They include nearly all driving offences. They also include common assault, criminal damage which has caused less than £5,000 damage and shoplifting where the value of the goods is less than £200.

> **Key term**
>
> Summary offence – an offence that can only be tried in the Magistrates' Court.

5.1.2 Triable-either-way offences

These are the middle range of crimes. As the name implies, these cases can be tried in either the Magistrates' Court or the Crown Court. They include a wide range of offences such as theft and assault causing actual bodily harm.

In order to decide whether a triable-either-way offence will be tried in the Magistrates' Court or the Crown Court, the defendant is first asked whether he is pleading guilty or not guilty. If the defendant is pleading guilty the case is heard by the magistrates. Where the plea is not guilty the defendant then has the right to ask for the case to be tried at the Crown Court by a jury.

The magistrates can also decide that the case is too serious for them and make the decision to send the case to the Crown Court.

> **Key term**
>
> Triable-either-way offence – an offence that can be tried in either the Magistrates' Court or the Crown Court.

5.1.3 Indictable offences

These are the most serious crimes and include murder, manslaughter and rape. The first preliminary hearing for such an offence will be at the Magistrates' Court, but then the case is transferred to the Crown Court. All indictable offences must be tried at the Crown Court by a judge and jury.

> **Key term**
>
> Indictable offence – an offence that has to be tried at the Crown Court.

Category of offence	Place of trial	Examples of offences
Summary	Magistrates' Court	Driving without insurance Taking a vehicle without consent Common assault
Triable either way	Magistrates' Court OR Crown Court	Theft Assault causing actual bodily harm Obtaining property by deception
Indictable	Crown Court	Murder Manslaughter Rape Robbery

Figure 5.1 The three categories of offence

5.2 Pre-trial procedure in criminal cases

The criminal law is set down by the state. A breach of the criminal law can lead to a penalty such as imprisonment or a fine being imposed on the defendant in the name of the state. Therefore, bringing a prosecution for a criminal offence is usually seen as part of the role of the state. Indeed, the majority of criminal prosecutions are conducted by the Crown Prosecution Service which is the state agency for criminal prosecutions.

The first hearing of all criminal cases is at the Magistrates' Court.

5.2.1 Pre-trial procedure for summary offences

Under the better case management scheme now operating in the Magistrates' Court, the aim is to complete the case at the earliest possible hearing. So where the defendant pleads guilty and is either already legally represented or does not want legal representation, the magistrates will go ahead with the case and, wherever possible, decide on the sentence there and then.

Many driving offences can be dealt with at a first hearing through a procedure under which the defendant can plead guilty by post, so that attendance at court is not necessary.

If the defendant is pleading not guilty, the magistrates must at this first hearing try to discover the issues involved in the case, so that it can proceed as quickly and efficiently as possible.

5.2.2 Pre-trial procedure for triable-either-way offences

Since triable-either-way offences can be tried at either the Magistrates' Court or the Crown Court, the pre-trial procedure has first to decide where the case will be tried. There has to be a plea before venue hearing.

Plea before venue

Under this procedure, the defendant is first asked whether he pleads guilty or not guilty. If the plea is guilty then the defendant has no right to ask for the case to be heard at the Crown Court. However, the magistrates may decide to send the defendant to the Crown Court for sentence.

Mode of trial

If the defendant pleads not guilty then the magistrates must carry out 'mode of trial' proceedings to decide whether the case will be tried in the Magistrates' Court or the Crown Court.

The magistrates first decide if they think the case is suitable for trial in the Magistrates' Court and whether they are prepared to accept jurisdiction. Under s 19 of the Magistrates' Court Act 1980, they must consider the nature and seriousness of the case, their own powers of punishment and any representations of the prosecution and defence.

Cases involving complex questions of fact or law should be sent to the Crown Court. Other relevant factors which may make a case more suitable for trial at the Crown Court include:
- where there was a breach of trust by the defendant
- where the crime was committed by an organised gang.

Defendant's election

If the magistrates are prepared to accept jurisdiction, the defendant is then told he has the right to choose trial by jury, but may be tried by the magistrates if he agrees to this course. However, he is also warned that if the case is tried by the magistrates and at the end of the case he is found guilty, the magistrates can send him to the Crown Court for sentence if they feel their powers of punishment are insufficient.

Once the magistrates have decided to send the case to the Crown Court or the defendant elects trial there, the case will be sent to the Crown Court and all other pre-trial matters dealt with there.

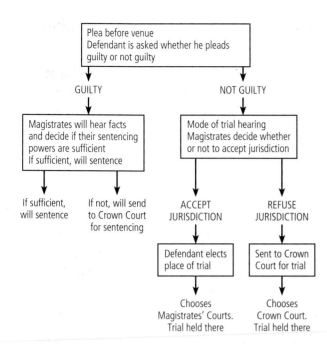

Figure 5.2 Flow chart of procedure for triable-either-way offences

5.2.3 Evaluation of trial court choices

A main point for discussion is whether defendants should be allowed to choose the court in which they will be tried. This involves the right to trial by jury. The only offences for which there is a choice of who should try the case are triable-either-way offences

Remember that cases where the defendant pleads not guilty to a summary offence can never be tried by a jury. These are always tried by magistrates. Also remember that cases where the defendant pleads not guilty to an indictable offence are always tried by jury.

In triable-either-way cases, most defendants choose to be tried by magistrates in the Magistrates' Courts. However, there are some reasons why defendants may prefer to be tried by a jury in the Crown Court.

Advantages of trial in the Crown Court

Defendants are more likely to be acquitted (found not guilty) at the Crown Court than in the Magistrates' Court. Only about 15 per cent of defendants who plead not guilty in the Magistrates' Courts are found not guilty. At the Crown Court, over 60 per cent of defendants are acquitted.

An interesting point on the number of acquittals in the Crown Court is that most are as a result of the judge discharging the case or directing that the defendant be found not guilty. This will happen where the prosecution drops the case or witnesses fail to attend court, so there is no evidence against the defendant.

However, juries do acquit in more cases than magistrates. They acquit in about 35 per cent of cases, compared with the 15 per cent acquittal rate in the Magistrates' Courts.

Research conducted into the reasons why defendants chose trial at the Crown Court found that most did so as the result of advice from their lawyers. The main factor in the choice was the higher chance of an acquittal.

However, there were other factors influencing the choice, including (where defendants were held in custody awaiting trial) a wish to serve part of the sentence in a remand prison!

Another reason for choosing trial at the Crown Court is that the defendant is more likely to receive legal aid. This means that the state will pay for his legal representation.

The legal representative at the Crown Court must have a certificate of advocacy giving the right to present cases at the Crown Court. This is likely to mean that the lawyer is more experienced at presenting cases in court.

Disadvantages of trial in the Crown Court

There is usually a longer wait before the case is dealt with at the Crown Court than for cases in the Magistrates' Courts. If the defendant is not given bail, this waiting period is spent in prison.

The stress of a trial in the Crown Court is much greater and the trial is likely to last considerably longer than a trial in the Magistrates' Court. Cases in the Crown Court usually take several days whereas cases in the Magistrates' Court are rarely more than half a day.

Cases in the Crown Court are also more likely to be reported in the media than cases in the Magistrates' Courts.

The costs of the case are much great than those in the Magistrates' Court. If the defendant has to pay for his own lawyers, this will be expensive. In addition, if the defendant is ordered to pay part of the prosecution costs, this will be a greater amount than in the Magistrates' Court.

Another disadvantage is that, for defendants who are found guilty, the judge at the Crown Court has the power to give a greater sentence than the magistrates.

5.2.4 Pre-trial procedure for indictable offences

Even for indictable offences which are the most serious classification of offences, the first hearing is in the Magistrates' Court. This may deal with whether the defendant wants to apply for legal aid and issues of bail. All indictable offences are then sent to the Crown Court immediately.

All other pre-trial and case management issues are dealt with by a judge at the Crown Court.

5.3 Magistrates' Courts

There are about 240 Magistrates' Courts in England and Wales. They are local courts so there will be a Magistrates' Court in almost every town, while big cities will have several courts. Each court deals with cases that have a connection with its geographical area and they have jurisdiction over a variety of matters involving criminal cases.

Cases are heard by magistrates, who are either qualified District Judges or unqualified lay justices. There is also a legally qualified clerk attached to each court to assist the magistrates.

See Chapter 7 for further details on magistrates.

Magistrates are limited in the sentences they can impose. The maximum prison sentence they can give is six months for one offence or 12 months for two offences. Magistrates can also impose fines. For the top end of the range of offences there is no limit on the amount magistrates can fine, but for other offences there are limits. Magistrates can also impose a range of other penalties such as community orders or a conditional discharge.

See Chapter 6 for more details on sentencing.

5.3.1 Jurisdiction of the Magistrates' Courts

In criminal cases the Magistrates' Courts deal with a variety of matters. They have a very large workload as they do the following:

- try all summary cases
- try any triable-either-way offences in which the magistrates are prepared to accept jurisdiction and where the defendant agrees to summary trial by the magistrates.

These two categories account for about 97 per cent of all criminal cases, and about 1.5 million cases take place each year in Magistrates' Courts. As well as these duties, the magistrates also:

- deal with the preliminary hearings of any triable-either-way offence which is going to be tried in the Crown Court
- deal with the first preliminary hearing of all indictable offences
- deal with all the side matters connected to criminal cases, such as issuing warrants for arrest and deciding bail applications
- try cases in the youth court where the defendants are aged 10–17 inclusive.

Giving evidence in a Magistrates' Court

5.4 The Crown Court

5.4.1 Jurisdiction of the Crown Court

The Crown Court currently sits in about 90 different centres throughout England and Wales. Each year the Crown Court deals with about 80,000 cases. These cover:

- triable-either-way offences where the defendant has elected to be tried in the Crown Court or where the magistrates have decided the case is too serious for them and sent it to the Crown Court
- all indictable offences
- appeals from the Magistrates' Court.

5.4.2 Dealing with cases at the Crown Court

If a defendant pleads guilty at the Crown Court a judge decides the sentence. If a defendant pleads not guilty at the Crown Court the case is tried by a judge and a jury of 12. The judge decides points of law. The jury decides on the facts whether the defendant is guilty or not guilty. If the defendant is found guilty, the judge then decides the appropriate sentence.

For appeals from the Magistrates' Court to the Crown Court, the case is heard by a judge sitting with two lay magistrates.

5.5 Appeals and appellate courts

It is possible for a defendant to appeal against conviction and/or sentence in any criminal case. The prosecution rights of appeal are more limited. The appeal routes from the Magistrates' Court and from the Crown Court are completely different.

5.6 Appeals from the Magistrates' Courts

There are two different routes of appeal from the Magistrates' Court. The route used will depend on whether the appeal is only on a point of law or whether it is for other reasons.

5.6.1 Appeals to the Crown Court

This is the normal route of appeal from the Magistrates' Court. It is only available to the defence. If the defendant pleaded guilty at the Magistrates' Court, then he can only appeal against sentence.

If the defendant pleaded not guilty and was convicted then the appeal can be against conviction and/or sentence. In both cases the defendant has an automatic right to appeal and does not need to get leave (permission) to appeal.

At the Crown Court the case is completely reheard by a judge and two magistrates. They can come to the same decision as the magistrates and confirm the conviction or they can decide that the case is not proved and reverse the decision. In some cases it is possible for them to vary the decision and find the defendant guilty of a lesser offence.

Where the appeal is against sentence, the Crown Court can confirm the sentence or they can increase or decrease it. However, any increase can only be up to the magistrates' maximum powers for the case.

If it becomes apparent that there is a point of law to be decided, then the Crown Court can decide that point of law, but there is the possibility of a further appeal by way of case stated being made to the Administrative Court (see below).

5.6.2 Case stated appeals

A case stated appeal goes to the Administrative Court. Both the prosecution and the defence can use this appeal route. The appeal can be made direct from the Magistrates' Court or following an appeal to the Crown Court.

This route is only used by the defendant against a conviction or by the prosecution against an acquittal in situations where they claim the magistrates came to the wrong decision because they made a mistake about the law.

The magistrates (or the Crown Court) are asked to state the case by setting out their findings of fact and their decision. The appeal is then argued on the basis of what the law is on those facts; no witnesses are called. Although the appeal is made to the Administrative Court, the case can be (and usually is) sent to be heard by a panel of two High Court Judges from the Queen's Bench Division in the Divisional Court. There are usually only about 100 case stated appeals each year.

The Divisional Court may confirm, vary or reverse the decision or remit (send back) the case to the Magistrates' Court for the magistrates to implement the decision on the law.

Further appeal to the Supreme Court

From the decision of the Queen's Bench Divisional Court there is a possibility of a further appeal to the Supreme Court. Such an appeal can only be made if:
a   the Divisional Court certifies that a point of law of general public importance is involved and
b   the Divisional Court or the Supreme Court gives permission to appeal because the point is one which ought to be considered by the Supreme Court.

Only a very small number of cases will go to the Supreme Court. An example of a case which followed this appeal route was *C v DPP* (1994).

A diagram setting out the appeal routes from the Magistrates' Court is shown in Figure 5.3.

Key case

C v DPP (1994)

This case concerned the legal point about the presumption of criminal responsibility of children from the age of ten up to their fourteenth birthday. Until this case, it had been accepted that a child of this age could only be convicted if the prosecution proved that the child knew he was doing wrong. The Divisional Court held that times had changed, children were more mature and the rule was not needed. They decided that children of this age were presumed to know the difference between right and wrong, and that the prosecution did not need to prove 'mischievous discretion'.

The case was then appealed to the House of Lords who overruled the Divisional Court, holding that the law was still that a child of this age was presumed not to know he was doing wrong, and therefore not to have the necessary intention for any criminal offence. A child of this age could only be convicted if the prosecution disproved this presumption by bringing evidence to show that the child was aware that what he was doing was seriously wrong. The House of Lords ruling was on the basis that it was for Parliament to make such a major change to the law, not the courts. The courts were bound by precedent.

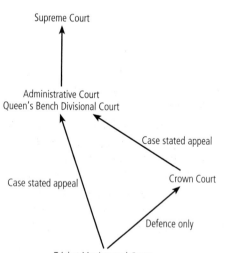

Figure 5.3 Appeal routes from the Magistrates' Court

5.7 Appeals from the Crown Court

The rights of appeal are for the defendant and the prosecutor.

5.7.1 Appeals by the defendant

The defendant has the possibility of appealing against conviction and/or sentence to the Court of Appeal (Criminal Division). So, at the end of any trial in which a defendant has been found guilty, his lawyer should advise him on whether there should be an appeal.

Leave to appeal

In all cases the defendant must get leave to appeal from the Court of Appeal or a certificate that the case is fit for appeal from the trial judge. The idea is that cases which are without merit are filtered out and the court's time saved.

The application for leave to appeal is considered by a single judge of the Court of Appeal in private, although if he refuses it is possible to apply to a full Court of Appeal for leave.

Grounds for appeal

The Criminal Appeal Act 1995 simplified the grounds under which the court can allow an appeal. The Act states that the Court of Appeal:

a shall allow an appeal against conviction if they think that the conviction is unsafe; and

b shall dismiss such an appeal in any other case.

New evidence

Any new evidence which the defence wants to produce at the appeal must appear to be capable of belief and would afford a ground for an appeal. Also it has to be considered whether it would have been admissible at the trial and why it was not produced at that trial.

Court of Appeal's powers

If the Court of Appeal decide that the conviction is unsafe, they can allow the defendant's appeal and quash the conviction. Alternatively they can vary the conviction to that of a lesser offence of which the jury could have convicted the defendant. If the Court of Appeal decides that the conviction is safe, then they will dismiss the appeal.

The Court of Appeal also has the power to order that there should be a retrial of the case in front of a new jury. The power was given to the court in 1988. Initially it was not often used; in 1989 only one retrial was ordered. However, its use has increased, with between 50 and 70 retrials being ordered each year.

If the appeal is against sentence, the court can decrease the sentence but cannot increase it on the defendant's appeal.

5.7.2 Appeals by the prosecution

Originally the prosecution had no right to appeal against either the verdict or sentence passed in the Crown Court. Gradually, however, some limited rights of appeal have been given to it by Parliament.

Against a judge's ruling

If the trial judge gives a ruling on a point of law which effectively stops the case against the defendant, the prosecution now has the right to appeal against that ruling. This right was given by the Criminal Justice Act 2003. It makes sure that an error of law by the judge does not lead to an acquittal.

Against acquittal

There are only two limited situations in which the prosecution can appeal against an acquittal by a jury.

1 Where the acquittal was the result of the jury being 'nobbled'.

This is where one or more jurors are bribed or threatened by associates of the defendant. In these circumstances, provided there has been an actual conviction for jury nobbling, the Criminal Procedure and Investigations Act 1996 allows the prosecution to appeal and the Court of Appeal can order a retrial.

Once the acquittal is quashed, the prosecution could then start new proceedings for the same offence.

2 Where there is new and compelling evidence of the acquitted person's guilt and it is in the public interest for the defendant to be retried.

This power is given by the Criminal Justice Act 2003 and it is only available for some 30 serious offences, including murder, manslaughter, rape and terrorism offences. It is known as double jeopardy, since the defendant is being tried twice for the same offence.

The DPP has to consent to the reopening of investigations in the case. Once the evidence has been found, then the prosecution has to apply to the Court of Appeal for the original acquittal to be quashed.

This power has been used in cases where new techniques of DNA testing now show that a defendant who is acquitted is in fact the offender. The first case in which this power was used is shown in the article in the next column.

Another case in which this power was used was in 2011 when two defendants who had been previously acquitted of the murder of black teenager, Stephen Lawrence, were retried and convicted some 19 years after his murder. Part of the new evidence was a DNA match with Stephen's blood found on the clothing of one of the defendants. This evidence became available due to improved DNA testing techniques.

Referring a point of law

Where the judge may have made an error in explaining the law to the jury, the prosecution have the right to refer a point of law to the Court of Appeal if the defendant is acquitted. This right is under s 36 of the Criminal Justice Act 1972 which allows the Attorney General to refer the point of law to the Court of Appeal in order to get a ruling on the law. The decision by the Court of Appeal on that point of law does not affect the acquittal but it creates a precedent for any future case involving the same point of law.

Against sentence

Under s 36 of the Criminal Justice Act 1988 the Attorney General can apply for leave to refer an unduly lenient sentence to the Court of Appeal for re-sentencing. The victim or members of the public can submit cases to the Attorney General for consideration. If the Attorney General thinks the sentence is unduly lenient then that case will be referred to the Court of Appeal. About 120 cases are referred each year and the sentence is increased in about 80 per cent of these cases.

In the news

Man admits murder in first UK double jeopardy case

Fifteen years after he was cleared of murder, the first person in Britain to face a retrial under new double jeopardy rules admitted today that he killed his victim.

Billy Dunlop, 43, pleaded guilty to murdering pizza delivery girl Julie Hogg, 22, in Billingham, Teeside, when he appeared at the Old Bailey today.

Dunlop stood trial twice in 1991 for her murder but each time a jury failed to reach a verdict. He was formally acquitted under the convention that the prosecution do not ask for a third trial in such circumstances.

But in April last year the double jeopardy rule – which prevented a defendant who had been acquitted from being tried again for the same offence – was changed under the Criminal Justice Act 2003.

The following November the Director of Public Prosecutions announced the legal process to retry Dunlop had begun. The case was sent to the Court of Appeal where his acquittal was quashed.

Source: Taken from an article in the *Daily Mail*, 11 September 2006

43

Most increases are of an extra year or two being added to the sentence. However, there are some cases in which much greater increases are made. Examples of such increases include one defendant whose sentence for two offences of rape was increased from 3.5 years' imprisonment to 11 years' imprisonment and another defendant whose sentence for assault, conspiracy to kidnap and false imprisonment was increased from 3 years and 9 months to 9 years and 9 months.

Extension activity

Look at the Attorney General's website to find recent cases which have been referred to the Court of Appeal. (It is probably easiest to search the internet using 'Attorney General lenient sentences'.)

● What is the biggest increase in sentence you can find and what offence was it for?
● Find a case where the Court of Appeal did not increase the sentence.

5.7.3 Further appeals to the Supreme Court

Both the prosecution and the defence may appeal from the Court of Appeal to the Supreme Court, but it is necessary to have the case certified as involving a point of law of general public importance and to get permission to appeal, either from the Supreme Court or from the Court of Appeal. Only a few criminal appeals go to the Supreme Court each year.

Activity

Explain whether an appeal (and if so to what court) or other action can be made in the following cases.

1 Conroy was found guilty of theft in the Magistrates' Court and sentenced to 3 months' imprisonment. He wants to appeal against this sentence.
2 Smartshops Ltd have been found guilty of an offence involving regulations about the sale of goods. They wish to appeal because they believe the magistrates have made a mistake about the way the law operates.
3 Anika has been tried and found guilty of robbery at the Crown Court. She has been sentenced to 4 years' imprisonment. She wishes to appeal against both the conviction and the sentence.
4 Monty pleaded guilty to an offence of causing grievous bodily harm (s 18 Offences Against the Person Act 1861) and was sentenced to 2 years' imprisonment. The prosecution believe that this sentence is too lenient.

Tip

Appeal routes are complicated to remember. Try using the diagrams as a help to identifying the different appeal routes

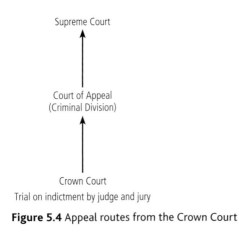

Figure 5.4 Appeal routes from the Crown Court

Summary

- There are three categories of offence:
  - summary offences
  - triable-either-way offences
  - indictable offences.
- The Magistrates' Court deals with summary offences and triable-either-way offences where the defendant elects trial there.
- The Crown Court deals with all indictable offences and with triable-either-way offences where the defendant has elected trial in the Crown Court or where the magistrates decide the case is too serious for them.
- Trial at the Crown Court is by judge and jury: the jury decide guilty or not guilty on the facts of the case.

- Appeals:
  - Appeals from the Magistrates' Court normally go to the Crown Court but appeals on points of law go to the Administrative Court.
  - Appeals from the Crown Court go to the Court of Appeal.
  - The defendant can appeal against conviction and/or sentence.
  - The prosecution has limited rights of appeal. The Court of Appeal can only appeal against an acquittal by a jury where:
    - the acquittal was the result of the jury being 'nobbled'
    - there is new and compelling evidence of the acquitted person's guilt and it is in the public interest for the defendant to be retried.

Chapter 6

Sentencing

After reading this chapter you should be able to:
- Understand the aims of sentencing
- Understand the factors courts take into consideration when sentencing an offender
- Understand the sentences the court can impose
- Evaluate the different types of sentence

6.1 Aims of sentencing

When judges or magistrates have to pass a sentence they will not only look at the sentences available, they will also have to decide what they are trying to achieve by the punishment they give. Section 142 of the Criminal Justice Act 2003 sets out the purposes of sentencing for those aged 18 and over saying that a court must have regard to:
- the punishment of offenders
- the reduction of crime (including its reduction by deterrence)
- the reform and rehabilitation of offenders
- the protection of the public and
- the making of reparation by offenders to persons affected by their offences.

In addition to the purposes of sentencing given in the 2003 Act, denunciation of crime is also recognised as an aim of sentencing. Each of the aims will now be examined in turn.

6.1.1 Retribution/Punishment

Retribution is based on the idea of punishment. The offender deserves punishment for his acts. This aim of sentencing does not seek to reduce crime or alter the offender's future behaviour. A judge using this aim is only concerned with the offence that was committed and making sure that the sentence given is in proportion to that offence.

The crudest form of retribution can be seen in the old saying 'an eye for an eye and a tooth for a tooth and a life for a life'. This was one of the factors used to justify the death penalty for the offence of murder.

> **Key term**
>
> Retribution – imposing a punishment because the offender has broken the law.

Tariff sentences

Retribution, today, is based more on the idea that each offence should have a certain tariff or level of sentencing. The Sentencing Council produces guidelines for all the main categories of offence. Judges have to take notice of these guidelines and should not normally give a lower sentence than the minimum set out in the guidelines.

6.1.2 Deterrence

This can be individual deterrence or general deterrence. Individual deterrence is intended to ensure that the offender does not reoffend, through fear of future punishment. General deterrence is aimed at preventing other potential offenders from committing crimes. Both are aimed at reducing future levels of crime.

> **Key term**
>
> Deterrence – giving a punishment aimed at putting off the defendant from reoffending because of fear of punishment or preventing other potential offenders from committing similar crimes.

Individual deterrence

There are several penalties that can be imposed with the aim of deterring the individual offender from

STEP ONE Determining the offence category

The court should determine the offence category using the table below	
Category 1	Greater harm (serious injury must normally be present) **and** higher culpability
Category 2	Greater harm (serious injury must normally be present) **and** lower culpability; **or** lesser harm **and** higher culpability
Category 3	Lesser harm **and** lower culpability
The guidelines then give factors which indicate higher or lower culpability. They also give factors to help decide the level of harm.	

STEP TWO Starting point and category range

Having determined the category, the court should use the corresponding starting points to reach a sentence within the category range below. The starting point applies to all offenders irrespective of plea or previous convictions. A case of particular gravity, reflected by multiple features of culpability in step one, could merit upward adjustment from the starting point before further adjustment for aggravating or mitigating features, set out below.

Offence category	Starting point (applicable to all offenders)	Category range (applicable to all offenders)
Category 1	1 year 6 months' custody	1–3 years' custody
Category 2	26 weeks' custody	Low level community order – 51 weeks' custody
Category 3	Medium level community order	Band A fine – high level community order

Figure 6.1 Sentencing Council's Guidelines

Source: Adapted from guidelines for assault occasioning actual bodily harm

committing similar crimes in the future. These include a prison sentence, a suspended sentence or a heavy fine. However, prison does not appear to deter as about 55 per cent of adult prisoners reoffend within two years of release. With young offenders, custodial sentences have even less of a deterrent effect. Over 70 per cent of young offenders given a custodial sentence reoffend within two years.

General deterrence

The value of this is even more doubtful as potential offenders are rarely deterred by severe sentences passed on others. However, the courts do occasionally resort to making an example of an offender in order to warn other potential offenders of the type of punishment they face.

Examples of deterrent sentencing were those imposed following rioting in the summer of 2011. Many offenders were given custodial sentences for relatively minor theft offences as these occurred during the looting of shops in the riots. This was sending a clear message to others that offenders committing offences during riots would be given severe sentences.

General deterrence is in direct conflict with the principle of retribution, since it involves sentencing an offender to a longer term than is deserved for the specific offence. It is probably the least effective and least fair principle of sentencing.

6.1.3 Reform/Rehabilitation

Under this aim of sentencing the main aim of the penalty is to reform the offender and **rehabilitate** him into society. It is a forward-looking aim, with the hope that the offender's behaviour will be altered by the penalty imposed, so that he will not offend in the future (it aims to reduce crime in this way).

Key term

Rehabilitate – trying to alter the offender's behaviour so that he will conform to community norms and not offend in future.

Reformation is a very important element in the sentencing philosophy for young offenders, but it is also used for some adult offenders. The court will be given information about the defendant's background, usually through a pre-sentence report prepared by the probation service. Where relevant, the court will consider other factors, such as school reports, job prospects, or medical problems.

Offenders will usually be given a community order with various requirements aimed at rehabilitating them.

Key term

Reformation – trying to reform the offender's behaviour so that he will not offend in future.

6.1.4 Protection of the public

The public needs to be protected from dangerous offenders. For this reason life imprisonment or a long term of imprisonment is given to those who commit murder or other violent or serious sexual offences.

The Criminal Justice Act 2003 introduced a provision for serious offences that where the court is of the opinion that there is a significant risk to members of the public of serious harm being caused by the defendant in the future, the court must send the defendant to prison for the protection of the public.

For less serious offences there are other ways in which the public can be protected. For example, dangerous drivers are disqualified from driving. Another method is to include an exclusion order as a requirement in a community order. This will ban the offender from going to places where he is most likely to commit an offence.

A good example of this is where the defendant committed an affray in Manchester when attending a football match in which Oldham Athletic, the team he supported, was playing. The judge banned the defendant from going into Oldham town centre on home match days and also banned him from approaching within half a mile of any football stadium. Both bans were for a period of six years.

Another method of protecting the public is to impose a curfew order on the offender ordering him to remain at home for certain times of the day or night. The curfew can be monitored by an electronic tag, which should trigger an alarm if the offender leaves his home address during a curfew period.

6.1.5 Reparation

This is aimed at compensating the victim of the crime, usually by ordering the offender to pay a sum of money to the victim or to make restitution, for example, by returning stolen property to its rightful owner. The courts are required to consider ordering compensation to the victim of a crime, in addition to any other penalty they may think appropriate. There are also projects to bring offenders and victims together, so that the offenders may make direct reparation.

> ### Key term
>
> Reparation – where an offender compensates the victim or society for the offending behaviour.

The concept also includes making reparation to society as a whole. This can be seen mainly in the use of an unpaid work requirement where offenders are required to do so many hours' work on a community project under the supervision of the probation service.

6.1.6 Denunciation

This is society expressing its disapproval of criminal activity. A sentence should indicate both to the offender and to other people that society condemns certain types of behaviour. It shows people that justice is being done.

Theory	Aim of theory	Suitable punishment
Retribution/Punishment	Punishment imposed only on ground that an offence has been committed	• Tariff sentences • Sentence must be proportionate to the crime
Deterrence	Individual – the offender is deterred through fear of further punishment General – potential offenders warned as to likely punishment	• Prison sentence • Heavy fine • Long sentence as an example to others
Rehabilitation	Reform offender's behaviour	• Individualised sentence • Community order
Protection of the public	Offender is made incapable of committing further crime Society is protected from crime	• Long prison sentences • Tagging • Banning orders
Reparation	Repayment/Reparation to victim or to community	• Compensation order • Unpaid work • Reparation schemes
Denunciation	Society expressing its disapproval Reinforces moral boundaries	• Reflects blameworthiness of the offence

Figure 6.2 Aims of sentencing

Denunciation also reinforces the moral boundaries of acceptable conduct and can mould society's views on the criminality of particular conduct; for example, drink driving is now viewed by the majority of people as unacceptable behaviour. This is largely because of the changes in the law and the increasingly severe sentences that are imposed. By sending offenders to prison, banning them from driving and imposing heavy fines, society's opinion of drink driving has been changed.

> **Key term**
>
> **Denunciation** – expressing society's disapproval of an offender's behaviour.

6.2 Factors in sentencing

When deciding what sentence to pass on a defendant, the courts consider the following matters:
- the offence
- sentencing guidelines
- the offender's background.

6.2.1 Aggravating factors in sentencing

In looking at the offence, the most important point to establish is how serious was it, of its type? This is now set out in s 143(1) of the Criminal Justice Act 2003 which states that:

> In considering the seriousness of the offence, the court must consider the offender's culpability in committing the offence and any harm which the offence caused, or was intended to cause or might reasonably foreseeably have caused.

The Act goes on to give certain factors which are considered as aggravating factors making an offence more serious. These are:
- previous convictions for offences of a similar nature or relevant to the present offence
- the fact that the defendant was on bail when he committed the offence
- racial or religious hostility being involved in the offence
- hostility to disability or sexual orientation being involved in the offence.

As well as these points in the Criminal Justice Act 2003, there are also other factors which are regarded as aggravating features for specific offences.

For example where the defendant has committed an assault, aggravating features include:
- the offender being part of a group attacking the victim
- a particularly vulnerable victim, e.g. a young child or an elderly person
- a victim serving the public, e.g. an attack on a nurse in a hospital emergency unit
- the fact that the assault was premeditated.

Where there is an aggravating factor the court will pass a more severe sentence than it would normally have given.

Magistrates and judges all have a copy of the guidelines issued by the Sentencing Council. These give a starting point for an offence, depending on certain factors, in particular whether the magistrates should be thinking of a custodial sentence or a community order. The guidelines also give a sentencing range.

6.2.2 Mitigating factors available in sentencing

A mitigating factor is one which allows the court to give a lighter sentence than would normally be given.

If the offender co-operates with the police, for example helping identify others involved in the crime, then the court can take this into account when deciding sentence.

Other factors taken into account in mitigation include:
- mental illness of the defendant
- physical illness of the defendant
- the fact that a defendant has no previous convictions
- evidence of genuine remorse.

Reduction in sentence for a guilty plea

There will also be a reduction in sentence for a guilty plea, particularly where the defendant made that plea early in the proceedings. The Sentencing Council guidelines on this are that the reduction for a guilty plea at the first reasonable opportunity should attract a reduction of up to one-third, while a plea of guilty after the trial has started would only be given a one-tenth reduction. The amount of reduction is on a sliding scale as shown in Figure 6.3.

The only exception is where the evidence is overwhelming and the defendant's guilt is clear. In these circumstances, even if the defendant pleads guilty at the earliest possible opportunity, the judge need only give a 20 per cent discount for that plea of guilty.

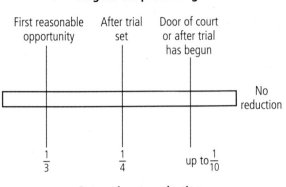

Stage in the proceedings

First reasonable opportunity — After trial set — Door of court or after trial has begun

No reduction

$\frac{1}{3}$ $\frac{1}{4}$ up to $\frac{1}{10}$

Proportionate reduction

Figure 6.3 Reduction in sentence for a guilty plea

6.2.3 Background of the offender

Previous convictions

An important fact about the defendant is whether he has previous convictions or not. Where he has a previous conviction for the same or similar type of offence, then he is likely to receive a heavier sentence.

A defendant who has no previous convictions is usually treated more leniently.

Reports

The courts will often have a report prepared by the probation service on the offender and his background. If the defendant is ill, then the court may also ask for a medical report. These reports will be considered with all other factors in deciding what sentence to impose on the defendant.

6.3 Types of sentence available for adult offenders

6.3.1 Custodial sentences

A custodial sentence is the most serious punishment that a court can impose. Custodial sentences range from a few weeks to life imprisonment. They include:
- mandatory and discretionary life sentences
- fixed-term sentences
- suspended sentences.

Custodial sentences are meant to be used only for serious offences. The Criminal Justice Act 2003 says that the court must not pass a custodial sentence unless it is of the opinion that the offence (or combination of offences) 'was so serious that neither a fine alone nor a community sentence can be justified'.

Mandatory life sentences

For murder the only sentence a judge can impose is a life sentence. However, the judge is allowed to state the minimum number of years' imprisonment that the offender must serve before being eligible for release on licence. This minimum term is now governed by the Criminal Justice Act 2003. This gives judges clear starting points for the minimum period to be ordered. The starting points range from a full life term down to 12 years depending on the facts of the case.

The types of murder a full life term has to be given include:
- the murder of a child if it involves the abduction of the child or a sexual motive; or
- a murder done for the purpose of advancing a political, religious, racial, religious or ideological cause.

Where a full life sentence does not have to be given the judge will consider any aggravating or mitigating circumstances. Aggravating factors include where:
- there is a significant degree of planning or premeditation
- the victim was particularly vulnerable
- the defendant inflicted mental or physical abuse on the victim before killing them.

Mitigating factors include where there was:
- an intention to cause grievous bodily harm rather than to kill
- lack of premeditation
- a belief by the offender that the murder was an act of mercy.

Discretionary life sentences

For other serious offences such as an offence under s 18 of the Offences Against the Person Act 1861, the maximum sentence is life imprisonment but the judge does not have to impose it. The judge has discretion in sentencing and can give any lesser sentence where appropriate. For certain serious offences, a life sentence should be given for a second offence.

Winchester prison

Fixed-term sentences

For other crimes, the length of the sentence will depend on several factors, including the maximum sentence available for the particular crime, the seriousness of the crime and the defendant's previous record. Imprisonment for a set number of months or years is called a 'fixed-term' sentence.

Prisoners do not serve the whole of the sentence passed by the court. Anyone sent to prison is automatically released after they have served half of the sentence. Only offenders aged 21 and over can be given a sentence of imprisonment.

Prison population

A problem is that prisons in England and Wales are overcrowded. There has been a big increase in the number of people in prison and there are not enough prison places. Figure 6.4 shows the increase in the prison population between 1951 and 2016.

Overcrowding in prisons can lead to rioting and violence, as shown by the riots in some prisons at the end of 2016.

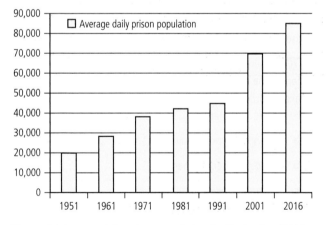

Figure 6.4 Average daily prison population for England and Wales 1951–2016

Look online

Look up the current prison population on the internet. You should be able to find it by searching for 'prison population'.

Suspended prison sentences

An adult offender may be given a suspended prison sentence of up to two years (six months' maximum in the Magistrates' Court). This means that the sentence does not take effect immediately. The court will fix a time during which the sentence is suspended; this can be for any period up to two years. If, during this time, the offender does not commit any further offences, the prison sentence will not be served. However, if the offender does commit another offence within the period of suspension, then the prison sentence is 'activated' and the offender will serve that sentence together with any sentence for the new offence.

A suspended sentence should only be given where the offence is so serious that an immediate custodial sentence would have been appropriate, but there are exceptional circumstances in the case that justify suspending the sentence.

6.3.2 Community orders

The Criminal Justice Act 2003 created one community order under which the court can combine any requirements it thinks are necessary. These requirements are listed below. The sentences can 'mix and match' requirements, allowing them to fit the restrictions and rehabilitation to the offender's needs. The sentence is available for offenders aged 16 and over. The full list of requirements available to the courts is set out in s 177 of the Criminal Justice Act 2003. This states:

177(1) Where a person aged 16 or over is convicted of an offence, the court by or before which he is convicted may make an order imposing on him any one or more of the following requirements:

a an unpaid work requirement,

b an activity requirement,

c a programme requirement,

d a prohibited activity requirement,

e a curfew requirement,

f an exclusion requirement,

g a residence requirement,

h a mental health treatment requirement,

i a drug rehabilitation requirement,

j an alcohol treatment requirement,

k a supervision requirement, and

l in the case where the offender is aged under 25, an attendance centre requirement.

Each of these is defined within the Criminal Justice Act 2003. Most are self-explanatory from their name, such as drug rehabilitation and alcohol treatment. Much crime is linked to drug and alcohol abuse and the idea behind these two requirements is to tackle the causes of crime, and hopefully prevent further offences. Mental health treatment is also aimed at the cause of the offender's behaviour. The main other requirements are explained briefly below.

THIS IS THE GOVERNMENT'S LATEST IDEA FOR A COMMUNITY SENTENCE

Unpaid work requirement

This requires the offender to work for between 40 and 300 hours on a suitable project organised by the probation service. The exact number of hours will be fixed by the court, and those hours are then usually worked in eight-hour sessions, often at weekends. The type of work involved will vary, depending on what schemes the local probation service has running. The offender may be required to paint school buildings, help build a play centre or work on conservation projects.

Prohibited activity requirement

This requirement allows a wide variety of activities to be prohibited. The idea is to try to prevent the defendant from committing another crime of the type he has just been convicted of. Often the defendant is forbidden to go into a certain area where he has caused trouble. In some cases the defendant has been banned from wearing a 'hoodie'. In 2006, a defendant who was found guilty of criminal damage was banned from carrying paint, dye, ink or marker pens.

Curfew requirement

Under these, an offender can be ordered to remain at a fixed address for between 2 and 16 hours in any 24-hour period. This order can last for up to six months and may be enforced by electronic tagging (where suitable). Courts can only make such an order if there is an arrangement for monitoring curfews in their area. Such monitoring can be done by spot-checks, with security firms sending someone to make sure that the offender is at home or offenders may be electronically tagged. Satellite technology may be used to track those who are tagged.

Supervision requirement

For this requirement the offender is placed under the supervision of a probation officer for a period of up to three years. During the period of supervision the offender must attend appointments with the supervising officer or with any other person decided by the supervising officer.

6.3.3 Fines

This is the most common way of disposing of a case in the Magistrates' Court. In the Crown Court only a small percentage of offenders are dealt with by way of a fine. Usually the offender is ordered to pay the fine at a set rate each week.

6.3.4 Discharges

These may be either:
● a conditional discharge or
● an absolute discharge.

A conditional discharge means that the court discharges an offender on the condition that no further offence is committed during a set period of up to three years. It is intended to be used where it is thought that punishment is not necessary. If an offender reoffends within the time limit, the court can then impose another sentence in place of the conditional discharge, as well as imposing a penalty for the new offence. Conditional discharges are widely used by Magistrates' Courts for first-time minor offenders.

An absolute discharge means that, effectively, no penalty is imposed. Such a penalty is likely to be used where an offender is technically guilty but morally blameless. So, in the unlikely situation of someone being prosecuted for this, the magistrates, who would have to impose some penalty, would most probably decide that an absolute discharge was appropriate.

Activity

Read the following facts taken from 'Proven Re-offending Statistics Quarterly April 2014 to March 2015', published January 2017, and answer the questions below.

● Adult offenders had a proven reoffending rate of 24.3 per cent.
● Around 352,000 proven offences were committed by adults over the one-year follow-up period. Those that reoffended committed on average 3.22 reoffences each.
  ○ Adult offenders with 11 or more previous offences have a higher reoffending rate than those with no previous offences – 44.7 per cent compared to 7.5 per cent.
  ○ The proven reoffending rate for adults starting a court order (community sentence or suspended sentence order) was 32 per cent.
  ○ The proven reoffending rate for adult offenders released from custody was 44.7 per cent.

● The rate for those released from short custodial sentences has been consistently higher compared to those released from longer sentences. Adults who served sentences of less than 12 months reoffended at a rate of 59.7 per cent compared to 33.4 per cent for those who served determinate sentences of 12 months or more.

Questions

1 What is the average reoffending rate for adults?
2 How many previous offences had been committed by those with the highest rate of reoffending?
3 What was the reoffending rate for those released from a custodial sentence? How does that compare with the reoffending rate for those given a community sentence or suspended sentence order?
4 How did the length of prison sentence served affect the reoffending rate?

6.3.5 Other powers of the court

The court has other orders it can make when sentencing an offender. These include:

- disqualifying the defendant from driving for a certain length of time – this is mostly used for motoring offences such as drink driving or dangerous driving but it can also be used for other offences such as theft of a car
- compensation order – the court can order the offender to pay a sum of money to the victim of the crime
- forfeiture order – this orders that certain property in the possession of the offender be taken from him, for example, cans of spray paint (where a defendant is guilty of criminal damage involving the use of the paint).

Victim surcharge

In addition, when a court passes a sentence it must also order that the relevant surcharge is paid. The amount of the surcharge depends on the sentence and whether at the time the offence was committed the offender was an adult or a youth. Revenue raised from the victim surcharge is used to fund victim services through the Victim and Witness General Fund.

6.4 Evaluation: penal policies and their effects

Sentencing policies have an effect on the number of offenders who are sent to prison. The UK sends a higher percentage of its population to prison than any other EU country. The changes in sentencing policy over the last few years are reflected in the changing size of the prison population as the various governments have attempted to reduce the number of defendants sent to prison for relatively minor offences, and then (to some extent) reversed their policies in an effort to be seen as the party of 'law and order'.

6.4.1 Prison population

There has been concern at the number of people in prison (known as the prison population).

In 1951 there were only 50 per 100,000 of the population in prison; by 2001 this had risen to 136. By 2004 the UK had the highest rate of prison population per 100,000 in the whole of Europe.

The Criminal Justice Act 2003 introduced tougher community penalties to try to avoid using custodial sentences. The prison population continued to increase for the next few years, but has been fairly stable since 2011, though it is still the highest in Europe.

6.4.2 Reoffending

The statistics in the Activity earlier in this chapter show that 44.75 per cent of adults who serve a prison sentence reoffend within one year from their release from prison. The statistics also show that those who served a short prison sentence (less than 12 months) are nearly twice as likely to reoffend (59.7 per cent) than those who serve a sentence of 12 months or more (33.4 per cent).

Adult offenders who are given community orders are less likely to reoffend than those given custodial sentences. Overall, 32.4 per cent of those given a community order reoffend with one year of that penalty being imposed.

6.4.3 Women and sentencing

Numerically there are far fewer women in prison than men. In 2016 there were about 4,000 women in prison, compared to about 82,000 men. It is also true that, for indictable offences, women are more likely to be given a discharge or a community sentence than men, and are less likely to be fined or sentenced to custody.

The Fawcett Society, a leading charity for women's equality and rights, is very critical of the number of women sent to prison. It points out that custodial sentences for women are:

- **inappropriate** – over half of women in prison have suffered domestic violence and one in three has experienced sexual abuse
- **damaging to the women** – prison causes damage and disruption to the lives of vulnerable women – 70 per cent of women prisoners have mental health problems, and one in three has attempted to commit suicide
- **damaging to their families** – approximately two-thirds of women in prison have dependent children; over 17,000 children a year are separated from their mothers by imprisonment
- **ineffective** – prison is an ineffective way of cutting women's offending – the most common offences for which women are sent to prison are theft and handling stolen goods, and 65 per cent reoffend on release.

Summary

- The aims of sentencing are:
  - punishment of offenders
  - reduction of crime (including its reduction by deterrence)
  - reform and rehabilitation of offenders
  - protection of the public
  - making of reparation by offenders
  - denunciation of offending behaviour.

- Factors taken into account when sentencing include:
  - aggravating factors
  - mitigating factors
  - plea of guilty
  - offender's background
  - reports on the offender.

- Types of sentences for adult offenders include:
  - custodial sentences
  - community orders
  - fines
  - discharges.

- Other powers of the court include:
  - disqualification from driving
  - compensation order
  - forfeiture order.

Chapter 7

Lay magistrates

After reading this chapter you should be able to:
- Understand the qualifications, selection, appointment and training of lay magistrates
- Understand the role of lay magistrates in criminal cases
- Evaluate the use of lay magistrates in the criminal courts.

7.1 Lay magistrates

There are about 17,500 **lay magistrates** sitting as unpaid, part-time judges in the Magistrates' Courts; another name for lay magistrates is Justices of the Peace. They sit to hear cases as a bench of two or three magistrates. A single lay magistrate sitting on his own has very limited powers. He can, however, issue search warrants and warrants for arrest and conduct Early Administrative Hearings.

Key term 🔑

Lay magistrates – these are unpaid, part-time judges who have no professional legal qualifications.

7.1.1 Qualifications

Lay magistrates do not have to have any qualifications in law. There are, however, some requirements as to their character. Candidates should have the following six key qualities:
- good character
- understanding and communication
- social awareness
- maturity and sound temperament
- sound judgment
- commitment and reliability.

They must have certain 'judicial' qualities – it is particularly important that they are able to assimilate factual information and make a reasoned decision upon it. They must also be able to take account of the reasoning of others and work as a team.

There are also formal requirements as to age and residence: lay magistrates must be aged between 18 and 65 on appointment and can sit as magistrates until they are 70. Not many younger people are appointed. Since the age for appointment was reduced to 18 in 2003, a few more young magistrates have been appointed. However, the statistics for 2016 show that only 3 per cent of magistrates were under the age of 40.

Activity ❓

1. Put the list of the six key qualities into order, with the one you think is the most important first and the least important last.
2. Compare your list with those of other people.
3. Explain what other qualities you think that magistrates might need.

7.1.2 Area

Up to 2003 it was necessary for lay magistrates to live within 15 miles of the commission area for the court which they sat in. In 2003 the Courts Act abolished commission areas. Instead there is now one commission area for the whole of England and Wales. However the country is divided into local justice areas. These areas are specified by the Lord Chancellor and lay magistrates are expected to live or work within or near to the local justice area to which they are allocated. The local justice areas are used to determine which Magistrates' Courts may hear a particular case. Cases are heard in the area where:
- the offence is alleged to have been committed; or
- the person charged with the offence lives; or

- the witnesses, or the majority of the witnesses, live; or
- other cases raising similar issues are being dealt with.

7.1.3 Commitment

The other requirement is that lay magistrates are prepared to commit themselves to sitting at least 26 half days each year. It is thought that this level of commitment deters many people from becoming lay magistrates. Lay magistrates are only paid expenses.

7.1.4 Restrictions on appointment

Some people are not eligible to be appointed. These include people with serious criminal convictions, though a conviction for a minor motoring offence will not automatically disqualify a candidate. Others who are disqualified include undischarged bankrupts, members of the forces and those whose work is incompatible with sitting as a magistrate, such as police officers and traffic wardens.

Relatives of those working in the local criminal justice system are not likely to be appointed as it would not appear 'just' if, for example, the wife or husband of a local police officer were to sit to decide cases. In addition people whose hearing is impaired, or who by reason of infirmity cannot carry out all the duties of a justice of the peace cannot be appointed. Close relatives will not be appointed to the same bench.

7.2 Selection and appointment

About 700 new lay magistrates are appointed each year. Since 2013, appointments are made by the Lord Chief Justice, who can delegate these powers. The current Lord Chief Justice has delegated these powers to the Senior Presiding Judge. In order to decide who to appoint, this judge relies on recommendations made by the local advisory committees.

7.2.1 Local advisory committees

The membership of the committees must be published. The members tend to be current or ex-Justices of the Peace. About half the members have to retire in rotation every three years. The committees should have a maximum of 12 members and these should include a mixture of magistrates and non-magistrates.

Anyone can apply to become a magistrate. The process is explained online at **www.gov.uk**.

Advertisements are used to try to encourage as wide a range of potential candidates as possible. Advertisements have been placed in local papers, or newspapers aimed at particular ethnic groups, and even on buses! People are also encouraged to go to open evenings at their local Magistrates' Court. All this is aimed at getting as wide a spectrum of potential candidates as possible. The intention is to create a panel that is representative of all aspects of society.

The aim is for membership to reflect a balance of occupations. The Lord Chancellor set down 11 broad categories of occupations, and advisory committees are recommended that they should not have more than 15 per cent of the bench coming from any one category.

7.2.2 Interview panels

There is usually a two-stage interview process. At the first interview the panel tries to find out more about the candidate's personal attributes, in particular looking to see if he has the six key qualities required. The interview panel will also explore the candidate's attitudes on various criminal justice issues such as youth crime or drink driving. The second interview is aimed at testing candidates' potential judicial aptitude and this is done by a discussion of at least two case studies which are typical of those heard regularly in Magistrates' Courts. The discussion might, for example, focus on the type of sentence which should be imposed on specific case facts.

The advisory committees will then submit names of those they think are suitable to the Lord Chief Justice or his delegate, who will then appoint new magistrates from this list. Once appointed, magistrates may continue to sit until the age of 70.

7.3 Composition of the bench today

The traditional image of lay justices is that they are 'middle-class, middle-aged and middle-minded'. However, in many respects the bench is well balanced. About 53 per cent of magistrates are women. This is a higher percentage than anywhere else in the judiciary. Only 22 per cent of judges in the High Court and above are women, though there are more at the lower levels. For example, about 32 per cent of District Judges in the Magistrates' Court are women.

Also, ethnic minorities are reasonably well represented in the magistracy. About 11 per cent of magistrates are from ethnic minorities. This compares very favourably to the professional judiciary where less than 5 per cent are from ethnic minority backgrounds.

The relatively high level of ethnic minority magistrates is largely a result of campaigns to attract a wider range of candidates. Adverts are placed in national newspapers and also in TV guides and women's magazines. In an effort to encourage those from ethnic minorities to apply, adverts have also appeared in such publications as the *Caribbean Times*, the *Asian Times* and *Muslim News*. This has led to an increase in the numbers of ethnic minority appointments.

Disabled people are encouraged to apply to become magistrates. This has included appointing blind persons as lay magistrates. About 4 per cent of magistrates have a disability.

Look online

Look up the composition of the magistracy for your area. This is on **www.judiciary.gov.uk** but it may be easier to search the internet for 'Magistrates in post'.

Find out:
1 How many male and female magistrates are there in your area?
2 How many magistrates from an ethnic minority are there in your area?

7.4 The role of magistrates

Magistrates have a very wide workload connected to criminal cases. They deal with all summary cases. They also deal with triable-either-way offences where the defendant chooses to be tried in the Magistrates' Court. These two categories account for about 94 per cent of all criminal cases.

The magistrates deal with all the preliminary work in these cases. This includes Early Administrative Hearings, remand hearings (where the case is put back to a later date for some reason) and bail applications. Where the defendant pleads not guilty, the magistrates will hold a trial and decide whether the defendant is guilty or not guilty. Where the defendant pleads guilty or is found guilty the magistrates also decide the sentence.

They have the power to imprison an offender for six months for one offence or 12 months for two offences. They also have other wide sentencing powers including making community orders, fining a defendant, ordering a conditional or absolute discharge and disqualifying a defendant from driving.

Lay magistrates also deal with the first hearing of indictable offences but then transfer these to the Crown Court for trial.

Leeds Magistrates' Court

7.4.1 Youth Court

Specially nominated and trained justices from the Youth Court panel hear most criminal charges against young offenders aged 10–17 years old inclusive. The panel must usually include at least one man and one woman.

7.4.2 Appeal hearings

Lay magistrates also sit at the Crown Court to hear appeals from the Magistrates' Court. In these cases two lay justices (who were not at the original trial) form a panel with a qualified judge. They hear all the evidence in the case and decide whether the appellant is guilty or not guilty. If the finding is one of guilt then they will also decide on the sentence.

7.5 Training of lay magistrates

The training of lay magistrates is supervised by the Magisterial Committee of the Judicial College. This Committee has drawn up a national syllabus of the topics which lay magistrates should cover in their training. However, because of the large numbers of lay magistrates, the actual training is carried out in local areas, sometimes through the clerk of the court, sometimes through weekend courses organised by universities with magistrates from the region attending.

7.5.1 Training for new magistrates

There is a syllabus for new magistrates which is divided into three parts:

1 Initial introductory training – this covers such matters as understanding the organisation of the bench and the administration of the court and the roles and responsibilities of those involved in the Magistrates' Court.
2 Core training – this provides the new magistrate with the opportunity to acquire and develop the key skills, knowledge and understanding required of a competent magistrate.
3 Activities – these will involve observations of court sittings and visits to establishments such as a prison or a probation office.

After doing the core training and observing cases, a new magistrate will sit as a 'winger' to hear cases. This means that he will be one of a panel of three. The chairman (who sits in the middle) is a very experienced magistrate and the magistrates who sit on either side of the chairman are known as 'wingers'.

7.5.2 Appraisal

During the first two years of the new magistrate sitting in court, some of the sessions will be mentored. In the same period the magistrate is also expected to attend more training sessions. After two years, or whenever it is felt that the magistrate is ready, an appraisal will take place to check if he has acquired the competencies.

Any magistrate who cannot show that he has achieved the competencies will be given extra training. If he still cannot achieve the competencies, then the matter is referred to the local advisory committee,

Qualifications	Between ages of 18 and 65 on appointment Have the six key qualities Live or work near the area in which they sit Be prepared to sit 26 half days a year
Appointment	Local advisory committee recommend for appointment Appointment by Lord Chief Justice or anyone to whom the LCJ has delegated this power
Training	Supervised by the Magisterial Committee of the Judicial College Most training delivered locally Appraisal
Composition of bench	17,500 lay magistrates: 47% men, 53% women Good representation of ethnic minorities Only 3% under the age of 40
Role of magistrates	Deal with all summary offences Deal with triable-either-way offences where defendant chooses trial in the Magistrates' Court Deal with preliminary issues: remands and bail Transfer indictable cases to the Crown Court Youth Court Appeals in the Crown Court

Figure 7.1 Lay magistrates

who may recommend to the Lord Chancellor that the magistrate is removed from sitting.

7.6 The magistrates' clerk

Every bench is assisted by a clerk, also known as a legal adviser. The senior clerk in each court has to be qualified as a barrister or solicitor for at least five years. The clerk's duty is to guide the magistrates on questions of law, practice and procedure. This is set out in s 28(3) of the Justices of the Peace Act 1979 which says:

> It is hereby declared that the functions of a justices' clerk include the giving to the justices ... of advice about law, practice or procedure on questions arising in connection with the discharge of their functions.

The clerk is not meant to assist in the decision making and should not normally retire with the magistrates when they go to make their decision.

Clerks deal with routine administrative matters. They can also issue warrants for arrest, extend police bail, adjourn criminal proceedings and deal with Early Administrative Hearings.

7.7 Evaluation of lay magistrates

7.7.1 Advantages of lay magistrates

Cross-section of society

The system involves members of the community and provides a wider cross-section on the bench than would be possible with the use of professional judges. This is particularly true of women, with 53 per cent of magistrates being women. Also, there is considerable involvement of ethnic minorities.

There are a small number of younger magistrates in their twenties and even a few eighteen- or nineteen-year-olds. This again contrasts with professional judges who will be considerably older.

Local knowledge

Since lay magistrates have to live or work near the court, it is intended that they should have local knowledge of particular problems in the area. Their main value is that they will have more awareness of local events, local patterns of crime and local opinions than a professional judge from another area.

Cost

The use of unpaid lay magistrates is cheap. The cost of replacing them with paid judges has been estimated at £100 million a year (there would also be the problem of recruiting sufficient qualified lawyers to be such judges). The cost of a trial in the Magistrates' Court is also much cheaper than in the Crown Court.

Training

Improved training means that lay magistrates are not complete 'amateurs'. The majority of decisions require common sense rather than professional training.

Legal adviser

All magistrates' clerks have to be legally qualified. This brings a higher level of legal skill to the Magistrates' Court. The availability of a legal adviser gives the magistrates access to any necessary legal advice on points that may arise in any case. This overcomes any criticism of the fact that lay magistrates are not themselves legally qualified.

Few appeals

Comparatively few defendants appeal against the magistrates' decisions, and many of the appeals that are made are against sentence, not against the finding of guilt. From a total workload of about one and a half million cases there are only a small number of appeals. In most years there are about 11,000 appeals each year and less than half of these appeals are successful.

There are also very few instances where an error of law is made. This is shown by the fact that there are fewer than 100 appeals by way of case stated to the Administrative Court each year. Of this very small number of appeals, less than half are allowed. From this it can be argued that, despite the amateur status of lay magistrates, they do a remarkably good job.

7.7.2 Disadvantages of lay magistrates

Middle-aged, middle class

Lay magistrates are often perceived as being middle-aged and middle class. This is largely true as their average age is over 50 and they are often from professional backgrounds.

Inconsistency in sentencing

Magistrates in different areas often pass very different sentences for what appear to be similar offences. This is something which has not really improved over the years, despite the training they receive. In some areas magistrates are four times as likely to send defendants to prison as in other areas.

For example, courts in Northamptonshire and Derbyshire imposed immediate custodial sentences in more than 6 per cent of the cases they heard during 2011. This was four times the rate recorded in Warwickshire (1.5 per cent) and Northumbria (1.6 per cent).

Reliance on the clerk

The lack of legal knowledge of the lay justices should be offset by the fact that a legally qualified clerk is available to give advice. However, this will not prevent inconsistencies in sentencing since the clerk is not allowed to help the magistrates decide on a sentence. In some courts it is felt that the magistrates rely too heavily on their clerk.

Prosecution bias

It is often said that lay magistrates tend to be prosecution-biased, believing the police too readily. However, part of the training is aimed at eliminating this type of bias. It is also true that at courts outside London they will see the same Crown Prosecution Service prosecutor frequently and this could affect their judgment. There is a low acquittal rate in Magistrates' Courts with only 20 per cent of defendants being acquitted. By comparison 60 per cent of defendants pleading not guilty at the Crown Court are acquitted.

Summary

- Lay magistrates are not legally qualified but must have certain key qualities.
- They must be between 18 and 65 on appointment.
- Local advisory committees interview candidates and make recommendations for appointment.
- Lay magistrates are more representative of the community than professional judges with slightly more women than men and good representation of ethnic minorities.
- Magistrates deal with:
  - all summary cases
  - triable-either-way offences where the defendant chooses to be tried in the Magistrates' Court
  - all work connected to such cases, including bail applications and remands
  - first hearings of indictable offences which are then transferred to the Crown Court
  - youth cases for 10–17 year olds
  - appeals at the Crown Court.
- Where a defendant pleads not guilty magistrates hear the case and decide if he is guilty or not guilty.

- When a defendant pleads guilty or is found guilty the magistrates decide the sentence.
- Magistrates have to attend training courses and are appraised on their work.
- Magistrates are assisted on points of law by a legally qualified clerk.
- Advantages of using lay people as magistrates are:
  - they are a cross-section of society
  - they have local knowledge
  - they are much cheaper than using professional judges
  - they are well trained and also have a clerk as legal adviser
  - they do their job well as there are relatively few appeals from their decisions.
- Disadvantages of using lay people as magistrates are:
  - they are middle-aged and middle class
  - there is inconsistency in sentencing
  - they may rely too heavily on the clerk
  - there may be prosecution bias.

Chapter 8

Juries

> After you have read this chapter you should be able to:
> - Understand the qualifications for being a juror and how jurors are selected
> - Describe the role of the jury in a criminal case
> - Evaluate the use of juries to decide criminal cases

8.1 History of the jury system

Juries have been used in the legal system for over 1,000 years. Originally they were used for providing local knowledge and information, and acted more as witnesses than decision makers. By the middle of the fifteenth century juries had become independent assessors and assumed their modern role as deciders of fact.

8.1.1 The independence of the jury

The independence of the jury became even more firmly established following *Bushell's Case* (1670).

> **Key case**
>
> **Bushell's Case (1670)**
>
> Several jurors refused to convict Quaker activists of unlawful assembly. The trial judge would not accept the not guilty verdict, and ordered the jurors to resume their deliberations without food or drink. When the jurors persisted in their refusal to convict, the court fined them and committed them to prison until the fines were paid. On appeal, the Court of Common Pleas ordered the release of the jurors, holding that jurors could not be punished for their verdict.

This case established that the jury was the sole arbiter of fact and the judge could not challenge its decision. A more modern example, demonstrating that judges must respect the independence of the jury, is *R v McKenna* (1960).

> **Key case**
>
> **R v McKenna (1960)**
>
> The judge at the trial threatened the jurors that if they did not return a verdict within another ten minutes they would be locked up all night. The jury then returned a verdict of guilty, but the defendant's conviction was quashed on appeal because of the judge's interference.

8.1.2 Juries in criminal cases

The most important use of juries today is in the Crown Court where they decide whether the defendant is guilty or not guilty. Jury trials, however, account for about 2 per cent of all criminal trials. This is because about 94 per cent of cases are dealt with in the Magistrates' Court and of the cases that go to the Crown Court, about two out of every three defendants will plead guilty. A jury in the Crown Court has 12 members.

8.2 Jury qualifications

8.2.1 Basic qualifications

The qualifications are set out in the Juries Act 1974 (as amended) so that to qualify for jury service a person must be:
- aged between 18 and 75 inclusive (age increased from 70 by the Criminal Justice and Courts Act 2015)
- registered as a parliamentary or local government elector
- ordinarily resident in the United Kingdom, the Channel Islands or the Isle of Man for at least five years since his thirteenth birthday.

However, certain people are not permitted to sit on a jury even though they are within these basic qualifications; these are people who are disqualified or mentally disordered.

8.2.2 Disqualification

Disqualified permanently from jury service are those who at any time have been sentenced to:

- imprisonment for life, detention for life or custody for life
- detention during Her Majesty's pleasure (given to offenders under 21 for very serious offences)
- imprisonment for public protection or detention for public protection
- an extended sentence
- a term of imprisonment of five years or more or a term of detention of five years or more.

Those in the following categories are disqualified for ten years if in the last ten years they have:

- served a sentence of imprisonment
- had a suspended sentence passed on them
- had a community order or other community sentence passed on them.

In addition anyone who is currently on bail in criminal proceedings is disqualified from sitting as a juror.

If a disqualified person fails to disclose that fact and turns up for jury service, he may be fined up to £5,000.

8.2.3 Mentally disordered persons

This category includes:

- those who suffer from mental illness or mental handicap and on account of that condition are resident in a hospital or similar institution, or regularly attend for treatment; or
- a person who is under guardianship under section 7 of the Mental Health Act 1983; or
- a person who has been determined by a judge to be incapable of administering his property and affairs.

None of these is allowed to do jury service.

8.2.4 The right to be excused jury service

Full-time serving members of the forces will be excused from jury service if their commanding officer certifies their absence from duty (because of jury service) would be prejudicial to the efficiency of the service.

8.2.5 Discretionary excusals

Anyone who has problems which make it very difficult for them to do their jury service may ask to be excused or for their period of service to be put back to a later date. The court has discretion to grant such an excusal but will only do so if there is a sufficiently good reason. Such reasons include being too ill to attend court or suffering from a disability that makes it impossible for the person to sit as a juror, or being a mother with a small baby. Other reasons could include business appointments that cannot be undertaken by anyone else, examinations or holidays that have been booked.

In these situations the court is most likely to defer jury service to a more convenient date, rather than excuse the person completely. This is stated in the current guidance for summoning officers which is aimed at preventing the high number of discretionary excusals. The guidance states that:

> The normal expectation is that everyone summoned for jury service will serve at the time for which they are summoned. It is recognised that there will be occasions where it is not reasonable for a person summoned to serve at the time for which they are summoned. In such circumstances the summoning officer should use his/her discretion to defer the individual to a time more appropriate. Only in extreme circumstances, should a person be excused from jury service.

If a person is not excused from jury service he must attend on the date set or he may be fined up to £1,000 for non-attendance.

8.2.6 Lawyers and police officers

There used to be a category of people who were ineligible for jury service. This included judges and others who had been involved in the administration of justice within the previous ten years. This category was abolished by the Criminal Justice Act 2003. This means that judges, lawyers, police, etc. are now eligible to serve on juries. Many people feel that this could lead to bias or to a legally well-qualified juror influencing the rest of the jury.

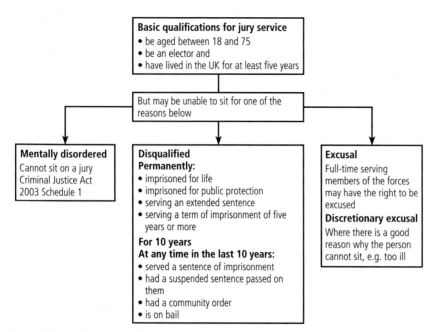

Figure 8.1 Qualifications of jurors

Basic qualifications for jury service
- be aged between 18 and 75
- be an elector and
- have lived in the UK for at least five years

But may be unable to sit for one of the reasons below

Mentally disordered
Cannot sit on a jury
Criminal Justice Act
2003 Schedule 1

Disqualified
Permanently:
- imprisoned for life
- imprisoned for public protection
- serving an extended sentence
- serving a term of imprisonment of five years or more

For 10 years
At any time in the last 10 years:
- served a sentence of imprisonment
- had a suspended sentence passed on them
- had a community order
- is on bail

Excusal
Full-time serving members of the forces may have the right to be excused
Discretionary excusal
Where there is a good reason why the person cannot sit, e.g. too ill

Activity

Discuss whether you think the following people should sit on a jury:

1 A woman who was fined for shoplifting a month ago.
2 A man who was fined and disqualified from driving for taking cars without the consent of the owner.
3 A doctor who works in general practice.
4 A doctor who works in an accident and emergency unit of a busy city hospital.
5 A Circuit Judge who frequently tries cases in the Crown Court.

8.2.7 Lack of capacity

A judge at the court may discharge a person from being a juror for lack of capacity to cope with the trial. This could be because the person does not understand English adequately or because of some disability which makes him unsuitable as a juror. This includes anyone who is blind, and who would be unable to see plans and photographs produced in evidence. Section 9B(2) of the Juries Act 1974 (which was added into the Act by the Criminal Justice and Public Order Act 1994, s 41) makes it clear that the mere fact of a disability does not prevent someone from acting as a juror. The judge can only discharge

the juror if he is satisfied that the disability means that that juror is not capable of acting effectively as a juror.

Deaf jurors

Those who are deaf and need a sign-language interpreter cannot sit as jurors. This is because the law does not allow a thirteenth person – a sign-language interpreter – to be present in the jury room.

8.3 Selecting a jury

At each Crown Court there is an official who is responsible for summoning enough jurors to try the cases that will be heard in each two-week period. This official will arrange for names to be selected at random from the electoral registers for the area which the court covers. This is done through a computer selection at a central office. It is necessary to summons more than 12 jurors as most courts have more than one courtroom and it will not be known how many of those summonsed are disqualified or may be excused. In fact, at the bigger courts up to 150 summonses may be sent out each fortnight.

Those summonsed must notify the court if there is any reason why they should not or cannot attend. All others are expected to attend for two weeks' jury service, though, of course, if the case they are trying goes on for more than two weeks they will have to stay until the trial is completed. Where it is known that a trial may be exceptionally long, such as a complicated fraud trial, potential jurors are asked if they will be able to serve for such a long period.

8.3.1 Vetting

Once the list of potential jurors is known, both the prosecution and the defence have the right to see that list. In some cases it may be decided that this pool of potential jurors should be 'vetted', i.e. checked for suitability. There are two types of vetting:
- police checks and
- wider background checks.

Police checks

Routine police checks are made on prospective jurors to eliminate those disqualified. In *R v Crown Court at Sheffield, ex parte Brownlow* (1980) the defendant was a police officer and the defence sought permission to vet the jury panel for convictions. The judge gave permission but the Court of Appeal, while holding that they had no power to interfere, said that vetting was 'unconstitutional' and a 'serious invasion of privacy' and not sanctioned by the Juries Act 1974.

However, in *R v Mason* (1980) where it was revealed that the Chief Constable for Northamptonshire had been allowing widespread use of unauthorised vetting of criminal records, the Court of Appeal approved of this type of vetting. Lawton LJ pointed out that, since it is a criminal offence to serve on a jury while disqualified, the police were only doing their normal duty of preventing crime by checking for criminal records. Furthermore, the court said that, if in the course of looking at criminal records convictions were revealed which did not disqualify, there was no reason why these should not be passed on to prosecuting counsel, so that this information could be used in deciding to stand by individual jurors (see section 8.3.3 for information on the right of stand by).

Juror's background

A wider check is made on a juror's background and political affiliations. This practice was brought to light by the 'ABC' trial in 1978 where two journalists and a soldier were charged with collecting secret information. It was discovered that the jury had been vetted for their loyalty. The trial was stopped and a new trial ordered before a fresh jury. Following this, the Attorney General published guidelines in 1980 on when political

vetting of jurors should take place. These guidelines state that:

a vetting should only be used in exceptional cases involving:
  - national security where part of the evidence is likely to be given in camera
  - terrorist cases
b vetting can only be carried out with the Attorney General's express permission.

8.3.2 Selection at court

The jurors are usually divided into groups of 15 and allocated to a court. At the start of a trial the court clerk will select 12 out of these 15 at random.

8.3.3 Challenging

Once the court clerk has selected the panel of 12 jurors, these jurors come into the jury box to be sworn in as jurors. At this point, before the jury is sworn in, both the prosecution and defence have certain rights to challenge one or more of the jurors. These are:
- to the array
- for cause
- prosecution right to stand by (put to one side) jurors.

To the array

This right to challenge is given by s 5 of the Juries Act 1974 and it is a challenge to the whole jury on the basis that it has been chosen in an unrepresentative or biased way. A **challenge to the array** was used in *R v Ford* (1989) when it was held that if the jury was chosen in a random manner then it could not be challenged simply because it was not multi-racial.

> **Key term**
>
> **Challenge to the array** – a challenge to the whole jury on the basis it has been chosen in an unrepresentative way.

For cause

This involves challenging the right of an individual juror to sit on the jury. To be successful the challenge must point out a valid reason why that juror should not serve on the jury. An obvious reason is that the juror is disqualified, but a challenge for cause can also be made if the juror knows or is related to a witness or defendant. If such people are not removed from the jury there is a risk that any subsequent conviction could be quashed.

Prosecution right to stand by jurors

This is a right that only the prosecution can exercise. It allows the juror who has been stood by to be put to the end of the list of potential jurors, so that he will not be used on the jury unless there are not enough other jurors. The prosecution does not have to give a reason for 'standing by', but the Attorney General's guidelines make it clear that this power should be used sparingly.

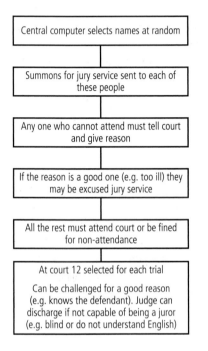

Figure 8.2 Selecting a jury

8.4 The jury's role in criminal cases

The jury is used only at the Crown Court for cases where the defendant pleads not guilty. This means that a jury is used in fewer than 30,000 cases each year.

8.4.1 Split function

The trial is presided over by a judge and the functions split between the judge and jury. The judge decides points of law and the jury decides the facts. At the end of the prosecution case, the judge has the power to direct the jury to acquit the defendant if he decides that, in law, the prosecution's evidence has not made out a case against the defendant. This is called a **directed acquittal**.

Where the trial continues, the judge will sum up the case at the end, to the jury and direct it on any law involved. The jury retires to a private room and makes the decision on the guilt or innocence of the accused in secret. Initially the jury must try to come to a unanimous verdict, i.e. one on which the jurors are all agreed. The judge must accept the jury verdict, even if he or she does not agree with it. The jury does not give any reasons for its decision.

8.4.2 Majority verdicts

If, after at least two hours (longer where there are several defendants), the jury has not reached a verdict, the judge can call it back into the courtroom and direct it that he can now accept a majority verdict. Majority verdicts have been allowed since 1967. Where there is a full jury of 12, the verdict can be 10:2 or 11:1 either for guilty or for not guilty. If the jury has fallen below 12 for any reason (such as the death or illness of a juror during the trial) then only one can disagree with the verdict. That is, if there are 11 jurors, the verdict can be 10:1; if there are 10 jurors it can be 9:1. If there are only nine jurors the verdict must be unanimous. A jury cannot go below nine.

Majority verdicts were introduced because of the fear of jury 'nobbling', that is jurors being bribed or intimidated by associates of the defendant into voting for a not guilty verdict. When a jury had to be unanimous, only one member need be bribed to cause a 'stalemate' in which the jury was unable to reach a decision. It was also thought that the acquittal rates in jury trials were too high and majority decisions would result in more convictions.

Where the jury convicts a defendant on a majority verdict, the foreman of the jury must announce the numbers both agreeing and disagreeing with the verdict in open court. This provision is contained in s 17(3) of the Juries Act 1974 and is aimed at making sure the jury has come to a legal majority, and not one, for example of 8:4, which is not allowed. About 20 per cent of convictions by juries each year are by majority verdict.

Court	Crown Court
Qualifications	Aged 18–75 Registered to vote Resident in UK for at least five years since age 13
Disqualified	Sentenced to five years' or more imprisonment – disqualified for life Served a prison sentence OR suspended sentence OR a community order – disqualified for ten years On bail – disqualified while on bail
Excusals	Members of the armed forces Discretionary – ill, business commitments, or other 'good reason'
Selection	A central office selects names from the lists of electors Summons sent to these people Must attend unless disqualified, ineligible or excused
Vetting	May be checked for criminal record – *R v Mason* (1980) In cases of national security may be subject to a wider check on background subject to Attorney General's guidelines
Challenges	Individual juror may be challenged for cause, e.g. knows defendant Whole panel may be challenged for biased selection – but no right to a multi-racial jury (*R v Ford* (1989)) Prosecution may 'stand by' any juror
Function	Decide verdict – 'Guilty' or 'Not guilty' Sole arbiters of fact but judge directs them on law
Verdict	Must try for a unanimous verdict BUT if cannot reach a unanimous verdict then a majority verdict of 10:2 or 11:1 can be accepted

Figure 8.3 The use of juries in criminal cases

8.4.3 Secrecy

The jury discussion takes place in secret and there can be no inquiry into how the jury reached its verdict. The Criminal Justice and Courts Act 2015 makes it a criminal offence to intentionally disclose or ask about anything that happens in the jury room. This includes any opinions expressed or votes cast by members of a jury in the course of their deliberations. Disclosure is allowed in situations where it is in the interests of justice, such as reporting juror misconduct.

The Criminal Justice and Courts Act 2015 also gives power to the judge to ask jurors to hand in their mobile phones or other electronic communication devices. Where the judge makes such an order and a juror disobeys it, then the juror is in contempt of court.

8.5 Evaluation of using juries

8.5.1 Advantages of jury trial

Public confidence

On the face of it, asking 12 strangers who have no legal knowledge and without any training to decide what may be complex and technical points is an absurd one. Yet the jury is considered one of the fundamentals of a democratic society. The right to be tried by one's peers is a bastion of liberty against the state and has been supported by eminent judges. For example, Lord Devlin said juries are 'the lamp that shows that freedom lives'. The tradition of trial by jury is very old and people seem to have confidence in the impartiality and fairness of a jury trial.

Jury equity

Since jurors are not legal experts, they are not bound to follow the precedent of past cases or even Acts of Parliament, and do not have to give reasons for their verdict, it is possible for them to decide cases on their idea of 'fairness'. This is sometimes referred to as jury equity. Several cases have shown the importance of this, in particular *Ponting's case* (1984).

> **Key case**
>
> ### *Ponting's case* (1984)
>
> A civil servant was charged under the old wide-ranging s 2 of the Official Secrets Act 1911. He had leaked information on the sinking of the ship, The *General Belgrano*, in the Falklands war to an MP. At his trial he pleaded not guilty, claiming that his actions had been in the public interest. The jury refused to convict him even though the judge ruled there was no defence. The case also prompted the government to reconsider the law and to amend s 2.

More recently, a jury acquitted a mother of attempting to murder her daughter who had committed suicide. Her daughter was aged 31 and had been ill for 17 years. She had injected herself with an overdose of morphine. The mother had given her daughter some medication to ease her suffering in her final hours. She had pleaded guilty to assisting the daughter's suicide, but the prosecution had insisted on continuing to prosecute her for attempted murder. The jury found her not guilty.

Open system of justice

The use of a jury is viewed as making the legal system more open. Justice is seen to be done as members of the public are involved in a key role and the whole process is public. It also helps to keep the law clearer as points have to be explained to the jury, enabling the defendant to understand the case more easily.

Secrecy of the jury room

This can be seen as an advantage, since the jury is free from pressure in its discussion. Jurors are protected from outside influences when deciding on the verdict. This allows juries to bring in verdicts that may be unpopular with the public as well as allowing jurors the freedom to ignore the strict letter of the law. It has been suggested that people would be less willing to serve on a jury if they knew that their discussions could be made public.

Impartiality

A jury should be impartial as it is not connected to anyone in the case. The process of random selection should result in a cross-section of society and this should also lead to an impartial jury, as the jurors will have different prejudices and so should cancel out each other's biases. No one individual person is responsible for the decision. A jury is also not case-hardened since it sits for only two weeks and is unlikely to try more than three or four cases in that time.

8.5.2 Disadvantages of jury trial

Perverse decisions

In section 8.5.1 we looked at the idea of jury equity and the case of *Ponting*. In that case the refusal of the jury to convict might be seen as a fair decision. However, in some circumstances this type of decision can be seen as a perverse decision: that is one which ignores the evidence and gives a wrong decision. An example of this is *R v Randle and Pottle* (1991).

Key case

R v Randle and Pottle (1991)

The defendants were charged with helping a spy to escape from prison and flee to Russia. Their prosecution did not occur until 25 years after the escape, when they wrote about what they had done. The jury acquitted them, possibly as a protest over the time lapse between the offence and the prosecution.

Another case where the evidence was clear, yet the jury acquitted the defendants was *R v Kronlid and others* (1996).

Key case

R v Kronlid and others (1996)

The defendants admitted they had caused £1.5 million damage to a plane. They pleaded not guilty to charges of criminal damage on the basis that they were preventing the plane from being sent to Indonesia where it would have been used in attacks against the people of East Timor. The jury acquitted them.

Secrecy

Earlier we considered how the secrecy of the jury protects jurors from pressure. However, the secrecy of the jury room is also a disadvantage because as no reasons have to be given for the verdict, there is no way of knowing if the jury understood the case and came to the decision for the right reasons.

In *R v Mirza* (2004) the House of Lords ruled that it could not inquire into discussions in a jury room. Two separate cases were considered in the appeal. These were *R v Mirza* and *R v Connor and Rollock*.

Key case

R v Mirza (2004)

The defendant was a Pakistani who had had an interpreter to help him in the trial. During the trial the jury sent notes asking why he needed an interpreter. He was convicted on a 10:2 majority. Six days after the jury verdict, one juror wrote to the defendant's counsel alleging that from the start of the trial there had been a 'theory' that the use of an interpreter was a 'ploy'. The juror also said that she had been shouted down when she objected and reminded her fellow jurors of the judge's directions.

R v Connor and Rollock (2004)

A juror wrote to the Crown Court stating that while many jurors thought it was one or other of the defendants who had committed the stabbing, they should convict both to 'teach them a lesson'. The House of Lords held that:
- confidentiality was essential to the proper functioning of the jury process
- there was merit in finality
- jurors had to be protected from harassment.

Exceptions

There are two exceptions where the courts will inquire into the conduct of the jury in coming to its verdict. The first is where there has been a complete repudiation of the oath taken by the jurors to try the case according to the evidence. In other words, they have used another method to make their decision.

The best known example of this is the case of *R v Young (Stephen)* (1995).

> **Key case**
>
> ### *R v Young (Stephen)* (1995)
>
> The defendant was charged with the murder of two people. The jury had to stay in a hotel overnight as it had not reached a verdict by the end of the first day of deliberations. At the hotel, four of the jurors held a séance using a ouija board to try to contact the dead victims and ask them who had killed them. The next day, the jury returned a guilty verdict.
>
> When the use of the ouija board became known, the Court of Appeal quashed the conviction and ordered a retrial. The Court also felt able to inquire into what had happened as it had occurred in a hotel and was not part of the jury room deliberations.

The second exception is where extraneous material has been introduced into the jury room. Examples have included telephone calls in and out of the jury room, papers mistakenly included in the set of papers given by the court to the jury and information from the internet. A case in which this happened is *R v Karakaya* (2005).

> **Key case**
>
> ### *R v Karakaya* (2005)
>
> The defendant was accused of rape. A juror did an internet search at home and brought into the jury room the printed-out results of the search. The jury convicted Karakaya, but this conviction was quashed because of the outside information that the jury had access to during its deliberations. A retrial was ordered and the defendant was acquitted by the jury in the second trial.

Jurors and the internet

Judges direct jurors not to look at the internet for information. However, internet research by jurors has become more common. In 2010, a report, 'Are Juries Fair?', by Cheryl Thomas was published. She found that 12 per cent of jurors admitted they had looked on the internet for information about cases they were trying. Such information may be prejudicial to the defendant. For example, doing a search on a defendant's name may find newspaper reports of previous convictions, which the jury should not know about.

Section 71 of the Criminal Justice and Courts Act 2015 makes it a criminal offence for a juror to search the internet intentionally for information relevant to the case. Section 72 of the Act also makes it a criminal offence to disclose such information to another member of the jury. Both these offences have a maximum penalty of two years' imprisonment. This shows how seriously this issue is viewed.

Racial bias

Although jurors have no direct interest in a case, and despite the fact that there are 12 of them, they may still have prejudices which can affect the verdict. Some jurors may be biased against the police – this is one of the reasons that those with certain criminal convictions are disqualified from sitting on a jury.

In particular there is the worry that some jurors are racially prejudiced. One case that raised the problem of racial bias was *Sander v United Kingdom* (2000).

Key case

Sander v United Kingdom (2000)

One juror had written a note to the judge raising concern over the fact that other jurors had been making openly racist remarks and jokes. The European Court of Human Rights held that in the circumstances of the case the judge should have discharged the jury as there was an obvious risk of racial bias and a breach of the right to a fair trial under Article 6 of the European Convention on Human Rights.

Media influence

Media coverage may influence jurors. This is especially true in high-profile cases, where there has been a lot of publicity about police investigations into a case. One case where media coverage was held to have influenced the jury was *R v Taylor and Taylor* (1993).

Key case

R v Taylor and Taylor (1993)

Two sisters were charged with murder. Some newspapers published still photos taken from a video which gave a false impression of what was happening. After the jury had convicted the sisters, the judge gave leave to appeal because of the possible influence the pictures could have had on the jury's verdict and the Court of Appeal quashed the convictions.

Lack of understanding

There are worries that jurors may not understand the case which they are trying.

The report 'Are Juries Fair?' also looked at jurors' understanding of cases. In order to test understanding, a series of simulated trials was used. A total of 797 jurors in three different areas all saw the same simulated trial and heard exactly the same judicial directions on the law.

The research found that in most cases about two-thirds of the jurors thought they had understood the judge's directions. However, when the jurors' understanding of the directions was tested, it was found that only 31 per cent of the jurors had actually understood the directions fully. Matters improved when the jurors were given a written summary of the instructions. With this written aid, 48 per cent of the jurors understood the directions. This study shows that, even with a written summary, less than half of jurors fully understood the judge's directions.

Fraud trials

Fraud trials with complex accounts being given in evidence can create special problems for jurors. Even jurors who can easily cope with other evidence may have difficulty understanding a fraud case. These cases are also often very long, so that the jurors have to be able to be away from their own work for months. A long fraud trial can place a great strain on jurors. Such cases also become very expensive, both for the prosecution and for the defendants.

In the Domestic Violence, Crime and Victims Act 2004, there is a special provision for cases where there is a large number of counts on the indictment. This allows a trial of sample counts with a jury and then, if the defendant is convicted on those, the remainder can be tried by a judge alone. This does help prevent long jury trials in very complex fraud cases.

Jury tampering

In a few cases, friends of the defendant may try to interfere with the jury. This may be by bribing jury members to bring in a not guilty verdict or by making threats against jury members so that they are too afraid to find the defendant guilty. In such cases, police may be used to try to protect the jurors, but this may not be effective and is also expensive and removes the police from their other work.

To combat this, s 44 of the Criminal Justice Act 2003 provides that where there has already been an effort to tamper with a jury in the case, the prosecution can apply for the trial to be heard by judge alone. The first trial without a jury was approved in *R v Twomey and others* (2009).

Key case

R v Twomey and others (2009)

The defendants were charged with various offences connected to a large robbery from a warehouse at Heathrow. Three previous trials had collapsed and there had been a 'serious attempt at jury tampering' in the last of these. The prosecution applied to a single judge for the trial to take place without a jury. The judge refused, but the Court of Appeal overturned this decision, ordering that the trial should take place without a jury.

However, in other cases the Court of Appeal have not granted trial by judge alone. An example is *KS v R* (2010).

Case	Facts	Law
Bushell's case (1670)	A jury refused to convict Quaker activists They were fined and imprisoned They were released after an appeal	The jury makes the decision on the facts The judge must not challenge that decision
Ponting's case (1984)	A civil servant leaked information to an MP The jury refused to convict him even though the judge ruled he had no defence	A jury is independent and if it decides cases on the basis of fairness, its decision cannot be challenged
R v Mirza (2004)	One juror complained that the other members of the jury had shown racial bias in coming to their decision	Discussions in the jury room are secret and the court will not normally inquire into them
R v Young (Stephen) (1995)	Four jurors held a séance to try to contact two murder victims and find out who had murdered them	The court was able to inquire into what had happened as it was at a hotel where the jurors were staying and not in the jury room discussions
R v Karakaya (2005)	A juror did an internet search on the defendant and brought the printed out results into the jury room	The court could inquire into this as outside information had been used in the jury room
R v Twomey and others (2009)	There was a serious attempt at interfering with the jury and three previous trials had collapsed	Section 44 of the Criminal Justice Act 2003 applied and a retrial was ordered by judge alone
KS v R (2010)	There was an effort to interfere with the jury, but it had only occurred because jurors and members of the public were taking breaks in the same area	An application under s 44 of the Criminal Justice Act 2003 for trial without a jury was refused The approach was opportunistic rather than a deliberate targeting of jurors

Figure 8.4 Cases on juries

Key case

KS v R (2010)

There had been several trials on various allegations of fraud committed by the defendant. It was not until the tenth trial that jury tampering occurred. It occurred because jurors and members of the public who wished to smoke during breaks were directed to the same area. During one of these breaks, a friend of the defendant approached a juror. The Court of Appeal refused an application for trial by judge alone. They pointed out that the casual arrangements at the Crown Court which had allowed the contact would not be repeated. Also the approach had been opportunistic rather than a deliberate targeting of jurors. For these reasons, there was no need to order trial by judge alone.

High acquittal rates

Juries are often criticised on the grounds that they acquit too many defendants. The figures usually quoted in support of this are that about 60 per cent of those who plead not guilty at the Crown Court are acquitted. However, this figure does not give a true picture of the workings of juries as it includes cases discharged by the judge and those in which the judge directed an acquittal.

The Criminal Court statistics (published quarterly by the Government) show that in most years about a third of acquittals are ordered by the judge without a jury even being sworn in to try the case. This happens where the prosecution drops the case at the last minute and offers no evidence against the defendant. Another 5 per cent of acquittals are by a jury but on the direction of a judge. This occurs where the judge rules that there is no case against the defendant; it might be because of a legal point or because the prosecution evidence is not sufficient in law to prove the case.

When these decisions are excluded from the statistics it is found that juries actually acquit in about 35 per cent of cases.

Other disadvantages

The compulsory nature of jury service is unpopular, so that some jurors may be against the whole system, while others may rush their verdict in order to leave as quickly as possible. Jury service can be a strain, especially where jurors have to listen to horrific evidence. Jurors in the Rosemary West case, where several young women and girls had been murdered by West and her husband, were offered counselling after the trial to help them cope with the evidence they had seen and heard.

Advantages	Disadvantages
Public confidence Considered to be a fundamental part of a democratic society New qualifications for jury service mean that almost everyone can serve on a jury	High acquittal rates undermine confidence in the criminal justice system Doing jury service is unpopular
Jury equity: *Ponting's case*	Perverse verdicts: *Randle and Pottle* (1991) *R v Kronlid* (1996)
Open system of justice Involves members of the public	Media influence Reporting may influence the decision: *Taylor and Taylor* (1993)
Secrecy of the jury room protects jurors from pressure	Secrecy means that: • the reasons for the decision are not known • the jury's understanding of the case cannot be checked *(Mirza* (2004)) Exception: Complete repudiation of oath *(Young (Stephen)* (1995)); extraneous material used *(Karakaya* (2005))
Impartiality Having 12 members with no direct interest in the case should cancel out any bias	Bias In some cases there has been racial bias: *Sander v UK* (2000)

Figure 8.5 Advantages and disadvantages of jury trial

Summary

- Juries have been used for over 1,000 years in the English legal system.
- The jury is the sole decider of fact in a case and is independent in its decision making: *Bushell's case, R v McKenna*.
- Juries are used at the Crown Court in criminal cases.
- Jurors must be:
  - aged between 18 and 75 inclusive
  - registered as a parliamentary or local elector
  - ordinarily resident in the UK for at least five years since their thirteenth birthday.
- Those who have at any time been sentenced to a prison sentence of at least five years are disqualified for life from jury.
- Also disqualified are those who have at any time in the last ten years:
  - served a sentence of imprisonment
  - had a suspended sentence
  - been given a community order.
- People on bail are also disqualified from being a juror.
- The court can give a discretionary excusal to anyone chosen for jury service but there must be a very good reason.

- Jurors are selected at random from the registers of electors.
- Jurors can be vetted by a police check or, in exceptional cases, by a wider background check.
- The jury decides the verdict of guilty or not guilty in cases at the Crown Court where the defendant pleads not guilty.
- The verdict can be a majority one, of 10:2.
- Advantages of jury trial are:
  - public confidence
  - jury equity
  - open system of justice
  - decision made in secret
  - impartiality.
- Disadvantages of jury trial are:
  - perverse decisions
  - secrecy of the decision
  - racial bias
  - media influence
  - lack of understanding of jurors, especially in fraud trials
  - the possibility of jury tampering
  - high acquittal rates
  - jury service is unpopular and can be a strain.

Chapter 9

Legal personnel 1 – Barristers, solicitors, legal executives and legal services

> After reading this chapter you should be able to:
> - Understand the roles of barristers, solicitors and legal executives
> - Understand the differences in these roles – their qualifications, training and work
> - Understand in outline the regulation of legal personnel
> - Understand some of the changes and trends in legal services, including the impact of technology and globalisation
> - Evaluate the legal professions

9.1 Types of legal personnel

In England and Wales there are two types of lawyers (barristers and solicitors), jointly referred to as the legal profession.

There are also legal executives who work in solicitors' firms, who have qualifications in law but are not as fully qualified as solicitors.

9.2 Barristers

There are about 12,700 barristers who are self-employed in independent practice in England and Wales. In addition there are about 3,000 barristers employed by organisations such as the Crown Prosecution Service, independent businesses, local government and the Civil Service.

Collectively barristers are referred to as 'the Bar' and they are controlled by their own professional body – the General Council of the Bar. All barristers must also be a member of one of the four Inns of Court: Lincoln's Inn, Inner Temple, Middle Temple and Gray's Inn, all of which are situated near the Royal Courts of Justice in London.

9.2.1 Qualifications and training of barristers

Entry to the Bar is normally degree-based. If the degree is not in law, it is necessary to take the Graduate Diploma in Law (GDL).

A barrister

All student barristers also have to pass the Bar Professional Training Course. On this course students study:
- case preparation
- opinion writing (giving written advice) and legal research
- drafting documents such as claim forms

- conference skills (interviewing clients)
- negotiation
- advocacy (speaking in court)
- knowledge which includes civil litigation, criminal litigation, sentencing and evidence.

> ### Key term 🔑
>
> Advocacy – the art of speaking in court on behalf of another; conducting a case in court as the legal representative of another person.

Once a student has passed the Bar Professional Training Course, he is then 'called to the Bar'. This means that he is officially qualified as a barrister. However, there is still a practical stage to his training which must be completed. This is called pupillage.

Pupillage

After the student has passed the Bar Professional Training Course there is 'on the job' training where the trainee barrister becomes a pupil to a qualified barrister. This effectively involves 'work shadowing' that barrister, and can be with the same barrister for 12 months or with two different Pupil Supervisors for six months each.

The method of applying for pupillage has recently been changed so that an application is made to a central point, the Pupillage Gateway. All pupillage vacancies are notified to the Gateway and advertised on their site. Applications for pupillage are usually made about 18 months before the start of the pupillage. Applications can be made for up to 12 of the advertised vacancies. This system is much more open and allows applicants to know about all possible vacancies.

9.2.2 Evaluation of the training process

The main problem is a financial one. Students will normally have to pay the fees of the Bar Professional Training Course (about £15,000). The result is that students from less well-off families cannot afford to take the course and are therefore prevented from becoming barristers. If they have a degree in a subject other than law and have had to do the GDL, they will also have had to pay for that course.

The financial problem has increased since universities have increased their fees to £9,000 a year, so that students are already in debt from their degree course.

Another criticism is that non-law graduates do only one year of formal law for the GDL. The Ormrod Committee which reported on legal education in 1971 thought that the main entry route should be via a law degree, but in practice not all barristers will have taken a law degree. One critic posed the question of whether the public would be satisfied with doctors who have only studied medicine for one year, concentrating on only six subjects. Yet this is precisely what is occurring in the legal profession

Yet another problem is that of over-supply. There are not enough pupillage places for the number of students who pass the Bar Professional Training Course. In 2014–15 there were over 1,500 students taking the BPTC but only 422 pupillages available. So some students will have run up massive debts and yet be unable to complete their training as a barrister.

9.2.3 Role of barristers

Barristers practising at the Bar are self-employed, but usually work from a set of chambers where they can share administrative expenses with other barristers. Most sets of chambers are fairly small, with about 15–20 barristers. They will employ a clerk as a practice administrator – booking in cases and negotiating fees – and they will have other support staff.

After a barrister has practised for at least ten years, an application to be made a Queen's Counsel (QC) can be made. (See section 9.5 for details on Queen's Counsel.) If they are appointed as a QC this means that they will take on more difficult and complex cases and their earnings will be more.

The majority of barristers will concentrate on advocacy. Advocacy is presenting cases in court. Barristers have full rights of audience. This means they can present cases in any court in England and Wales. However, there are some barristers who specialise in areas such as tax and company law, and will rarely appear in court. Even those who specialise in advocacy will do a certain amount of paperwork, writing opinions on cases, giving advice and drafting documents for use in court.

> ### Key term 🔑
>
> Rights of audience – the right to present a case in court on behalf of another person.

Direct access

Originally it was necessary for anybody who wished to instruct a barrister to go to a solicitor first. The solicitor would then brief the barrister. This was thought to create unnecessary expense for clients, as it meant they had to use two lawyers instead of one. It is no longer necessary to go to a solicitor in order to instruct a barrister for civil cases, although in the majority of cases this will still happen. Direct access is still not allowed for criminal cases or family work. To do direct access work, a barrister must do additional training.

Employed barristers

Barristers can be employed by government organisations, the Civil Service, local government and businesses. In particular the Crown Prosecution Service employs a large number to prosecute cases in the criminal courts. Employed barristers have the same rights of audience (i.e. the right to present cases in court) as self-employed barristers.

Criminal advocacy

In 2015 a proposed new system for lawyers doing advocacy in the higher courts was announced. All lawyers will have to get accreditation under the Quality Assurance Scheme for Advocates (QASA). The intention is that advocates will only be allowed to act in serious cases when they have shown competency in lower level cases.

9.3 Solicitors

There are about 136,000 solicitors practising in England and Wales and they are controlled by their own professional body, the Law Society. Of the 136,000, about 90,000 are in private practice and the remainder are in employed work, such as for local government, the Civil Service, the Crown Prosecution Service or private businesses.

9.3.1 Qualifications and training of solicitors

To become a solicitor it is usual to have a law degree, although those with a degree in a subject other than law can take the Graduate Diploma in Law (GDL). The next stage is the Legal Practice Course (LPC). This includes training in skills such as client interviewing, negotiation, advocacy, drafting documents and legal research. There is also an emphasis on business management, for example keeping accounts.

The training requirements are overseen by the Solicitors' Regulatory Authority.

Period of authorised training

Even when this course has been passed, the student is still not a qualified solicitor. He must next do a period of authorised training in which he works in a solicitors' firm for two years, getting practical experience. This training

period can also be undertaken in certain other legal organisations such as the Crown Prosecution Service or the legal department of a local authority. Once the trainee has completed his training period he will be admitted as a solicitor by the Law Society.

9.3.2 Evaluation of the training process

As with barristers, the main problem is financial. Students will normally have to pay the fees of the Legal Practice Course (about £14,000) and support themselves while doing the course. The result is that students from less well-off families cannot afford to take the course and are therefore prevented from becoming solicitors, even though they may have obtained a good law degree. If they have a degree in a subject other than law and have had to do the GDL, they will also have had to pay for that course.

Again, the problem has increased since universities have increased their fees to £9,000 a year, so that students are already in debt from their degree course. In order to try to help would-be solicitors, the GDL can be taken as a part-time course over two years, instead of the one-year full-time course. Doing the course part-time allows students to work as well, easing their financial problems. Often this work will be as a para-legal in a law firm, so that the student is also getting practical experience at the same time.

The same criticism that applied to barristers that non-law graduates only do one year of formal law for the GDL also applies to solicitors.

Another problem is that newly qualified solicitors are competing against legal executives and paralegals for jobs.

A solicitor meeting with clients

9.3.3 Role of solicitors

The majority of those who succeed in qualifying as a solicitor will then work in private practice in a solicitors' firm. However, there are other careers available, and some newly qualified solicitors may go on to work in the Crown Prosecution Service or for a local authority or government department. Others will become legal advisers in commercial or industrial businesses. About 40,000 solicitors are employed.

In a law firm the newly qualified solicitor will initially be an assistant/associate solicitor. They will hope to progress to being a partner in the firm. Initially this is likely to be a non-equity partner or junior partner which means that they do not 'buy in' to become a partner, but equally they do not receive as big a share of the profits as an equity partner. The most senior position in a firm of solicitors is as an equity partner.

A solicitor in private practice may work as a sole practitioner or in a partnership. About a quarter of firms are sole practitioner firms. In January 2017 there was a total of 10,370 firms of solicitors, ranging from the small 'high street' practice to the big city firms. The number of partners is not limited, and some of the biggest firms will have over a hundred partners as well as employing assistant solicitors.

The type of work done by a solicitor will largely depend on the type of firm he is working in. A small high street firm will probably be a general practice advising clients on a whole range of topics such as consumer problems, housing and business matters and family problems. A solicitor working in such a practice is likely to spend some of his time interviewing clients in his office and negotiating on their behalf, and a large amount of time dealing with paperwork. This will include:

- writing letters on behalf of clients
- drafting contracts, leases or other legal documents
- drawing up wills
- dealing with conveyancing (the legal side of buying and selling flats, houses, office buildings and land).

The solicitor may also, if he wishes, act for some of his clients in court. Standing up in court, putting the client's case and questioning witnesses is known as advocacy. Some solicitors will specialise in this and spend much of their time in court.

Specialising

Although some solicitors may be general practitioners handling a variety of work, it is not unusual, even in small firms, for a solicitor to specialise in one particular field. The firm itself may handle only certain types of cases (perhaps only civil actions) and not do any criminal cases, or a firm may specialise in matrimonial cases. Even within the firm the solicitors are likely to have their own field of expertise.

In large firms there will be an even greater degree of specialisation, with departments dealing with one aspect of the law. The large city firms usually concentrate on business and commercial law.

Briefing barristers

Where it is necessary to go to court, the solicitor may decide to brief a barrister to do the case. A solicitor may also go to a barrister for an opinion on a complex case.

Rights of advocacy

All solicitors have always been able to act as advocates in the Magistrates' Courts and the County Courts, but their rights of audience in the higher courts used to be very limited. This was changed by the Courts and Legal Services Act 1990. Solicitors in private practice now have the right to apply for a certificate of advocacy which enables them to appear in the higher courts. Such a certificate is granted if the solicitor already has experience of advocacy in the Magistrates' Court and the County Court, takes a short training course and passes examinations on the rules of evidence.

Solicitors with an advocacy qualification are also eligible to be appointed as Queen's Counsel (see section 9.5).

9.4 Overlap of roles of barristers and solicitors

Until the end of the last century the roles of barristers and solicitors were to a large degree quite different. Barristers specialised in presenting cases in courts and could appear in any court. Solicitors generally did office-based work and only had limited rights to present cases in court. The changes over the last few years mean that now:

Both barristers and solicitors can present cases in court. However, there are only about 6,500 solicitors with higher rights. So, although the rules allow barristers and solicitors to carry out the same advocacy work, in practice there is still a difference in the work they do.

In civil cases the public can go direct to either a barrister or a solicitor but there is no direct access to a barrister in criminal cases or family work.

Both barristers and solicitors can do the preparatory work in civil cases, such as interviewing the client, writing letters to the other side and negotiating; previously only solicitors could do this.

9.5 Queen's Counsel

After at least ten years as a barrister or as a solicitor with an advocacy qualification, it is possible to apply to become a Queen's Counsel (QC). About 10 per cent of the barristers practising at the Bar are Queen's Counsel. Becoming a Queen's Counsel is known as 'taking silk'. QCs usually take on more complicated and high-profile cases than junior barristers (all barristers who are not Queen's Counsel are known as 'juniors'), and they can command higher fees for their recognised expertise. Often a QC will have a junior barrister to assist with the case.

9.5.1 Appointment system

Until 2004 Queen's Counsel were appointed by the Lord Chancellor. However, the Lord Chancellor's criteria for selecting QCs were criticised as being too secretive. There was also the fact that under this selection process less than 10 per cent of QCs were women and only a very small number were from ethnic minorities. In turn, this had an effect on the composition of the judiciary since senior judges are usually chosen from the ranks of Queen's Counsel.

In 2004 the Lord Chancellor, the Bar Council and the Law Society agreed a new system for appointment.

Selection of who should become a QC is now made by an independent selection panel. Lawyers apply to become QCs. They have to pay an application fee of £2,160 and, if successful, an appointment fee of £3,600 (2016–17 figures). Applicants must provide references (these can include references from clients). The applicants are interviewed by members of the independent selection panel. The panel then recommends those who should be appointed to the Lord Chancellor.

The first appointments of QCs under the new system were made in 2006. Since then the number of women and ethnic minority lawyers appointed has increased. In 2016 a total of 107 new QCs were appointed. Of these, 25 were women from the 48

women who had applied. There were 32 ethnic minority applicants and nine of these were successful. Only nine solicitors applied and three were successful.

As a result of the new appointment system, the diversity of QCs is slowly improving. About 15 per cent of QCs are women and 6.5 per cent are from an ethnic minority.

9.6 Legal executives

Legal executives work in solicitors' firms as assistants. They are qualified lawyers who have passed the Institute of Legal Executives' Professional Qualification in Law. They specialise in a particular area of law. There are over 20,000 legal executives practising.

9.6.1 Qualifications and training of legal executives

To become a legal executive it is necessary to pass the Professional Diploma in Law and the Professional Higher Diploma in Law. As well as passing the PHDL examinations, it is also necessary to have worked in a solicitors' firm (or other legal organisation such as the Crown Prosecution Service or local government) for at least five years. When all the qualifications have been achieved the person becomes a Fellow of the Chartered Institute of Legal Executives.

A Fellow of the Chartered Institute of Legal Executives can go on to become a solicitor. In order to do this he will have to pass the Law Society's Legal Practice Course, but he may be given exemption from the two-year training contract.

9.6.2 Role of legal executives

Legal executives specialise in a particular area of law. Within that area of law their day-to-day work is similar to that of a solicitor, though they tend to deal with the more straightforward matters. For example, they can:

- handle various legal aspects of a property transfer
- assist in the formation of a company
- draft wills
- advise people with matrimonial problems
- advise clients accused of serious or petty crime.

They also have some rights of audience. They can appear to make applications where the case is not defended in family matters and civil cases in the County Court.

Since 2008 legal executives have been able to do a course on advocacy and obtain wider rights

	Barristers	Solicitors	Legal executives
Training and qualifications	Degree: if not in law then must pass GDL Bar Professional Training Course Pupillage	Degree: if not in law then must pass GDL Legal Practice Course Training contract	Professional Higher Diploma in Law Work for at least five years
Role	Self-employed in chambers OR employed Mostly court work Also write opinions and draft documents Briefed by solicitors Direct access by clients in civil cases	Private practice in solicitors' firm OR employed Wide variety of work mostly office-based Contracts, leases, wills, conveyancing Direct access by clients May brief a barrister where it is necessary to go to court	Work in a solicitors' firm OR in other legal organisation Similar work to solicitors Deal with more straightforward matters
Advocacy	Full rights of audience in all courts	Automatic rights of audience in Magistrates' Court or County Court Can get advocacy qualification to do cases in higher courts	Very limited rights of audience: applications in undefended cases Can obtain advocacy certificate to make some applications in Magistrates' Court or County Court
Queen's Counsel	Can apply to become a QC after at least ten years in practice Will then do more complicated cases	If have an advocacy qualification can apply to become a QC after at least ten years in practice Will then do more complicated cases	

Figure 9.1 Comparing barristers, solicitors and legal executives

of audience. There are three different practising certificates: a Civil Proceedings Certificate, a Criminal Proceedings Certificate and a Family Proceedings Certificate. These allow legal executives to do such matters as make an application for bail or deal with cases in the Youth Court or the Family Court of the Magistrates' Courts.

Legal executives are fee earners. This means that where a legal executive works for a firm of solicitors in private practice, that legal executive's work is charged an hourly rate directly to clients. In this way a legal executive makes a direct contribution to the income of the law firm. The partners of the firm are responsible for the legal executive's work.

9.7 Regulation of legal personnel

Barristers, solicitors and legal executives all have their own regulatory bodies. All of these bodies are overseen by the Legal Services Board.

9.7.1 The General Council of the Bar

The General Council of the Bar represents barristers in England and Wales. It promotes the Bar's high-quality specialist advocacy and advisory services. It fulfils the function of what might be called a 'trade union', representing the interests of the Bar. It makes the Bar's

view on issues, such as legal aid payment rates, known to the appropriate government department.

The Council also promotes fair access to justice for all, the highest standards of ethics, equality and diversity across the profession, and the development of business opportunities for barristers at home and abroad.

The Council also used to be responsible for disciplining barristers who breached the Code of Practice. This was seen as creating a conflict in its roles, so the independent Bar Standards Board was created to deal with disciplinary matters and also oversee training and education requirements.

9.7.2 Bar Standards Board

This is the body which regulates the profession of barristers. It sets training and entry standards. It also sets out a Code of Conduct which barristers should comply with.

The Board investigates any alleged breach of the Code of Conduct. It can discipline any barrister who is in breach of the Code. If the matter is serious it will be referred to a Disciplinary Tribunal arranged by an independent Bar Tribunals and Adjudication service. A tribunal has several sanctions it can impose including:

- reprimand the barrister (that is, formally warn him about his behaviour)

- make the barrister complete further professional development training
- order the barrister to pay a fine of up to £50,000
- suspend the barrister for up to 12 months
- disbar (strike off) the barrister: this can only be done in extreme cases.

If the complainant is unhappy with the decision of the Bar Standards Board, he may take the matter to the Legal Ombudsman (see section 9.7.7 below).

Making a complaint against a barrister

The chambers from which the barrister practises should have a complaints procedure and this should be used first. If the complaint is not satisfactorily resolved than a complaint can be made to the Bar Standards Board.

It is also possible to sue a barrister in the civil courts for negligence. This was decided in *Saif Ali v Sydney Mitchell and Co.* (1980) where it was held that a barrister could be sued for negligence in respect of written advice and opinions. In that case a barrister had given the wrong advice about who to sue, with the result that the claimant was too late to start proceedings against the right person.

In *Hall (a firm) v Simons* (2000) the House of Lords held that lawyers could also be liable for negligence in the conduct of advocacy in court. This decision overruled the earlier case of *Rondel v Worsley* (1969) in which barristers were held not to be liable because their first duty was to the courts and they must be 'free to do their duty fearlessly and independently'.

The Law Lords in *Hall (a firm) v Simons* (2000) felt that in light of modern conditions it was no longer in the public interest that advocates should have immunity from being sued for negligence. They pointed out that doctors could be sued and they had a duty to an ethical code of practice and might have difficult decisions to make when treating patients. There was no reason why advocates should not be liable in the same way.

9.7.3 The Law Society

The Law Society is the governing body of solicitors. All practising solicitors must be members of the Law Society. On its website the Law Society states that it

> exists to support, promote and represent all solicitors so they can help their clients. We also work to ensure no one is above the law and to protect everyone's right to have access to justice.

It has supported the interests of solicitors in England and Wales for almost 200 years. It leads the debate on issues affecting solicitors throughout England and Wales. In particular it speaks to government, Parliament and the public on a range of legal issues and works to influence policy and legislation to make sure that it protects its members, the public and the justice system

The Law Society makes sure the profession's voice is heard with the right people – government, industry and in international jurisdictions. It helps raise the profile of the profession through campaigns and networking and promotes the UK legal sector locally and globally.

9.7.4 Solicitors Regulatory Authority

This deals with complaints about professional misconduct of solicitors. The Authority will investigate the matter. If there is evidence of serious professional misconduct, it can put the case before the Solicitors Disciplinary Tribunal. If the tribunal upholds the complaint, it can fine or reprimand the solicitor or, in more serious cases, it can suspend a solicitor from the Roll, so that he cannot practise for a certain time. In very serious cases, the tribunal can strike off a solicitor from the Roll so that he is prevented from practising as a solicitor.

If the complainant is unhappy with the decision of the Solicitors Regulatory Authority he may take the matter to the Legal Ombudsman (see section 9.7.7 below).

Complaints against solicitors

A client who wishes to complain about a solicitor should first use the complaints procedure of the firm of solicitors involved. If the matter is not resolved through this then the complaint can be made to the Solicitors Regulatory Authority.

In addition there is the possibility of suing the solicitor in the civil courts. This is because a solicitor deals directly with clients and enters into a contract with them. This means that if the client does not pay, the solicitor has the right to sue for his fees. It also means that the client can sue his solicitor for breach of contract if the solicitor fails to do the work.

A client can also sue his solicitor for negligence. This happened in *Griffiths v Dawson* (1993) where solicitors for the plaintiff had failed to make the correct application in divorce proceedings against her husband. As a result the plaintiff lost financially and the solicitors were ordered to pay her £21,000 in compensation.

It used to be held that a solicitor presenting a case in court could not be sued for negligence. However, in *Hall (a firm) v Simons* (2000), the House of Lords decided that advocates can be liable for negligence.

Other people affected by the solicitor's negligence may also have the right to sue in certain circumstances. An example of this was the case of *White v Jones* (1995) where a father wanted to make a will leaving each of his daughters £9,000. The solicitors did nothing about it, so as a result the daughters did not inherit any money. They successfully sued the solicitor for the £9,000 they had each lost.

9.7.5 Chartered Institute of Legal Executives

All legal executives are members of the Chartered Institute of Legal Executives (CILEx). This organisation provides education, training and development of skills for legal executives. It also protects the status and interests of legal executives. Another aim is to 'promote and secure professional standards of conduct among Fellows and those who are registered with the Institute'.

CILEx publishes a code of conduct and guides to good practice but regulation of members is done by the CILEx Regulation Board.

9.7.6 CILEx Regulation Board

The CILEx Regulation Board is the independent regulator of members of CILEx and investigates complaints about legal executives.

When an investigation is complete a summary of the issues is prepared and the matter is put to the Professional Conduct Panel for consideration. The Panel will decide if there has been misconduct. If there has not it will reject the complaint. If there has been misconduct it may reprimand or warn a member. It will refer serious matters to the Disciplinary Tribunal.

The Disciplinary Tribunal has the power to:
- exclude a person from membership
- reprimand or warn the member.

In addition the tribunal can order the legal executive to pay a fine up to £3,000 and costs.

9.7.7 The Legal Ombudsman

The Legal Ombudsman's office was set up by the Office for Legal Complaints to deal with complaints against the legal profession. It deals with complaints against the handling of complaints by the Bar Standards Board, the Solicitors Regulatory Authority and CILEx Regulatory Board. It can order the legal professional who was complained about to:
- apologise to the client
- give back any documents the client might need
- put things right if more work can correct what went wrong
- refund or reduce the legal fees or
- pay compensation of up to £30,000.

The main complaints made include excessive costs, deficient information on costs, delay, failure to follow instructions and failure to keep informed.

	Barristers	Solicitors	Legal executives
Representative body	Bar Council	Law Society	Chartered Institute of Legal Executives (CILEx)
Regulatory body	Bar Standards Board	Solicitors Regulatory Authority	CILEx Regulation Board
Complaints	Complaints about decisions of the regulatory bodies go to the Legal Ombudsman		

Figure 9.2 Regulation of legal personnel

Look online

Look at the Legal Ombudsman's website, **www.legalombudsman.org.uk**, and find a case study of a complaint. You could use this as the basis of a presentation to your class.

9.8 Evaluating the composition of the legal profession

The legal profession has an image of being white male-dominated. In fact this is becoming less and less true as increasing numbers of women and those from an ethnic minority are entering the profession.

9.8.1 Women

Women are forming an increasing number of the entrants to the profession. There are now more women than men graduating in law. In 2016 60 per cent of those getting a law degree were women.

This has led to an increase in the number of women entrants to both barristers' and solicitors' professions. Well over half of new solicitors are women and about half of new entrants to the Bar. About one-third of practising barristers and 49 per cent of solicitors are female.

Despite this there are very few women at the higher levels in either profession. For example, at the Bar only about 15 per cent of QCs are women although this is slowly increasing. Women solicitors tend to be in junior positions as assistant solicitors or junior partners. Recent statistics show that 45 per cent of women working in solicitors' practices are assistant solicitors. By comparison, only 20 per cent of men are working as assistant solicitors. Women are much less likely to be partners in firms. Only 22 per cent of women are partners. This figure showed some improvement in the first part of this century but it has been fairly static in recent years.

A report, 'Obstacles and Barriers to the Career Development of Women Solicitors', was published by the Law Society in 2010. The following factors were the main reasons why women were less likely than men to progress in the profession:

- lack of flexible working hours
- the organisational culture, which was perceived as being traditional, conservative and male-dominated
- the long working hours with the 24/7 mindset
- the fact that the measurement of success was strongly linked to the number of hours billed to clients – measuring quantity rather than quality
- the fact that women were not prepared to challenge the status quo or push themselves forward for promotion.

These factors lead to many women leaving solicitors' firms, often to become an 'in-house' lawyer in another organisation where there is a different work culture.

Women are better represented at the employed bar.

9.8.2 Ethnic minorities

Proportionate to the composition of the general population, black and minority ethnic groups (BME) are well represented at the Bar. In 2015, 13 per cent of practising barristers were from an ethnic minority. While they have experienced even more difficulty than women in achieving higher positions, with 6.5 per cent of QCs being of black or Asian ethnic minority, this is a great improvement from ten years ago and is likely to increase again in the future.

In the solicitors' profession ethnic minorities are well represented. In the last few years the number of ethnic minority entrants has risen substantially. The number of BME with a Practising Certificate rose from 5,009 in 2000 to 18,547 in 2015 making up 15 per cent of practising solicitors.

9.9 Changes and trends in legal services

9.9.1 Alternative Business Structures

In 2004, Sir David Clementi carried out a review of the legal profession. His report led to the passing of the Legal Services Act 2007 which brought about changes in the rules about the types of business structures allowed in the legal profession. Alternative Business Structures (ABSs) allowed are:

- legal businesses including lawyers and non-lawyers
- legal businesses including barristers and solicitors
- non-lawyers owning legal businesses
- legal businesses operating as companies.

In order to set up an ABS a licence must be applied for from the Legal Services Board. The first three licences under the Act were given in April 2012. Two of these were to 'high street' solicitors who wished to bring in a non-lawyer practice manager to their practices. The third was to the Co-operative Society, a big business with shops nationwide.

As more ABSs are set up, the style of legal advice and services is likely to change considerably. Traditional solicitors' firms will face competition from commercial firms such as the Co-operative Society.

Arguments in favour of ABSs

There are several arguments in favour of allowing ABSs. These include:

- there is a demand for a 'one-stop' facility
- ABSs give direct access to a range of specialists in the same business
- ABSs allow free market competition and this should keep fees at a lower level

- it gives clients a choice of a traditional firm or an ABS
- solicitors and barristers should have the choice of how to practise.

Arguments against ABSs

Equally, there a number of concerns about ABSs. These include:

- the legal profession must be independent in order to maintain its role of protecting individual liberties
- there is an increased risk of conflict of interest
- there may be problems regulating lawyers' and non-lawyers' professional conduct
- there is a risk that all the best lawyers would be concentrated in a small number of firms – at the moment all solicitors have access to the top barristers at the independent bar.

9.9.2 Technology and globalisation and the legal profession

Information technology is an important aspect of our modern world. The number of internet users and email account holders is numbered in billions worldwide. Computers are increasingly becoming more powerful and cloud computing has dramatically increased the amount of data-storage.

Already the working practices of legal professionals have changed with the use of technology. Case decisions can be accessed online. There is no longer the need to have a set of printed law reports or to go to a legal library to look up cases in the printed version.

The work of the courts has also been affected by technology. Claims can be filed online. Documents are stored on computer. Computers can be used in court to access documents instead of having a large amount of paperwork in court.

Storage of information can be done electronically. Legal documents, including forms for starting legal actions in the courts, are available online. Automated document systems can generate customised first drafts of documents. This all saves time. For lawyers who charge by the hour, this can mean less income since what took hours in the past can now be done in minutes.

Computer systems also exist to carry out Intelligent Searches of legal documents. This means

that large amounts of documents can be reviewed and categorised. Again, this is major saving of time as lawyers no longer have to go through such documents manually. And again this is reducing the time that can be charged to clients.

Information technology also threatens to reduce the work of lawyers in other ways. Online Dispute Resolution (ODR) services already exist. These allow people to resolve a dispute from the comfort of their own homes and without the need for lawyers.

See Chapter 4 at 4.3.4 for more detail on ODR.

There is also a proposal for an online court to operate in the English legal system. This will probably start in 2020. Again there would be no need for lawyers.

Advances in technology, especially in communications, also mean that it is easier for law firms to become international in a process known as 'globalisation'.

Globalisation

Globalisation proved a tremendous boon to many law firms. As their clients internationalised, the law firms moved into new markets to support them. In this way the largest law firms have entered the global market. Examples of such firms include Baker McKenzie, Clifford Chance and Freshfields. Many firms have offices in several other countries. They also have relationships with large firms abroad so that they effectively operate one firm all over the world.

However, this has created some problems. It is expensive and large firms can rarely charge the same rates in new markets as they do in their home jurisdictions. It can also be difficult to identify and develop high-quality talent in distant locations.

Globalisation has also occurred at the Bar with at least one set of Chambers, 20 Essex Street, establishing a permanently staffed office in Singapore.

Globalisation has also resulted in a change in focus of the law. Mass communication encourages the world to face challenges, such as climate, terrorism and human rights, together. Such issues have encouraged the rise of international law alongside national law.

However, the effect on the legal profession is only felt in the bigger city firms. It is not an issue which affects smaller firms or local high street solicitors. It also has very little impact on the criminal Bar.

Summary

- Barristers
  - can be self-employed or work for an organisation: they must be a member of one of the four Inns of Court
  - have to pass the Bar Professional Training Course and do pupillage before they can practise
  - most do court work: they have full rights of audience
  - are represented by the General Council of the Bar: their regulatory body is the Bar Standards Board.

- Solicitors
  - can work in a solicitors' firm or for an organisation: they must belong to the Law Society
  - have to pass the Legal Training Course and do a two-year training contract
  - do mostly office-based work, but can present cases in the Magistrates' Court and County Court; can also qualify for rights of audience in higher courts
  - are represented by the Law Society: their regulatory body is the Solicitors Regulatory Authority.

- Legal executives
  - work in a solicitors' firm or other legal organisation
  - have to pass the Professional Higher Diploma in Law and work for at least five years
  - do the more straightforward matters: have very limited rights of audience
  - are represented by CILEx: their regulatory body is the CILEx Regulation Board.

- Queen's Counsel
  - barristers of ten years' standing and solicitors with higher rights of advocacy can apply to become a Queen's Counsel
  - do more complex cases.

- Complaints against the legal profession: the Legal Ombudsman
  - hears complaints about the regulatory bodies' failure to deal properly with clients' complaints
  - can order an apology, putting things right, a refund or reduction in legal fees, compensation.

- Women and ethnic minorities in the legal profession
  - The number of women has increased: they make up over half the number of entrants: nearly half of practising solicitors and one-third of practising barristers.
  - Women are not so well represented at the higher levels of the professions.
  - Ethnic minorities are well represented in the lower levels of the professions.
  - Ethnic minorities are not so well represented at the higher levels of the professions.

- Changes and trends in legal services
  - Alternative Business Structures pose a challenge to traditional legal firms.
  - Working practices have had to change with the increasing use of information technology.
  - Globalisation has led to large city firms becoming international.

Chapter 10

Legal personnel 2 – The judiciary

After reading this chapter you should be able to:
- Understand the different types of judge
- Understand their qualifications, selection and appointment
- Understand training for judges and their role in civil and criminal courts
- Understand procedures for judges' retirement and removal
- Explain the doctrine of the separation of powers
- Understand how the independence of the judiciary is ensured
- Comment on the reasons for and the advantages of judicial independence

10.1 Types of judge

When speaking of judges as a group they are referred to as the judiciary. There are many different levels of judges, but their basic function is the same. Their main role is to make decisions in respect of disputes. This they must do in a fair, unbiased way, applying the law and the legal rules of England and Wales.

The judiciary is divided into what are known as 'superior' judges (those in the High Court and above) and 'inferior' judges (those in the lower courts). This distinction affects training, work and, in particular, the terms on which they hold office. So it is important to start by understanding which judges sit in which court.

10.1.1 Superior judges

Superior judges are those in the Supreme Court, the Court of Appeal and the High Court. They are:
- the Justices of the Supreme Court
- the Lord Justices of Appeal in the Court of Appeal
- High Court Judges (also known as puisne (pronounced 'pew-nay') judges) who sit in the three divisions of the High Court; judges in the Queen's Bench Division of the High Court also sit to hear serious cases in the Crown Court.

The head of the judiciary is the Lord Chief Justice.

Judges walking to the Houses of Parliament

10.1.2 Inferior judges

The inferior judges include:
- Circuit Judges who sit in both the Crown Court and the County Court
- Recorders who are part-time judges who usually sit in the Crown Court, though some hear cases in the County Court
- District Judges who hear small claims and other matters in the County Court
- District Judges (Magistrates' Courts) who sit in Magistrates' Courts in London and other major towns and cities
- tribunal judges.

10.2 Qualifications, selection and appointment

10.2.1 Qualifications

The relevant qualifications for the different judicial posts are set out in the Courts and Legal Services Act 1990 as amended by the Tribunals, Courts and Enforcement Act 2007. Qualifications to become a judge are based on legal qualifications plus relevant legal experience for a number of years.

10.2.2 Selection

Up to 2005, selection of superior judges was done by the Lord Chancellor. The system was secretive. In addition, the Lord Chancellor is a political appointment. This meant selection of judges was not independent from political influence.

The system was changed by the Constitutional Reform Act 2005 which established the Judicial Appointments Commission to deal with the selection of judges.

The Lord Chancellor is still nominally involved in appointments to the High Court, the Supreme Court and Court of Appeal. However, for lower court judgeships the process is now completely separate from the government and executive. The Crime and Courts Act 2013 transferred the Lord Chancellor's power in respect of all judges below the High Court to the Lord Chief Justice.

The Judicial Appointments Commission

The Commission is responsible for selecting over 500 people each year for appointment to judicial posts. The Commission advertises its selection exercises on their website, through their email newsletter and on Twitter.

The key features of the process for appointing judges are:
- Appointments are made solely on merit.
- The Commission is entirely responsible for assessing the merit of the candidates and selecting candidates for appointment.
- No candidate can be appointed unless recommended by the Commission.
- The Commission must consult with the Lord Chief Justice and another judge of equivalent experience before recommending a candidate for appointment.

Judicial qualities

The Commission has listed five qualities that are desirable for a good judge. These are:
- intellectual capacity
- personal qualities including integrity, independence of mind, sound judgement, decisiveness, objectivity and willingness to learn
- ability to understand and deal fairly
- authority and communication skills
- efficiency.

It is also important the potential judge is of good character. If a person has a criminal conviction, they would not be considered for a judicial appointment. The only exception is for minor motoring offences, but even here the person must not have too many of these as shown by the case of *R (Graham Stuart Jones) v Judicial Appointments Commission* (2014) where an applicant for appointment as a District Judge had seven penalty points on his driving licence for motoring offences. He was said by the Judicial Appointments Commission to be an outstanding candidate, but the Commission rejected his application because their guidelines state that having more than six points 'normally prevents selection'. He took judicial review proceedings challenging the Commission's decision but the High Court upheld the decision.

Process of selection

All candidates have to fill in an application form. Candidates are also asked to nominate between three and six referees. In addition, the Commission has published a list of people whom it may consult about candidates. These include existing judges.

For all judicial posts below that of Circuit Judge, there is an extra filtering process. All applicants must do an online qualifying test at the start of their application. These tests are designed to assess candidates' ability to perform judicial roles. Candidates are then short-listed on the basis of their performance in these tests along with their application form and qualifications.

A shortlist will then be made of candidates and these will be interviewed. The interview process may include role play or taking part in a formal, structured discussion.

The Commission then selects those to be appointed and recommends them to the Lord Chancellor for appointment.

10.2.3 Appointment

Once a candidate has been selected the appointment is made by the Queen. This keeps selection and appointment separate from the government.

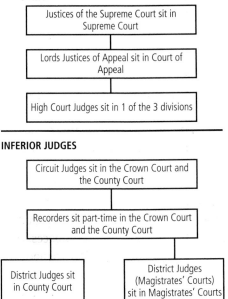

SUPERIOR JUDGES

Justices of the Supreme Court sit in Supreme Court

Lords Justices of Appeal sit in Court of Appeal

High Court Judges sit in 1 of the 3 divisions

INFERIOR JUDGES

Circuit Judges sit in the Crown Court and the County Court

Recorders sit part-time in the Crown Court and the County Court

District Judges sit in County Court

District Judges (Magistrates' Courts) sit in Magistrates' Courts

Figure 10.1 The hierarchy of judges

10.3 Training of judges

The training of judges is carried out by the Judicial College which was set up in 2011 by bringing together the Judicial Studies Board, which had previously trained judges, and the Tribunals Judicial Training Group, which had previously trained tribunal members.

The Judicial College points out that there are three main elements to training. These are:

- knowledge of substantive law, evidence and procedure
- the acquisition and improvement of judicial skills
- the social context within which judging occurs.

On first appointment, all new judges have to go through an induction programme. This normally consists of a residential course of three to five days. New judges at the lower levels are assigned an experienced judge to act as mentor and support them at the start of their judicial career.

Where judges are promoted to a high level in the judiciary, then they will have to attend the induction course for that level.

For experienced judges continuing education is given by a mixture of residential and non-residential courses supplemented by e-learning. Continuing education will include the effect of any new legislation.

There is also training in human awareness, including gender, racial and disability issues. The training explores the perceptions of unrepresented parties, witnesses, jurors, victims and their families. It is aimed at making judges more aware of other people's viewpoints.

10.4 Role of judges

10.4.1 Justices of the Supreme Court

Judges in the Supreme Court hear about 100 cases each year. These are appeals. They can be in civil or criminal cases. However, the majority of cases are civil appeals. A case can only be appealed to the Supreme Court if there is a point of law involved. Often civil cases involve complicated and technical areas of law such as planning law or tax law.

The Justices of the Supreme Court must sit as an uneven number panel (minimum three judges) to hear a case. In the Brexit case in December 2016, the court unusually comprised eleven judges. This was because the issue was such an important one.

Any decision the Supreme Court makes on a point of law becomes a precedent for all lower courts to follow. You can find reports of cases decided by the Supreme Court at **www.supremecourt.uk**.

Courtroom 1 of the Supreme Court

10.4.2 Lords Justices of Appeal

All their work is concerned with appeals. The Lords Justices of Appeal sit in both the civil and criminal divisions of the Court of Appeal, so they deal with both civil and criminal cases. Their workload is much heavier than the Supreme Court.

Court of Appeal judges usually sit as a panel of three to hear cases. On rare occasions in important cases, there may be a panel of five. Decisions by the Court of Appeal on points of law become precedents which lower courts must follow.

10.4.3 High Court Judges

The main function of High Court Judges is to try cases. These are known as cases at first instance because it is the first time the case has been heard by a court. They will hear evidence from witnesses, decide what the law is and make the decision as to which side has won the case. If the claim is for damages (an amount of money) the judge decides how much should be awarded to the winning claimant.

When hearing first instance cases, judges usually sit alone.

High Court Judges also hear some appeals. These are mainly from civil cases tried in the County Court. The judges in the Queen's Bench Division also hear criminal appeals from the Magistrates' Courts by way of case stated. These are appeals on law only. When sitting to hear appeals, there will be a panel of two judges.

Judges from the Queen's Bench Division also sit in the Crown Court to hear criminal trials. When they do this they sit with a jury. The jury decides the facts and the judge decides the law. Where a defendant pleads guilty or is found guilty by a jury, the judge then has to decide on the sentence.

10.4.4 Inferior judges

Circuit Judges sit in the County Court to hear civil cases and also in the Crown Court to try criminal cases. In civil cases they sit on their own. They decide the law and the facts. They make the decision on who has won the case.

In criminal cases they sit with a jury. The jury decides the facts and the judge decides the law. Where a defendant pleads guilty or is found guilty by a jury, the judge then has to decide on the sentence.

Recorders are part-time judges who are appointed for a period of five years. They are used mainly in the Crown Court to try criminal cases, but some sit in the County Court to help with civil cases.

District Judges sit in the County Court to deal with small claims cases (under £10,000) and can also hear other cases for larger amounts.

District Judges (Magistrates' Courts) try criminal cases in the Magistrates' Courts. They sit on their own and decide facts and law. When a defendant pleads guilty or is found guilty, they also have to decide on the sentence.

In appellate courts	Hear appeals for the decision of the court below. The reasons for the decision can form a precedent which has to be followed in later cases
In civil courts	Sit alone to decide facts and law, make decision of which party wins case, award damages
In criminal courts	**Crown Court** Sit with a jury of 12. Judge decides law: jury decides facts and verdict: if defendant is guilty, judge decides sentence **Magistrates' Court** District Judge sits on own and makes decisions about law and facts: decides if defendant is guilty or not guilty; decides sentence where defendant is guilty

Figure 10.2 The role of judges

10.5 Retirement and removal

It is important that judges should be impartial in their decisions and, in particular, that the government cannot force a judge to resign if that judge makes a decision with which the government of the day disagrees. In this country judges are reasonably secure from political interference.

10.5.1 Retirement

Since the Judicial Pensions and Retirement Act 1993 all judges now have to retire at the age of 70, though there are some situations in which authorisation can be given for a judge to continue beyond that age. Prior to this Act judges in the High Court and above could remain sitting as judges until they were 75. The Lord Chancellor may authorise retired senior judges to sit part-time until the age of 75. All inferior judges also retire at 70.

10.5.2 Removal

Superior judges have security of tenure in that they cannot be removed by the Lord Chancellor or the government. This right originated in the Act of Settlement 1700 which allowed them to hold office while of good behaviour (previously the monarch could dismiss judges at will).

The same provision is now contained in the Senior Courts Act 1981 for High Court Judges and Lords Justices of Appeal, and in the Constitutional Reform Act 2005 for the Justices of the Supreme Court. As a result they can only be removed by the monarch following a petition presented to her by both Houses of Parliament. This gives superior judges protection from political whims and allows them to be independent in their judgments.

This power to remove a superior judge has never been used for an English judge, though it was used in 1830 to remove an Irish judge, Jonah Barrington, who had misappropriated £700 from court funds.

The Lord Chief Justice can, however, after consulting with the Lord Chancellor, declare vacant the office of any judge who (through ill health) is incapable of carrying out his work and of taking the decision to resign. This power was first introduced in the Administration of Justice Act 1973 and is now contained in the Senior Courts Act 1981.

In fact what has happened on two occasions in the past is that pressure has been put on unsatisfactory High Court Judges to resign. The first of these was in 1959 when the Lord Chancellor asked Mr Justice Hallett to resign; the second in 1998 when Mr Justice Harman resigned after criticisms by the Court of Appeal.

10.5.3 Removal of inferior judges

These do not have the same security of tenure of office as superior judges since the Lord Chancellor has the power to remove inferior judges for incapacity or misbehaviour. A criminal conviction for dishonesty would obviously be regarded as misbehaviour and would lead to the dismissal of the judge concerned.

This happened in the 1970s when Bruce Campbell, a Circuit Judge, was convicted of evading customs duty on cigarettes and whisky. Other matters such as drunken driving would probably be seen as misbehaviour, as would racial or sexual harassment.

In 2014 it also happened in the case of Constance Briscoe, a Recorder who was convicted and imprisoned for perverting the course of justice. She had lied and then altered her statement regarding her involvement in a case where she was a witness.

Examples of other reasons for dismissal include the following cases:

- In April 2009, Judge Margaret Short was dismissed in this way for 'inappropriate, petulant and rude' behaviour in one case and 'intemperate and ill-judged' behaviour in another case.
- In 2015, one District judge and two Deputy District judges were removed from office for viewing pornographic material on their official judicial IT accounts.

Under the Constitutional Reform Act 2005, the Lord Chancellor must comply with set procedures and have the consent of the Lord Chief Justice before he can remove any judge from office.

In addition under the Constitutional Reform Act 2005, the Lord Chief Justice has the power to suspend a person from judicial office if he is subject to criminal proceedings or has been convicted. The Lord Chief Justice can only exercise this power if the Lord Chancellor agrees, and must use set procedures. Any judge who is suspended or disciplined in any other way can make a complaint to an Ombudsman if the procedures have not been carried out correctly and fairly.

Judges	Court/s	Tenure
Justices of the Supreme Court	Supreme Court	'during good behaviour' Constitutional Reform Act 2005
Lords Justices of Appeal	Court of Appeal	'while of good behaviour' Senior Courts Act 1981
High Court Judges	High Court Crown Court for serious cases	'while of good behaviour' Senior Courts Act 1981
Circuit Judges	County Court Crown Court	Can be dismissed by the Lord Chancellor (with the consent of the Lord Chief Justice) for incapacity or misbehaviour Courts Act 1971
District Judges	County Court Magistrates Court	Can be dismissed by the Lord Chancellor (with the consent of the Lord Chief Justice) for incapacity or misbehaviour Courts Act 1971
Recorders	Crown Court Some may sit in the County Court	Appointed for a period of five years. The Lord Chief Justice can decide not to re-appoint

Figure 10.3 Judges and their tenure

10.6 Evaluation of the judiciary

One of the main criticisms of the bench has always been that it is dominated by elderly, white, upper-class males. There are very few women judges in the upper ranks of judges, and even fewer judges from ethnic minorities. Also, it is unusual for any judge to be appointed under the age of 40, with superior judges usually being well above this age.

10.6.1 Women in the judiciary

The system of selection by the Judicial Appointments Commission has led to improved diversity in the judiciary. This can be seen by comparing the percentage of women and ethnic minority judges now with those of past times.

In the early 1990s there were no women judges in the Court of Appeal and only three in the High Court. At the beginning of 2016 there were eight women judges in the Court of Appeal and 23 in the High Court.

In the lower level of the judiciary there has also been a great increase in the number of female judges. In the early 1990s only about 5 per cent of Circuit Judges and Recorders were women. At the beginning of 2016, 25 per cent of Circuit Judges and 17 per cent of Recorders were female. It was also very notable that of the newly appointed Recorders in January 2016 over half were women.

The biggest increase has been in the post of District Judges. In the early 1990s only 2 per cent of District Judges were female. By 2016 this had increased to 30 per cent.

The increasing number of women judges is partly due to the open and competitive method of selection. But it is also partly due to the fact that there is an increasing number of women barristers and solicitors, and so more possible applicants for judicial posts.

10.6.2 Ethnic minorities

There has also been an increase in the number of judges from black and minority ethnic background (BME). In the early 1990s there were no BME judges in the Court of Appeal or High Court and very few in the lower judicial posts.

By 2016 there were three BME High Court Judges and 17 Circuit Judges. At the lower levels of the judiciary the numbers are much greater with 7 per cent of Recorders and 8 per cent of District Judges (County Court) from BME backgrounds.

10.6.3 Educational and social background

At the higher levels judges tend to come from the upper levels of society, with many having been educated at public school and nearly all attending Oxford University or Cambridge University. A survey

by the magazine Labour Research found that of the 85 judges appointed from 1997 to mid-1999, 73 per cent had been to public school and 79 per cent to Oxbridge.

In 2007, Penny Darbyshire surveyed 77 judges from different levels of the judiciary. She found that there were marked differences in background between superior judges and those at a lower level. For example, none of the District Judges (Magistrates' Court) had been to private school, while 11 out of 16 High Court Judges and 8 out of the 10 Court of Appeal/House of Lords Judges she interviewed had been privately educated.

University

There was also a major difference in the universities that senior judges had attended compared to judges at a lower level. Ninety per cent of Court of Appeal/House of Lords Judges had been to Oxford or Cambridge, but only one of six District Judges (Magistrates' Court) and four out of thirteen District Judges (County Court) had attended Oxford or Cambridge. However, as the judges in the Court of Appeal and House of Lords decide complex cases and law, Darbyshire pointed out that 'It would surely be a matter of concern if senior judges were not highly educated and exceptionally intelligent'.

10.6.4 Should there be a career judiciary?

In many continental countries becoming a judge is a career choice made by students once they have their basic legal qualifications. They will usually not practise as a lawyer first, but instead are trained as judges. Once they have qualified as a judge they will sit in junior posts and then hope to be promoted up the judicial ladder. This has two distinct advantages over the system in use in this country:

- The average age of judges is much lower, especially in the bottom ranks where they will be in their twenties. In this country an Assistant Recorder will normally be in his late thirties or early forties when appointed, and the average age for appointment to the High Court Bench tends to be late forties/early fifties.
- Judges have had far more training in the specific skills they need as judges.

The disadvantage of the continental system is that judges may be seen as too closely linked to the government as they are civil servants. In this country judges are generally considered as independent from the government. This point of judicial independence is explored more fully in section 10.8.

10.7 Separation of powers

The doctrine of the separation of powers was first put forward by Montesquieu, a French political theorist, in the eighteenth century. The theory states that there are three primary functions of the state and that the only way to safeguard the liberty of citizens is by keeping these three functions separate. As the power of each is exercised by independent and separate bodies, each can keep a check on the others and thus limit the amount of power wielded by any one group. Ideally this theory requires that individuals should not be members of more than one 'arm of the state'.

Some countries, for example the USA, have a written constitution which embodies this theory. In the United Kingdom there is no such written constitution, but even so the three organs of state are roughly separated. There is some overlap, especially in the fact that the Lord Chancellor is involved in all three functions of the state. However, the Lord Chancellor's role in relation to the judiciary is now much reduced.

The three arms of the state identified by Montesquieu are:

1   **The legislature**
   This is the law-making arm of the state and in the British system this is Parliament.
2   **The executive**
   This is the body administering the law. In the British political system this is the government of the day which forms the Cabinet.
3   **The judiciary**
   This refers to the judges who apply the law. There is an overlap between the executive and the legislature, in that the ministers forming the government also sit in Parliament and are active in the law-making process. With the exception of the Lord Chancellor, there is very little overlap between the judiciary and the other two arms of the state. This is important because it allows the judiciary to act as a check and ensure that the executive does not overstep its constitutional powers. This is in accordance with Montesquieu's theory. However, it is open to debate whether the judiciary is truly independent from the other organs of government.

10.8 Independence of the judiciary

Judges in the English system can be thought of as being independent in a number of ways.

10.8.1 Security of tenure

Superior judges

Superior judges have security of tenure in that they cannot be dismissed by the government. They can only be removed by the monarch following a petition presented to her by both Houses of Parliament. This gives superior judges protection from political whims and allows them to be independent in their judgments.

Inferior judges

Inferior judges do not have the same security of tenure of office as superior judges. The Lord Chancellor, with the consent of the Lord Chief Justice, has the power to dismiss inferior judges for incapacity or misbehaviour.

10.8.2 Immunity from suit

Judges are given immunity from prosecution for any acts they carry out in performance of their judicial function.

They also have immunity from being sued in a civil case for actions taken or decisions made in the course of their judicial duties. This was confirmed in *Sirros v Moore* (1975) and is a key factor in ensuring judicial independence in decision making.

> **Key case**
>
> ### *Sirros v Moore* (1975)
>
> In a case in the Crown Court, the judge wrongly ordered someone's detention. That person started a claim for false imprisonment against the judge.
>
> The Court of Appeal held that, although the detention had been unlawful, no action could be taken against the judge as he had acted in good faith, believing he had the power to imprison.

Judges also benefit from immunity from being sued for defamation for the things they say about parties or witnesses in the course of hearing cases. Immunity from suit allows a judge to perform his duties without fear of repercussions. It gives judges complete independence. A judge would only be liable if he was not acting in a judicial capacity or if he knew that he had no jurisdiction to do what he did.

10.8.3 Independence from the executive

Superior judges cannot be dismissed by the government and in this way they can truly be said to be independent of the government. They can make decisions which may displease the government without the threat of dismissal.

Judicial independence is now guaranteed under s 3 of the Constitutional Reform Act 2005. This states that the Lord Chancellor, other ministers in the government and anyone with responsibility for matters relating to the judiciary or the administration of justice must uphold the continued independence of the judiciary.

The section also specifically states that the Lord Chancellor and other ministers must not seek to influence particular judicial decisions.

The fact that judges are now recommended for appointment by the Judicial Appointments Commission also helps to keep judges independent from the executive.

A good example of this was seen in the Brexit case: *R (Miller) v Secretary of State for Exiting the European Union* (2016).

In 2016 following the referendum decision to leave the European Union, the government announced it would start the process for leaving. There was then a challenge as to whether the executive could do this without consulting Parliament.

The courts held that the government could not start the process for leaving without consulting Parliament. This decision was attacked by some people who felt that the judiciary should not interfere.

However, the Prime Minister, Theresa May, publically upheld the right of the judiciary to be independent.

10.8.4 Independence from the legislature

Judges generally are not involved in the law-making functions of Parliament. Full-time judges are not allowed to be members of the House of Commons, although the rule is not as strict for part-time judges so that Recorders and Assistant Recorders can be Members of Parliament. There used to be judges in the House of Lords when the Appellate Committee of the House of Lords was the final court of appeal. The main reason for the creation of the Supreme Court in 2009 was to separate the judiciary from the legislature. The Supreme Court has its own building and support staff.

10.8.5 Independence from the case

Judges must not try any case where they have any interest in the issue involved. The *Pinochet case* in 1998 reinforced this rule. In that case the House of Lords judges heard an appeal by Augusto Pinochet, the former head of the state of Chile. There was a claim to extradite him to Chile to face possible trial for crimes involving torture and deaths which had occurred there while he was head of state.

Amnesty International, the human rights movement, had been granted leave to participate in the case. After the House of Lords ruled that Pinochet could be extradited, it was discovered that one of the judges, Lord Hoffmann, was an unpaid director of Amnesty International Charitable Trust. Pinochet's lawyers asked for the decision to be set aside and to have the case reheard by a completely independent panel of judges.

Way in which independence is protected	Facts	Comment
Security of tenure	Superior judges can only be removed by the monarch following a petition presented to her by both Houses of Parliament Inferior judges can be removed by the Lord Chancellor and Lord Chief Justice for misbehaviour or incapacity	Allows judges to make decisions against the government without fear of being dismissed
Immunity from suit	Cannot be sued for decisions they make in cases, even if they make a mistake *Sirros v Moore* (1975)	Allows a judge to perform his duties without fear of repercussions
Independence from the executive	Judicial independence is guaranteed under s 3 of the Constitutional Reform Act 2005	The Lord Chancellor and other ministers must not seek to influence particular judicial decisions
Independence from case	Must not try any case where they have any interest in the issue involved *Pinochet case* (1998)	Judges must be completely impartial when making decisions

Figure 10.4 Judicial independence

The Law Lords decided that their original decision could not be allowed to stand. Judges had to be seen to be completely unbiased. The fact that Lord Hoffmann was connected with Amnesty meant that he might be considered not to be completely impartial. The case was retried with a new panel of judges.

10.8.6 Evaluating judicial independence

An independent judiciary is seen as important in protecting the liberty of the individual from abuse of power by the executive. If the government could make judges decide the way the government wanted this could lead to opponents of the government being imprisoned without reasonable cause. An independent judiciary is vital in a democracy.

In 2016 following the referendum in which the people voted to leave the European Union, the government announced that in 2017 it would start the process for leaving. There was then a challenge as to whether the executive could do this without consulting Parliament.

This challenge was first heard in the courts and the High Court held that the government could not start the process for leaving without consulting Parliament. This decision was attacked by some people who felt that the judiciary should not interfere. However, the Prime Minister, Theresa May, publicly upheld the right of the judiciary to be independent.

It is also important that the government cannot force a judge to resign if that judge makes a decision with which the government of the day disagrees. In judicial review cases, judges often have to decide if an act or decision by a government department is reasonable. It is important that the judges can carry out this function without fear of repercussions.

It is important that judges should be impartial in their decisions. It is vital that each judge is able to decide cases solely on the evidence presented in court by the parties and in accordance with the law.

Judges must be free to exercise their judicial powers without interference from litigants, the state, the media or powerful individuals or entities, such as large companies.

Judicial independence is important whether the judge is dealing with a civil or a criminal case. Individuals involved in any kind of case before the courts need to be sure that the judge dealing with their case cannot be influenced by an outside party or by the judge's own personal interests.

Advantages of judicial independence

Because judges are independent, decisions are made only on the basis of the facts of the case and law. This ensures fairness in all cases and is an important advantage of judicial independence.

Another important advantage is that the judiciary is able to protect citizens against unlawful acts of government. There can be an impartial judicial review of acts or decisions by the government.

Also the public have confidence in our judicial system. They know that their cases will be decided fairly and in accordance with the law.

Summary 🖉

- There are different types of judge in each level of the courts.
- Judges are selected by the Judicial Appointments Commission and recommendation made to the Lord Chancellor.
- The role of judges varies according to the court they are sitting in:
  - appellate courts – judges hear appeals – these can involve points of law and decisions may create precedents
  - civil courts at first instance – judge decides facts, law and awards appropriate remedy
  - criminal courts
  - Crown Court: judge decides law, jury decides verdict, judge passes sentence
  - Magistrates' Court: judge decides law, verdict and passes sentence.
- Judges normally retire at 70.
- Removal of judges
  - Superior judges can be only be removed by the monarch following a petition from both Houses of Parliament.
  - Inferior judges can be removed by the Lord Chancellor with the consent of the Lord Chief Justice.
- The doctrine of the separation of powers states that the three functions of the state, legislative, executive and judiciary must be kept separate.
- For the independence of the judiciary it is important that judges:
  - have security of tenure
  - are immune from suit
  - are independent from the executive
  - are impartial in all cases.
- Judicial independence is needed to protect the liberty of the individual and for judges to be able to act without pressure and without fear of repercussions.
- The advantages of judicial independence are:
  - ensures fairness in all cases
  - protects citizens against unlawful acts of government
  - public confidence.

Chapter 11

Access to justice

After reading this chapter you should be able to:
- Understand government funding available in civil and criminal cases
- Understand private funding, conditional fees and other advice agencies
- Evaluate access to justice.

11.1 Access to justice

When faced with a legal problem, most people need expert help from a lawyer. Often the need is only for advice, but some people may need help in starting court proceedings and/or presenting their case in court. For the ordinary person seeking legal assistance, there are three main difficulties:

1 Lack of knowledge – many people do not know where their nearest solicitor is located or, if they do know this, they do not know which solicitor specialises in the law involved in their particular case.

2 Fear of dealing with lawyers – people feel intimidated when dealing with lawyers.

3 Cost – solicitors charge from about £150 an hour for routine advice from a small local firm, to over £600 an hour for work done by a top city firm of solicitors in a specialist field.

Where a person cannot get the help he needs, he is being denied access to justice. Access to justice involves both an open system of justice and also being able to fund the costs of a case.

Various schemes have aimed at making the law more accessible to everyone. One of the earliest was the Citizens Advice Bureaux which started in 1938 and now operates in most towns (see section 11.7.1 for more information).

However, the problem of cost still remains a major hurdle. The cost of civil cases in the High Court may run into hundreds of thousands or even millions of pounds. Even in the cheaper County Court, the cost will possibly be more than the amount of money recovered in damages. There is the additional risk in all civil cases that the loser has to pay the winner's costs.

In criminal cases, a person's liberty may be at risk and it is essential that he should be able to defend himself properly.

11.1.1 Government schemes

The government has run schemes to help those in lower income brackets with the funding of cases. The first scheme for civil cases was started in 1949 and altered many times over the years. The first full scheme for criminal cases was started in 1964 and again altered many times over the years.

In 2000, the Legal Services Commission was set up by the government to run legal aid for both civil and criminal cases. However, in March 2010, the House of Commons Committee of Public Accounts criticised the Legal Services Commission for its financial management.

In 2012, the government decided to abolish the Legal Services Commission and bring legal aid under the control of the Ministry of Justice. This was done by passing the Legal Aid, Sentencing and Punishment of Offenders (LASPO) Act 2012 which set up the Legal Aid Agency.

Under this Act there are various services available. The main services are:
- Legal Help under which advice can be given
- Legal Representation which gives full legal services for the whole case.

There are also services aimed at specific types of case, for example Family Mediation, which allows both advice and representation in mediation proceedings and Legal Representation in immigration cases.

11.2 Government-funded advice

When someone has a legal problem it is important that he should be able to get help and advice about it. The government-funded Legal Aid Agency provides various advice schemes for both civil and criminal cases.

11.2.1 Help lines

Civil Legal Advice (CLA) is a government-funded scheme for providing advice in civil cases. It is possible to get telephone help from CLA for problems such as:
- debt, if your home is at risk
- housing, e.g. if you are homeless or at risk of being evicted
- domestic abuse
- family issues, e.g. family mediation or if your child is being taken into care
- special education needs
- discrimination.

In the 12 months from July 2015 to June 2016, nearly 160,000 people rang the CLA telephone service.

11.2.2 Help in civil cases

The Legal Aid Agency has contracts with law firms and not-for-profit organisations such as some Citizens Advice offices. Under these contracts they can give free advice to people on lower incomes. However, the income limits are very low. No one who is above the limits can use any of these services.

11.2.3 Advice in criminal cases

Anyone held as a suspect at a police station has the right to free legal advice. There is a duty solicitor scheme available 24 hours a day. This is a government-funded service. In 2016 advice was given to over 650,000 suspects at police stations. The advice may be by telephone or face to face. There is no means test for this service.

11.3 Government funding in civil cases

The funding for legal aid comes from the government's budget. This means that a set amount is made available each year. Also the amount set has to be considered against all the other claims on the budget, such as hospitals, health care and education. As a result, the government cannot afford to make legal aid available to everyone.

11.3.1 Criteria for civil legal aid services

LASPO 2012 gave the Lord Chancellor the power to set criteria for making civil legal aid services available. It also sets out the factors the Lord Chancellor must consider when setting the criteria. These factors are set out in s 10(3) of the Act. They include:
- the likely cost of providing the services and the benefit which may be obtained by them
- the availability of resources to provide the services
- the importance for the individual of the matters in relation to which the services would be provided
- the availability of other services, such as mediation
- where the services are sought by an individual in relation to a dispute, the individual's prospect of success in the dispute
- the public interest.

In order to qualify, there is also a strict means test; see section 11.4.2 below.

11.3.2 Availability of legal aid

Under previous legal aid systems, aid was available for all cases except those specifically excluded. There always were certain types of case excluded, for example small claims.

Under LASPO 2012, the starting point is that legal aid is not available for civil cases unless it is in a category specifically mentioned in the Act or other regulations.

The types of cases for which legal aid is allowed include those involving children's rights and those involving liberty of the individual. This includes cases being heard at Mental Health Tribunals as these are about whether a person should continue to be detained in a mental hospital and cases involving claims for asylum.

Public funding is not available for breach of contract cases; nor is it available for claims in tort, such as claims for personal injury, trespass to the person, to land or to property. These contract and tort cases used to be government-funded prior to the 2012 Act.

11.3.3 Means testing

A person applying for government-funded advice or representation must show that he does not have enough money to pay for his own lawyer. In order to decide if the applicant is poor enough to qualify for government-funded help, his income and capital are considered.

People receiving Income Support or Income-based Job Seekers' Allowance automatically qualify, assuming their disposable capital is below the set level. For all other applicants, their gross income is considered first. If a person's gross income is above a set amount per month, then he does not qualify.

Disposable income

If the person's gross income is below the set amount per month, then his disposable income has to be calculated by starting with his gross income and taking away:

- tax and National Insurance
- housing costs
- childcare costs or maintenance paid for children
- an allowance for himself and for each dependant.

If the amount left after making all deductions is below a minimum level, the applicant does not have to pay any contribution towards his funding. If the amount left is above a maximum level, the person will not qualify for any of the schemes provided by the Legal Aid Agency.

Where the disposable income is between the minimum level and the maximum level, the person applying for legal help has to pay a monthly contribution. The more in excess of the minimum, the greater the amount of the contribution. This idea of minimum and maximum levels is shown in Figure 11.1.

Look online

The figures for the limits on income are increased slightly each year. Find the current figures on the Ministry of Justice's website: **www.justice.gov.uk**.

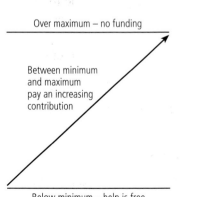

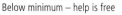

Figure 11.1 Increasing contributions for legal aid

Disposable capital

Disposable capital is the assets of the person, such as money in a bank or savings account, stocks and shares or expensive jewellery. In order to qualify for funding to take a court case, there is a maximum limit for disposable capital of £8,000.

If the assets are over £8,000, he must use his own money to fund any legal case, although once he has spent the money in excess of £8,000 he can become eligible for funding. Even where the disposable capital is below £8,000, he can be asked to pay a contribution towards his case.

Where a person owns a home, the value of that home is taken into account in deciding the disposable capital. This is so even though the person may have a large mortgage. Only the first £100,000 of any mortgage is deducted from the value of the home. This rule means that any person can be regarded as having too much disposable capital because of the value of his house, although in reality he might have no spare money.

11.4 Public funding in criminal cases

Since 2013, criminal legal aid services have been under the Legal Aid Agency in the Ministry of Justice. The agency makes contracts with law firms to provide legal services to people charged with criminal offences. Most service providers are solicitors.

In order to get representation at court for a criminal case, the defendant has to qualify under the 'interests of justice' test. There is also a means test.

11.4.1 Interests of justice

A defendant will only get help with legal funding for representation in court if he can show that he comes within at least one of the five 'interests of justice' factors. These factors are:

1 Whether, if any matter arising in the proceedings is decided against him, the individual would be likely to lose his liberty or livelihood or suffer serious damage to his reputation.
2 The case will involve consideration of a point of law.
3 The individual is unable to understand the proceedings in court or to state his own case.
4 The case may involve the tracing, interviewing or expert cross-examination of witnesses.

5 It is in the interests of another person that the individual be represented (such as in a rape case).

11.4.2 Magistrates' Court means testing

As well as having to qualify under the 'interests of justice' test, there is a strict means test in the Magistrates' Court. It is often described as the 'in or out' scheme, where applicants are either:

- eligible for legal aid (because they pass the initial or full means test) or
- ineligible (because they fail the initial or full means test) and are therefore expected to pay for legal representation privately.

Those who are on income support, defendants under the age of 16 and those under 18 in full-time education automatically pass the means test. For everyone else, the test starts with a first-stage simple means test which is calculated on gross annual income. If their income is too high on this test then the defendant does not qualify for legal aid. If a defendant's income is below a certain level, he qualifies. For those in the middle bracket, they are further means tested to calculate their disposable income and if they are above the set limit, they will not get legal aid.

The levels allowed are very low. This means that about three-quarters of adults do not qualify for legal aid in criminal cases in the Magistrates' Courts.

11.4.3 Crown Court means testing

The main difference from the Magistrates' Courts is that there is no upper limit on disposable income. Most defendants can receive legal aid. It is free for those on low incomes. Those on higher incomes (but below £37,500 disposable income) have to pay towards their legal aid. Those whose disposable income is above £37,500 (figure in 2016) are ineligible for legal aid and will have to pay privately for representation in court.

Where a defendant has to pay, then the higher his income, the higher the contribution he will have to pay towards the case. The maximum amount he has to pay through contributions from his income is set by the type of case. If a defendant is found guilty, he may also have to pay extra from his capital.

If a defendant is found not guilty, any contributions paid will normally be refunded.

11.5 Problems with government funding of cases

11.5.1 'Advice deserts'

There is evidence that not enough legal service providers have contracts. This is partly due to the smaller numbers of contracts made with providers by the Legal Services Commission (and now by the Legal Aid Agency) and also to the fact that many solicitors are finding that the rates of pay are so low, it is not economically viable for them to continue in the scheme. This has created what have been called 'advice deserts'.

The problem of advice deserts was considered by the Constitutional Affairs Select Committee as long ago as 2004. In the evidence to the Committee, even the Legal Services Commission acknowledged that 'It is clear that there are parts of England and Wales in which the need for publicly funded legal services is not currently being met'.

Since 2004, the position has been getting worse as more solicitors have stopped doing government-funded legal work. With so few legal service providers in certain areas, people who want help may have to travel long distances to find it.

The continuing lack of lawyers to undertake certain types of case has been confirmed by a survey carried out in 2008–09 by the Legal Action Group. For example, it quotes one person from South Wales as saying she had 'contacted dozens of solicitors in the last month, but no help was forthcoming as none specialised in welfare benefits'.

The availability of legal aid for housing cases has fallen dramatically. LASPO 2012 alters the criteria for which cases would be funded and this caused the number of cases in which legal aid was granted to fall by half. The number has continued to decline and dropped by another 18 per cent between 2015 and 2016, and as an example, in Suffolk and Shropshire there are currently no solicitors' firms doing government-funded housing work.

The numbers of law firms doing legal aid work has decreased dramatically this century. When the Legal Services Commission started in 2000, there were about 5,000 law firms doing civil legal aid work. By 2016, there were only 1,500 firms.

11.5.2 Non-availability

As set out in section 11.3.2, funding is not available for many civil claims. Claims for damages for personal injury are excluded from the scheme. Any such case has to be paid for privately or through a conditional fee agreement (see section 11.6.3). This works well where people have suffered minor injuries, but it can be argued that it creates difficulties for people who have been left with serious disabilities. They need all the help they can get to make sure they receive adequate compensation.

It can also be argued that people bringing employment claims against large companies are disadvantaged by being unable to receive public funding to bring their case. The company will be able to afford a lawyer and will be at an advantage in the case.

11.5.3 Eligibility levels

Even where there are enough legal services providers in an area, only people with very low levels of income and capital can qualify for help.

In March 2016, over 20 senior lawyers and directors of legal aid charities wrote a letter to the *Guardian* newspaper. In this letter they stated that:

> Every day, our members and the people we support see the impact of the measures implemented in the Legal Aid, Sentencing and Punishment of Offenders Act. We believe the legal aid reforms have had a severe impact on the ability of vulnerable people to access justice since they came into effect on 1 April 2013 ... the cuts have limited access to justice for some of those who need legal aid the most. Too much effort has focused on the point of crisis rather than prevention, and the number of people who have no choice but to represent themselves in court has risen sharply.

11.5.4 Criteria set by the Lord Chancellor

In 2013 the Lord Chancellor set criteria for making legal aid services available to individuals. These criteria aimed to restrict the circumstances in which legal aid was to be granted and have proved very controversial. In particular the Guidance for Exceptional Case Funding stated:

> The overarching question to consider is whether the withholding of legal aid would make the assertion of the claim practically impossible or lead to an obvious unfairness in proceedings. This is a very high threshold.

The legality of this guidance was challenged in the courts in the case of *R (Gudanavicene and others) v The Director of Legal Aid Casework; The Lord Chancellor* (2014). The Court of Appeal ruled that the Exceptional Case Funding Guidelines were unlawful as they set the bar for the provision for legal aid too high. The Court of Appeal held that s 10(3) of LASPO 2012 required legal aid to be granted where failure to provide such legal aid would constitute a breach of European Union law or the European Convention on Human Rights.

As a result of this judgment, the guidance was revised.

11.5.5 Lack of funds

Each year the government sets a budget for all its departments. Clearly services such as health and education have to have large amounts of money. This means that government money for legal cases is limited.

Levels of help and representation available	• Advice only • Legal representation – covers all aspects of a case
Means test	Generally strict means test on gross income, disposable income and capital Only scheme that is not means tested is advice for those being held as a suspect at a police station
Merits test for representation	**Civil cases** Whether the case has a reasonable chance of success and that the damages will be worth more than the costs Other criteria include: • Can the matter be funded in another way? • Are there funds available? **Criminal cases** Interests of justice test
Problems	• Number of solicitors is decreasing • In civil cases only available for specified types of cases • Means tests very strict so only those with very low levels of income and capital qualify • Criteria set by Lord Chancellor too strict • Lack of government funds – in particular civil cases may be refused because the money has run out

Figure 11.2 Public funding in civil and criminal cases

In addition, the fact that criminal cases take priority on funding means there may not be enough left for civil cases. This can lead to civil cases which have merit being refused funding just because the money has run out.

11.6 Private funding of cases

11.6.1 Own resources

Anyone who can afford it can pay for a solicitor and/or a barrister to deal with a legal matter.

There are firms of solicitors in most towns. However, some solicitors specialise in certain types of work. If your legal problem is in an unusual area of law, then it may be necessary to travel to another town to find a solicitor who can deal with it.

The bigger firms of solicitors work in the major cities, in particular London. They often specialise in commercial law and the majority of their clients are businesses.

Consulting a solicitor can be expensive. The average cost of a solicitor outside London is about £150 an hour. For a big London firm of solicitors, the charges are usually at least £600 an hour and can be as much as £1,000 an hour.

On issues of civil law, it is also possible to consult a barrister directly, without going to a solicitor first. This can be cheaper than using a solicitor because barristers do not have such high business expenses as solicitors.

11.6.2 Insurance

Another way of funding a court case is by legal insurance. Most motor insurance policies offer cover (for an additional small amount) for help with legal fees in cases arising from road accidents. Policies for home insurance will offer cover for any legal claims arising such as a visitor being injured on the premises.

There are also policies purely for insurance against legal costs. These can be 'before the event', that is when there is no known legal claim. More common is 'after the event' insurance where someone who is taking a case to court insures against losing the case and having to pay the other side's costs. After the event insurance is often used alongside a conditional fee agreement.

11.6.3 Conditional fee agreements

One of the main problems of taking a case to court is that it is difficult to estimate how long it will last or

how much it will cost. If a person is funding his own case, this is a major problem for him. Also, if he loses the case, he may have to pay the costs of the other party. The combined costs of the case can be many thousands of pounds. In order to overcome these problems, a conditional fee agreement (CFA) can be used in all civil cases except family cases.

CFAs cannot be used in criminal cases.

How conditional fees work

The solicitor and client agree on the fee that would normally be charged for such a case. The agreement will also set out what the solicitor's success fee will be if he wins the case.

Many conditional fee agreements will be made on the basis that if the case is lost, the client pays nothing. Because of this sort of agreement, the scheme is often referred to as 'no win, no fee'. However, some solicitors may prefer to charge a lower level fee, for example half the normal fee, even if the case is lost.

If the case is won, the client has to pay the normal fee plus the success fee.

Success fee

The success fee could be up to 100 per cent of the normal fee. However, most agreements will include a 'cap' on the success fee, which prevents it from being more than 25 per cent of the damages (amount of money) that the client wins as compensation. This protects the client from having to pay more than he won as compensation. Even so, it can mean that the client is left with very little of his damages. This is easier to understand by looking at the examples given in Figure 11.3.

A winning claimant cannot claim the success fee back from the losing defendant.

Agreement	
Normal fee	£4,000
Fee if case is lost	NIL
Success fee	£2,000
Cap on success fee	25% of damages
Possible results of case	**Client pays**
Case is lost	Nothing
Case is won: client gets £50,000 damages	£6,000 (£4,000 + £2,000)
Case is won: client gets £6,000 damages	£5,500 (£4,000 + £1,500*)
*This £1,500 is because the success fee cannot be more than 25% of the damages	

Figure 11.3 Illustration of conditional fees

Insurance premiums

Although the client will often not have to pay anything to his own lawyer if the case is lost, he will usually have to pay the costs of the other side. This can leave the client with a very large bill to pay. To help protect against this, it is possible to insure against the risk. This type of insurance is known as 'after the event' insurance. So, if the case is lost, your insurers will pay the other side's costs.

11.6.4 Are conditional fees working?

Conditional fee agreements have helped thousands of people to bring cases to court and obtain justice. One area in which they have been particularly useful for claimants has been in defamation cases. Legal aid has never been available for such cases and only the rich could risk pursuing defamation claims. CFAs have enabled ordinary people to take such cases.

However, there are problems with CFAs. Low value cases are not attractive to lawyers who need to be able to make a profit for their legal business to survive. Lawyers are also more likely to take on cases where there is a very high chance of success.

LASPO 2012 has made CFAs less attractive for two reasons:

1 The cost of after the event insurance can no longer be claimed back from the defendant by a claimant who wins the case.
2 Success fees can no longer be claimable from the defendant by a claimant who wins the case.

These two points mean that a winning claimant will have to bear more of the cost of taking a case. As a result, a large proportion of the amount of damages he receives may well be used up by his costs.

11.7 Other advice agencies

As well as the government-funded advice services set out in section 11.2, there are a number of other advice schemes. These only usually deal with civil matters. Some of them are by telephone or on a website. Others also provide face-to-face advice. Important sources of advice include Citizens Advice Bureaux and law centres.

In addition, there are other agencies which offer specialist advice on certain topics; for example trade unions will help members with legal problems, particularly in work-related matters. There are also charities, such as Shelter which offers advice to people with housing problems.

11.7.1 Citizens Advice Bureaux

These were first set up in 1939 and today they give advice in over 2,500 locations throughout the country, with a bureau existing in most towns. They give general advice free to anyone on a variety of issues mostly connected to social welfare problems and debt, but they also advise on some legal matters. They can provide information on which local solicitors do legal aid work or give cheap or free initial interviews. Many have arrangements under which solicitors may attend at the bureau once a week or fortnight to give more qualified advice on legal matters.

The Citizens Advice Bureaux (CABx) is very important in providing legal advice. In 2014–15 they provided advice to 2.5 million people. Forty-eight per cent of these were by face-to-face contact, 45 per cent on the telephone and 7 per cent by email or webchat.

The main areas that CABx help with are:
- entitlement to benefits
- debt problems
- consumer issues
- housing issues
- employment issues.

11.7.2 Law centres

These offer a free, non-means-tested legal service to people in their area. The first law centre opened in North Kensington in 1970. This stated its aims as providing:

> a first class solicitor's service to the people … a service which is easily accessible, not intimidating, to which they can turn for guidance as they would to their family doctor, or as someone who can afford it would turn to his family solicitor.

Their aim is to provide free legal advice (and sometimes representation) in areas where there are few solicitors. Many of their clients are disadvantaged. In 2016 there were 44 law centres in operation.

Funding

Law centres have always struggled to secure enough funding. Cuts by local authorities in their budgets have meant the withdrawal or reduction of funding from this source. As a result, some law centres have had to close. They also receive some funding from central government, but cuts have also been made to this funding. Some centres have received funds from the

National Lottery fund where the law centre is part of a community project.

Look online

Look at the website of the Law Centres Federation at www.lawcentres.org.uk. Find out the present number of law centres and see if there is one near you, and collect more information about the work they do.

11.7.3 Trade unions

Trade unions usually offer their members free legal advice for all work-related problems. Many trade unions also offer free legal advice for other legal problems such as personal injury cases. This help may be available even where the injury was not connected to work. Unite, the biggest trade union in the country, gives its members free legal advice and also free legal representation for any personal injury case.

11.7.4 Schemes run by lawyers

Some solicitors offer a free half-hour first interview. Local CABx will have a list of solicitors who offer the service.

Bar Pro Bono Unit

Since 1996, volunteer barristers have staffed the Bar Pro Bono Unit. This unit, situated in London, gives free advice to those who cannot afford to pay and who cannot get legal aid. They will give advice on any area of law and will also, where necessary, represent the client in court proceedings.

11.8 Evaluation of advice agencies

The most useful agency is CABx. It has offices in most towns and deals with a large number of cases.

It generally only deals with limited areas of law, but those areas are ones which affect the most vulnerable people. CABx can refer people to solicitors but this will only be for advice. If the matter needs to go to court the person will have to find a way of funding the case.

Law centres also give advice on issues that affect the most vulnerable people in society. They also sometimes provide representation. The main problem is the lack of funding and the limited number of law centres operating. Many areas have no law centre.

Trade unions provide advice and representation. But this service is limited to their own members.

Solicitors' schemes are only for a short session of free advice. If government funding is available for the issue, the solicitor will help with an application for legal help and representation. But with the reduction of legal aid availability, only a few cases will come into this category. For other cases, the half-hour free advice is not particularly helpful if the matter is complicated or it needs to go to court.

The Bar Pro Bono Unit offers advice and representation on any area of law, but the scheme is a small one and only available in London.

Activity ❓

Advise where it might be possible for each of the following people to get legal advice:
1 Aylmer has been arrested and taken to a police station to be questioned about a robbery the police suspect him of being involved in.
2 Benjamin has a dispute with his employers regarding his employment contract.
3 Charity has been injured when a car in which she was a passenger overturned because the driver was driving too fast.
4 Denzil has a dispute with his landlord. Denzil is unemployed.

Source	Fact	Comment
Help line	Civil Legal Advice – government run	Nearly 160,000 calls in year
Citizens Advice Bureaux	Operates in about 2,500 locations throughout the country	Provide advice to about 2.5 million people a year
Law centres	Funding cuts have reduced numbers	Operate in disadvantaged areas
Trade unions	Offer members free legal advice	Usually only for work-related issues, but may also include personal injury cases
Schemes run by lawyers	Solicitors may offer a free half-hour interview Bar Pro Bono Unit	London based but will advise on any area of law

Figure 11.4 Where to get advice in civil cases

Summary

- Government-funded schemes are available for advice in civil issues but only for those with very low incomes and low capital.
- Free advice in criminal cases is available under the government scheme for those being questioned at a police station.
- Government-funded representation in civil cases is limited:
  - there are strict criteria as to when it will be given
  - it is only available for a few categories of case
  - it is means tested.
- Government funding for representation in criminal cases is also limited:
  - it must be in the interest of justice
  - it is means tested.
- There are also problems in that:
  - fewer solicitors do government-funded work
  - the means tests only allow the very poorest access to justice
  - the legal budget set by the government is limited.
- Legal advice and representation can be paid for privately through the person's own resources.
- Insurance can help pay for the costs of a case, especially in cases arising from road accidents.
- Conditional fee agreements can be used to fund a case – these often operate on a 'no win, no fee' basis.
- Legal advice is also available from:
  - Citizens Advice Bureaux
  - law centres
  - trade unions
  - schemes run by lawyers, especially free half-hour offered by solicitors and Bar Pro Bono Unit.

Component 1

SECTION B

Chapter 12

Rules of criminal law

> After reading this chapter you should be able to:
> - Understand the definition of a crime
> - Have an outline understanding of the theory and rules of criminal law including:
>   - the theory of criminal law
>   - the concept of the elements of *actus reus* and *mens rea* in crimes
>   - the standard of proof in criminal cases
>   - the burden of proof in criminal cases

12.1 Defining a crime

Virtually everyone can identify these as criminal offences. But how many others can you name? There are thousands of different offences. They vary from the most serious, such as murder and manslaughter, to minor breaches of regulations, such as selling a lottery ticket to someone who is under the age of 16.

With such a wide range, it is difficult to have a general definition covering all offences. The only way in which it is possible to define a crime is to say that it is conduct which is:
- forbidden by the state and
- for which there is a punishment.

Lord Atkin supported this definition when, in the case of *Proprietary Articles Trade Association v Attorney-General for Canada* (1931), he said:

> " The criminal quality of an act cannot be discerned by intuition (made out by 'gut feeling'); nor can it be discovered by reference to any standard but one: is the act prohibited with penal consequences? "

This is the only definition which covers all crimes. However, there have been other definitions. An American legal writer, Herbert Packer, thought that, to be a crime:
- the conduct must be wrongful and
- it must be necessary to condemn or prevent such conduct.

However, what is considered criminal will change over time. This can be caused, for example, by changing views in society, or changes in technology which lead to the need for new offences to cover new situations.

Changing views on what is criminal can be demonstrated by the changes in the law on consenting homosexual acts. In 1885 the Criminal Law Amendment Act made consenting homosexual acts criminal even if they were in private. This remained as the law until 1967 when the Sexual Offences Act 1967 decriminalised such behaviour between those aged 21 and over. The age was reduced to 18 in 1994 and finally, in 2000, it was further reduced to 16. This age brings the law into line with consenting sexual acts between heterosexuals.

New technology can lead to new areas of criminal law. For example, the invention of the motor car over a hundred years ago led to new road traffic laws. These have been added to over the years so that we now have such offences as driving without a licence, driving while over the legal limit of alcohol, having tyres which do not have the right level of tread, and causing death by dangerous driving.

Computers and the internet have led to new offences being created, to protect people from internet fraud and to prevent pornographic material from being viewed or downloaded.

12.1.1 Brief overview of the theory of criminal law

The question of why an act is considered a criminal act or why it is not a criminal act is a matter for moral philosophy. The relationship between law and morality is examined in greater depth in Book 2, but examples are given below where Parliament enacts that something is a crime or changes the law to make something no longer a crime. Similarly there are examples given below where judges have established that some behaviour is or is not criminal. The jury system also reflects this when so called perverse verdicts are reached as in the case of Ponting (1985) where a civil servant was charged with breaching the Official Secrets Act for releasing privileged information about the sinking of the Argentinian warship General Belgrano. The judge told the jury that any public interest in the information did not provide a defence. However, the jury acquitted him.

The relationship of law and justice, is again explored in detail in Book 2. Suffice it to say that criminal law is often seen as **retributive justice**, a theory of justice that considers proportionate punishment a morally acceptable response to crime. This has been seen in the biblical view of an eye for an eye, but also with the idea of forgiveness. Most other religions have a view of a similar nature.

> **Key term**
>
> **Retributive justice** – a system of criminal justice based on the punishment of offenders rather than on rehabilitation.

Modern criminal law is no longer a purely retributive exercise – it is not just about punishment.

The idea of deterrence is much more to the fore as well as the idea of **corrective justice**.

> **Key term**
>
> **Corrective justice** – the idea that liability rectifies the injustice inflicted by one person on another. This is also a major part of the theory of the law of tort.

If a person is found guilty of a crime, then justice demands the offender is sentenced. The aims of sentencing are taken into account as well as aggravating and mitigating factors. There may be the purpose of punishment, deterrence to the offender or others, rehabilitation of the offender or even to ensure denunciation of the offender.

The criminal law also provides a form of social control over society. This may reflect the general morality of the time as well as the use of nudges to push society in a particular way. This can be seen in the changed attitude of the public to the offence of drink (or drug) driving and the changing view of society about the use of mobile phones while driving. Social control is also apparent in that alcohol is a legal substance but most other drugs are not and there is a balance between the possible harm to the individual and their desires and the need to raise revenue through taxation.

12.1.2 The role of the state

The criminal law is mainly set down by the state. This can be by passing an Act of Parliament such as the Theft Act 1968 or by the issuing of regulations.

A breach of criminal law can lead to a penalty, such as imprisonment or a fine, being imposed on the defendant in the name of the state. Therefore, bringing a prosecution for a criminal offence is usually seen as part of the role of the state. Indeed, the majority of criminal prosecutions are conducted by the Crown Prosecution Service (CPS) which is the state agency for criminal prosecutions.

However, it is also possible for a private organisation to start a prosecution. For example, the RSCPA regularly brings prosecutions against people for offences of cruelty towards or neglect of animals.

12.1.3 Conduct criminalised by the judges

Although, in the vast majority of offences, the state decides what conduct is considered to be criminal, some conduct is criminalised by judges rather than the state. This occurs where judges create new criminal offences through case law. In modern times this only happens on rare occasions because nearly all law is made by Parliament. An example of conduct criminalised by judges is the offence of conspiracy to corrupt public morals. This offence has never been enacted by Parliament. However, the judges recognised that it existed in *Shaw v DPP* (1962).

> ### Key case
>
> #### *Shaw v DPP* (1962)
>
> The defendant published a Ladies Directory which advertised the names and addresses of prostitutes, with their photographs and details of the 'services' they were prepared to offer. He was charged with conspiracy to corrupt public morals. The House of Lords accepted that there was an offence of conspiracy to corrupt public morals, as there did not appear to be an offence which covered the situation.

Another offence which has been created by the judges in modern times is marital rape. This was declared a crime in *R v R* (1991). Before that case, the law held that a husband could not be guilty of raping his wife, as she was assumed, by the fact of marriage, to consent to sexual intercourse with him. When the House of Lords decided the case of *R v R* they pointed out that society's views on the position of women had changed. The House of Lords said:

> 66 The status of women and the status of married women in our law have changed quite dramatically. A husband and wife are now for all practical purposes equal partners in marriage. 99

The House of Lords ruled that if a wife did not consent to intercourse, then the husband could be guilty of raping her.

12.2 Elements of a crime

There are many offences aimed at different 'wrong' behaviour. For OCR AS you have to study non-fatal offences against the person. For A Level you will also have to study murder, manslaughter, theft, robbery and burglary. However, there are general principles which apply to all offences.

The most important principle is that for all crimes, except crimes of strict liability (see Chapter 14), there are two elements which must be proved by the prosecution. These are:

- *actus reus* and
- *mens rea*.

These terms come from a Latin maxim (*actus non facit reum nisi mens sit rea*) which means 'the act itself does not constitute guilt unless done with a guilty mind'. Both an act (or omission) and a guilty mind must be proved for most criminal offences.

12.2.1 *Actus reus*

'*Actus reus*' has a wider meaning than 'an act', as it can cover omissions or a state of affairs. The term '*actus reus*' has been criticised as misleading. Lord Diplock in *Miller* (1983) preferred the term 'prohibited conduct', while the Law Commission in the Draft Criminal Code (1989) used the term 'external element'.

We will look at the concept of *actus reus* in detail in Chapter 13.

> ### Key term
>
> *Actus reus* – this is an act, an omission or a state of affairs that is the prohibited conduct in an offence.

12.2.2 *Mens rea*

'*Mens rea*' translates as 'guilty mind' but this is also misleading. The Law Commission in the Draft Criminal Code (1989) used the term 'fault element'. The levels of 'guilty mind' required for different offences vary from the highest level, which is specific intention for some crimes, to much lower levels, such as negligence or knowledge of a certain fact, for less serious offences.

The levels of *mens rea* are explained in detail in Chapter 14.

> ### Key term
>
> *Mens rea* – this is the mental element (guilty mind) or the fault element in an offence.

Figure 12.1 The elements of an offence

Examples

The *actus reus* and *mens rea* will be different for different crimes. For example, in murder the *actus reus* is the killing of a human being, and the *mens rea* is causing the death 'with malice aforethought' which means that the killer must have intended to kill or to cause grievous bodily harm. For theft, the *actus reus* is the appropriation of property belonging to another, while the *mens rea* is doing this dishonestly and with the intention permanently to deprive the other of the property.

The *actus reus* and the *mens rea* must be present together, but if there is an ongoing act, then the existence of the necessary *mens rea* at any point during that act is sufficient.

This is explained fully in Chapter 14.

However, even where the *actus reus* and *mens rea* are present, the defendant may be not guilty if he has a defence (see section 12.3).

12.2.3 Strict liability offences

There are some crimes which are an exception to the general rule that there must be both *actus reus* and *mens rea*. These are crimes of strict liability, where the prosecution need prove only the *actus reus*; no mental element is needed for guilt.

12.3 Defences

Although the defendant may have done the required act, there are a number of defences that may be available which will lead to a 'not guilty' verdict. A defence is relevant to the issue as to whether a person is guilty of the offence, whereas mitigation is relevant to the question of punishment. There are general defences that apply to all offences and specific defences that apply only to specific offences.

For A Level, you have to study some defences but these are not required for AS. They are covered in Book 2.

12.4 The rules of the standard of proof

The prosecution has to prove the case against the defendant. There are rules on the level to which the case has to be proved. This is referred to as the 'standard of proof'. The standard of proof in criminal cases is 'beyond reasonable doubt'. This is usually explained by the judge telling the jury that it should only convict if it is satisfied on the evidence, so that it is sure of the defendant's guilt.

This is a higher standard than the one used in civil cases. Civil cases have to be proved only 'on the balance of probabilities'. The reason that criminal cases require a higher standard of proof is because the defendant is at risk of losing his liberty if he is found guilty.

12.5 The rules of the burden of proof

An accused person is presumed innocent until proven guilty. The burden of proof is on the prosecution. This means that the prosecution must prove both the required *actus reus* and the required *mens rea*. An important case on these principles is *Woolmington* (1935).

Key case

Woolmington v DPP (1935)

The defendant's (D's) wife had left him and gone to live with her mother. D went to the mother's house and shot his wife dead. He claimed that he had decided to ask his wife to come back to him and, if she refused, that he would commit suicide. For this reason he was carrying under his coat a loaded sawn-off shotgun. When his wife indicated that she would not return to him, he threatened to shoot himself and brought the gun out to show her he meant it. As he brought it out, it somehow went off, killing his wife. He claimed that this was a pure accident.

The judge at the trial told the jury that the prosecution had to prove beyond reasonable doubt that the defendant killed his wife. He then went on to tell them that, if the prosecution satisfied them of that, the defendant had to show that there were circumstances which made that killing pure accident. This put the burden of proof on the defendant to prove the defence. In the House of Lords it was held that this was not correct.

The decision in this case made several important points which the House of Lords regarded as fixed matters on English law. These were:

- the prosecution must prove the case
- this rule applies to all criminal cases
- the rule must be applied in any court where there is a criminal trial (currently the Magistrates' Court and the Crown Court)
- guilt must be proved beyond reasonable doubt and
- a reasonable doubt can be raised by evidence from either the prosecution or the defence.

12.5.1 Raising a defence

If the defendant raises a defence then it is for the prosecution to disprove that defence. In *Woolmington v DPP* (1935) the defendant stated that the gun had gone off accidentally, thus raising the defence of accident. The prosecution was obliged to disprove this if the defendant was to be found guilty.

For all common law defences, except insanity, there must be some evidence of the key points of the defence given at the trial. This can be from evidence given by the defence or by the prosecution. If evidence of a defence is given at the trial then, even where the defendant has not specifically raised the defence, the prosecution must disprove at least one element of that defence. The trial judge must direct the jury to acquit unless it is satisfied that the defence has been disproved by the prosecution.

Reverse burden

For certain defences, the burden of proof is on the defendant. For example, if the defendant claims that he was insane at the time of the crime, the burden of proving this is on him. This shifting of the burden of proof to the defendant is known as the 'reverse onus'. As well as applying to the common law defence of insanity, it also applies to some defences which have been created by statute. One of these is the defence of diminished responsibility in the Homicide Act 1957 where s 2(2) states:

> On a charge of murder, it shall be for the defence to prove that the person charged is, by virtue of this section, not liable to be convicted of murder.

Where a statute places the burden of proof on the defendant to prove a defence, the standard is the civil one of 'on the balance of probabilities'.

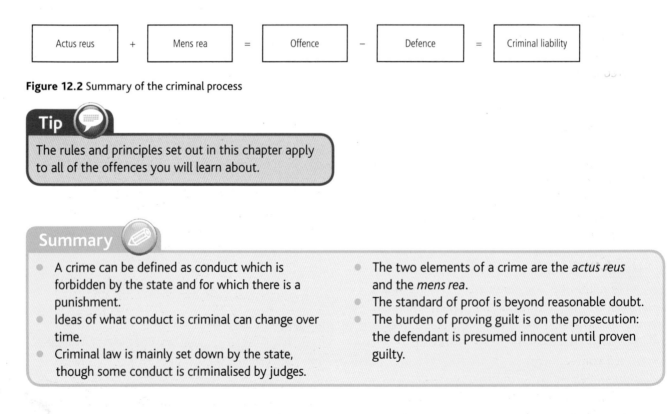

Figure 12.2 Summary of the criminal process

Tip

The rules and principles set out in this chapter apply to all of the offences you will learn about.

Summary

- A crime can be defined as conduct which is forbidden by the state and for which there is a punishment.
- Ideas of what conduct is criminal can change over time.
- Criminal law is mainly set down by the state, though some conduct is criminalised by judges.

- The two elements of a crime are the *actus reus* and the *mens rea*.
- The standard of proof is beyond reasonable doubt.
- The burden of proving guilt is on the prosecution: the defendant is presumed innocent until proven guilty.

Chapter 13

Actus reus

After reading this chapter you should be able to:
- Understand the concept of *actus reus*, and conduct and consequences crimes
- Understand voluntariness and involuntariness
- Understand when criminal liability can be imposed for a failure to act (omission)
- Understand the legal rules on causation
- Apply the law to factual situations

13.1 What is *actus reus*?

As already stated in Chapter 12, the *actus reus* is the physical element of a crime. It can be:
- an act or
- a failure to act (an omission) or
- a 'state of affairs'.

In most cases the *actus reus* will be something the defendant does, but there are situations in which a failure to act is sufficient for the *actus reus*. These are set out at section 13.2. 'State of affairs' cases are considered at section 13.1.3.

13.1.1 Conduct crimes

Conduct crimes are those where the *actus reus* is the prohibited conduct itself. For example, the *actus reus* of the offence of drink driving is a criminal offence under s 5(a) of the Road Traffic Act 1988. Merely driving with excess alcohol in your bloodstream is the offence. No consequence (such as causing an accident) is required.

13.1.2 Consequence crimes

For some crimes the *actus reus* must also result in a consequence. This means that the *actus reus* is only committed where, as well as the defendant doing (or failing to do) something, there is also a particular prohibited consequence.

This can be seen in the offence of assault occasioning actual bodily harm (s 47 of the Offences against the Person Act 1861). There must be an application or threat of unlawful force but there must also be a consequence of 'actual bodily harm', in other words some injury to the victim. This could be a bruise, a broken nose or broken arm. It could even be psychiatric injury. But without the consequence of 'actual bodily harm' there cannot be a s 47 offence. The *actus reus* for s 47 is not complete.

However, it is not enough that there is a consequence. There must also be an *actus reus* causing that consequence. This was shown by the case of *Marchant and Muntz* (2003).

Key case

Marchant and Muntz (2003)

A farmer, defendant 1 (D1), owned an agricultural vehicle with a grab with one-metre long spikes attached at the front for lifting and moving large round hay bales. The vehicle was authorised for use on public roads and the farmer gave instructions to an employee, defendant 2 (D2), to take the vehicle onto a public road to deliver some hay bales. D2 was stopped waiting to make a turn onto a farm track when the victim (V), a motorcyclist, approached at high speed (estimated at 80 mph) from the opposite direction, collided with the vehicle and was impaled on one of the spikes. He suffered injuries described as 'catastrophic' and died. D1 and D2 were convicted, respectively, of causing death by dangerous driving and procuring the offence. There was no suggestion that D2's driving was dangerous. The Court of Appeal quashed the convictions.

So, in this case, although a death had happened, there was no act of dangerous driving, so there was no offence.

13.1.3 'State of affairs' crimes

In other crimes the *actus reus* can be a state of affairs for which the defendant is responsible. An example is having an offensive weapon in a public place (s 1 of the Prevention of Crime Act 1953). The defendant does not have to do anything with the weapon, nor does it have to be visible. It is enough that he has it with him in a public place.

Another example is being in possession of a controlled drug (s 5 of the Misuse of Drugs Act 1971). It does not matter whether the defendant is going to use the drug himself or is going to hand it over to someone else. The fact that he is in possession of it is sufficient for the *actus reus* of the offence.

There are some rare instances in which the defendant has been convicted even though he did not act voluntarily. These situations involve a 'state of affairs', but not one that the defendant entered into voluntarily. They are sometimes considered offences for which there is absolute liability. An example of this is the case of *R v Larsonneur* (1933).

Key case

R v Larsonneur (1933)

The defendant, a Frenchwoman, was ordered to leave the UK. She decided to go by boat to the Irish Republic. On landing, she was immediately deported and sent back to the UK. She was not acting voluntarily. When she landed in the UK she was immediately arrested and charged with being 'an alien to whom leave to land in the UK had been refused was found in the UK'. She was convicted because (1) she was an alien who had been refused leave to land and (2) she was 'found in the UK'. It did not matter that she had been sent back against her will.

13.1.4 Voluntary nature of *actus reus*

The act or omission must be voluntary on the part of the defendant. If the defendant has no control over his actions then he has not committed the *actus reus*. In *Hill v Baxter* (1958) the court gave examples of where a driver of a vehicle could not to be said be doing the act of driving voluntarily. These included where a driver lost control of his vehicle because he was stung by a swarm of bees, or if he was struck on the head by a stone or had a heart attack while driving.

Other examples of an involuntary act include where the defendant hits another person because of a reflex action or a muscle spasm. Yet another is where one person pushes a second person, causing them to bump into a third person. In this situation the act of the second person who has been pushed is involuntary. Even though he has hit the third person, he has not committed the *actus reus* for any assault offence. Of course, the original 'pusher' can be liable. This was shown in the case of *R v Mitchell* (1983).

Key case

R v Mitchell (1983)

D tried to push his way into a queue at the post office. A 72-year-old man told him off for this. D punched this man, causing him to stagger backwards into an 89-year-old woman. The woman was knocked over and injured, and a few days later died of her injuries. D was convicted of unlawful act manslaughter. The man who had been punched and fallen against the woman was not liable for any criminal act.

This also illustrates that the criminal law is concerned with fault on the part of the defendant. Where there is an absence of fault, then the defendant is usually not liable.

13.1.5 'Involuntariness'

We have seen that an act needs to be voluntary if there is to be liability in criminal law, with the exception of state of affairs crimes and the unusual case of *R v Larsonneur* (1933). This idea is also present when considering the lack of *mens rea* which is explored later.

Tip

Actus reus is one of the essential elements needed to prove an offence. So make sure you understand the basic concepts as you will need to show understanding and/or apply these rules in examination questions on criminal law.

13.2 Omissions as *actus reus*

The normal rule is that an omission cannot make a person guilty of an offence. This was explained by Stephen J, a nineteenth-century judge, in the following way.

> " A sees B drowning and is able to save him by holding out his hand. A abstains from doing so in order that B may be drowned. A has committed no offence. "

Activity

Read the following scenario:

Zoe is sitting by a swimming pool in the grounds of a hotel. Jason is swimming in the pool. He is the only person in the water and there are no other people near the pool. Jason gets out of the pool and while walking around it slips and falls into the water. He is knocked unconscious. Zoe sees this happen but she does nothing. Jason drowns.

Discuss these points:

- Should Zoe be found guilty of an offence?
- Would it make any difference to your answer if Zoe could not swim?

A 'Good Samaritan' law?

Some other countries have a law which is known as a 'Good Samaritan' law. It makes a person responsible for helping other people in an 'emergency situation', even though they are complete strangers. French law has this and an example was seen when Princess Diana's car crashed in Paris in 1997. Journalists who had been following her car took photographs of her, injured, in the car. They did not try to help her, even though she was critically injured. The French authorities threatened to charge these journalists under the French 'Good Samaritan' law.

There are problems in enforcing such a law. What if a 'rogue' pretends to be seriously hurt in order to lure a stranger to his assistance, so that the rogue can then rob the stranger? There is also the risk that an untrained person, by intervening, could do more harm to an injured person. Also, what is an 'emergency situation'? Who decides that there is an emergency so that the 'Good Samaritan' law is operating?

A problem would also arise if several people witnessed the incident. Do all of them have to help? Or is it enough if one of them helps? If one person helps, are the others still under a duty to help?

Finally, there is the question of whether would-be rescuers have to put themselves at risk in order to help. It seems unlikely that the law would require this. In the case of *Miller* (1983) (see section 13.2.1), the House of Lords thought that a defendant who has created the risk would only be expected to take reasonable steps. He would not be expected to put himself at risk. If

this is the situation for the person who has caused the problem, then surely the same would have to apply to innocent passers-by?

13.2.1 Exceptions to the rule

There are exceptions to the rule that an omission cannot make a person guilty of an offence. In some cases it is possible for a failure to act (an omission) to be the *actus reus*.

An omission is only sufficient for the *actus reus* where there is a duty to act. There are six ways in which such a duty can exist:

- a statutory duty
- a contractual duty
- a duty because of a relationship
- a duty which has been taken on voluntarily
- a duty through one's official position
- a duty which arises because the defendant has set in motion a chain of events.

A statutory duty

An Act of Parliament can create liability for an omission. Examples include the offences of failing to stop or report a road traffic accident (s 170 of the Road Traffic Act 1988) and of failing to provide a specimen of breath (s 6 of the Road Traffic Act 1988). In fact, these offences can only be committed by failing to do something.

Another example where an Act of Parliament creates a duty is in s 1 of the Children and Young Persons Act 1933. This section puts parents who are legally responsible for a child under a duty to provide food, clothing, medical aid and lodging for their children. If a parent fails (omits) to do this, he can be guilty of the offence of wilful neglect.

A more recent example is the offence of allowing the death of a child or vulnerable adult under s 5 of the Domestic Violence, Crime and Victims Act 2004. This applies where a person in the same household fails to take such steps as he reasonably could have been expected to take to protect the victim.

A contractual duty

In *R v Pittwood* (1902) a railway-crossing keeper omitted to shut the gates, with the result that a person crossing the line was struck and killed by a train. The keeper was guilty of manslaughter.

A more modern example would be of a lifeguard at a pool who leaves his post unattended. His failure to do his duty could make him guilty of an offence if a swimmer were injured or drowned.

A duty because of a relationship

This is usually a parent–child relationship as a parent has a duty to care for young children. A duty can also exist the opposite way round, where a grown-up child is caring for his elderly parent. A case involving a parent–child duty is *R v Gibbins and Proctor* (1918).

Key case

R v Gibbins and Proctor (1918)

The father of a seven-year-old girl lived with a partner. The father had several children from an earlier marriage. He and his partner kept the girl separate from the father's other children and deliberately starved her to death. They were both convicted of murder.

The father had a duty to feed her because he was her parent and the mistress was held to have undertaken to look after the children, including the girl, so she was also under a duty to feed the child. The omission or failure to feed her was deliberate with the intention of killing or causing serious harm to her. In these circumstances they were guilty of murder. The failure to feed the girl was enough for the *actus reus* of murder.

A duty which has been undertaken voluntarily

In the above case of *Gibbins and Proctor* (1918) the partner had voluntarily undertaken to look after the girl. She therefore had a duty towards the child. When she failed to feed the child she was guilty of murder because of that omission.

Another example of where a duty had been undertaken voluntarily is *R v Stone and Dobinson* (1977).

Key case

R v Stone and Dobinson (1977)

Stone's elderly sister, Fanny, came to live with the defendants. Fanny was eccentric and often stayed in her room for several days. She also failed to eat. She eventually became bedridden and incapable of caring for herself. On at least one occasion Dobinson, Stone's partner, helped to wash Fanny and also occasionally prepared food for her. Fanny died from malnutrition. Both defendants were found guilty of her manslaughter.

As Fanny was Stone's sister, he owed a duty of care to her. Dobinson had undertaken some care of Fanny and so also owed her a duty of care. The duty was either to help her themselves or to summon help from other sources. Their failure to do either of these meant that they were in breach of their duty.

A more recent case where a mother was guilty of manslaughter through her failure to act is *R v Evans* (2009).

Key case

R v Evans (2009)

V, aged 16 and a heroin addict, lived with her mother and her older half-sister. The half-sister, D, bought some heroin and gave it to V who self-injected. Later it became obvious that V had overdosed. Neither the mother nor the half-sister tried to get medical help. Instead they put V to bed and hoped she would recover. V died.

Both the mother and D were convicted of gross negligence manslaughter. The mother clearly owed a duty of care to V as she was her daughter. D appealed, claiming that she did not owe a duty of care to a sister. The Court of Appeal upheld the conviction on the basis that D had created a state of affairs which she knew or ought reasonably to have known was threatening the life of V.

A duty through one's official position

This is very rare but it did happen in *R v Dytham* (1979).

Key case

R v Dytham (1979)

D was a police officer who was on duty. He saw a man (V) being thrown out of a nightclub about 30 yards from where he was standing. Following the throwing out, there was a fight in which three men kicked V to death. D took no steps to intervene or to summon help. When the fight was over, D told a bystander that he was going off-duty and left the scene. He was convicted of misconduct in a public office.

Because D was a police officer, he was guilty of wilfully and without reasonable excuse neglecting to perform his duty.

A duty which arises because the defendant set in motion a chain of events

This concept of owing a duty and being liable through omission was created in the case of *R v Miller* (1983) where a squatter had accidentally started a fire.

Key case

R v Miller (1983)

D was living in a squat. He fell asleep while smoking a cigarette. He awoke to find his mattress on fire. He did not attempt to put out the fire or to summon help but went into another room and went back to sleep. The house caught fire. He was convicted of arson.

It was not the setting of the mattress on fire which made him guilty. Instead, it was the fact that he had failed to take reasonable steps to deal with the fire when he discovered that his mattress was on fire. This failure or omission meant that he had committed the *actus reus* for arson. The House of Lords pointed out that Miller was only expected to take reasonable steps. He did not have to put himself at risk. So, if, when he woke and found the fire, it was very small and could easily be put out then he was expected to do that. However, if it was too dangerous for him to deal with it personally, then his duty was to summon the fire brigade.

Why should I bother to call the fire brigade?

Another case where the defendant knew that there was a dangerous situation but failed to take any steps is *DPP v Santa-Bermudez* (2003).

Key case

DPP v Santa-Bermudez (2003)

A policewoman, before searching the defendant's pockets, asked him if he had any needles or other sharp objects on him. The defendant said 'no', but when the police officer put her hand in his pocket she was injured by a needle which caused bleeding. The defendant was convicted of assault occasioning actual bodily harm under s 47 of the Offences Against the Person Act 1861.

In this case it was the failure to tell the police officer of the needle which made the defendant liable. He knew that there was danger to the police officer but failed to warn her about it. This failure was enough for the *actus reus* for the purposes of an assault causing actual bodily harm.

The case of *Evans* (2009) also illustrates the principle of a defendant being liable for failing to act after creating a state of affairs. In this case the half-sister who had supplied V with heroin which V then self-injected was found guilty of manslaughter. She had created a state of affairs which she knew or ought reasonably to have known was threatening the life of V, but she did nothing about it. She could easily have called for medical assistance for V. The failure to do so made her liable for V's death.

Source	Examples
Statutory duty	Failing to provide a specimen of breath (s 6 Road Traffic Act 1988). Wilful neglect (s 1 Children and Young Persons Act 1933)
Under a contract, especially of employment	*Pittwood* (1902)
Because of a relationship such as parent and child	*Gibbins and Proctor* (1918) *Evans* (2009)
A duty voluntarily undertaken, e.g. care of an elderly relative	*Stone and Dobinson* (1977)
Because of a public office, e.g. police officer	*Dytham* (1979)
As a result of a dangerous situation created by the defendant	*Miller* (1983) *Santa-Bermudez* (2003) *Evans* (2009)

Figure 13.1 When omissions can be *actus reus*

13.2.2 The duty of doctors

There can be cases where doctors decide to stop treating a patient. If this discontinuance of treatment is in the best interests of the patient then it is not an omission which can form the *actus reus*. This was decided in *Airedale NHS Trust v Bland* (1993).

Key case

Airedale NHS Trust v Bland (1993)

Bland was a young man who had been crushed by the crowd at the Hillsborough football stadium tragedy in 1989. This had stopped oxygen getting to his brain and left him with severe brain damage. He was in a persistent vegetative state (PVS), unable to do anything for himself and unaware of what was happening around him. He was fed artificially through tubes. He had been in this state for three years and the doctors caring for him asked the court for a ruling that they could stop feeding him.

The court ruled that the doctors could stop artificially feeding Bland even though it was known that he would die as a result. This was held to be in his best interests.

13.3 Causation

Where a consequence must be proved, then the prosecution has to show that:

- the defendant's conduct was the factual cause of that consequence
- it was the legal cause of that consequence and
- there was no intervening act which broke the chain of causation.

13.3.1 Factual cause

The defendant can only be guilty if the consequence would not have happened 'but for' the defendant's conduct. This 'but for' test can be seen in operation in the case of *R v Pagett* (1983).

Key case

R v Pagett (1983)

The defendant took his pregnant girlfriend from her home by force. He then held the girl hostage. Police called on him to surrender. D came out, holding the girl in front of him and firing at the police. The police returned fire and the girl was killed by police bullets. D was convicted of manslaughter.

Pagett was guilty because the girl would not have died 'but for' him using her as a shield in the shoot-out.

The opposite situation was seen in *White* (1910) where the defendant put cyanide in his mother's drink, intending to kill her. She died of a heart attack before she could drink it. The defendant was not the factual cause of her death. So, he was not guilty of murder, although he was guilty of attempted murder.

In *R v Hughes* (2013) the Supreme Court held that factual causation is not necessarily enough on its own for liability. They distinguished between 'cause' in the 'but for' sense without which a consequence would not have occurred, and 'cause' in the sense of something which was a legally effective cause of that consequence.

Key case

R v Hughes (2013)

D was driving his camper van. His driving was faultless. As he rounded a right-hand bend on his correct side of the road a car came towards him swerving all over the road and crossing on to D's side of the road. The car smashed into D's camper van and tipped it over. The other driver, who was found to be under the influence of heroin, suffered fatal injuries as a result.

D was not insured and did not have a full driving licence. He was charged under s 3ZB of the Road Traffic Act 1988 with causing death by driving without a licence and while uninsured and convicted. The Supreme Court quashed the conviction on the ground that although D was the 'cause' of the other driver's death in the sense that but for D's camper van being on the road there would have been no collision, this was not enough to be a legal effective cause. It was the merest chance that what the other driver hit was the van that D was driving.

13.3.2 Legal cause

There may be more than one act contributing to the consequence. Some of these acts may be made by people other than the defendant. The rule is that the defendant can be guilty if his conduct was more than a 'minimal' cause of the consequence. But the defendant's conduct need not be a substantial cause. In some cases the courts have stated that the conduct must be more than *de minimis*. In *R v Kimsey* (1996) the Court of Appeal held that instead of using this Latin phrase '*de minimis*' it was acceptable to tell the jury it must be 'more than a slight or trifling link'.

R v Kimsey (1996)

D was involved in a high-speed car chase with a friend. She lost control of her car and the other driver was killed in the crash. The evidence about what happened immediately before D lost control was not very clear. The trial judge directed the jury that D's driving did not have to be 'the principal, or a substantial cause of the death, as long as you are sure that it was a cause and that there something more than a slight or trifling link'. The Court of Appeal upheld D's conviction for causing death by dangerous driving.

In *R v Hughes* (2013) the Supreme Court further explained the minimum threshold requirement for legal causation as follows:

> Where there are multiple legally effective causes, it suffices if the act or omission under consideration is a significant (or substantial) cause, in the sense that it is not *de minimis* or minimal. It need not be the only or the principle cause. It must, however, be a cause which is more than *de minimis*, more than minimal.

Multiple causes

There may be more than one person whose act contributed to the death. The defendant can be guilty even though his conduct was not the only cause of the death. In *Kimsey* both drivers were driving at high speed, but the defendant could be found guilty.

The 'thin-skull' rule

The defendant must also take the victim as he finds him. This is known as the 'thin-skull' rule. It means that if the victim has something unusual about his physical or mental state which makes an injury more serious, then the defendant is liable for the more serious injury. So, if the victim has an unusually thin skull which means that a blow to his head gives him a serious injury, then the defendant is liable for that injury. This is so even though that blow would have only caused bruising in a 'normal' person. An example is the case of *R v Blaue* (1975).

R v Blaue (1975)

A young woman was stabbed by the defendant. She was told that she needed a blood transfusion to save her life but she refused to have one as she was a Jehovah's Witness and her religion forbade blood transfusions. She died and the defendant was convicted of her murder.

So, the fact that the victim was a Jehovah's Witness made the wound fatal, but the defendant was still guilty because he had to take his victim as he found her.

13.3.3 Intervening acts

There must be a direct link from the defendant's conduct to the consequence. This is known as the chain of causation. In some situations something else happens after the defendant's act or omission and, if this is sufficiently separate from the defendant's conduct, it may break the chain of causation.

Figure 13.2 Breaking the chain of causation

An example would be where the defendant has stabbed the victim who needs to be taken to hospital for treatment. On the way to hospital, the ambulance carrying the victim is involved in an accident and crashes, causing fatal head injuries to the victim.

Under the 'but for' test it could be argued that the victim would not have been in the ambulance but for the defendant's act in stabbing him. However, the accident is such a major intervening act that the defendant would not be liable for the death of the victim.

The chain of causation can be broken by:
- an act of a third party
- the victim's own act or
- a natural but unpredictable event.

In order to break the chain of causation so that the defendant is not responsible for the consequence, the intervening act must be sufficiently independent of the defendant's conduct and sufficiently serious.

Where the defendant's conduct causes a foreseeable action by a third party, then the defendant is likely to be held to have caused the consequence. This principle was applied in *Pagett* (1983) where his girlfriend was shot when he held her as a shield against police bullets (see section 13.3.1).

13.3.4 Medical treatment

Medical treatment is unlikely to break the chain of causation unless it is so independent of the defendant's acts and 'in itself so potent in causing death' that the defendant's acts are insignificant. The following three cases show this.

Key case

R v Smith (1959)

Two soldiers had a fight and one was stabbed in the lung by the other. The victim was carried to a medical centre by other soldiers, but was dropped on the way. At the medical centre the staff gave him artificial respiration by pressing on his chest. This made the injury worse and he died. The poor treatment probably affected his chances of recovery by as much as 75 per cent. However, the original attacker was still guilty of his murder.

In this case it was held that a defendant would be guilty, provided that the injury caused by D was still an 'operating' and 'substantial' cause of death. Smith was guilty because the stab wound to the lung was still 'operating' (it obviously had not healed up) and it was a substantial cause of V's death.

Key case

R v Cheshire (1991)

D shot the victim in the thigh and the stomach. V needed major surgery. He developed breathing problems and was given a tracheotomy (i.e. a tube was inserted in his throat to help him breathe). Some two months after the shooting, V died from rare complications left by the tracheotomy. These complications were not diagnosed by the doctors. By the time V died, the original wounds had virtually healed and were no longer life-threatening. The defendant was still held to be liable for V's death.

In this case the Court of Appeal held that even though treatment for injuries was 'short of the standard expected of a competent medical practitioner', D could still be criminally responsible for the death. The prosecution had only to prove that D's acts contributed to the death. D's acts need not be the sole cause or even the main cause of death, provided that his acts contributed significantly to the death.

In the first two cases the doctors were carrying out treatment for the injuries in an attempt to save the victim's life. The victims would not have needed treatment if they had not been seriously injured by the defendant. In such situations the attacker is still liable even though the medical treatment was not very good. This was pointed out in R v Cheshire (1991) by Beldam LJ:

> Even though negligence in the treatment of the victim was the immediate cause of death, the jury should not regard it as excluding the responsibility of the accused unless the negligent treatment was so independent of his acts, and in itself so potent in causing death, that they regard the contribution made by his acts as insignificant.

Key case

R v Jordan (1956)

The victim had been stabbed in the stomach. He was treated in hospital and the wounds were healing well. He was given an antibiotic but suffered an allergic reaction to it. One doctor stopped the use of the antibiotic but the next day another doctor ordered that a large dose of it be given. The victim died from the allergic reaction to the drug. In this case the actions of the doctor were held to be an intervening act which caused the death. The defendant was not guilty of murder.

In the third case of Jordan (1956), the fact that the victim was given a large amount of a drug when the doctors knew he was allergic to it was a sufficiently independent act to break the chain of causation. However, if a normal dose of a drug is given as part of emergency treatment and the doctors do not know that the victim is allergic to it, then the giving of the drug would not break the chain of causation.

Life-support machines

Switching off a life-support machine by a doctor when it has been decided that the victim is brain-dead does not break the chain of causation. This was decided in R v Malcherek (1981).

Key case

R v Malcherek (1981)

D stabbed his wife in the stomach. In hospital she was put on a life-support machine. After a number of tests showed that she was brain-dead, the machine was switched off. D was charged with her murder. The trial judge refused to allow the issue of causation to go to the jury. D was convicted and the Court of Appeal upheld his conviction.

13.3.5 Victim's own act

If the defendant causes the victim to react in a foreseeable way, then any injury to the victim will be considered to have been caused by the defendant. This occurred in R v Roberts (1971).

Case	Facts	Law
Smith (1959)	Soldier stabbed another soldier V's medical treatment very poor and affected chances of recovery	D liable if the injuries he caused are still an operating and substantial cause
Cheshire (1991)	D shot V V needed a tracheotomy V died because of complications from the tracheotomy His wounds were virtually healed	Medical treatment would only break the chain of causation if it is 'so independent' of D's acts and 'in itself so potent in causing death'
Jordan (1956)	V was stabbed When his wounds were almost healed he was given a large dose of a drug to which it was known he was allergic	The chain of causation was broken in this case
Malcherek (1981)	D stabbed his wife She was put on a life-support machine but when tests showed she was brain-dead, the machine was switched off	Switching off a life-support machine does not break the chain of causation

Figure 13.3 Medical intervention and causation

Key case

R v Roberts (1972)

A girl jumped from a car in order to escape from Roberts' sexual advances. The car was travelling at between 20 and 40 mph and the girl was injured by jumping from it. The defendant was held to be liable for her injuries.

Another case in which it was held that D was liable if V's action was reasonably foreseeable was *R v Marjoram* (2000).

Key case

R v Marjoram (2000)

Several people, including D, shouted abuse and kicked the door of V's hostel room. They eventually forced the door open. V then fell (or possibly jumped) from the window of the room and suffered serious injuries. D's conviction for inflicting grievous bodily harm was upheld by the Court of Appeal.

In this situation it was reasonably foreseeable that V would fear that the group was going to use violence against him and that the only escape route for him was the window.

V's action was also reasonably foreseeable in *Bristow, Dunn and Delay* (2012) where the owner of a motor repair business in remote farm buildings tried to stop robbers and was run over and killed by them.

The victim's own act breaks the chain of causation. This is particularly relevant in cases where a supplier of illegal drugs leaves the victim who then dies as a result of administering the drugs to himself as in the case of *R v Kennedy* (2007).

Key case

R v Kennedy (2007)

The defendant had supplied a class A drug to a friend who then died taking it. The victim had a choice, knowing the facts, whether to inject himself or not. The heroin was self-administered, not jointly administered. The defendant supplied but did not administer the drug. He did not cause the drug to be administered to or taken by the victim. Therefore, he had not caused the death of the victim.

Activity

In a small group brainstorm a list of similarities and differences between the cases of *R v Kennedy* (2007) and *R v Khan and Khan* (1998).

Unreasonable reaction

However, if the victim's reaction is unreasonable, then this may break the chain of causation. In *R v Williams and Davis* (1992) a hitch-hiker jumped from Williams' car and died from head injuries caused by his head hitting the road. The car was travelling at about 30 mph. The prosecution alleged that there had been an attempt to steal the victim's wallet and that was the reason for his jumping from the car. The Court of Appeal said that the victim's act had to be foreseeable and also had to be in proportion to the threat. The question to be asked was whether the victim's conduct was:

> within the ambit of reasonableness and not so daft as to make his own voluntary act one which amounted to a *novus actus interveniens* (a new intervening act) and consequently broke the chain of causation.

This makes it necessary to consider the surrounding circumstances in deciding whether the victim's conduct has broken the chain of causation. Where the threats to the victim are serious, then it is more likely for it to be reasonable for him to jump out of a moving car (or out of a window or into a river etc.). Where the threat is very minor and the victim takes drastic action, it is more likely that the courts will hold that it broke the chain of causation.

The main rules on causation are shown in a flowchart in Figure 13.4.

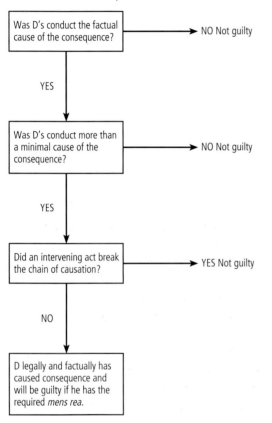

Figure 13.4 Flowchart of rules on causation

Tip

The law on causation is complex. Make sure you have understood the section and then do the activity below to test your ability to apply the law.

Activity

Read the following situations and explain whether causation would be proved.

1 Aled has been threatened by Ben in the past. When Adam sees Ben approaching him in the street, Aled runs across the road without looking and is knocked down and injured by a car. Is Ben liable for Aled's injuries?
2 Toyah stabs Steve in the arm. His injury is not serious but he needs stitches, so a neighbour takes Steve to hospital in his car. On the way to the hospital, the car crashes and Steve sustains serious head injuries. Is Toyah liable for the head injuries?
3 Lewis has broken into Katie's third-floor flat. He threatens to rape her, and in order to escape from him she jumps from the window and is seriously injured. Is Lewis liable for her injuries?
4 Ross stabs Panjit in the chest. Panjit is taken to hospital where he is given an emergency blood transfusion. Unfortunately, he is given the wrong type of blood and he dies. Is Ross liable for Panjit's death?

Summary

- *Actus reus* is the physical element of a crime and it can include conduct, circumstances or consequences.
- *Actus reus* can be a failure to act (an omission) – this usually occurs where D is under a duty to act. There is no general duty to act in English law but specific duties have been recognised. These are:
  - statutory
  - under a contract
  - by a relationship
  - a duty voluntarily undertaken

  - because of an official position
  - through the creation of a dangerous situation.
- In consequence crimes, the act or omission by D must have caused consequence:
  - There must be factual and legal causation.
  - D need not be the only cause or even the main cause, but it must be more than a minimal cause.
  - D is not liable if the chain of causation is broken.
  - Medical treatment does not normally break the chain of causation.

Chapter 14

Mens rea

After reading this chapter you should be able to:
- Understand the law of intention, both direct and oblique
- Understand the law of subjective recklessness
- Understand the law of negligence
- Understand the principle of transferred malice
- Understand the need for coincidence of *actus reus* and *mens rea*
- Apply the legal principles to factual situations

14.1 *Mens rea* and fault

In criminal law, there is a general presumption that liability is based upon fault. This is consistent with our sense of justice: a person should not be held liable for a criminal offence unless he is to some extent blameworthy, or at fault. The *mens rea* of a criminal offence examines the state of mind of the defendant at the time of committing the offence. Generally speaking, it is what is in a person's mind that distinguishes between a mere accident and a criminal offence.

For example, breaking another's fingers in a sport such as cricket or rugby will not normally incur criminal liability. However, breaking another's fingers with an iron bar in a fight will normally incur criminal liability. The injury is the same; the defendant's mind frame is completely different. Further, the level of *mens rea* may vary between charges.

Mens rea is an essential element of all serious criminal offences. Unless the offence is one of strict liability, the absence of *mens rea* will result in an acquittal as in the case of *R v Clarke* (1972).

Key case

R v Clarke (1972)
A woman transferred some items from her shopping basket into her own bag before paying for them. She was able to show that she suffered from absent-mindedness due to depression. She therefore lacked *mens rea* for theft and was acquitted.

14.2 Levels of *mens rea*

Mens rea is the mental element of an offence. Each offence has its own *mens rea* or mental element. The only exceptions are offences of strict liability.

These offences do not require proof of a mental element in respect of at least part of the *actus reus*. In criminal cases it is for the prosecution to prove the required *mens rea*.

There are different levels of *mens rea*. To be guilty, the accused must have at least the minimum level of *mens rea* required for the offence.

The highest level of *mens rea* is intention. This is also referred to as 'specific intention'. The other main types of *mens rea* are recklessness, negligence and knowledge.

14.3 Intention (specific intent)

In the case of *Mohan* (1975) the court defined 'intention' as:

> a decision to bring about, in so far as it lies within the accused's power, [the prohibited consequence], no matter whether the accused desired that consequence of his act or not.

This makes it clear that the defendant's motive or reason for doing the act is not relevant. The important point is that the defendant decided to bring about the prohibited consequence.

This can be illustrated by looking at the offence set out in s 18 of the Offences Against the Person Act 1861. For this offence, the defendant must wound or cause grievous bodily harm. The *mens rea* is that the defendant must intend to cause grievous bodily harm or intend to resist arrest. If the defendant did not intend either of these then he cannot be guilty of this offence. For example, if a person opens a door very suddenly and hits and seriously injures someone on the other side of the door whom they did not know was there, then they do not intend to 'bring about' the prohibited consequence.

Motive

Mohan (1975) also makes it clear that motive is not the same as intention and is not relevant in deciding whether the defendant had intention. For example, a person may feel very strongly that the banking system in the Western world is causing poverty in poorer nations. That person then steals millions of pounds from a bank so that he can give it to people in poorer nations. His motive is to make sure that the poor receive money. This is irrelevant in deciding whether the defendant has the *mens rea* required for theft.

14.3.1 Direct and oblique intent

In the majority of cases the defendant has what is known as direct intent. This means that he intends the specific consequence to occur. For example, D decides to kill V. He aims a gun directly at V's head and pulls the trigger. Here D has the direct intent to kill V.

However, there can be situations where the defendant intends one thing but the actual consequence which occurs is another thing. This is known as oblique intent or indirect intent.

An example of this is if the defendant intends to frighten someone so as to stop him going to work, but does not intend to kill or seriously injure him. This occurred in the case of *Hancock and Shankland* (1986). The actual consequence was that the driver of the car taking the person to work was killed. This is shown in diagram form in Figure 14.1.

14.3.2 Foresight of consequences

The main problem with proving intention is in cases where the defendant's main aim was not the prohibited consequences. He intended something else. If, in achieving the other thing, the defendant foresaw that he would also cause those consequences, then he may be found guilty. This idea is referred to as 'foresight of consequences'.

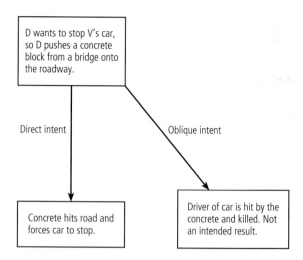

Figure 14.1 Direct intent/oblique intent

An example of this type of situation is where the defendant decides to set fire to his shop in order to claim insurance. His main aim is damaging the shop and getting the insurance. Unfortunately, he starts the fire when members of staff are still in the shop and some of them are seriously injured. Has the defendant the intention for the s 18 offence of causing grievous bodily harm?

The starting point for foresight of consequences is s 8 of the Criminal Justice Act 1967 which states that:

A court or jury, in determining whether a person has committed an offence–

a shall not be bound in law to infer that he intended or foresaw a result of his actions by reason only of its being a natural and probable consequence of those actions; but

b shall decide whether he did intend or foresee that result by reference to all the evidence, drawing such inferences from the evidence as appear proper in the circumstances.

This wording has been the subject of several cases over the last 20 years or so. These are mainly cases where defendants have been charged with murder. The important point is that the defendant must intend or foresee a result. In a murder case this means that the defendant must foresee that death or really serious injury will be caused. The leading case on this is now *Woollin* (1998), but to understand the law and the problems it is necessary to look at cases which came before *Woollin*. The first of these was *Moloney* (1985).

Key case

Moloney (1985)

D and his step-father had drunk a considerable amount of alcohol at a family party. After the party, they were heard talking and laughing. Then there was a shot. D phoned the police, saying that he had just murdered his step-father. D said that they had being seeing who was the faster at loading and firing a shotgun. He had loaded his gun faster than his step-father. His step-father then said that D hadn't got 'the guts' to pull the trigger. D said 'I didn't aim the gun. I just pulled the trigger and he was dead.' D was convicted of murder but this conviction was quashed on appeal.

In the case of *Moloney* the House of Lords ruled that foresight of consequences is only evidence of intention. It is not intention in itself. This part of the House of Lords' judgment is still law.

However, other parts of this judgment have been overruled by later cases. This was because Lord Bridge stated that jurors should be told to consider two questions:

1 Was death or really serious injury a natural consequence of the defendant's act?
2 Did the defendant foresee that consequence as being a natural result of his act?

The problem with these questions (which are often referred to as the *Moloney* guidelines) is that the word 'probable' is not mentioned.

If you look back to s 8 of the Criminal Justice Act 1967, you will see that the section uses the phrase 'natural and probable consequence'. Lord Bridge referred only to a 'natural' result. This omission of the word 'probable' was held in *Hancock and Shankland* (1986) (see below) to make the guidelines defective. The guidelines are therefore no longer law.

Key case

Hancock and Shankland (1986)

Ds were miners who were on strike. They tried to prevent another miner from going to work by pushing a concrete block from a bridge onto the road along which he was being driven to work in a taxi. The block struck the windscreen of the taxi and killed the driver. The trial judge used the *Moloney* guidelines to direct the jury, and Ds were convicted of murder. On appeal, the Court of Appeal quashed their convictions. This was upheld by the House of Lords.

The problem with *Moloney* (1985) was explained by Lord Scarman who stated that the guidelines in that case were unsafe and misleading. He said:

> In my judgment, therefore, the Moloney guidelines as they stand are unsafe and misleading. They require a reference to probability. They also require an explanation that the greater the probability of a consequence the more likely it is that the consequence was foreseen and that if that consequence was foreseen the greater the probability is that that consequence was also intended.

The next case was *Nedrick* (1986) where the Court of Appeal thought that the judgments in the two earlier cases of *Moloney* (1985) and *Hancock and Shankland* (1986) needed to be made clearer.

Key case

Nedrick (1986)

D had a grudge against a woman. He poured paraffin through the letter box of her house and set it alight. A child died in the fire. D was convicted of murder but the Court of Appeal quashed the conviction and substituted one of manslaughter.

In the case of *Nedrick*, the Court of Appeal tried to make the law decided in *Moloney* and *Hancock and Shankland* easier for jurors to understand and apply in murder trials. The Court of Appeal said that it was helpful for a jury to ask themselves two questions:

1 How probable was the consequence which resulted from D's voluntary act?
2 Did D foresee that consequence?

It was necessary for the consequence to be a virtual certainty and for D to have realised that. If this was so then there was evidence from which the jury could infer that D had the necessary intention. Lord Lane CJ put it this way:

> The jury should be directed that they are not entitled to infer the necessary intention unless they feel sure that death or serious bodily harm was a virtual certainty (barring some unforeseen intervention) as a result of the defendant's actions and that the defendant appreciated that such was the case.

This remained the law until 1998 and the case of *Woollin* (1998). This went to the House of Lords who

123

felt that the Court of Appeal's views in *Nedrick* (1986) were not helpful.

Key case

Woollin (1998)

D threw his three-month-old baby towards his pram which was against a wall some three or four feet away. The baby suffered head injuries and died. The court ruled that the consequence must have been a virtual certainty and the defendant must have realised this. Where the jury was satisfied on both these two points, then there was evidence on which the jury could find intention.

In *Woollin* the Law Lords stated that the two questions in *Nedrick* were not helpful. They held that the model direction from *Nedrick* should be used, but that the word 'find' should be used rather than the word 'infer'. So the model direction to be given to a jury considering foresight of consequences should now be:

> the jury should be directed that they are not entitled to find the necessary intention unless they feel sure that death or serious bodily harm was a virtual certainty (barring some unforeseen intervention) as a result of the defendant's actions and that the defendant appreciated that such was the case.

Problems with the decision in *Woollin*

The decision in *Woollin* causes some problems. First of all, the word 'infer' is used in s 8 of the Criminal Justice Act 1967 and this is presumably why it was used in *Nedrick*. Does the substitution of the word 'find' improve the clarity of the direction to the jury? Another problem is whether the use of the word 'find' means that foresight of consequence is intention and not merely evidence of it.

In his judgment Lord Steyn also went on to say that the effect of the direction is that 'a result foreseen as virtually certain is an intended result'. He also pointed out that in *Moloney* the House of Lords had said that if a person foresees the probability of a consequence as little short of overwhelming, this 'will suffice to establish the necessary intent'. Lord Steyn emphasised

the word 'establish'. This seems to suggest that the House of Lords in *Woollin* regarded foresight of consequences as the same as intention, when *Moloney* had clearly stated that it was not.

In later cases there have been conflicting decisions on this point. In the civil case of *Re A* (2000), doctors asked the courts whether they could operate to separate conjoined twins when they foresaw that this would kill the weaker twin. The Court of Appeal (Civil Division) clearly thought that *Woollin* laid down the rule that foresight of consequences is intention.

In the criminal case of *Matthews and Alleyne* (2003) the Court of Appeal held that the judgment in *Woollin* meant that foresight of consequences is not intention: it is a rule of evidence. If a jury decides that the defendant foresaw the virtual certainty of death or serious injury, it is entitled to find intention but does not have to do so.

Key case

Matthews and Alleyne (2003)

The defendants dropped the victim 25 feet from a bridge, into the middle of a deep river. The victim had told them that he could not swim. They watched him 'dog paddle' towards the bank but left before seeing whether he reached safety. The victim drowned.

The trial judge had directed the jury that the defendants' intention to kill could be proved either by direct intention to kill or by the defendants' appreciation that V's death was a virtual certainty (barring an attempt to save him) together with the fact that the defendants did not intend to save the victim.

The Court of Appeal stated that the trial judge had been wrong to say that an appreciation of a virtual certainty constituted intention.

However, they upheld the convictions because, if the jury were sure that the defendants appreciated the virtual certainty of death if they did not attempt to save V and that at the time of throwing V off the bridge they had no intention of saving him, then it was impossible to see how the jury could not have found that the defendants intended V to die.

Case	Brief facts	Law
Moloney (1985)	D shot step-father in 'quick on the draw' incident	Foresight of consequences is not intention; it is evidence of intention
Hancock and Shankland (1986)	Miner dropped lumps of concrete onto road, killing taxi driver.	The greater the probability of a consequence, the more likely it is that the consequence was foreseen and if that consequence was foreseen the greater the probability is that that consequence was also intended
Nedrick (1986)	Poured paraffin through letter box, causing fire in the house in which a child died	Jury not entitled to infer the necessary intention unless sure that death or serious bodily harm was a virtual certainty and that the defendant appreciated this
Woollin (1998)	Threw baby at pram, causing its death	The direction in *Nedrick* should not use the word 'infer'. Instead, the jury should be told it is entitled to find intention
Re A (2000)	Doctors wanted to operate on conjoined twins but knew this would cause one of them to die	Court thought that *Woollin* made it law that foresight of consequences is intention
Matthews and Alleyne (2003)	Threw V into river where he drowned	*Woollin* meant that foresight of consequences is not intention. It is a rule of evidence. If a jury decides that the defendant foresaw the virtual certainty of death or serious injury then it is entitled to find intention but it does not have to do so

Figure 14.2 Cases on foresight of consequences

A chart of the cases on foresight of consequences is included to help keep the cases clear; see Figure 14.2.

14.3.3 Evaluating foresight of consequences as intention

It can be seen from the above that the courts have struggled with the concept of intention where foresight of consequences is involved. For example:

- natural and probable consequence
- difficulty for jurors in applying the tests after the cases of *Moloney* and *Hancock and Shankland*

- the change in *Woollin* from inferring intention to finding intention
- the fact that there are still two interpretations of the judgment in *Woollin*.

Natural and probable consequences

It is necessary to include both words in the test for intention. This is because something can be a natural consequence without being a probable consequence. For example, a natural consequence of sexual intercourse is that the girl becomes pregnant. However, it is not a probable consequence. Pregnancy only occurs in a small percentage of cases.

The difficulty for jurors applying the law

Following the cases of *Moloney* and *Hancock and Shankland*, where jurors had to be directed on the level of probability, the law was left in a state which made it difficult for judges to explain it to jurors and for jurors to apply the law. The difficulties it caused were emphasised when the Court of Appeal in *Nedrick* thought it necessary to try to make the law easier for jurors to understand and apply.

Infer or find

The use of the two question test from *Nedrick* operated for some 12 years until the case of *Woollin*. Then the House of Lords said that they thought the two questions from *Nedrick* were not helpful. They also held that the direction to the jury should use the word 'find' instead of 'infer'. As already discussed in the previous section, the decision in *Woollin* appears to create more problems than it solved.

Two interpretations of *Woollin*

There are still problems in the law on intention as shown by the fact that the Court of Appeal in two different cases has interpreted the decision of the House of Lords in *Woollin* in different ways.

In *Re A* (2001) the Court of Appeal thought that *Woollin* meant that foresight of consequences is intention, whereas in *Matthews and Alleyne* they stated that foresight of consequences is only evidence of intention.

It can be seen from this that the law on intention is still not in a satisfactory state.

14.4 Subjective recklessness

This is a lower level of *mens rea* than intention. **Subjective recklessness** is where the defendant knows there is a risk of the consequence happening but takes that risk.

> ### Key term 🔑
>
> **Subjective recklessness** – where the defendant knows there is a risk of the consequence happening but takes that risk.

14.4.1 The case of *Cunningham*

The explanation of subjective recklessness comes from the case of *Cunningham* (1957).

> ### Key case
>
> #### *Cunningham* (1957)
>
> D tore a gas meter from the wall of an empty house in order to steal the money in it. This caused gas to seep into the house next-door, where a woman was affected by it. Cunningham was charged with an offence under s 23 of the Offences Against the Person Act 1861, of maliciously administering a noxious thing. It was held that he was not guilty since he did not realise the risk of gas escaping into the next-door house. He had not intended to cause the harm, nor had he taken a risk he knew about.

The offence involved in *Cunningham* uses the word 'maliciously' to indicate the *mens rea* required. The court held that this word meant that to have the necessary *mens rea* the defendant must either intend the consequence or realise that there was a risk of the

consequence happening and decide to take that risk. Knowing about a risk and taking it can also be referred to as 'subjective recklessness'. It is subjective because the defendant himself realised the risk.

The case of *Savage* (1992) confirmed that the same principle applies to all offences where the definition in an Act of Parliament uses the word 'maliciously'. The Law Lords said that 'maliciously' was a term of legal art. In other words, it has a special meaning when used in an Act of Parliament, not its normal dictionary definition. It means doing something intentionally or being subjectively reckless about the risk involved.

Do not forget that if the defendant has the higher level of intention he will, of course, be guilty. For example, if the defendant intends to punch the victim in the face, that defendant has the higher level of intention and is guilty of a battery. It is only when the defendant does not have the higher level that recklessness has to be considered.

Offences for which recklessness is sufficient for the *mens rea* include:

- assault and battery
- assault occasioning actual bodily harm (s 47 of the Offences Against the Person Act 1861)
- malicious wounding (s 20 of the Offences Against the Person Act 1861).

14.5 Negligence

A person is negligent if he fails to meet the standards of the reasonable man. This means it is an objective test. The defendant will be guilty because he did not act as a reasonable man would have done in the circumstances. What the defendant intended or thought is not relevant. This makes it a much lower level of fault to the two levels of fault, intention and recklessness, that we have already looked at.

> ### Key term 🔑
>
> **Neglience** – failure to meet the standards of the reasonable man.

The concept of **negligence** making a person liable is well known in the civil law, but it is not widely used in the criminal law. It occurs in some statutory offences, for example s 3 of the Road Traffic Act 1988 which makes it an offence to drive without due care and attention.

Level of mens rea	Explanation	Case/Example
Intention (specific intent)	'A decision to bring about, in so far as it lies within the accused's power, [the prohibited consequence], no matter whether the accused desired that consequence of his act or not'	*Mohan* (1975)
Recklessness (basic intent)	The defendant must realise that there is a risk of the consequences occurring and decide to take that risk	*Cunningham* (1957)
Negligence	A failure to meet the standards of the reasonable man	*Adomako* (1994)

Figure 14.3 Key facts chart on levels of *mens rea*

The only mainstream offence for which negligence is relevant is manslaughter. One form of manslaughter can be committed by 'gross negligence'. This means there has to be a very high degree of negligence. The leading case is *Adomako* (1994). The level used in civil cases is not enough. Manslaughter is explained in more detail in Book 2 as it is only required for the full A Level specification.

14.6 The concept of strict liability

Strict liability offences are those offences where *mens rea* is not required to be proved in respect of at least one aspect of the *actus reus*.

Key term

Strict liability offences – offences where *mens rea* is not required in respect of at least one aspect of the *actus reus*.

An example demonstrating strict liability is *Pharmaceutical Society of Great Britain v Storkwain Ltd* (1986).

Key case

Pharmaceutical Society of Great Britain v Storkwain Ltd (1986)

D was charged under s 58(2) of the Medicines Act 1968 which states that no one shall supply certain drugs without a doctor's prescription. D had supplied drugs on prescriptions, but the prescriptions were later found to be forged. There was no finding that D had acted dishonestly, improperly or even negligently. The forgery was sufficient to deceive the pharmacists. Despite this, the House of Lords held that the Divisional Court was right to direct the magistrates to convict D. The pharmacists had supplied the drugs without a genuine prescription and this was enough to make him guilty of the offence.

14.6.1 Requirement of *actus reus*

For nearly all strict liability offences, it must be proved that the defendant did the relevant *actus reus*. For *Storkwain*, this meant proving that the chemist had supplied drugs without a genuine prescription. It also has to be proved that the doing of the *actus reus* was voluntary. If the chemist had been forced at gunpoint to provide the drug, then the act would not have been voluntary.

However, there are a few rare cases where the defendant has been found guilty even though he did not do the *actus reus* voluntarily. These are known as crimes of absolute liability, an example of which we have seen earlier in *R v Larsonneur* (see section 13.1.3).

14.6.2 Strict liability and *mens rea*

For all offences there is a presumption that *mens rea* is required. The courts will always start with this presumption, but if they decide that the offence does not require *mens rea* for at least part of the *actus reus* then the offence is one of strict liability. This idea of not requiring *mens rea* for part of the offence is illustrated by two cases: *R v Prince* (1875) and *R v Hibbert* (1869). In both these cases the charge against the defendant was that he had taken an unmarried girl under the age of 16 out of the possession of her father, against his will, contrary to s 55 of the Offences against the Person Act 1861.

In both cases the girls willingly went with the respective defendants and both were under 16. The issue was whether *mens rea* was required in respect of two points: first, whether the defendant had to know the girl was under 16 and second, whether the defendant had to know he was taking the girl from the 'possession' of her father.

Key cases

R v Prince (1875)

Prince knew that the girl he took was in the possession of her father but believed, on reasonable grounds, that she was aged 18. He was convicted as he had the intention to remove the girl from the possession of her father. *Mens rea* was required for this part of the *actus reus* and he had the necessary intention. However, the court held that knowledge of her age was not required. On this aspect of the offence there was strict liability.

R v Hibbert (1869)

The defendant met a girl aged 14 on the street. He took her to another place where they had sexual intercourse. He was acquitted of the offence as it was not proved that he knew the girl was in the custody of her father. Even though the age aspect of the offence was one of strict liability, *mens rea* was required for the removal aspect and, in this case, the necessary intention was not proved.

These cases were, of course, in Victorian times when the law was very different to what it is today. However, they illustrate that *mens rea* may be required for one part of an offence, but that another element of the offence is one of strict liability.

14.6.3 No fault

As already stated, the *actus reus* must be proved and the defendant's conduct in doing the *actus reus* must be voluntary. However, a defendant can be convicted if his voluntary act inadvertently caused a prohibited consequence. This is so even though the defendant was totally blameless in respect of the consequence. An example was the case of *Callow v Tillstone* (1900).

Key case

Callow v Tillstone (1900)

A butcher asked a vet to examine a carcass to see if it was fit for human consumption. The vet assured him that it was all right to eat and so the butcher offered it for sale. In fact, it was unfit and the butcher was convicted of the offence of exposing unsound meat for sale.

Because it was a strict liability offence the butcher was guilty, even though he had taken reasonable care not to commit the offence. The butcher was not at fault in any way.

This is the case even where all reasonable precautions have been taken, sometimes known as **due diligence**, as can be seen in the case of *Harrow LBC v Shah and Shah* (1999).

Key term 🔑

Due diligence – where the defendant has done all that was within his power not to commit an offence.

Key case

Harrow LBC v Shah and Shah (1999)

The defendants owned a newsagents' business where lottery tickets were sold. They had told their staff not to sell tickets to anyone under 16 years old. They frequently reminded their staff that if there was any doubt about a customer's age, the staff should ask for proof of age, and if still in doubt should refer the matter to the defendants. One of their staff sold a lottery ticket to a 13-year-old boy, without asking for proof of age. The salesman mistakenly believed the boy was over 16 years old. D1 was in a back room of the premises at the time: D2 was not on the premises. The defendants were charged with selling a lottery ticket to a person under 16, contrary to s 13(1)(c) of the National Lottery Act 1993. The magistrates dismissed the charges, but the prosecution appealed to the Divisional Court which held that the offence was one of strict liability. This meant that the defendants were guilty.

As the offence did not require any *mens rea*, then the act of selling the ticket to someone who was actually under 16 was enough to make the defendants guilty. This was so, even though the defendants had done their best to prevent the selling of lottery tickets in their shop to those under age.

There is no defence of mistake so the defendant cannot be acquitted when he made an honest mistake. This can be seen in the case of *Cundy v Le Cocq* (1884).

Key cases

Cundy v Le Cocq (1884)

D was charged with selling intoxicating liquor to a drunken person. The magistrate trying the case found as a fact that the defendant and his employees had not noticed that the person was drunk. The magistrate also found that while the person was on the licensed premises he had been 'quiet in his demeanour and had done nothing to indicate insobriety; and that there were no apparent indications of intoxication'. However, the magistrate held that the offence was complete on proof that a sale had taken place and that the person served was drunk, and convicted the defendant. The defendant appealed against this but the Divisional Court upheld the conviction.

14.6.4 Summary of strict liability

So, where an offence is held to be one of strict liability, the following points apply:

- The defendant must be proved to have done the *actus reus*.
- This must be a voluntary act on his part.
- There is no need to prove *mens rea* for at least part of the *actus reus*.
- No 'due diligence' defence will be available.
- The defence of mistake is not available.

These factors are well established. The problem lies in deciding which offences are ones of strict liability.

14.7 Methods used to establish whether an offence is a strict liability offence

14.7.1 Presumption of *mens rea*

In order to decide whether an offence is one of strict liability, the courts start by assuming that *mens rea* is required, but they are prepared to interpret the offence as one of strict liability if Parliament has expressly or by implication indicated this in the relevant statute.

The judges often have difficulty in deciding whether an offence is one of strict liability or not. The first rule is that where an Act of Parliament includes words indicating *mens rea* (e.g. 'knowingly', 'intentionally', 'maliciously' or 'permitting'), the offence requires *mens rea* and is not one of strict liability. However, if an Act of Parliament makes it clear that *mens rea* is not required, the offence will be one of strict liability.

However, in many instances a section in an Act of Parliament is silent about the need for *mens rea*. Parliament is criticised for this. If it made clear in all sections which create a criminal offence whether *mens rea* was required or not, then there would be no problem. As it is, where there are no express words indicating *mens rea* or strict liability, the courts have to decide which offences are ones of strict liability.

14.7.2 Principle in *Sweet v Parsley*

Where an Act of Parliament does not include any words indicating *mens rea*, the judges will start by presuming that all criminal offences require *mens rea*. This was made clear in the case of *Sweet v Parsley* (1969).

Key case

Sweet v Parsley (1969)

D rented a farmhouse and let it out to students. The police found cannabis at the farmhouse and D was charged with 'being concerned in the management of premises used for the purpose of smoking cannabis resin'. D did not know that cannabis was being smoked there. It was decided that she was not guilty as the court presumed that the offence required *mens rea*.

The important point of this case is that, in giving judgment, Lord Reid said:

> There has for centuries been a presumption that Parliament did not intend to make criminals of persons who were in no way blameworthy in what they did. That means that whenever a section is silent as to *mens rea* there is a presumption that ... we must read in words appropriate to require *mens rea*.

Although the courts start with the presumption that *mens rea* is required, they look at a variety of points to decide whether the presumption should stand or should be displaced and the offence made one of strict liability.

14.7.3 The *Gammon* tests

In *Gammon (Hong Kong) Ltd v Attorney-General of Hong Kong* (1984) the appellants had been charged with deviating from building work in a material way from the approved plan, contrary to the Hong Kong Building Ordinances. It was necessary to decide whether it had to be proved that they knew that their deviation was material or whether the offence was one of strict liability on this point.

The Privy Council started with the presumption that *mens rea* is required before a person can be held guilty of a criminal offence and that this presumption of *mens rea* applies to statutory offences.

They went on to give four other factors to be considered. These were that:

- The presumption can only be displaced if this is clearly or by necessary implication the effect of the words of the statute.
- The presumption is particularly strong where the offence is 'truly criminal' in character.
- The presumption can only be displaced if the statute is concerned with an issue of social concern such as public safety.

129

- Strict liability should only apply if it will help enforce the law by encouraging greater vigilance to prevent the commission of the prohibited act.

14.7.4 Looking at the wording of an Act

As already stated, where words indicating *mens rea* are used, the offence is not one of strict liability. If the particular section is silent on the point then the courts will look at other sections in the Act. Where the particular offence has no words of intention, but other sections in the Act do, then it is likely that this offence is a strict liability offence.

In *Storkwain* (1986) (see section 14.6), the relevant section, s 58(2) of the Medicines Act 1968, was silent on *mens rea*. The court looked at other sections in the Act and decided that, as there were express provisions for *mens rea* in other sections, Parliament had intended s 58(2) to be one of strict liability.

Where other sections allow for a defence of 'due diligence' but another section does not, then this is another possible indicator from within the statute that the offence is meant to be one of strict liability.

In *Harrow LBC v Shah and Shah* (1999) the defendants were charged under s 13(1)(c) of the National Lottery Act 1993. This subsection does not include any words indicating either that *mens rea* is required or that it is not, nor does it contain any provision for a defence of 'due diligence'. However, another subsection, s 13(1)(a), clearly allows a defence of 'due diligence'. The inclusion of a 'due diligence' defence in subsection (1)(a) of s 13 but not in the subsection under which the defendants were charged, was an important point in the Divisional Court coming to the decision that s 13(1)(c) was an offence of strict liability.

14.7.5 Quasi-criminal offences

In *Gammon* (1984) the Privy Council stated that the presumption that *mens rea* is required is particularly strong where the offence is 'truly criminal' in character. Offences which are regulatory in nature are not thought of as being truly criminal matters and are, therefore, more likely to be interpreted as being of strict liability.

Regulatory offences are also referred to as 'quasi-crimes'. They affect large areas of everyday life. They include offences such as breaches of regulations in a variety of fields such as:
- selling food, as in *Callow v Tillstone* (1900)
- the selling of alcohol, as in *Cundy v le Cocq* (1884)
- building regulations, as occurred in *Gammon* (1984)

- sales of lottery tickets to an under-age child, as in *Harrow LBC v Shah and Shah* (1999) and
- regulations preventing pollution from being caused, as in *Alphacell Ltd v Woodward* (1972).

Key case

Alphacell Ltd v Woodward (1972)

The company was charged with causing polluted matter to enter a river, contrary to s 2(1)(a) of the Rivers (Prevention of Pollution) Act 1951, when pumps which it had installed failed, causing polluted effluent to overflow into a river. There was no evidence either that the company knew of the pollution or that it had been negligent. The offence was held by the House of Lords to be one of strict liability and the company was found guilty because it was of the 'utmost public importance' that rivers should not be polluted.

14.7.6 Penalty of imprisonment

Where an offence carries a penalty of imprisonment, it is more likely to be considered 'truly criminal' and so less likely to be interpreted as an offence of strict liability. This was an important factor in *B v DPP* (2000).

Key case

B v DPP (2000)

D, a 15-year-old boy, asked a 13-year-old girl on a bus to give him a 'shiner' (i.e. have oral sex with him). He believed she was over the age of 14. He was charged with inciting a child under the age of 14 to commit an act of gross indecency, under s 1(1) of the Indecency with Children Act 1960. The House of Lords quashed his conviction, as *mens rea* was required for the offence.

The offence, inciting a child under the age of 14 to commit an act of gross indecency, carried a maximum penalty of two years' imprisonment. Lord Nicholls pointed out that this was a serious offence and that:

the more serious the offence, the greater was the weight to be attached to the presumption [of *mens rea*], because the more severe was the punishment and the graver the stigma that accompanied a conviction.

However, some offences carrying imprisonment have been made strict liability offences. For example in *Storkwain* (1986) (see section 14.6) the offence carried a maximum sentence of two years' imprisonment. Despite this, the House of Lords still held that the offence was one of strict liability.

It appears unjust that an individual should be liable to imprisonment even though the offence does not require proof of any fault by the defendant.

14.7.7 Issues of social concern

The type of crime and whether it is 'truly criminal' are linked to another condition laid down by the case of *Gammon* (1984): that is the question of whether the crime involves an issue of social concern. The Privy Council ruled that the only situation in which the presumption of *mens rea* can be displaced is where the statute is concerned with an issue of social concern.

This allows strict liability to be justified in a wide range of offences, as issues of social concern can be seen to cover any activity which is a 'potential danger to public health, safety or morals'.

Regulations covering health and safety matters in relation to food, drink, pollution, building and road use are obviously issues of social concern, but other issues such as possession of guns are also regarded as matters of public safety.

Even transmitting an unlicensed broadcast has been held to be a matter of social concern. This was decided in *R v Blake* (1997).

Key case

R v Blake (1997)

D was a disc jockey who was convicted of using a station for wireless telegraphy without a licence, contrary to s 1(1) of the Wireless Telegraphy Act 1949. His defence was that he believed he was making a demonstration tape and did not know he was transmitting. He was convicted on the basis that the offence was one of strict liability. He appealed to the Court of Appeal but his appeal was dismissed.

14.7.8 Promoting enforcement of the law

In *Gammon* (1984) the final point in considering whether strict liability should be imposed, even where the statute is concerned with an issue of social concern, was whether it would be effective to promote the objects of the statute by encouraging greater vigilance to prevent the commission of the prohibited act. If the imposition of strict liability will not make the law more effective then there is no reason to make the offence one of strict liability.

In *Lim Chin Aik v The Queen* (1963) the appellant had been convicted under s 6(2) of the Immigration Ordinance of Singapore of remaining (having entered) in Singapore when he had been prohibited from entering by an order made by the minister under s 9 of the same Ordinance.

The Ordinance was aimed at preventing illegal immigration. However, the appellant had no knowledge of the prohibition and there was no evidence that the authorities had even tried to bring it to his attention. The Privy Council thought that it was not enough to be sure that the statute dealt with a grave social evil in order to infer strict liability. It was also important to consider whether the imposition of strict liability would assist in the enforcement of the regulations. If it did not, then the offence should not be one of strict liability.

	Law	Cases
Presumption of *mens rea*	Unless the words make it clear that *mens rea* is not required, the courts will always start with the presumption that *mens rea* is required	*Sweet v Parsley* (1969)
Looking at the rest of the Act	If other subsections state that *mens rea* is required but the section being considered does not state this, it is likely that the offence will be held to be one of strict liability	*Storkwain* (1986)
Quasi-criminal offences	Regulatory crimes (not truly criminal) are *more* likely to be held to be strict liability offences	*Harrow LBC v Shah and Shah* (1999)
Penalty of imprisonment	Where an offence is punishable by imprisonment, it is *less* likely that it will be held to be one of strict liability	*B v DPP* (2000)
Issue of social concern	Where the offence involves potential danger to public health, safety or morals then it is *more* likely to be held to be a strict liability offence	*Blake* (1997)
Would strict liability promote enforcement of the law?	If making the offence one of strict liability would *not* help law enforcement then there is no reason to make the offence a strict liability one	*Lim Chin Aik v The Queen* (1963)

Figure 14.4 How the courts decide whether strict liability applies

Case	Facts	Law/Comment
Pharmaceutical Society of Great Britain v Storkwain Ltd (1986)	Pharmacists did not realise that a prescription was a forgery	Supplying the drugs without a genuine prescription made them guilty of the offence, even though the forgery was very difficult to spot An example of strict liability
R v Larsonneur (1933)	D, having left the UK, was sent back in police custody	Even though her return was not voluntary she was guilty of being 'found in the UK' An example of absolute liability
Callow v Tillstone (1900)	A butcher sold meat that had been passed fit to sell by a vet The meat was found to be unfit	The butcher was guilty even though he was not at fault in any way No defence of no fault
Harrow LBC v Shah and Shah (1999)	Ds had told their staff to ask for proof of age Despite this a lottery ticket was sold to an under-age boy Ds were guilty	The offence was one of strict liability. Ds were guilty even though they had done their best to prevent such an offence happening
Sweet v Parsley (1969)	Tenants in a farmhouse owned by D smoked cannabis there The landlord did not know	D was not guilty as there was a presumption that *mens rea* was required
Alphacell Ltd v Woodward (1972)	Pumps at D's factory failed, causing polluted effluent to overflow into a river There was no evidence either that the company knew of the pollution or that it had been negligent	Ds were guilty because the offence was one of strict liability It was important to protect against pollution
B v DPP (2000)	The conviction of D, a 15-year-old boy, for inciting a child under the age of 14 to commit an act of gross indecency was quashed	*Mens rea* was required for the offence as it carried a maximum penalty of two years' imprisonment

Figure 14.5 Cases on strict liability

14.8 Transferred malice

This is the principle that the defendant can be guilty if he intended to commit a similar crime but against a different victim. An example is aiming a blow at one person with the necessary *mens rea* for an assault causing actual bodily harm, but actually hitting another person. This occurred in *Latimer* (1886).

Key case

Latimer (1886)

D aimed a blow with a belt at a man in a pub because that man had attacked him. The belt bounced off the man and struck a woman in the face. D was guilty of an assault against the woman, although he had not meant to hit her.

Where the *mens rea* is for a completely different type of offence, then the defendant may not be guilty. This was the situation in *Pembliton* (1874), where the defendant threw a stone, intending it to hit people with whom he had been fighting. The stone hit and broke a window. The intention to hit people could not be transferred to the window.

A more recent case on transferred malice is *Gnango* (2011).

Key case

Gnango (2011)

Gnango and another man, known only as 'Bandana Man', shot at each other. Bandana Man hit an innocent passerby and killed her. Gnango was tried and convicted of her murder. The Court of Appeal quashed the conviction but it was reinstated by the Supreme Court. They held he was guilty of the murder of the passerby as, by agreeing to the shoot-out with Bandana Man, he was attempting to murder Bandana Man and also aiding and abetting Bandana Man's attempt to murder him. Bandana Man would have been guilty of the murder of the passerby under the doctrine of transferred malice. This meant that Gnango, because of his participation in the attempted murder of himself, was also guilty of the murder of the passerby under the principle of transferred malice.

14.8.1 General malice

In some cases the defendant may not have a specific victim in mind: for example, a terrorist who plants a bomb in a pub, intending to kill or injure anyone who happens to be there. In this case the defendant's *mens rea* is held to apply to the actual victim.

14.9 Coincidence of *actus reus* and *mens rea*

In order for an offence to take place, both the *actus reus* and the *mens rea* must be present at the same time. For example, if you decide to go round to your next-door neighbour, intending to assault him, but when you get to his house you change your mind and do not actually assault him, you cannot be guilty of an assault even though you had the *mens rea*.

If, two hours later, you are driving your car out of your driveway and knock down your neighbour because you did not see him, you have now done what could be the *actus reus* for an assault. However, you are not guilty of any criminal offence since at the moment you hit your neighbour you did not have the necessary *mens rea*. The *mens rea* and the *actus reus* were not present at the same time.

In *Thabo Meli v R* (1954) the court had to decide whether the *actus reus* and *mens rea* were present together.

Key case

Thabo Meli v R (1954)

Ds attacked a man and believed they had killed him. They then pushed his body over a low cliff. In fact, the man had survived the attack but died of exposure when unconscious at the foot of the cliff. It was held that Ds were guilty of murder.

The defendants in this case were guilty as the required *mens rea* and *actus reus* were combined in a series of acts. A similar situation occurred in *Church* (1965).

Key case

Church (1965)

D had a fight with a woman and knocked her out. He tried, unsuccessfully, for about half an hour to bring her round. He thought she was dead and he put her in the river. She drowned. His conviction for manslaughter was upheld.

14.9.1 Continuing act

Where there is a continuing act for the *actus reus* and at some point while that act is still going on the defendant has the necessary *mens rea*, then the two do coincide and the defendant will be guilty. This may be seen as the mirror image of the *mens rea* and *actus reus* in *Thabo Meli and Church*. This is illustrated by the case of *Fagan v Metropolitan Police Commissioner* (1986).

Key case

Fagan v Metropolitan Police Commissioner (1986)

Fagan was told by a police officer to park by a kerb. In doing this Fagan drove on to the policeman's foot, without realising he had done so. Initially, Fagan refused to move the car. When the policeman pointed out what had happened, he asked Fagan several times to move the car off his foot. Eventually, Fagan did move the car. Fagan was convicted of assaulting the police officer in the execution of his duty.

The Court of Appeal held that once Fagan knew the car was on the police officer's foot he had the required *mens rea*. As the *actus reus* (the car putting force on the foot) was still continuing, the two elements were then present together. The *actus reus* in this case was a continuing act as, so long as the defendant developed the *mens rea* at some time while the act was continuing, then he could be guilty.

In the case of *R v Le Brun* (1991) the defendant knocked his wife unconscious in the course of an argument in the street. While he was trying to drag her body along the street to get her home and avoid detection, he lost his grip. Her head hit the pavement, fracturing her skull and causing her death.

Lord Lane CJ said: 'It seems to us that where the unlawful application of force and the eventual act causing death are parts of the same sequence of events, the same transaction, the fact that there is an appreciable interval of time between the two does not serve to exonerate the defendant from liability. That is certainly so where the appellant's subsequent actions which caused death, after the initial unlawful blow, are designed to conceal his commission of the original unlawful assault.

'It would be possible to express the problem as one of causation. The original unlawful blow to the chin was a *causa sine qua non* of the later *actus reus*. It was the opening event in a series which was to culminate in death: the first link in the chain of causation, to use another metaphor. It cannot be said that the actions of the appellant in dragging the victim away with the intention of evading liability broke the chain which linked the initial blow with the death.'

Activity

Explain in the following situations whether *actus reus* and *mens rea* are present. (Do not forget that there may be transferred malice.)

1 Bart has had an argument with Cara. He aims a punch at her head, but Cara dodges out of the way and Bart hits Homer who was standing behind Cara.
2 Desmond is sitting in a lecture. He pushes his chair back, but does not realise that one of the chair legs is pressing onto Mark's foot. Mark asks Desmond to move the chair, but Desmond thinks what has happened is funny and does not move but sits there laughing for several minutes.
3 Sian throws a stone at a cat. Her aim is very poor and the stone hits Ratinder who is standing several feet away.

Summary

- Different crimes require different levels of *mens rea*.
- Intention is the highest form of *mens rea*:
  - this may be direct intent where D's aim, purpose of desire is to bring about the consequence or
  - it may be oblique where D does not desire the consequence but foresees it as virtually certain
  - foresight of consequences is not the same as intention but it is evidence from which a jury may 'find' intention.
- Subjective recklessness requires proof that D, knowing of the risk, took that risk.
- Negligence is where D fails to meet the standards of the reasonable man.
- Transferred malice is where D intends to commit a crime against one person, but inadvertently commits it against another person.
- There must be coincidence of *actus reus* and *mens rea*: this can be through a continuing act.

Chapter 15

Non-fatal offences against the person

> After reading this chapter you should be able to:
> - Understand the common law offences of assault and battery under s 39 of the Criminal Justice Act 1988
> - Understand assault occasioning actual bodily harm – s 47 OAPA 1861
> - Understand malicious wounding or inflicting grievous bodily harm – s 20 OAPA 1861
> - Understand wounding or causing grievous bodily harm with intent – s 18 OAPA 1861
> - Analyse and evaluate the law on these offences
> - Apply the law to factual situations

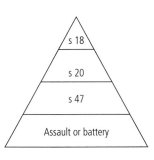

Figure 15.1 The hierarchy of non-fatal offences

15.1 Common assault under s 39 of the Criminal Justice Act 1988

There are two ways of committing common assault:

- assault
- battery.

Assault and battery are common law offences. There is no statutory definition for either assault or for battery. However, statute law recognises their existence as both of these offences are charged under s 39 of the Criminal Justice Act 1988 which sets out

that the maximum punishment for them is six months' imprisonment or a fine of £5,000, or both.

The act involved is different for assault and battery. For assault, there is no touching, only the fear of immediate, unlawful force. For battery, there must be actual force. There are often situations in which both occur, for example where the defendant approaches the victim shouting that he is going to 'get him', then punches the victim in the face. The approaching, shouting and raising his arm prior to the punch constitute an assault, while the punch is the battery. As the act is different for each it is easier to consider assault and battery separately.

15.1.1 Definition of assault

An **assault** is an act which causes the victim to apprehend the infliction of immediate, unlawful force with either an intention to cause another to fear immediate unlawful personal violence or recklessness as to whether such fear is caused.

In *R v Nelson* (2013) the Court of Appeal stated that 'What is required for common assault is for [D] to have done something of a physical kind which causes someone else to apprehend that they are about to be struck'.

Assault – an act which causes the victim to apprehend the infliction of immediate, unlawful force with either an intention to cause another to fear immediate unlawful personal violence or recklessness as to whether such fear is caused.

15.1.2 *Actus reus* of assault

An assault is also known as a technical assault or a psychic assault. There must be:

- an act
- which causes the victim to apprehend the infliction of immediate, unlawful force.

'An act'

An assault requires some act or words. An omission is not sufficient to constitute an assault. However, words are sufficient for an assault. These can be verbal or written. In *R v Constanza* (1997) the Court of Appeal held that letters could be an assault. The defendant had written 800 letters and made a number of phone calls to the victim. The victim interpreted the last two letters as clear threats. The Court of Appeal said there was an assault as there was a 'fear of violence at some time, not excluding the immediate future'.

In *R v Ireland* (1997) it was held that even silent telephone calls can be an assault. It depends on the facts of the case.

'Apprehend immediate unlawful force'

The important point is that the act or words must cause the victim to apprehend that immediate force is going to be used against him. There is no assault if the situation is such that it is obvious that the defendant cannot actually use force. For example, where the defendant shouts threats from a passing train there is no possibility that he can carry out the threats in the immediate future.

It was decided in *R v Lamb* (1967) that pointing an unloaded gun at someone who knows that it is unloaded cannot be an assault. This is because the other person does not fear immediate force. However, if the other person thought the gun was loaded then this could be an assault.

Fear of immediate force is necessary; immediate does not mean instantaneous, but 'imminent', so an

assault can be through a closed window, as in *Smith v Chief Superintendent of Woking Police Station* (1983).

Key case

Smith v Chief Superintendent of Woking Police Station (1983)

D broke into a garden and looked through V's bedroom window on the ground floor at about 11 p.m. one evening. V was terrified and thought that D was about to enter the room. Although D was outside the house and no attack could be made at that immediate moment, the court held that V was frightened by his conduct. The basis of the fear was that she did not know what he was going to do next, but that it was likely to be of a violent nature. Fear of what he might do next was sufficiently immediate for the purposes of the offence.

Words indicating that there will be no violence may prevent an act from being an assault. This is a principle which comes from the old case of *Tuberville v Savage* (1669) where the defendant placed one hand on his sword and said, 'If it were not assize time, I would not take such language from you'. This was held not to be an assault, because what he said showed he was not going to do anything.

However, it will depend on all the circumstances. For example, in *R v Light* (1857) the defendant raised a sword above the head of his wife and said, 'Were it not for the bloody policeman outside, I would split your head open.' It was held that this was an assault. The wife feared that force was going to be used on her and the words in the circumstances were not enough to negate that fear.

Fear of any unwanted touching is sufficient: the force or unlawful personal violence which is feared need not be serious.

There are many examples of assault:

- raising a fist as though about to hit the victim
- throwing a stone at the victim which just misses
- pointing a loaded gun at someone within range
- making a threat by saying 'I am going to hit you'.

Unlawfulness of the force

The force which is threatened must be unlawful. If it is lawful, there is no offence of common assault. Whether force is lawful or unlawful is discussed in detail under the *actus reus* of battery in the next section.

15.1.3 *Mens rea* of assault

The *mens rea* for an assault is either an intention to cause another to fear immediate unlawful personal violence, or recklessness as to whether such fear is caused.

The test for recklessness is subjective; the defendant must realise there is a risk that his acts/words could cause another to fear unlawful personal violence.

15.1.4 Definition of battery

Battery is the application of unlawful force to another person intending either to apply unlawful physical force to another or being recklessness as to whether unlawful force is applied.

> ### Key term 🔑
>
> **Battery** – the application of unlawful force to another person intending either to apply unlawful physical force to another or recklessness as to whether unlawful force is applied.

15.1.5 *Actus reus* of battery

The *actus reus* of battery is the application of unlawful force to another person. Force is a slightly misleading word as it can include the slightest touching, as shown by the case of *Collins v Wilcock* (1984).

> ### Key case
>
> #### *Collins v Wilcock* (1984)
>
> Two police officers saw two women apparently soliciting for the purposes of prostitution. They asked the appellant to get into the police car for questioning but she refused and walked away.
>
> As she was not known to the police, one of the officers walked after her to try to find out her identity. She refused to speak to the officer and again walked away. The officer then took hold of her by the arm to prevent her leaving. She became abusive and scratched the officer's arm. She was convicted of assaulting a police officer in the execution of his duty. She appealed against that conviction on the basis that the officer was not acting in the execution of his duty, but was acting unlawfully by holding her arm as the officer was not arresting her. The court held that the officer had committed a battery and the defendant was entitled to free herself.

In this case, the court pointed out that touching a person to get his attention was acceptable, provided that no greater degree of physical contact was used than was necessary. However, physical restraint was not acceptable.

A similar point arose in *Wood v DPP* (2008) where a police officer took hold of Wood's arm to check his identity.

> ### Key case
>
> #### *Wood (Fraser) v DPP* (2008)
>
> The police had received a report that a man named Fraser had thrown an ashtray at another person in a public house. The ashtray had missed the person but had been smashed. Three police officers went to the scene. They saw a man (the appellant, W) who fitted the description of 'Fraser' leave the public house. One of the police officers took hold of W by the arm and asked if he was Fraser. W denied this and struggled, trying to pull away. At that point another officer took hold of W's other arm. W was charged with assaulting two of the police officers while they were acting in the execution of their duty.
>
> The police officer who had first caught hold of W's arm said that he had done this in order to detain W, but was not at that point arresting him. It was held that as the officer had not arrested W, there was a technical assault (battery) by the police officers. This meant that W was entitled to struggle and was not guilty of any offence of assault against the police.

Even touching the victim's clothing can be sufficient to form a battery. In *R v Thomas* (1985) the defendant touched the bottom of a woman's skirt and rubbed it. The Court of Appeal said, *obiter*, 'There could be no dispute that if you touch a person's clothes while he is wearing them that is equivalent to touching him'.

Continuing act

A battery may be committed through a continuing act, as in *Fagan v Metropolitan Police Commissioner* (1968) where the defendant parked his car with one of the tyres on a police officer's foot. When he parked he was unaware that he had done this, but when the police officer asked him to remove it, he refused to do so for several minutes. The court said that at the start there was an act which could be a battery but the full offence of battery was not committed at that point because there was no element of intention. However, it became an offence of battery the moment the intention was formed to leave the wheel on the officer's foot.

Indirect act

A battery can also be through an indirect act such as a booby trap. In this situation the defendant causes force to be applied, even though he does not personally touch the victim. This occurred in *R v Martin* (1881) where the defendant placed an iron bar across the doorway of a theatre. He then switched off the lights. In the panic which followed several of the audience were injured when they were trapped and unable to open the door. Martin was convicted of an offence under s 20 of the Offences Against the Person Act (OAPA) 1861.

A more modern example is *DPP v K* (1990).

Key case

DPP v K (1990)

D was a 15-year-old schoolboy who took sulphuric acid without permission from his science lesson, to try its reaction on some toilet paper. While he was in the toilet he heard footsteps in the corridor, panicked and put the acid into a hot-air hand drier to hide it. He returned to his class intending to remove the acid later. Before he could do so another pupil used the drier and was sprayed by the acid. D was charged with assault occasioning actual bodily harm (s 47). The magistrates acquitted him because he said he had not intended to hurt anyone (see section 15.2.3 for the *mens rea* of s 47). The prosecution appealed, by way of case stated, to the Queen's Bench Divisional Court which held that a common assault (which includes both an assault and a battery) could be committed by an indirect act.

Another example of indirect force occurred in *Haystead v Chief Constable of Derbyshire* (2000) where the defendant caused a small child to fall to the floor by punching the woman holding the child. The defendant was found guilty because he was reckless as to whether or not his acts would injure the child. It is worth noting that, in this case, the conviction could also be justified by the principle of transferred malice.

Omissions

Criminal liability can arise by way of an omission, but only if the defendant is under a duty to act. Such a duty can arise out of a contract, a relationship, from the assumption of care for another or from the creation of a dangerous situation. As the *actus reus* of battery is the application of unlawful force it is difficult to think how examples could arise under these duty situations, but there has been one reported case, *DPP v Santa-Bermudez* (2003).

Key case

DPP v Santa-Bermudez (2003)

In this case a policewoman, before searching D's pockets, asked him if he had any needles or other sharp objects on him. D said 'no', but when the police officer put her hand in his pocket she was injured by a needle which caused bleeding. The Divisional Court held that the defendant's failure to tell her of the needle could amount to the *actus reus* for the purposes of an assault causing actual bodily harm.

Other scenarios which could make a defendant liable by way of omission are where the defendant has created a dangerous situation which may lead to force being applied to the victim. This can be seen by analogy with *R v Miller* (1983) where D accidentally set fire to his mattress but failed to do anything to prevent damage to the building in which he was sleeping. He was convicted of arson.

No other person was involved, but if there had been someone else asleep in the room and Miller had failed to wake him and warn him of the danger, then he could have been liable for a battery if there had been any problem. For example, if the person was hit by plaster falling from the ceiling as a result of the fire, then there appears to be no reason why Miller could not have been charged with battery of that person.

Unlawful force

For a battery to be committed, the force must be unlawful. If the victim gives genuine consent to it then the force may be lawful. Force may also be lawful where it is used in self-defence or prevention of crime. This can only be so if the force used is reasonable in the situation as the defendant believed it to be. If the force is lawful, then the person using the force is not guilty of a battery.

Another situation where force may be lawful is in the correction of a child by a parent. English law recognises that moderate and reasonable physical chastisement of a child is lawful. However, in *A v UK* (1998) where a jury had acquitted a father who had beaten his son with a garden cane, the European Court of Human Rights ruled that a law allowing force to be used on children offends Article 3 of the European Convention on Human Rights. This article prohibits torture and inhuman or degrading treatment of punishment.

However, the Children Act 2004 now provides that a battery committed on a child is unlawful if it results in any injury.

Battery without an assault

It is possible for there to be a battery even though there is no assault. This can occur where the victim is unaware that unlawful force is about to be used on him, such as where the attacker comes up unseen behind the victim's back. The first thing the victim knows is when he is struck; there has been a battery but no assault.

Activity

Explain whether there is an assault and/or battery in the following situations.

1 At a party Tanya sneaks up behind Wilhelm, whom she knows well, and slaps him on the back.
2 Vince throws a stone at Delyth, but misses. He picks up another stone and this time hits the edge of Delyth's coat.
3 Imram turns round quickly without realising that Harry is standing just behind him, and bumps into Harry. Harry shouts at him, 'If you were not wearing glasses, I would hit you in the face.'
4 Ramsey and Sue are having an argument. During the argument, Ramsey says, 'If you don't shut up, I'll thump you.' Sue is so annoyed at this that she gets out a penknife and waves it in front of Ramsey's face. Ramsay pushes her away.

15.1.6 *Mens rea* of battery

The *mens rea* for battery is either an intention to apply unlawful physical force to another or recklessness as to whether unlawful force is applied.

For a battery the defendant must realise there is a risk that his act (or omission) could cause unlawful force to be applied to another.

Case	Facts	Law
Constanza (1997)	D wrote 800 letters and made phone calls to V	Written words can be an assault if they cause V to fear immediate violence
Smith v Chief Superintendent (Woking) (1983)	D looked through V's bedroom window late at night	Fear of what D would do next was sufficient for the *actus reus* of assault
Tuberville v Savage (1669)	D put hand on sword and said 'Were it not assize time, I would not take such language from you'	Words can prevent an act from being an assault, but it depends on the circumstances
Collins v Wilcock (1984)	A police officer held a woman's arm to prevent her walking away	Any touching may be a battery, and always is if there was physical restraint
Wood (Fraser) v DPP (2008)	An officer took hold of W's arm to check his identity	This was a battery by the police and W was entitled to struggle to release himself
Fagan v MPC (1968)	D, unknowingly, stopped his car with a wheel on a policeman's foot and refused to move when requested	The *actus reus* of assault can be an ongoing act so that the complete offence is committed when D forms the *mens rea*
DPP v K (1990)	D put acid in a hand drier – the next person to use it was sprayed with acid	An indirect act can be the *actus reus* of assault
DPP v Santa-Bermudez (2003)	D failed to tell a policewoman that he had a needle in his pocket – she was injured when she searched him	An omission is sufficient for the *actus reus* of assault

Figure 15.2 Cases on assault and battery

15.2 Section 47 OAPA 1861: assault occasioning actual bodily harm

We now look at assaults where an injury is caused. The lowest level of injury is referred to in the Offences Against the Person Act 1861 as 'actual bodily harm' under s 47. It is a triable-either-way offence. The section states:

> Whosoever shall be convicted of any assault occasioning actual bodily harm shall be liable ... to imprisonment for five years.

As can be seen from this very brief section, there is no definition of 'assault' or 'actual bodily harm'. Nor is there any reference to the level of *mens rea* required. For all these points it is necessary to look at case law.

15.2.1 Definition of assault occasioning actual bodily harm

An assault occasioning actual bodily harm is an assault or battery which causes actual bodily harm. It must be done with the intention of causing the victim to fear unlawful force, or with the intention of subjecting the victim to unlawful force, or being subjectively reckless as to whether the victim fears or is subjected to unlawful force.

15.2.2 *Actus reus* of s 47

It is necessary to prove that there was an assault or battery and that this caused actual bodily harm.

Actual bodily harm

In *Miller* (1954) it was said that actual bodily harm is 'any hurt or injury calculated to interfere with the health or comfort of the victim'. In *T v DPP* (2003) loss of consciousness, even momentarily, was held to be actual bodily harm.

Key case

T v DPP (2003)

D and a group of other youths chased V. V fell to the ground and saw D coming towards him. V covered his head with his arms and was kicked. He momentarily lost consciousness and remembered nothing until being woken by a police officer. D was convicted of assault occasioning actual bodily harm.

So, s 47 can be charged where there is any injury. Bruising, grazes and scratches all come within this offence. As we have seen in *T v DPP* (2003) it was held that loss of consciousness, even for a very short time, could be actual bodily harm. In *DPP v Smith (Michael)* (2006) it was held that cutting the victim's hair can amount to actual bodily harm.

Key case

DPP v Smith (Michael) (2006)

The defendant had had an argument with his girlfriend. He cut off her ponytail and some hair from the top of her head without her consent. He was charged with an offence under s 47 of the Offences Against the Person Act 1861. The magistrates found there was no case to answer as they thought that cutting hair could not amount to actual bodily harm. The prosecution appealed and the Divisional Court held that cutting off a substantial amount of hair could be actual bodily harm.

In *Smith* the court held that physical pain was not a necessary ingredient of actual bodily harm. Hair is attached to the head and this makes it a part of the body so that harm to the hair comes within the meaning of 'actual bodily harm'. However, the court did stress that a substantial amount of hair has to be cut off for the harm to be 'actual' as opposed to trivial or insignificant harm.

Actual bodily harm: psychiatric injury

Psychiatric injury is also classed as 'actual bodily harm'. This was decided by the Court of Appeal in *R v Chan Fook* (1994). However, they pointed out that actual bodily harm does not include 'mere emotions such as fear, distress or panic' nor does it include 'states of mind that are not themselves evidence of some identifiable clinical condition'.

This decision was approved by the House of Lords in *R v Burstow* (1997) where it was said that 'bodily harm' in ss 18, 20 and 47 OAPA 1861 must be interpreted so as to include recognisable psychiatric illness.

15.2.3 *Mens rea* of s 47

The section in the Act makes no reference to *mens rea* but, as the essential element is assault or battery, the courts have held that the *mens rea* for the underlying assault or battery is sufficient for the *mens rea* of a s 47 offence.

This means the defendant must, for example, intend or be subjectively reckless as to whether the victim fears or is subjected to unlawful force. This is the same *mens rea* as for an assault or a battery. It is important to note that there is no need for the defendant to intend or be reckless as to whether actual bodily harm

is caused. This is demonstrated by the case of *R v Roberts* (1971).

Key case

R v Roberts (1971)

D, who was driving a car, made advances to the girl in the passenger seat and tried to take her coat off. She feared that he was going to commit a more serious assault and jumped from the car while it was travelling at about 30 miles per hour. As a result of this she was slightly injured. D was found guilty of assault occasioning actual bodily harm even though he had not intended any injury or realised there was a risk of injury. He had intended to apply unlawful force when he touched her as he tried to take her coat off. This satisfied the *mens rea* for a common assault and so he was guilty of an offence under s 47.

This decision was confirmed by the House of Lords in the combined appeals of *R v Savage* (1991) and *R v Parmenter* (1991).

Key case

R v Savage (1991)

D threw beer over another woman in a pub. In doing this the glass slipped from D's hand and V's hand was cut by the glass. D said that she had only intended to throw beer over the woman. D had not intended her to be injured, nor had she realised that there was a risk of injury. She was convicted of a s 20 offence but the Court of Appeal quashed that and substituted a conviction under s 47 (assault occasioning actual bodily harm). She appealed against this to the House of Lords. The Law Lords dismissed her appeal.

The fact that she intended to throw the beer over the other woman meant she had the intention to apply unlawful force and this was sufficient for the *mens rea* of the s 47 offence.

From all these cases, we can now get a definition for an *assault occasioning actual bodily harm* which is given below.

Key term

Assault occasioning actual bodily harm – an assault which causes V actual bodily harm and D intends or is subjectively reckless as to whether the victim fears unlawful force or is actually subjected to unlawful force.

Offence	Actus reus	Consequence (injury) required	Mens rea
Assault	Causing V to fear immediate unlawful violence. Requires an act but can be by silent telephone calls: *Ireland* (1997), or letters: *Constanza* (1997)	None needed	Intention of, or subjective reckless as to, causing V to fear immediate unlawful violence
Battery	Application of unlawful violence, even the slightest touching: *Collins v Wilcock* (1984)	None needed	Intention of, or subjective reckless as to, applying unlawful force
Assault occasioning actual bodily harm s 47 OAPA 1861	Assault, i.e. an assault or battery	Actual bodily harm (e.g. bruising) This includes: <ul><li>momentary loss of consciousness: *R(T) v DPP* (2003)</li><li>psychiatric harm: *Chan Fook* (1994)</li></ul>	Intention or subjective recklessness as to causing fear of unlawful violence or of applying unlawful force, i.e. the *mens rea* for an assault or battery

Figure 15.3 Assault, battery and s 47

15.3 Section 20 OAPA 1861: malicious wounding/ inflicting grievous bodily harm

This is the next offence in seriousness. It is an offence under s 20 OAPA 1861 which states:

> Whosoever shall unlawfully and maliciously wound or inflict any grievous bodily harm upon any other person, either with or without a weapon or instrument, shall be guilty of an offence and shall be liable ... to imprisonment for not more than five years.

There are two offences: malicious wounding and inflicting grievous bodily harm. S 20 is triable either way and the maximum sentence is five years. This is the same maximum sentence as for a s 47 offence, despite the fact that s 20 is seen as a more serious offence and requires both a higher degree of injury and *mens rea* as to an injury.

For the offence to be proved it must be shown that the defendant:

- wounded OR
- inflicted grievous bodily harm

and that he did this:

- intending some injury (but not serious injury) be caused OR
- being reckless as to whether any injury was inflicted.

15.3.1 What is a wound?

'Wound' means a cut or a break in the continuity of the whole skin. A cut of internal skin, such as in the cheek, is sufficient, but internal bleeding where there is no cut of the skin is not sufficient. In *JJC v Eisenhower* (1983) the victim was hit in the eye by a shotgun pellet. This did not penetrate the eye but did cause severe bleeding under the surface. As there was no cut, it was held that this was not a wound. The cut must be of the whole skin, so that a scratch is not considered a wound.

Even a broken bone is not considered a wound, unless the skin is broken as well. In the old case of *R v Wood* (1830) the victim's collar bone was broken but, as the skin was intact, it was held there was no wound.

15.3.2 What is grievous bodily harm?

Grievous bodily harm means really serious harm, which may be physical, psychiatric or by deliberate infection with a serious disease. This has developed over recent years to ensure that convictions can be achieved.

It was held in *DPP v Smith* (1961) that grievous bodily harm means 'really serious harm'. The harm does not have to be life-threatening and in *Saunders* (1985) it was held that it was permissible to direct a jury that there need be 'serious harm' not including the word 'really'.

In *R v Bollom* (2004) it was held that the severity of the injuries should be assessed according to the victim's age and health.

Key case

R v Bollom (2004)

A 17-month-old child had bruising to her abdomen, both arms and left leg. D was convicted of causing grievous bodily harm. The Court of Appeal quashed his conviction and substituted a conviction for assault occasioning actual bodily harm. However, the Court of Appeal stated that bruising could amount to grievous bodily harm.

However, bruising of this severity would be less serious on an adult in full health than on a very young child.

In *R v Burstow* (1997) where the victim of a stalker suffered a severe depressive illness as a result of his conduct, it was decided that serious psychiatric injury can be grievous bodily harm.

In *R v Dica* (2004) there was the first ever conviction for causing grievous bodily harm through infecting victims with the HIV virus.

Key case

R v Dica (2004)

The defendant had had unprotected sex with two women without telling them he was HIV-positive. Both women became infected as a result. Although on appeal the defendant's conviction was quashed on the question of consent and the case sent for re-trial, there was no doubt that infecting someone with HIV was inflicting grievous bodily harm. At his re-trial the defendant was convicted.

15.3.3 Inflicting grievous bodily harm

Section 20 uses the word 'inflict'. Originally, this was taken as meaning that there had to be a technical assault or battery. Even so it allowed the section to be interpreted quite widely, as shown in *R v Lewis* (1974) where D shouted threats at his wife through a closed door in a second-floor flat and tried to break his way through the door. The wife was so frightened that she jumped from the window and broke both her legs. D was convicted of a s 20 offence. The threats could be considered as a technical assault.

In *R v Burstow* (1997) it was decided that 'inflict' does not require a technical assault or a battery.

Key case

R v Burstow (1997)

D carried out an eight-month campaign of harassment against a woman with whom he had had a brief relationship some three years earlier. The harassment consisted of both silent and abusive telephone calls, hate mail and stalking. This caused V to suffer from severe depression. D's conviction under s 20 OAPA 1861 was upheld by the House of Lords.

This means that it need only be shown that the defendant's actions have led to the consequence of the victim suffering grievous bodily harm. The decision also means that there now appears to be little, if any, difference in the *actus reus* of the offences under s 20 and s 18 which uses the word 'cause'. In fact, in *R v Burstow* (1997) Lord Hope said that for all practical purposes there was no difference between the two words.

15.3.4 *Mens rea* of s 20

The word used in the section is 'maliciously'. In *Cunningham* (1957) it was held that 'maliciously' did not require any ill will towards the person injured. It simply meant either:

- an intention to do the particular kind of harm that was in fact done or
- recklessness as to whether such harm should occur or not (i.e. the accused has foreseen that the particular kind of harm might be done, and yet gone on to take the risk of it).

In *R v Parmenter* (1991) the House of Lords confirmed that the *Cunningham* meaning of recklessness applies to all offences in which the statutory definition uses the word 'maliciously'. So, for the *mens rea* of s 20 the prosecution can prove either that the defendant intended to cause another person some harm or that he was subjectively reckless as to whether another person suffered some harm.

This left another point which the courts had to resolve. What was meant by the particular kind of harm? Does the defendant need to realise the risk of a wound or grievous bodily harm? It was decided by the House of Lords in *Parmenter* that, although the *actus reus* of s 20 requires a wound or grievous bodily harm, there is no need for the defendant to foresee this level of serious injury.

Key case

R v Parmenter (1991)

D injured his three-month-old baby when he threw the child in the air and caught him. D said that he had often done this with slightly older children and did not realise that there was risk of any injury. He was convicted of an offence under s 20. The House of Lords quashed this conviction as there was no evidence that he foresaw any injury, but substituted a conviction for assault occasioning actual bodily harm under s 47.

This decision means that, although there are four offences which appear to be on a ladder in terms of seriousness, there is overlap in terms of the *mens rea*.

Tip

When explaining recklessness with respect to assault, battery, s 47 or s 20, make sure you explain it as recklessness as to the relevant consequence. So, for assault, causing V to fear immediate unlawful violence; for battery it is as to applying unlawful force; for s 47 it is the same as for the underlying assault or battery; for s 20 it is as to some harm.

15.4 Section 18 OAPA 1861: wounding or causing grievous bodily harm with intent

This offence under s 18 OAPA 1861 is often referred to as 'wounding with intent'. In fact, it covers a much wider range of offences than this implies.

It is considered a much more serious offence than s 20, as can be seen from the difference in the maximum punishments. Section 20 has a maximum of five years' imprisonment whereas the maximum for s 18 is life imprisonment. Also, s 20 is triable either way but s 18 must be tried on indictment at the Crown Court. The definition in OAPA 1861 states:

> 'Whosoever shall unlawfully and maliciously by any means whatsoever wound or cause any grievous bodily harm to any person, with intent to do some grievous bodily harm to any person, or with intent to resist or prevent the lawful apprehension or detainer of any person, shall be guilty of ... an offence.'

15.4.1 *Actus reus* of s 18

This can be committed in two ways:

- wounding or
- causing grievous bodily harm.

The meanings of 'wound' and 'grievous bodily harm' are the same as for s 20. The word 'cause' is very wide so that it is only necessary to prove that the defendant's act was a substantial cause of the wound or grievous bodily harm.

15.4.2 *Mens rea* of s 18

This is a specific intent offence. The defendant must be proved to have intended to:

- do some grievous bodily harm or
- resist or prevent the lawful apprehension or detainer of any person.

Note that an intention to wound is not enough for the *mens rea* of s 18. This was clearly stated in *R v Taylor* (2009).

Key case

R v Taylor (2009)

V was found with scratches across his face and a stab wound in his back. Photographs of the scratches showed no more than surface scratches and it was impossible to tell the depth of the wound. The medical evidence did not help in showing whether D had intended to cause really serious injury. The judge directed that the jury must be sure that the prosecution had proved that D had intended to cause grievous bodily harm or to wound. D was convicted of an s 18 offence. On appeal, the Court of Appeal quashed the conviction on the basis that the judge had misdirected the jury. An intention to wound was not sufficient for the *mens rea* of s 18. Instead the Court of Appeal substituted a conviction for s 20.

Intent to do some grievous bodily harm

Although the word 'maliciously' appears in s 18, it has been held that this adds nothing to the *mens rea* of this section where grievous bodily harm is intended. The important point is that s 18 is a specific intent crime. Intention must be proved; recklessness is not enough for the *mens rea* of s 18. 'Intention' has the same meaning as shown in the leading cases on murder.

Offence	*Actus reus*	Consequence (injury) required	*Mens rea*
Maliciously wounding or inflicting grievous bodily harm **s 20 OAPA 1861**	A direct or indirect act or omission: *Martin* (1881) No need to prove an assault: *Burstow* (1998)	Either a wound – a cutting of the whole skin: *JJC v Eisenhower* (1984) OR Grievous bodily harm (really serious harm) which includes psychiatric harm: *Burstow* (1998)	Intention or subjective recklessness as to causing some injury (though not serious): *Parmenter* (1991)
Wounding or causing grievous bodily harm with intent **s 18 OAPA 1861**	A direct or indirect act or omission which causes V's injury	A wound or grievous bodily harm (as above)	Specific intention to cause grievous bodily harm OR Specific intention to resist or prevent arrest plus recklessness as to causing injury: *Morrison* (1989)

Figure 15.4 Sections 20 and 18

So, as decided in *Moloney* (1985), foresight of consequences is not intention; it is only evidence from which intention can be inferred or found. Following the cases of *Nedrick* (1986) and *Woollin* (1998), intention cannot be found unless the harm caused was a virtual certainty as a result of the defendant's actions and the defendant realised that this was so.

See section 14.3 for a fuller discussion on these cases and the meaning of 'intention'.

Where the defendant is trying to resist or prevent arrest or detention then the level of intention regarding the injury is lower. The prosecution must prove that he had specific intention to resist or prevent arrest, but so far as the injury it needs only prove that he was reckless as to whether his actions would cause a wound or injury. This was decided in *R v Morrison* (1989).

Key case

R v Morrison (1989)

A police officer seized hold of D and told him that she was arresting him. He dived through a window, dragging her with him as far as the window so that her face was badly cut by the glass. The Court of Appeal held that as the word 'maliciously' is used in respect of this part of the section it must have the same meaning as in *Cunningham* (1957). This means that the prosecution must prove that the defendant either intended injury or realised there was a risk of injury and took that risk.

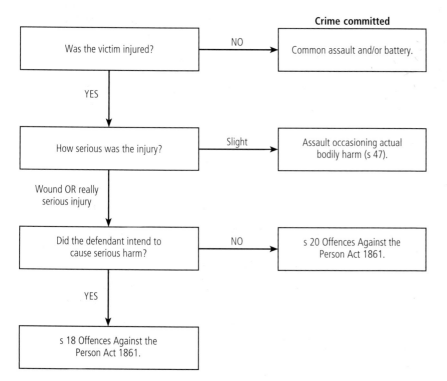

Figure 15.5 Flowchart on offences against the person

Activity

Explain in each of the situations below, what type of offence may have been committed.

1 In a football match Billy is kicked by Rio as Rio tries to get control of the ball. This causes bruising to Billy's leg. Billy is annoyed at this and punches Rio in the face causing a cut to his lip.
2 Anish is walking along a canal bank. Carol is in a hurry and pushes past him, knocking him into the canal. Anish hits his head on the side and suffers a fractured skull.
3 A police officer sees Jason damaging a parked car. The officer puts his hand on Jason's shoulder and says 'I am arresting you for criminal damage.' Jason punches the officer hard in the face breaking his jaw. Jason then runs off.
4 Karl waves a knife at Lily, saying 'I am going to cut that silly smile off.' Lily is very frightened and faints. She falls against Mary, who is knocked to the ground and suffers bruising.

15.5 Evaluation of non-fatal offences against the person

In the 1980s and 1990s many reports on this area of law were published. All of these emphasised the need for reform. They included:

- 'Criminal Law Revision Committee, Fourteenth Report, Offences Against the Person' (1980)
- 'Legislating the Criminal Code: Offences Against the Person and General Principles, Law Commission Report' (1993)
- 'Violence: Reforming the Offences Against the Person Act 1861', Home Office Consultation Paper with draft Bill (1998)
- 'Reform of Offences Against the Person', Law Commission (2015) Law Com No. 361.

None of these Reports, or the draft Bill have been implemented. It has not been seen as a government priority despite assertions by various Home Secretaries that it was a priority. The 2015 report sets out 28 main recommendations. It will be interesting to see if these latest proposals are adopted.

The reasons for the need for reform can be considered under a number of headings:

- The Offences Against the Person Act 1861 is out of date
- The different offences show inconsistencies between them
- There is no conformity with the correspondence principle
- Much of the language used is archaic.

15.5.1 Out of date

The 1861 Act is over 150 years old. This has caused a number of problems. For example, when it was created people did not have the understanding of mental health problems that we have today. So the Act only referred to 'bodily' harm in the offences and did not mention any mental harm.

As a result, for some time it was not sure that the offences could include those where the victim had suffered mental harm. To fill this gap in the law, the courts in *Chan Fook* (1994) and *Burstow* (1997) held that the meaning of 'bodily harm' did include injury to mental health. Since then defendants causing such injury can be convicted of offences under the 1861 Act.

Another area which has created problems is whether inflicting bodily harm could cover the situation of infecting another person with a disease. In 1861 there was only limited understanding of how some diseases were transmitted from person to person. The idea that a criminal offence could be committed by infecting someone with a disease was certainly not thought of then. Again the courts filled this gap by ruling in *Dica* (2004) that infecting someone with HIV did come within the wording of inflicting grievous bodily harm.

15.5.2 Inconsistency between offences

There are inconsistencies in the Act, especially with regard to the *mens rea* required for each offence. In particular, s 47 has the same *mens rea* as for an assault or battery. It does not require the defendant to intend or even realise that there is a risk of any injury. This appears unjust as s 47 carries a maximum sentence of five years' imprisonment while assault and battery only carry a maximum of six months' imprisonment.

It is also unjust that a person who causes a small cut can be charged with the more serious offence of s 20 instead of the offence of 'occasioning actual bodily harm' under s 47. This is because s 20 refers to 'wound or grievous bodily harm'. Yet clearly there are different levels of wound, and many of them do not equate with grievous bodily harm.

Another inconsistency is that the maximum sentence for both s 47 and s 20 offences is the same (five years' imprisonment). Yet the s 20 offence is clearly more serious than s 47 as it requires more serious injury. It also requires that D intends or is reckless as to causing V some harm whereas for s 47 it is not necessary to prove that D intended or was reckless as to whether he would cause some harm to V. It seems unjust that these two offences carry the same maximum penalty when the levels of blameworthiness are so different.

The 2015 Report points out that the above problems mean there is no clear hierarchy of offences.

Yet another inconsistency in the 1861 Act is that a defendant who intends or foresees the risk of minor injury, can be convicted of the very serious offence of s 18 if serious injury occurs when he intends to resist arrest. This is the effect of the decision in *Morrison* (1989) (see section 15.4.2). Is it right that by intending to resist arrest, the defendant becomes liable for the same offence as someone who has intended to cause very serious injuries?

15.5.3 Correspondence principle

The 2015 Report also points out that the offences in the Act do not conform to the 'correspondence principle'. Under this principle the results which D must intend or foresee should match the results which actually occur. D should not be held liable for a given kind and level of harm unless he meant to do it or at least knowingly ran the risk of it.

Under the 1861 Act a defendant can be guilty of a s 20 offence without intending or being reckless as to causing serious harm. Equally a defendant can be guilty of a s 47 offence without intending or being reckless as to causing any harm. Both these are clear breaches of the correspondence principle.

15.5.4 Need for modern, simplified language

Section 20 uses the word 'maliciously'. In modern language today, the word 'maliciously' suggests acting deliberately and with ill-will to the victim. Yet the meaning of the word in the 1861 Act has been held to be that D either intended to do the type of harm that was done or was reckless as to whether that type of harm occurred (see *Cunningham* (1957)). The Law Commission has recommended that the word 'reckless' should be used.

The Act is not consistent in that for s 20 the word 'inflict' is used, yet for s 18 the word 'cause' is used.

This led to considerable debate as to whether the word 'inflict' in s 20 meant that a technical assault had to take place. This was finally resolved by the case of *Burstow* (1997) (see section 15.3.3) in which the House of Lords ruled that it did not.

15.5.5 The 1998 draft Bill

In 1998 the Home Office issued a Consultation Document, 'Violence: Reforming the Offences Against the Person Act 1861'. This included a draft Bill which set out four main offences. These were intended to replace ss 18, 20, 47 and assault and battery. In order the clauses of the draft Bill, starting with the most serious are:

Clause 1

Intentional serious injury: where a person would be guilty if he intentionally caused serious injury to another.

Clause 2

Reckless serious injury: where a person would be guilty if he recklessly caused serious injury to another.

Clause 3

Intentional or reckless injury: where a person would be guilty if he intentionally or recklessly caused injury to another.

Clause 4

Assault: a person would be guilty if he intentionally or recklessly:

a applied force to or caused an impact on the body of another or

b caused the other to believe that any such force or impact is imminent.

In each of these the level of injury and the required *mens rea* are made clear by the wording. In addition, the draft Bill also defined the word 'injury', making it clear that both physical and mental injury were included.

15.5.6 Law Commission Report 2015

This Report set out several recommendations. The first one is that OAPA 1861 should be replaced by a 'comprehensive modern statute'.

Any new statute should respect the following principles:

● It should provide a clear hierarchy of offences from the most serious to the least. The place of each offence in the hierarchy should reflect:

- the harm caused
- the culpability of the defendant and
- the maximum penalty should be in proportion.
- Each offence should provide a clear and accurate label for the conduct in question and should be defined in language that is easy to understand.
- Each ingredient of an offence, whether an external element or a mental element, should be set out explicitly.

The Report also recommended that any new statute on crimes of violence should follow the scheme of the 1998 draft Bill, though it has also suggested some additions and modifications.

Draft Bill clauses 1–3

Clause 1 above would become the definition of the most serious non-fatal offence against the person replacing the present s 18 offence. The word 'wounding' is not used so that it would only be included if the wound caused a serious injury. The offence would carry a maximum sentence of life imprisonment.

Clause 2 would replace the existing s 20 offence. Under it the normal principles of recklessness would apply. So a defendant would only be guilty if he was aware, in the circumstances as he knew or believed them to be, that there was a risk of serious injury. This is a higher level of *mens rea* required than under the present s 20 where the defendant can be guilty if he is reckless about any injury (including minor injury) occurring. The recommendation is that this offence should carry a maximum sentence of seven years imprisonment (an increase on the present five years). This is justified because of the higher level of *mens rea* required by Clause 2.

Clause 3 would replace the existing s 47 offence. The defendant would be guilty if he intentionally or recklessly caused an injury to another person. The injury need not be serious. This offence would carry a maximum sentence of five years' imprisonment (the same as the present s 47).

For all of these three offences, injury would include both physical and mental illness. Mental injury should have the same limits as the existing law, namely recognised psychiatric conditions. Disease would still be considered a physical injury as in the case of *Dica* (2004) (see section 15.3.2). So a defendant who recklessly transmitted HIV could be charged with the offence in Clause 2, while a defendant who recklessly transmitted a less serious sexual disease could be charged under Clause 3.

Aggravated assault

The 2015 Report also recommended that there should be another offence where low-level injuries are involved. This would be 'aggravated assault'. The intention is that it should cover injuries such as superficial cuts, scratches, minor bruising, grazes and swellings. Although these are technically 'actual bodily harm' in the present law, the Crown Prosecution Service charging standards recommend that they should currently be charged as common assault.

The proposed new offence recognises that victims who have suffered a low-level injury can feel aggrieved when their case is only charged as a common assault. The *mens rea* would be the same as for the current common assault: that is that D must intend or be reckless as to whether V is put in fear of unlawful force or is subjected to unlawful force.

The Report recommends that this offence should have a maximum of 12 months' imprisonment.

Physical assault

The 2015 Report recommends that there should be an offence of physical assault to replace the common law battery. This should not be used for low-level injury, as happens at present. These would come under the aggravated assault offence. It would be where there is unwanted and unjustifiable touching of the victim, either direct physical contact between D and V or by D causing some object to come into contact with V such as throwing a stone or setting a trap.

The *mens rea* would be the same as for the current offence of common assault: that is that D must intend or be reckless as to whether V is put in fear of unlawful force or is subjected to unlawful force. The Report recommends that this offence should have a maximum of six months' imprisonment, the same as for the current offence of battery.

Threatened assault

The 2015 Report recommends that there should be an offence of threatened assault to replace the common law offence of assault. It would cover the same conduct as the present offence of assault and would be subject to the same penalty of a maximum of six months' imprisonment. The *mens rea* required would be the same as for the current offence of common assault: that is that D must intend or be reckless as to whether V is put in fear of unlawful force or is subjected to unlawful force.

The current law			The Commission's scheme		
Offence committed	*Actus reus*	*Mens rea*	Offence committed	*Actus reus*	*Mens rea*
s 18	Cause wounding or GBH to V	Intention to cause GBH	**Clause 1**	Cause serious injury to V	Intention to cause serious injury
s 20	Cause wounding or GBH to V	Intention or recklessness as to causing any harm	**Clause 2**	Cause serious injury to V	Recklessly causing serious injury
s 47	Common assault causing ABV to V	Intention or recklessness as to the common assault	**Clause 3**	Cause injury to V	Intentionally or recklessly causing injury
			Aggravated assault	Cause injury to V	Intentionally or recklessly causing a common assault
Common assault	D unlawfully touches V or D causes V to apprehend immediate unlawful violence	D intentionally or recklessly touches V, or D recklessly causes V to apprehend immediate personal violence	**Physical assault**	D unlawfully touches V	Intention or recklessness
			Threatened assault	D causes V to apprehend immediate unlawful violence	Intention or recklessness

Figure 15.6 From the Law Commission Report 2015

Causing serious harm intending to resist arrest

At the moment this offence is included in s 18. This means that it is subject to a maximum sentence of life imprisonment even though D need not intend or foresee serious injury. The 1998 draft Bill proposed a separate offence where D caused serious harm intending to resist arrest, prevent or terminate the lawful arrest or detention of himself or a third party. It was also thought that there should be a lower maximum penalty. This would recognise the fact the *mens rea* required is lower than for s 18.

Assault intending to resist arrest

The draft Bill also included a lower level of assault where D intends to resist arrest, prevent or terminate the lawful arrest or detention of himself or a third party. This would be charged where no serious harm was caused and it was proposed that the maximum penalty should be two years' imprisonment. The 2015 Report supports this proposal.

15.5.7 Comment on the 2015 Report

The recommendations in the Report would provide a more coherent set of offences than exists at present. There would be no overlap or inconsistency between the offences.

The *actus reus* and the *mens rea* for each proposed new offence are clearly set out. The offences conform to the 'correspondence principle' and defendants would only be held liable for a given kind and level of harm where they either meant to do it or knowingly ran the risk of it.

The law would be strengthened if the recommendation for a higher maximum penalty of seven years' imprisonment for Clause 2 is implemented. Also the proposed new offence of aggravated assault would carry a higher maximum penalty than common assault. This would give victims greater protection.

Tip

When applying the law to a scenario-based question, it is helpful to look to see what injury, if any, has occurred. If there is no injury then the offence can only be an assault or a battery. If there is slight injury then you need to consider s 47 OAPA 1861. If the injury is more serious, it is necessary to look at ss 20 and 18. Don't forget to discuss whether the necessary *mens rea* exists.

Look online

For further reading on this topic, look at the Law Commission's Report, 'Reform of Offences Against the Person' (Law Com No. 361). This can be found on the Law Commission's website: www.lawcom.gov.uk. Chapter 3 of the Report on the need for reform and Chapter 9 Recommendations are particularly useful.

- The present law on non-fatal offences against the person is mainly set out in the Offences Against the Person Act 1861.
- Common assault can be either an assault or battery.
- An assault is an act which intentionally or recklessly causes another to fear immediate and unlawful violence.
- Battery is the application, intentionally or recklessly, of unlawful force to another person.
- Assault occasioning actual bodily harm (s 47 OAPA 1861) is assault or battery which causes actual bodily harm. 'Actual bodily harm' is 'any hurt or injury calculated to interfere with the health or comfort' of the victim. It includes psychiatric injury.
- Unlawfully and maliciously wounding or inflicting grievous bodily harm upon another person (s 20 OAPA 1861). D must intend to cause another person some harm or be subjectively reckless as to whether he suffers some harm. There is no need for the defendant to foresee serious injury.

- Wounding or causing grievous bodily harm with intent to do so (s 18 OAPA 1861) is a specific intent offence. D must be proved to have intended to:
  - do some grievous bodily harm or
  - resist or prevent the lawful apprehension or detainer of any person.
- Where D intends to resist or prevent lawful apprehension or detainer there is no need for him to intend to cause grievous bodily harm. Recklessness as to injury is sufficient.
- For both ss 20 and 18 grievous bodily harm means 'really serious harm' but this does not have to be life-threatening: 'wound' means a cut or a break in the continuity of the whole skin.
- The law is in need of reform: the wording is old-fashioned and unclear; there are major inconsistencies between the offences.
- The Law Commission's Report (2015) proposes a new statute to replace the 1861 Act with a clearer hierarchy of offences.

Component 2

SECTION A

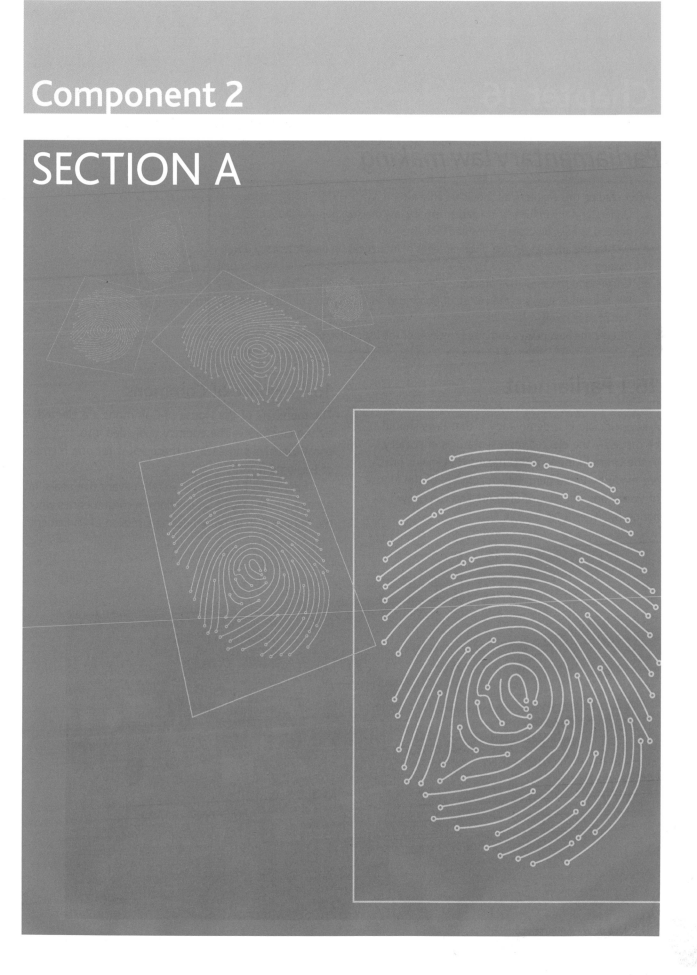

Chapter 16

Parliamentary law making

After reading this chapter you should be able to:
- Understand the influences on parliamentary law making: political, public opinion, media, pressure groups and lobbyists
- Discuss the advantages and disadvantages of influences on parliamentary law making
- Understand the legislative process – Green and White Papers, different types of Bill, legislative stages in the House of Commons and the House of Lords, and the role of the Crown
- Discuss the advantages and disadvantages of the legislative process

16.1 Parliament

A key principle in a democracy is that laws should be made by the elected representatives of society. In the United Kingdom this means that major laws are made by Parliament, which consists of the House of Commons, the House of Lords and the Crown all acting together.

16.1.1 House of Commons

The members of the House of Commons are elected by the electorate. The country is divided into constituencies and each of these votes for one Member of Parliament (MP).

There must be a general election every five years. In addition, there may be by-elections in constituencies where the MP has died or retired during a session of Parliament.

The Palace of Weshminster, London

The government of the day is formed by the political party which has a majority in the House of Commons, and it is the government which has the main say in formulating new Acts of Parliament.

16.1.2 House of Lords

The House of Lords is a non-elected body. Before 1999, there were over 1,100 members of the House of Lords of whom 750 were hereditary peers. The rest consisted of life peers (people who have been given a title for their service to the country), judges and bishops.

In 1999 the Labour Government reviewed membership of the House of Lords and decided that it should consist of some nominated members (the life peers) and some elected members. In particular it decided that an inherited title should not automatically allow that person to take part in the law-making process. Changes were made to the membership of the House of Lords so that it consisted of:

- 92 hereditary peers
- about 640 life peers
- the 26 most senior bishops in the Church of England.

This was meant to be a temporary solution while the government consulted on the final make-up of the House of Lords. However, there has not yet been agreement on how many of the House of Lords should be elected and how many should be nominated (and by whom). As a result the reform of the House of Lords has not been completed.

Note that the 12 most senior judges used to sit in the House of Lords, but they no longer do so. They are now separate from Parliament and sit as the Supreme Court (see Chapter 10).

16.2 The influences on Parliament

There are several influences that lead to Parliament deciding what new law to bring in or what law needs to be changed.

16.2.1 Political influence

Before a general election all the political parties publish a list of the reforms they would carry out if they were elected as the next government. This is called a manifesto, and it is one of the ways in which a party tries to persuade people to vote for them.

The party that has the most members of the House of Commons after a general election becomes the government. This party then has the whole life of the Parliament (this can be up to five years) to bring in the reforms they promised in their manifesto. Most of the reforms will gradually be put before Parliament to pass as an Act of Parliament.

Throughout any session of Parliament, the government has the major say on what new laws will be put before the House of Commons and the House of Lords for debate.

At the opening of each session of Parliament (usually about once a year) the government announces its plans for new laws in that session. This is done in the Queen's speech. This speech is written for the Queen by the Prime Minister and other senior ministers. This is shown in the speech as the Queen will usually use the words 'my government will ...'.

16.2.2 Public opinion/media

Where there is strong public opinion about a change to the law, the government may bow to such opinion. This is more likely towards the end of a term of government when there will be a general election soon and the government wants to remain popular with the majority of people.

The term 'media' means the ways in which information is supplied to the public. It includes television, radio, newspapers and magazines, the internet and increasingly social media. The media play a large role in bringing public opinion to the government's attention. Where an issue is given a high profile on television and in the newspapers, then this also brings it to the attention of other members of the public and may add to the weight of public opinion.

16.2.3 Pressure groups

These are groups which have a particular interest. They try to bring matters they are interested in to the attention of the general public and the government. There are two types of pressure group: sectional and cause.

Sectional pressure groups exist to represent the interests of a particular section of society. They often represent work groups or professions. Examples include the Law Society which represents solicitors' interests, the British Medical Association which represents doctors, and trade unions which represent workers such as train drivers.

Cause pressure groups exist to promote a particular cause. Examples of cause groups include environmental groups such as Greenpeace, animal welfare groups and human rights groups such as Amnesty and ASH, the anti-smoking group.

Pressure group activity may make the government reconsider the law on certain areas. This was seen in 2000 when the government finally agreed to reduce the age of consent for homosexual acts in private to 16. The League against Cruel Sports campaigned for the banning of hunting foxes with dogs and as a result of their campaign the Hunting Act 2004 was passed. In 2007 strict laws against smoking in public places were introduced because of public opinion and medical opinion.

Sometimes pressure groups will campaign against a proposed change to the law. An example was when the government tried to restrict the right to trial by jury. Pressure groups such as Justice and Liberty campaigned against this as they thought the changes infringed human rights.

Some pressure groups try to persuade individual MPs to support their cause. This is called lobbying: see the next section.

> ### Key term 🔑
>
> **Sectional pressure group** – a pressure group that represents the interests of a particular group of people.
> **Cause pressure group** – a pressure group that exists to promote a particular cause.

16.2.4 Lobbyists

Some people try to persuade individual Members of Parliament to support their cause. This is called lobbying. The name is used because members of the public can meet MPs in the lobbies (hallways) through which MPs go to get to the House of Commons.

Any individual can lobby his Member of Parliament. Lobbying is also used by pressure groups to highlight their concerns. However, most lobbying is done by professional lobbyists on behalf of businesses, trade associations and big charities. This type of lobbying can have a significant influence on legislation.

The usual form of lobbying is to persuade an MP to ask a question in the House of Commons so that the issue gets publicity.

Lobbyists may also try to persuade an MP who has won a place in the ballot to promote a Bill on the issues that concern the lobbyist.

16.3 Advantages and disadvantages of influences on law making

16.3.1 Political influences

Advantages

Each political party has its proposals for reform ready so that, if they are elected as the government, they and the electorate know what they wish to do. Also the fact that the government has a majority in the House of Commons means that virtually every law it proposes will be passed. In this way the government is reflecting the majority of the electorate.

Disadvantages

There are several disadvantages. If a different party is elected at the next general election, they may decide to repeal or alter some of the laws that the previous government passed. This is because their policies are likely to be quite different from the previous government. Changes in the law in this way can be costly and open to criticism.

Where the government has a very small majority it may be restricted in what laws it can propose. In particular, when there is a coalition government (that is, where two parties have to combine in order to have the majority of MPs in the House of Commons) then there will have to be a compromise on what policies are followed. This happened in the Coalition Government of 2010–15 where the Conservative and Liberal Democrat parties joined together to form the government. It could be said that the majority of the electorate did not vote for this coalition and compromise so the government did not reflect the will of the electorate.

16.3.2 Public opinion

Advantages

Sometimes public opinion will be affected by specific events and these may also play a role in formulating the law. A particularly tragic example was the massacre in 1996 of 16 young children and their teacher in Dunblane by a lone gunman with a legally owned gun. An enquiry into the ownership of guns was set up and a pressure group organised a campaign demanding the banning of handguns. Eventually, reflecting public opinion at the time, Parliament banned private ownership of most types of handguns.

The UK has a free press. This is an advantage as members of the press are able to criticise government policy or bring any other issue to the attention of the government. An example of the media highlighting bad practice was seen in 2009 over MPs' expenses claims. Expenses claims made by various MPs were detailed in a national newspaper. Some of the claims were for quite large amounts of money and some were even for items which the MP had not paid for. This caused a public outrage at the system of MPs' expenses. Parliament then had to reform the whole system.

Comments on social media can be made as soon as an issue has come to light. This allows the government to consider a law while it is fresh in the public consciousness.

Disadvantages

The government may respond too quickly to high-profile incidents (a 'knee-jerk reaction'). This can lead to law being created too quickly and not thought through, so that the law is poorly drafted. This was seen with the Dangerous Dogs Act 1991 where the wording in the Act has led to many disputed cases in the courts and an amending Act had to be introduced five years later. The purpose of the Act has also failed to protect people from attacks by dangerous dogs as thousands of people need hospital treatment each year after being attacked by dogs. Also each year there are incidents in which people, especially children, die as a result of being attacked by a dog.

In some cases, it can be argued that the media manipulate the news and create public opinion. An example of this could be said to be the *News of the World*'s 'name and shame' campaign against paedophiles.

16.3.3 Pressure groups

Advantages

Some pressure groups have large memberships that can exceed those of political parties. These large pressure groups, such as charities, the AA or the National Trust, can raise an issue of concern to a large number of people.

Pressure groups often raise important issues. Environmental groups have made the government much more aware of the damage being done to our environment by greenhouse gases, fuels and other pollutants.

Disadvantages

A disadvantage is that it can be argued that pressure groups are seeking to impose their ideas, even where the majority of the public do not support their views.

There are also occasions when two pressure groups have conflicting interests and want opposing things. This was seen when the ban against fox hunting was considered. The League Against Cruel Sports wanted it banned, but the Countryside Alliance wanted it to be allowed to continue.

16.3.4 Lobbyists

Advantages

Lobbyists bring issues to the attention of MPs. This may lead to a debate in Parliament, publicity for the issue and even to a change in the law. Professional lobbyists, particularly those used by pressure groups, are good at presenting the issues in the best way and making a case for the issue.

It is a system that can be used by anyone – individuals and large organisations. There are procedures to allow individuals to have access to their MP for the purpose of lobbying both at Parliament and at local constituency level.

Disadvantages

Using professional lobbyists can lead to an abuse of the process. This was especially seen when MPs were paid to ask questions. It means that financially successful businesses or other organisations have more influence than ordinary members of the public.

Look online

Look up websites of pressure groups such as Liberty (**www.liberty-human-rights.org.uk**) or Justice (**www.justice.org.uk**) or Greenpeace (**www.greenpeace.org.uk**). (These are only suggestions. You can find many other groups.) Choose one pressure group and write a brief summary of any changes in the law it is suggesting. Identify any success it has had in the past in bringing about a change in the law.

Tip

It is important not to just describe how each influence works, but to include at least one example of their work and to show whether the influence has been successful in bringing about a change in the law.

Influence	Explanation	Advantages	Disadvantages
Political	Each political party has its own policies and drafts a manifesto before a general election When elected as the government, these will be a major influence on the laws it introduces into Parliament	Each political party has its proposals known if they are elected A government majority means that most of the laws it introduces will be passed	New governments may repeal or alter laws made by a previous government
Public opinion/ Media	Strong public opinion or media reports can lead to a change in the law	Public opinion and the media play an important role in highlighting issues of social concern	Responding too quickly to high-profile incidents may lead to poorly drafted law Media can be accused of manipulating the news and creating public opinion
Pressure groups	Groups with a particular interest can bring issues to the attention of the general public and law makers	Raise important issues Wide range of issues is drawn to the attention of Parliament	Trying to impose their will on the majority Pressure groups may have conflicting interests
Lobbyists	People who meet MPs in the lobbies of Parliament in order to persuade them to support their cause, often by asking a question in Parliament	Brings issues to Parliament's attention Anyone can lobby their MP	Big businesses use professional lobbyists, giving them more influence than the general public Led to the cash-for-questions affair

Figure 16.1 Influences on parliamentary law making

16.4 The legislative process

16.4.1 Pre-legislative Process: Green and White Papers

Each government minister has a department of civil servants and advisers. The ministry which is responsible for the area in which a change in the law is being considered will draft ideas for change. A Green Paper may be issued by the minister with responsibility for that matter. This is a consultative document on a topic in which the government's view is put forward with outline proposals for reform. Interested parties are then invited to send comments to the relevant government department, so that a full consideration of all views can be made and necessary changes made to the government's proposals. Following this the government may publish a White Paper with its firm proposals for new law or will go ahead with draft legislation. A White Paper may be issued instead of a Green Paper setting out the government's firm proposals for new law before issuing legislation. There will be limited opportunity for comment on proposals in a White Paper.

Consultation before any new law is drafted is valuable as it allows time for mature consideration. Governments have been criticised for responding in a 'knee-jerk' fashion to incidents or proposals and, as a result, rushing law through that has subsequently proved to be unworkable.

Key term

Green Paper – a consultative document issued by the government putting forward proposals for reform of the law.
White Paper – a document issued by the government stating its decisions as to how it is going to reform the law.

Look online

Find an example of a recent Green Paper and of a recent White Paper. Has either led to a change in the law?

16.4.2 Different types of Bill

New laws are usually made through Acts of Parliament, which can also be known as statutes or legislation. There is often a long and formal process which has to be followed before an Act of Parliament becomes law.

The great majority of Acts of Parliament are introduced by the government and are known as Public Bills as they will affect everyone in the country. They are initially drafted by lawyers in the Civil Service who are known as parliamentary counsel to the Treasury or parliamentary draftsmen. The government department which is responsible for the new law gives instructions to the draftsmen as to what is to be included and the intended effect of the proposed law.

When the proposed law has been drafted it is published, and at this stage it is called a **Bill**. It will only become an **Act of Parliament** if it successfully completes all the necessary stages in Parliament. Where it is a Bill put forward by the government it will be introduced into Parliament by a government minister. For example, the Minister of Justice will introduce a Bill about the justice system, while the Minister for the Department for the Environment, Food and Rural Affairs will introduce a Bill on issues about the environment.

The draftsmen may face problems when preparing the Bill. It has to be drafted so that it represents the government's wishes, while using correct legal wording so that there will not be any difficulties in applying its provisions in the future. It must be unambiguous, precise and comprehensive. Achieving all this is not easy, and there may be unforeseen problems in the language used.

See Chapter 18 about statutory interpretation.

In addition, there is usually a pressure on time, as the government will have a timetable of when it wishes to introduce the draft Bill into Parliament.

Key terms

Bill – the name for a draft law going through Parliament before it passes all the parliamentary stages to become an Act of Parliament.

Act of Parliament – a law that has passed through all stages in Parliament and becomes part of the law of the land.

Private members' Bills

As well as Bills being introduced into Parliament by the government, it is possible for individual MPs to introduce a Bill into Parliament. These MPs will not be part of the government. They can be from any political party. They are also known as 'backbenchers' because they do not sit in the front row in the actual House of Commons. (The government ministers sit in the front row.)

There are two ways an MP can introduce a Bill. These are:

- by ballot
- through the 'ten-minute' rule.

Ballot

The parliamentary process allows for a ballot each parliamentary session in which 20 private members are selected who can then take their turn in presenting

a Bill to Parliament. The time for debate of private members' Bills is limited, usually only being debated on Fridays, so that only the first six or seven members in the ballot have a realistic chance of introducing a Bill on their chosen topic.

Relatively few private members' Bills became law, but there have been some important laws passed as the result of such Bills. The most famous example was the Abortion Act 1967 which legalised abortion in this country. Others include the Marriage Act 1994 which allows people to marry in any registered place, not only in Register Offices or religious buildings, and the Household Waste Recycling Act 2003 which places local authorities under a duty to recycle waste.

Ten-minute rule

Backbenchers can also try to introduce a Bill through the 'ten-minute' rule, under which any MP can make a speech of up to ten minutes supporting the introduction of new legislation. This method is rarely successful unless there is no opposition to the Bill, but some Acts of Parliament have been introduced in this way, for example the Bail (Amendment) Act 1993 which gave the prosecution the right to appeal against the granting of bail to a defendant. Members of the House of Lords can also introduce private members' Bills.

Public Bills

Most Bills introduced into Parliament involve matters of public policy which will affect either the whole country or a large section of it. These Bills are known as Public Bills. Most government Bills are in this category. For example the Legal Services Act 2007, the Legal Aid, Sentencing and Punishment of Offenders (LAPSO) Act 2012 and the Criminal Justice and Courts Act 2015 are all Public Bills. It is also possible for a private member to introduce a public Bill. The Abortion Act 1967, the Marriage Act 1994 and the Household Waste Recycling Act 2003 are all Public Bills.

Private Bills

A small number of Bills are designed to pass a law which will affect only individual people or corporations. These do not affect the whole community. They are known as Private Bills. A recent example of such a Bill was the Faversham Oyster Fishery Company Bill 2016. This Bill changes the way the company is run. This Bill should have been passed through Parliament by the

Type of Bill	Explanation	Example
Government Bill	Introduced by the government	Criminal Justice and Courts Act 2015
Private Members' Bill	Introduced by a private MP; likely to be a public Bill	Household Waste Recycling Act 2003
Public Bill	Involves matters of public policy which affect the general public	Legal Aid, Sentencing and Punishment Act 2012
Private	Affects a particular organisation, person or place	Faversham Oyster Fishery Company Bill 2016
Hybrid	Introduced by the government but likely to affect a single organisation, person or place	Crossrail and HS2 Acts

Figure 16.2 Types of Bill

time you read this textbook. Search for it as an Act on **www.legislation.gov.uk**.

Hybrid Bills

These are a cross between Public Bills and Private Bills. They are introduced by the government, but if they become law they will affect a particular person, organisation or place. Recent examples are the various Crossrail and HS2 Acts. These Acts allow for the construction of underground rail links in London and separately for the construction of a high speed railway, which affect people in the area. The Bills give power to acquire land, and give planning permission and authorisation of the necessary work. Individuals directly and specially affected by the construction of the route have been able to petition Parliament about it, so their views could be considered before the various Acts have been passed.

Role of the House of Commons

As the members of the House of Commons are democratically elected, most Bills are introduced into the House of Commons first. If the House of Commons votes against a Bill, then that is the end of the Bill.

During the course of a Bill through the House of Commons, there will be debates on issues of the policy behind the law as well as on the specific details of the Bill.

The government will have a majority in the House of Commons, so that it is likely that policies supported by the government will become law.

Role of the House of Lords

The House of Lords acts as a check on the House of Commons. All Bills go through the House of Lords and the members can vote against proposed changes to the law. In some cases this may alert the House of Commons to a problem with the proposal and it can be dropped or amended.

However, the power of the House of Lords is limited by the Parliament Acts 1911 and 1949. These allow a Bill to become law even if the House of Lords rejects it, provided that the Bill is reintroduced into the House of Commons in the next session of Parliament and passes all the stages again there. So the House of Lords can only delay a law by up to one year.

The principle behind the Parliament Acts is that the House of Lords is not an elected body. Its function is to refine and add to the law rather than oppose the will of the democratically elected House of Commons. In fact there have only been four occasions when this procedure has been used to by-pass the House of Lords after it had voted against a Bill. These were for the:

- War Crimes Act 1991
- European Parliamentary Elections Act 1999
- Sexual Offences (Amendment) Act 2000
- Hunting Act 2004.

Following the passing of the Hunting Act 2004, there was a challenge as to whether the Act was constitutionally valid. This was in *R (Jackson and others) v Attorney General* (2005). The challenge was on the basis that the Parliament Act 1949 could not be used as it had increased the House of Commons' power without the agreement of the House of Lords. It was held that the Parliament Act 1949 merely placed limits on the power of the unelected House of Lords and did not increase the power of the House of Commons. Therefore the Hunting Act 2004 had been validly enacted by Parliament.

16.4.3 Legislative stages in the House of Commons and the House of Lords

In order to become an Act of Parliament, the Bill will usually have to be passed by both Houses of Parliament and approved by the Crown. A Bill may start in either the House of Commons or the House of Lords. Finance Bills must start in the House of

Commons. All Bills must go through the following stages (for Bills starting in the House of Commons).

First reading

This is a formal procedure where the name and main aims of the Bill are read out. Usually no discussion or vote takes place.

Second reading

This is when the main debate on the whole Bill takes place. MPs can debate the main principles behind the Bill. At the end of the debate a vote is taken. The vote may be verbal or formal, in which MPs vote by leaving the Chamber and then walking back in through one of two special doors. There will be two 'tellers' positioned at each of these two voting doors to make a list of the members voting on each side. These tellers count up the number of MPs who voted for and against and declare these numbers to the Speaker in front of the members of the House. There must be a majority in favour for the Bill for it to progress any further.

Committee stage

At this stage a detailed examination of each clause of the Bill is undertaken by a committee of between 16 and 50 MPs. This is usually done by what is called a Standing Committee, which is chosen specifically for that Bill. In such a committee the government will have a majority and the opposition and minority parties are represented proportionately to the number of seats they have in the House of Commons.

The members of Parliament nominated for each Standing Committee will usually be those with a special interest in or knowledge of the subject of the Bill which is being considered. For Finance Bills the whole House will sit in committee.

Report stage

At the Committee stage amendments to various clauses in the Bill may have been voted on and passed, so this Report stage is where the committee reports back to the House on those amendments. (If there were no amendments at the Committee stage, there will not be a 'Report' stage – instead the Bill will go straight on to the Third reading.) The amendments will be debated in the House and accepted or rejected.

Further amendments may also be added. The Report stage has been described as 'a useful safeguard against a small committee amending a Bill against the wishes of the House, and a necessary opportunity for second thoughts'.

Third reading

This is the final vote on the Bill. It is almost a formality since a Bill that has passed through all previous stages is unlikely to fail at this late stage. In fact in the House of Commons there will only be an actual further debate on the Bill as a whole if at least six MPs request it.

The House of Lords

If the Bill started in the House of Commons, it is now passed to the House of Lords where it goes through the same five stages outlined above. If the House of Lords make amendments to the Bill, then it will go back to the House of Commons for them to consider those amendments. If the Commons do not accept the Lords' amendments, they then send those amendments back to the Lords. This sending to and fro can go on for some time and is referred to as 'ping-pong'. It will continue until all the proposed changes have been agreed by both Houses.

If the Bill starts in the House of Lords it will pass through similar stages as the Commons, though the Committee stage will be of the whole House. Once the Bill has passed through the Lords it will be passed to the Commons and pass through all the stages set out above until it is agreed by both Houses.

16.4.4 The role of the Crown

The final stage is where the monarch formally gives approval to the Bill and it then becomes an Act of Parliament and part of the law of the land. This is now a formality and, under the Royal Assent Act 1967, the monarch will not even have the text of the Bills to which she is assenting; she will only have the short title. The last time that a monarch refused assent was in 1707, when Queen Anne refused to assent to the Scottish Militia Bill.

These stages in the parliamentary procedure are shown in a flow chart in Figure 16.3.

It is important not just to accurately list each of the stages of the parliamentary process, but also to describe what happens at each stage.

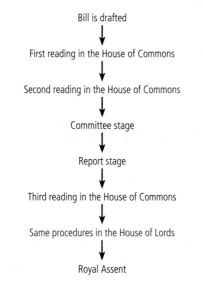

Bill is drafted

First reading in the House of Commons

Second reading in the House of Commons

Committee stage

Report stage

Third reading in the House of Commons

Same procedures in the House of Lords

Royal Assent

Figure 16.3 Flow chart of the passing of an Act of Parliament starting in the House of Commons

16.4.5 Commencement of an Act of Parliament

Following the Royal Assent the Act of Parliament will come into force on midnight of that day, unless another date has been set. However, very few Acts are implemented immediately. Instead the Act itself states the date when it will commence or passes responsibility on to the appropriate minister to fix the commencement date. In the latter case the minister will bring the Act into force by issuing a commencement order.

This can cause problems as it can be necessary to keep checking which sections have been brought into force. It may be that some sections or even a whole Act will never become law. An example of this is the Easter Act 1928, which was intended to fix the date of Easter Day. Although this Act passed all the necessary parliamentary stages, and was given the Royal Assent, it has never come into force.

Example of an Act of Parliament

Figure 16.4 reproduces an Act of Parliament – the Lords Spiritual (Women) Act 2015. The name of the Act is given immediately under the Royal coat of arms. Underneath the name, '2015 CHAPTER 18' means that it was the eighteenth Act to be passed in 2015.

Next follows a short statement, or preamble, about the purpose of the Act. Then there is a formal statement starting 'BE IT ENACTED' showing that the Act has been passed by both Houses of Parliament and received the Royal Assent. This is included in all Acts. After this comes the body of the Act, which is set out in sections. This is a very short Act with only two sections.

Section 1 has five subsections. The effect is to allow for women bishops to become members of the House of Lords when there is a vacancy. Remember that the 26 most senior bishops in the Church of England are entitled to sit in the House of Lords.

Section 2 has three subsections. These give the commencement (that is when the Act will come into force), the area of the country that it applies to – here it is England and Wales, Scotland and Northern Ireland. The final subsection states the name by which the Act is to be known.

ELIZABETH II   c. **18**

Lords Spiritual (Women) Act 2015

2015 CHAPTER 18

An Act to make time-limited provision for vacancies among the Lords Spiritual to be filled by bishops who are women.   [26th March 2015]

B E IT ENACTED by the Queen's most Excellent Majesty, by and with the advice and consent of the Lords Spiritual and Temporal, and Commons, in this present Parliament assembled, and by the authority of the same, as follows: —

1   Vacancies among the Lords Spiritual

(1)   This section applies where —

    (a)   a vacancy arises among the Lords Spiritual in the House of Lords in the 10 years beginning with the day on which this Act comes into force,

    (b)   at the time the vacancy arises there is at least one eligible bishop who is a woman, and

    (c)   the person who would otherwise be entitled to fill the vacancy under section 5 of the Bishoprics Act 1878 is a man.

(2)   If at the time the vacancy arises there is only one eligible bishop who is a woman, the vacancy is to be filled by the issue of writs of summons to her.

(3)   If at the time the vacancy arises there are two or more eligible bishops who are women, the vacancy is to be filled by the issue of writs of summons to the one whose election as a bishop of a diocese in England was confirmed first.

(4)   In this section "eligible bishop" means a bishop of a diocese in England who is not yet entitled in that capacity to the issue of writs of summons.

(5)   The reference in subsection (1) to a vacancy does not include a vacancy arising by the avoidance of the see of Canterbury, York, London, Durham or Winchester.

Figure 16.4 The Lords Spiritual (Women) Act 2015

2   Commencement, extent and short title

(1)   This Act comes into force on the day Parliament first meets following the first parliamentary general election after this Act is passed.

(2)   This Act extends to England and Wales, Scotland and Northern Ireland.

(3)   This Act may be cited as the Lords Spiritual (Women) Act 2015.

Figure 16.4 The Lords Spiritual (Women) Act 2015 (continued)

Look online

1. Look up a recent Act of Parliament on the internet. You can find Acts listed on **www.opsi.gov.uk**. Find the commencement section. Was the Act put into force when it was passed or at some later date? Who is given the power to set the commencement date?
2. Extension task – under the Browse tab there is a link to UK statutory instruments. Search this list of statutory instruments to find the commencement date(s).
3. Look up any Bill that is currently going through Parliament. These will be shown on **www.parliament.uk**. What stages in the parliamentary process has the Bill gone through so far?
4. Extension task – at revision time look at the progress of the Bill again. How many stages has it gone through now?

16.5 Advantages and disadvantages of the legislative process

16.5.1 Advantages

Democratic

The main advantage of parliamentary-made law is that it is made by our elected representatives. This means it is democratic. Parliament is answerable to the electorate, as there has to be a general election at least once every five years. A government can be voted out of office if it has not performed as the electorate expected.

Full reform

Another advantage is that Acts of Parliament can reform whole areas of law in one Act, which makes law simpler to find. An example is the Fraud Act 2006 which abolished all the old offences of deception and fraud and created a newer and, hopefully, simpler structure of offences. In contrast, judges using precedent can only change very small areas of law as they can only rule on the point of law in the case they are deciding.

Broad policy

Acts of Parliament can also set broad policies and give power to others (usually government ministers) to make detailed rules. This is known as delegated legislation (see Chapter 17). This is an advantage because the general structure is laid down by Parliament but it allows greater detail in the law than if it was just contained in an Act of Parliament.

Consultation

Before a Bill is presented to Parliament there will have been consultation on the proposed changes to the law. This allows the government to take into consideration subjections and objections to the proposals. The use of Green and White Papers also makes sure that the proposed law has received consultation.

Also, as all Bills have to be debated and considered by both Houses of Parliament, the new law will be thoroughly discussed in Parliament.

Law made by Parliament is also certain as it cannot be changed except through another Act of Parliament.

16.5.2 Disadvantages

Although there are major advantages to having law made in Parliament, there are also some disadvantages.

Lack of time

Parliament does not always have time, or political will, to consider all the reforms that are proposed. This is particularly true of 'lawyers' law' in areas such as criminal law or the law of contract.

An example of law that is still awaiting reform is the law on assaults and other offences against the person. The Law Commission proposed changes to the law on offences against the person in 1993. Reform was needed because the old law dates back to an Act of 1861 which was made in very different times and did not apply to modern life. In 1997 the government accepted that there was a need for reform and published a draft Bill in 1998. However, this was not put before Parliament and the law has still not been reformed.

Long process

Even where the government introduces a Bill into Parliament the process of becoming an Act with all the different reading, committee and report stages can take several months.

In addition the original Bill may be altered several times during the parliamentary legislative process. This can mean that the final Act is not as clear or comprehensive as it might have been.

Government control

The government is in control of the parliamentary timetable and allows very little time for private members' Bills, which often deal with important moral issues. Even when a private member does manage to introduce a Bill, it can be easily voted out by the government as they have the majority in the House of Commons. The result is that very few private members' Bills become law and few moral issues are legislated upon.

Complexity

Acts of Parliament are often very long and complex. This can make them difficult to understand. In fact many of the appeal cases that are heard by the Supreme Court deal with the interpretation of Acts of Parliament.

Where a lot of detailed rules are needed, it is not always possible to include them in an Act of Parliament. Even if detail is given it cannot be changed without another, later Act. It is often necessary to give power to other people (government ministers) to make detailed laws. It may be difficult to find these detailed laws which have to be read together with the original Act.

See Chapter 17 for detail on delegated legislation.

Pre-legislative process	Green Papers White Papers Consultation
Legislative process	First reading Second reading Committee stage Report stage Third reading Same procedure in the other House Royal Assent
Advantages and disadvantages of legislative process	**Advantages** Democratic Allows full reform of law Consultation before Bill is presented to Parliament Discussion in both Houses during legislative process **Disadvantages** Long process Limited parliamentary time may prevent some laws from being reformed Acts can be long and complex Wording of an Act may be difficult to understand and lead to court case on interpretation of meaning Not possible to include all the detail needed, may need to use delegated legislation
Influences on law making	Political policies Public opinion/media Pressure groups Lobbyists Law Commission

Figure 16.5 Parliament and Acts of Parliament

Summary

- Acts of Parliament are laws made by both Houses of Parliament and given Royal Assent.
- Parliament may be influenced in its law making by political policies, public opinion/media, pressure groups, lobbyists and law reform bodies, especially the Law Commission.
- There is usually pre-legislative consultation, and Green and White Papers will set out the government's proposals for changing the law.
- Bills can be put before Parliament by the government or by individual MPs.
- There are several formal stages in Parliament in both Houses before a Bill can become an Act. These are: First reading, Second reading, Committee stage, Report stage and Third reading.

- Advantages of parliamentary law making:
  - democratic
  - allows full reform of law
  - consultation before Bill is presented to Parliament
  - discussion in both Houses during legislative process.
- Disadvantages of parliamentary law making:
  - long process
  - limited parliamentary time may prevent some laws from being reformed
  - Acts can be long and complex
  - wording of an Act may be difficult to understand and lead to court cases on interpretation of meaning
  - may need to delegate power to other people to make law.

Chapter 17

Delegated legislation

After reading this chapter you should be able to:
- Understand and explain the different types of delegated legislation: Orders in Council, statutory instruments and by-laws
- Understand and explain controls on delegated legislation by Parliament and the courts, and their effectiveness
- Explain the reasons for the use of delegated legislation
- Discuss the advantages and disadvantages of delegated legislation

17.1 Types of delegated legislation

Parliament's authority to make **delegated legislation** is usually laid down in a 'parent' Act of Parliament known as an enabling Act. The enabling Act creates the framework of the law and then delegates power to others to make more detailed law in the area.

> ### Key term 🔑
>
> **Delegated legislation** – law made by some person or body other than Parliament, but with the authority of an Act of Parliament.

There are three different types of delegated legislation:
- Orders in Council
- statutory instruments
- by-laws.

Figure 17.1 shows these in diagram form.

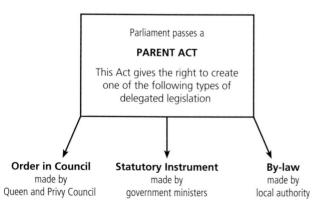

Figure 17.1 Different types of delegated legislation

17.1.1 Orders in Council

The Queen and the Privy Council have the authority to make Orders in Council. The Privy Council is made up of the Prime Minister and other leading members of the government. So this type of delegated legislation effectively allows the government to make laws without going through Parliament.

Orders in Council can be made on a wide range of matters, especially:

- transferring responsibility between government departments. For example, when the Ministry of Justice was created, the powers of the previous Department of Constitutional Affairs and some of the powers of the Home Office were transferred to what was then a new ministry;
- bringing Acts (or parts of Acts) of Parliament into force;
- giving legal effect to EU Directives
- dealing with some aspects of foreign affairs; and
- making law in times of national emergency when Parliament is not sitting under the authority of the Civil Contingency Act 2004.

2008 No. 3130

DANGEROUS DRUGS

The Misuse of Drugs Act 1971 (Amendment) Order 2008

Made   *10th December 2008*

Coming into force   *26th January 2009*

At the Court at Buckingham Palace, the 10th day of December 2008

Present,

The Queen's Most Excellent Majesty in Council

In accordance with section 2(5) of the Misuse of Drugs Act 1971 a draft of this Order has been laid before Parliament after consultation with the Advisory Council on the Misuse of Drugs and approved by a resolution of each House of Parliament.

Accordingly, Her Majesty, in exercise of the powers conferred upon Her by sections 2(2) and 2(4) of that Act, is pleased, by and with the advice of Her Privy Council, to order as follows:

Citation, commencement and revocation

1.—(1) This Order may be cited as the Misuse of Drugs Act 1971 (Amendment) Order 2008 and shall come into force on 26th January 2009.

(2) The Misuse of Drugs Act 1971 (Modification) (No. 2) Order 2003 is revoked.

Amendments to the Misuse of Drugs Act 1971

2.—(1) Schedule 2 to the Misuse of Drugs Act 1971 (which specifies the drugs which are subject to control under that Act) is amended as follows.

(2) In Part 2 (Class B drugs)—

(a) in paragraph 1(a), after "Amphetamine" insert—

"Cannabinol

Cannabinol derivatives

Cannabis and cannabis resin";

(b) after paragraph 2 insert—

"**2A**. Any ester or ether of cannabinol or of a cannabinol derivative."; and

(c) in paragraph 3, for "or 2" substitute ", 2 or 2A".

(3) In Part 3 (Class C drugs) the following words are repealed —

(a) in paragraph 1(a), "Cannabinol", "Cannabinol derivatives" and "Cannabis and cannabis resin"; and

(b) in paragraph 1(d), "or of cannabinol or a cannabinol derivative".

Judith Simpson
Clerk of the Privy Council

Figure 17.2 Example of an Order in Council

Orders in Council can also be used to amend or update existing law. For example, in 2003, an Order in Council was used to alter the Misuse of Drugs Act 1971 to make cannabis a class C drug. Five years later, the government decided that it had been a mistake to downgrade cannabis and another Order in Council was issued changing cannabis back to a class B drug (see Figure 17.2).

There must be an enabling Act allowing the Privy Council to make Orders in Council on the particular topic. For the change of category of cannabis, the enabling Act was the Misuse of Drugs Act 1971.

Another enabling Act giving power to make Orders in Council is the Constitutional Reform Act 2005. This allows the Privy Council to alter the number of judges in the Supreme Court.

Look online

Look up recent Orders in Council on the Privy Council website at **https://privycouncil.independent.gov.uk/**. On the home page, click on Privy Council, then click on Privy Council Meetings. There will be a list of years; choose a year and you should see a series of dates on which meetings took place. Click on a date of your choice to find an Order in Council. When you find one, identify which enabling Act has allowed the Order to be made. The enabling Act is usually given on the left-hand side of the list of Orders.

Extension activity – Find the Act that you have identified and in that Act identify the clause that gives the law-making power to the Privy Council.

17.1.2 Statutory instruments

Ministers and government departments are given authority to make regulations for areas under their particular responsibility. There are about 15 departments in the government. Each one deals with a different area of policy and can make rules and regulations in respect of matters it deals with. So the Minister for Work and Pensions will be able to make regulations on work-related matters, such as health and safety at work, while the Minister for Transport will be able to deal with necessary road traffic regulations.

Statutory instruments can be very short, covering one point such as making the annual change to the minimum wage. However, other statutory instruments may be very long with detailed regulations which were too complex to include in an Act of Parliament.

Key term

Statutory instruments – rules and regulations made by government ministers under the authority of an enabling Act.

Examples of statutory instruments which include a lot of detail are:

- Building Regulations 2010 – these have ten parts and six schedules. They have been amended a number of times by further regulations. They were made under the authority of the European Union Act 1972 and the Building Act 1984.
- Police Codes of Practice in relation to such powers as stop and search, arrest and detention. There are eight Codes. They are made by the Minister for Justice under powers in the Police and Criminal Evidence Act 1984 and are updated from time to time.

Statutory instruments are an important way of making law, as over 3,000 are made each year.

17.1.3 By-laws

These can be made by local authorities to cover matters within their own area: for example, a county council can pass laws affecting the whole county while a district or town council can only make by-laws for its district or town. Many local by-laws will involve traffic control, such as parking restrictions, or when dogs can be exercised on a beach. Other by-laws may be for such matters as banning the drinking of alcohol in public places or banning people from riding bicycles in local parks.

By-laws can also be made by public corporations and certain companies for matters within their jurisdiction, which involve the public. This means that bodies such as the British Airports Authority and railway companies can enforce rules about public behaviour on their premises.

Definition of delegated legislation	Law made by bodies other than Parliament, but with the authority of Parliament through an enabling or parent Act		
	Types of delegated legislation	Made by	Examples
	Orders in Council	Made by Queen and Privy Council	The Misuse of Drugs Act 1971 (Amendment) Order 2008
	Statutory instruments	Made by government ministers	Codes of Practice under PACE
	By-laws	Made by local authorities or public corporations	Local parking regulations

Figure 17.3 Different types of delegated legislation with examples

Activity

Look at the following two sources and answer the questions below.

Source A

STATUTORY INSTRUMENTS

2016 No. 719

PENSIONS

The Employers' Duties (Implementation) (Amendment) Regulations 2016

Made - - -	*7th July 2016*
Laid before Parliament	*11th July 2016*
Coming into force - -	*1st October 2016*

The Secretary of State makes the following Regulations in exercise of the powers conferred by sections 29(2) and (4) and 30(8) of the Pensions Act 2008(**a**):

Citation and commencement

1. These Regulations may be cited as the Employers' Duties (Implementation) (Amendment) Regulations 2016 and come into force on 1st October 2016.

Amendment of the Employers' Duties (Implementation) Regulations 2010

2.—(1) The Employers' Duties (Implementation) Regulations 2010(**b**) are amended as follows.

(2) In regulation 5 (transitional periods for money purchase and personal pension schemes)—

    (a) in paragraph (a) (prescription of first transitional period)—

        (i) omit "is five years and three months"; and

        (ii) after the words in parentheses, add ", ends on, but includes, 5th April 2018".

    (b) in paragraph (b) (prescription of second transitional period), for the words following the comma, substitute "beginning with 6th April 2018 and ending on, but including, 5th April 2019".

(3) In regulation 6 (transitional periods for defined benefits and hybrid schemes)—

    (a) omit "is five years and three months"; and

    (b) after the words "comes into force", add ", ends on, but includes, 30th September 2017".

Altmann
Minister of State,
Department for Work and Pensions

7th July 2016

(**a**) 2008 c. 30. Section 99 defines "prescribed" and "regulations".
(**b**) S.I. 2010/4. Regulations 5 and 6 were amended by S.I. 2012/1813.

Source B

Drinking ban zones

The Safer Croydon Partnership has implemented four drinking ban zones in four areas.

How do they work?

The correct term for a drinking ban zone is a Designated Public Place Order. These were introduced as part of the Criminal Justice and Police Act 2001. Prior to implementing a drinking ban zone, consultation must take place with the police and local residents, businesses and all of the licensed premises within the proposed area. Within the designated area, alcohol consumption is restricted in any open space, other than licensed premises.

It is important to note that this is a discretionary power, so where alcohol is being consumed without causing a problem (e.g. a family picnic in the park) the police would be unlikely to take action.

What happens to people who don't comply?

People are required to hand over alcohol in their possession when requested to do so by a police officer. The police officer will generally dispose of the alcohol by pouring it away. Failure to surrender alcohol on request may result in an arrest.

Source: Adapted from the Croydon Council website, August 2016

Questions

1 What type of delegated legislation is Source A?
2 Which Act is the enabling Act which allowed this delegated legislation to be made?
3 Which government department was responsible for producing the regulations?
4 To which type of delegated legislation does Source B refer?
5 Who made the orders referred to in the source?
6 What effect do these orders have?

17.2 Control of delegated legislation

As delegated legislation in many instances is made by non-elected bodies and, since there are so many people with the power to make delegated legislation, it is important that there should be some control over it. Control is exercised by Parliament and by the courts.

17.2.1 Control by Parliament

Checks on the enabling Act

Parliament has the initial control over what powers are delegated as the enabling Act sets out the limits within which any delegated legislation must be made. For example, the Act will state which government minister can make the regulations. It will also state the type of laws to be made and whether they can be made for the whole country or only for certain places. The Act can also set out whether the government department must consult other people before making the regulations.

Parliament also retains control over the delegated legislation as it can repeal the powers in the enabling Act at any time. If it does this then the right to make legislation will cease.

There are also various parliamentary committees, which scrutinise delegated legislation to see if it has been made appropriately. Examples of these committees are the Joint Committee on Statutory Instruments and the Secondary Legislation Scrutiny Committee in the House of Lords.

Affirmative resolutions

A small number of statutory instruments will be subject to an affirmative resolution. This means that the statutory instrument will not become law unless specifically approved by Parliament. The need for an affirmative resolution will be included in the enabling Act. For example, an affirmative resolution is required before new or revised police Codes of Practice under the Police and Criminal Evidence Act 1984 can come into force. One of the disadvantages of this procedure is that Parliament cannot amend the statutory instrument; it can only be approved, annulled or withdrawn.

Negative resolutions

Most other statutory instruments will be subject to a negative resolution, which means that the relevant statutory instrument will become law unless rejected by Parliament within 40 days. The main problem with this procedure is that very few of the statutory instruments will be looked at. They are available for parliamentary committees to scrutinise but, as there are so many statutory instruments made, it is likely that only a few will be looked at.

Super-affirmative resolution procedure

This procedure is available if delegated legislation has been made under the authority of the Legislative and Regulatory Reform Act 2006 when Parliament is given greater control as the Act gives Ministers very wide powers to amend Acts of Parliament (which Parliament itself can normally only do under the principle of parliamentary sovereignty).

Questioning of government ministers

Individual ministers may also be questioned by MPs in the House of Commons on the work of their departments. This can include questions about proposed or current delegated legislation.

Scrutiny Committees

A more effective check is the Joint Committee on Statutory Instruments, usually called the Scrutiny Committee. This committee reviews all statutory instruments and, where necessary, will draw the attention of both Houses of Parliament to points that need further consideration. However, the review is a technical one and not based on policy. The main grounds for referring a statutory instrument back to the Houses of Parliament are that:

- it imposes a tax or charge – this is because only an elected body has such a right;
- it appears to have retrospective effect which was not provided for by the enabling Act;
- it appears to have gone beyond the powers given under the enabling legislation;
- it makes some unusual or unexpected use of those powers;
- it is unclear or defective in some way.

The Scrutiny Committee can only report back its findings; it has no power to alter any statutory instrument.

The main problems with this form of scrutiny are that the review is only a technical one limited to the points set out above. Also, even if the Committee discovers a breach of one of these points, they cannot alter the regulations or stop them from becoming law. They can only draw the attention of Parliament to the matter.

Effectiveness of parliamentary controls

The sheer number of pieces of delegated legislation means that not all of them can be given proper scrutiny before they come into force. It is then very difficult to remove a piece of legislation once it has come into force. Also much legislation made in this way is very technical and those scrutinising it will often not have sufficient knowledge of, or expertise in, the relevant law to be able to assess whether it has been validly made. Finally the scrutiny committees can only make recommendations to Parliament who may or may not choose to act on the recommendation.

17.2.2 Control by the courts

Delegated legislation can be challenged in court by a person with sufficient standing or interest in the case. It can be challenged by judicial review on the ground that it is *ultra vires*. This means that it goes beyond the powers given by Parliament in the enabling Act.

The controls are:

1. It is ruled by the court to be *ultra vires* meaning it is void and of no effect. An example of this procedure is *R v Home Secretary, ex parte Fire Brigades Union* (1995) where changes made by the Home Secretary to the Criminal Injuries Compensation scheme were decided to have gone beyond the delegated powers given in the Criminal Justice Act 1988.

2. It is *ultra vires* because the correct procedure has not been followed. For example in the *Aylesbury Mushroom* case (1972) the Minister of Labour had to consult 'any organisation . . . appearing to him to be representative of substantial numbers of employers engaging in the activity concerned'. His failure to consult the Mushroom Growers' Association, which represented about 85% of all mushroom growers, meant that an order setting up a training board was invalid as it was against the interests of mushroom growers generally.
   In *R v Secretary of State for Education and Employment, ex parte National Union of Teachers* (2000) it was ruled that a statutory instrument setting conditions for appraisal and access to higher rates of pay for teachers was beyond the powers given to the Education Secretary by the Education Act 1996. In addition, the procedure used was unfair as only four days had been allowed for consultation.

3. It is *ultra vires* if it is unreasonable (often known as Wednesbury unreasonable after the case of *Associated Picture Houses v Wednesbury Corporation*). An example is *R (Rogers) v Swindon NHS Trust 2006* when a woman with breast cancer was prescribed the non-approved drug Herceptin. Her NHS Trust refused to provide her with the drug as it said her case was not exceptional, though it did provide the drug for some patients in its area. This decision was decided to be unreasonable and therefore *ultra vires*.

Key term 🔑

Ultra vires– the delegated legislation has (1) gone beyond the power given to make it in the enabling Act or (2) has been made after the incorrect procedure has been used or (3) a decision is made unreasonably. If *ultra vires* is found the legislation, or decision, will be void and of no effect.

Effectiveness of judicial control

A piece of delegate legislation can only be challenged by a person who has 'standing' – that is someone who is affected by the legislation or the decision. This person will usually have to challenge a public body or government department who are likely to have greater resources and funding to defend the legislation or decision.

While the UK remains a member of the European Union, statutory instruments can also be declared void if they conflict with European Union legislation.

17.3 Reasons for the use of delegated legislation

17.3.1 Detailed law

In our modern society there are a large number of rules and regulations. These are needed to make society work more safely and efficiently. Parliament does not have the time to deal with all the detail needed. Using delegated legislation means that Parliament has control, through the use of enabling Acts, of what regulations are passed.

17.3.2 Expert knowledge

Much legislation needs expert knowledge of the subject matter in order to draw up the most effective laws. It is impossible for Parliament to have all the knowledge needed to draw up laws for such things as controlling the use of technology, ensuring environmental safety, dealing with a vast array of different industrial problems or operating complex taxation schemes.

It is thought that it is better for Parliament to debate the main principles thoroughly, but leave the detail to be filled in by those who have expert knowledge of it.

17.3.3 Local knowledge

For by-laws, local councils know their own areas and can decide which areas need drinking bans or what local parking regulations there should be. It would be impossible for Parliament to deal with all the local requirements for every city, town and village in the country.

17.3.4 Consultation

Consultation is particularly important for rules on technical matters, where it is necessary to make sure that the legislation is technically accurate and workable. By creating law through delegated legislation, ministers can have the benefit of consultation before having regulations drawn up.

Also some enabling Acts giving the power to make delegated legislation set out that there must be consultation with interested persons before the regulations are created. For example, before any new or revised police Code of Practice under the Police and Criminal Evidence Act 1984 is issued, there must be consultation with a range of people including police and lawyers to ensure that any rules are workable for both sides.

17.4 Advantages and disadvantages of delegated legislation

17.4.1 Advantages

Saves parliamentary time

Parliament does not have time to consider and debate every small detail of complex regulations. Making such regulations through delegated legislation saves parliamentary time.

Access to technical expertise

Modern society has become very complicated and technical, so that it is impossible that members of Parliament can have all the knowledge needed to draw up laws on complex areas. By using delegated legislation, the necessary experts can be consulted.

Allows consultation

Ministers can have the benefit of further consultation before regulations are drawn up. Consultation is particularly important for rules on technical matters, where it is necessary to make sure that the regulations are technically workable.

Allows quick law making

As already seen the process of passing an Act of Parliament can take a considerable time and in an emergency Parliament may not be able to pass law quickly enough. Orders in Council, especially, can be made very quickly to deal with disasters or terrorist threats.

Easy to amend

Delegated legislation can be amended or revoked easily when necessary so that the law can be kept up to date. This is useful where monetary limits have to change each year as, for example, the minimum wage or the limits for legal aid. Ministers can also respond to new or unforeseen situations by introducing a statutory instrument. This is another reason why use of delegated legislation is sometimes preferred to an Act of Parliament.

17.4.2 Disadvantages

Undemocratic

The main criticism is that delegated legislation takes law making away from the democratically elected House of Commons and allows non-elected people to make law. This is acceptable provided there is sufficient control, but, as already seen, Parliament's control is fairly limited. This criticism cannot be made of by-laws made by local authorities since these are elected bodies and accountable to the local citizens.

Sub-delegation

Another problem is that of sub-delegation, which means that the law-making authority is handed down another level. This causes comments that much of our law is made by civil servants and merely 'rubber stamped' by the minister of that department.

Large volume and lack publicity

The large volume of delegated legislation also gives rise to criticism, since it makes it difficult to discover what the present law is. This problem is aggravated by a lack of publicity, as much delegated legislation is made in private and passed through Parliament without debate, in contrast to the public debates of statutory law.

Difficult wording

Finally, delegated legislation shares with Acts of Parliament the same problem of complex and obscure wording that can lead to difficulty in understanding what the law means. Rules of statutory interpretation may have to be used by the courts to understand the meaning of this form of legislation.

	Facts	Comment or case
Control by Parliament	• Enabling Act	Sets the limits of the power to make delegated legislation
	• Delegated Powers Scrutiny Committee	Can only report to Parliament, not amend
	• Affirmative resolutions	Must be approved by both Houses of Parliament before coming into force
	• Negative resolutions	Becomes law unless within 40 days there is an objection
	• Questioning of Ministers	MPs can question ministers in the House
	• Joint Select Committee on statutory instruments	Can thoroughly review but can only report back to Parliament
	• Super-affirmative resolutions	Only used for delegated legislation made under the Legislative and Regulatory Reform Act 2006
Control by the courts	Judicial review to decide if the delegated legislation is:	
	• beyond the powers given in the enabling Act	*R v Home Secretary, ex parte Fire Brigade Union* (1995)
	• unreasonable	*Strickland v Hayes* (1896)
	• failed to follow the correct procedure	*Aylesbury Mushroom case* (1972)
Reason for delegated legislation	• provides detailed and technical rules • expert knowledge used • local knowledge • consultation	
Advantages of delegated legislation	• Saves parliamentary time • Allows use of expert or local knowledge • Allows consultation • Quick to make • Easy to amend	
Disadvantages of delegated legislation	• Undemocratic • Risk of sub-delegation • Large volume and lack publicity • Complex wording requiring interpretation	

Figure 17.4 Delegated legislation

Summary

- There are three types of delegated legislation:
  - Orders in Council made by the Privy Council
  - statutory instruments made by government ministers and departments
  - by-laws made by local councils or other bodies such as the railways.
- Parliament controls delegated legislation by:
  - the enabling Act setting limits on the powers
  - Delegated Powers Scrutiny Committee
  - affirmative or negative resolutions
  - questioning of ministers
  - Joint Select Committee on statutory instruments
  - super-affirmative resolutions.
- The courts control delegated legislation through the judicial review process when it is *ultra vires* because:
  - it is beyond the powers given by the enabling Act
  - the decision made is unreasonable
  - it does not go through the correct procedure and consultation.
- Delegated legislation is needed because of the detail needed, consultation required, and for expert or local knowledge.
- Advantages of delegated legislation include: saving of parliamentary time, use of expert or local knowledge, use of consultation, relatively quick to make and easy to amend.
- Disadvantages of delegated legislation include: undemocratic, sub-delegation, large volume, lack of publicity and can be difficult to interpret.

Chapter 18

Statutory interpretation

After reading this chapter you should be able to:
- Understand why it may be necessary for judges to interpret the law
- Understand the three rules of statutory interpretation: the literal rule, the golden rule, the mischief rule
- Understand the purposive approach
- Understand aids to interpretation: rules of language, internal and external aids
- Understand the impact of European Union law on interpretation
- Understand the impact of the Human Rights Act 1998 on interpretation
- Discuss advantages and disadvantages of the different approaches and aids to interpretation

18.1 The need for statutory interpretation

As seen in Chapter 16, Acts of Parliament are passed after debate in Parliament. The meaning of the law in these statutes should be clear but this is not always the case. In order to help with understanding, an Act can include an interpretation section defining the meaning of certain words. In the Theft Act 1968, for example, the definition of theft is given in s 1, and then ss 2–6 define key words such as 'appropriate' and 'property'. To help judges with the meaning of general words the Interpretation Act 1978 makes it clear that, unless the contrary appears, 'he' includes 'she', and singular includes plural.

Many cases come before the courts each year because there is a dispute over the meaning of words in an Act of Parliament. In such cases the court's task is to decide the exact meaning of a particular word or phrase. There are many reasons why meaning may be unclear:
- A broad term

    There may be words designed to cover several possibilities. For example in the Dangerous Dogs Act 1991 there is a phrase 'any dog of the type known as the pit bull terrier'. This seems a simple phrase

but has led to problems. What is meant by 'type'? Does it mean the same as 'breed'? In *Brock v DPP* (1993) this was the key point in dispute and the Queen's Bench Divisional Court decided that 'type' had a wider meaning than 'breed'. It could cover dogs which were not pedigree pit bull terriers, but had a substantial number of the characteristics of such a dog.
- Ambiguity

    This is where a word has two or more meanings; it may not be clear which meaning should be used.
- A drafting error

    The draftsman who prepared the original Bill may have made an error which has not been noticed by Parliament or where the Bill was amended several times while going through Parliament.
- New developments

    New technology may mean that an old Act of Parliament does not apparently cover present day situations. This is seen in the case of *Royal College of Nursing v DHSS* (1981) where medical science and methods had changed since the passing of the Abortion Act in 1967. This case is discussed more fully at section 18.2.3.
- Changes in the use of language

The meaning of words can change over the years. This was one of the problems in the case of *Cheeseman v DPP* (1990). *The Times* law report of this case is set out in this chapter as an activity.

18.2 The three rules

In English law the judges have not been able to agree on which approach should be used, but instead, over the years three different rules of interpretation have been developed. These are:

- the literal rule
- the golden rule
- the mischief rule.

These rules take different approaches to interpretation and some judges prefer to use one rule, while other judges prefer another rule. This means that the interpretation of a statute may differ according to which judge is hearing the case. However, once an interpretation has been laid down, it may then form a precedent for future cases under the normal rules of judicial precedent. Since the three rules can result in very different decisions, it is important to understand them.

18.2.1 The literal rule

The **literal rule** developed in the early nineteenth century and was the main rule used for the first part of the twentieth century. It is still used as the starting point for interpreting any legislation.

Under this rule courts will give words their plain, ordinary or literal meaning, even if the result is not very sensible. This idea was expressed by Lord Esher in *R v Judge of the City of London Court* (1892) when he said:

> If the words of an act are clear then you must follow them even though they lead to a manifest absurdity. The court has nothing to do with the question whether the legislature has committed an absurdity.

Key term

Literal rule – a rule of statutory interpretation that gives the words their plain, ordinary, dictionary meaning.

Cases using the literal rule

The rule was used in *Whiteley v Chappell* (1868).

Key case

Whiteley v Chappell (1868)

In this case the defendant was charged under a section which made it an offence to impersonate 'any person entitled to vote'. The defendant had pretended to be a person whose name was on the voters' list, but who had died. The court held that the defendant was not guilty since a dead person is not, in the literal meaning of the words, 'entitled to vote'.

Using the literal rule in this case resulted in an absurd decision. The defendant was impersonating someone else in order to vote when he was not entitled to do so. That was what the law was aimed at preventing.

The rule can also lead to what are considered as harsh decisions. This occurred in *London & North Eastern Railway Co. v Berriman* (1946).

Key case

London & North Eastern Railway Co. v Berriman (1946)

A railway worker was killed while doing maintenance work, oiling points along a railway line. His widow tried to claim compensation because there had not been a look-out provided by the railway company in accordance with a regulation under the Fatal Accidents Act which stated that a look-out should be provided for men working on or near the railway line 'for the purposes of relaying or repairing' it. The court took the words 'relaying' and 'repairing' in their literal meaning and said that oiling points was maintaining the line and not relaying or repairing so that Mrs Berriman's claim failed.

Mr Berriman had been on the railway lines as part of his work and his safety should have been ensured. Literally, he was not 'repairing or relaying', but applying the words literally led to an unjust decision.

Activity

Read the following law report and answer the questions below.

Lurking policeman not 'passengers'

Cheeseman v Director of Public Prosecutions (1990)

Police officers who witnessed a man masturbating in a public lavatory were not 'passengers' within the meaning of section 28 of the Town Police Clauses Act 1847 when they had been stationed in the lavatory following complaints.

The Queen's Bench Divisional Court so held in allowing an appeal by way of case stated by Ashley Frederick Cheeseman against his conviction of an offence of wilfully and indecently exposing his person in a street to the annoyance of passengers.

Section 81 of the Public Health Acts Amendment Act 1907 extended the meaning of the word 'street' in section 28 to include, inter alia, any place of public resort under the control of the local authority.

LORD JUSTICE BINGHAM, concurring with Mr Justice Waterhouse, said that The Oxford English Dictionary showed that in 1847, when the Act was passed, 'passenger' had a meaning, now unusual except in the expression 'foot-passenger' of 'a passer-by or through; a traveller (usually on foot); a wayfarer'.

Before the meaning of 'street' was enlarged in 1907 that dictionary definition of passenger was not hard to apply: it clearly covered anyone using the street for ordinary purposes of passage or travel.

The dictionary definition could not be so aptly applied to a place of public resort such as a public lavatory, but on a commonsense reading when applied in context 'passenger' had to mean anyone resorting in the ordinary way to a place for one of the purposes for which people would normally resort to it.

If that was the correct approach, the two police officers were not 'passengers'. They were stationed in the public lavatory in order to apprehend persons committing acts which had given rise to earlier complaints. They were not resorting to that place of public resort in the ordinary way but for a special purpose and thus were not passengers.

Source: The Times, 2 November 1990

Questions

1. In this case the meaning of the word 'street' was important. Why did the court decide the word 'street' in the Act included a public lavatory?
2. The meaning of the word 'passenger' was also important. How did the court discover what this word meant in 1847?
3. The court decided that 'passenger' meant 'a passer-by or through; a traveller (usually on foot); a wayfarer'. Why did that definition not apply to the police officers who arrested the defendant?
4. The defendant was found not guilty because of the way the court interpreted 'passenger'. Do you think this was a correct decision? Give reasons for your answer.

18.2.2 The golden rule

The **golden rule** is a modification of the literal rule. It starts by looking at the literal meaning of the words but the court is then allowed to avoid an interpretation which would lead to an absurd result. There are two views on how far the golden rule should be used. The first is very narrow and is shown by Lord Reid's comments in *Jones v DPP* (1962) when he said:

> It is a cardinal principle applicable to all kinds of statutes that you may not for any reason attach to a statutory provision a meaning which the words of that provision cannot reasonably bear. If they are capable of more than one meaning, then you can choose between those meanings, but beyond this you cannot go.

So under the narrow application of the golden rule the court may only choose between the possible meanings of a word or phrase. If there is only one meaning then that must be taken.

The second and wider application of the golden rule is where the words have only one clear meaning, but that meaning would lead to a repugnant situation. This is a situation in which the court feels that using the clear meaning would produce a result which should not be allowed. In such a case the court will use the golden rule to modify the words of the statute in order to avoid this problem.

Key term

Golden rule – a modification of the literal rule to avoid an interpretation that is absurd.

Cases using the golden rule

The narrow view of the golden rule can be seen in practice in *Adler v George* (1964).

Key case

Adler v George (1964)

The Official Secrets Act 1920 made it an offence to obstruct Her Majesty's Forces 'in the vicinity' of a prohibited place. The defendant had caused an obstruction in the prohibited place. It was argued that he was not guilty as the literal wording of the Act did not apply to anyone **in** the prohibited place. It only applied to those 'in the vicinity', i.e. outside but close to it. Using the golden rule, the Divisional Court found the defendant guilty as it would be absurd if those causing an obstruction outside the prohibited place were guilty, but anyone inside were not. The words should be read as being 'in or in the vicinity of' the prohibited place.

A very clear example of the use of the wider application of the golden rule was the case of *Re Sigsworth* (1935).

Key case

Re Sigsworth (1935)

In this case the son had murdered his mother. The mother had not made a will, so normally her estate would have been inherited by her next of kin according to the rules set out in the Administration of Justice Act 1925. This meant that the murderer son would have inherited as her next of kin or 'issue'.

There was no ambiguity in the words of the Act, but the court was not prepared to let a murderer benefit from his crime. It was held that the literal rule should not apply; the golden rule would be used to prevent the repugnant situation of the son inheriting.

Although the meaning of 'issue' was clear, the court was giving a meaning that the 'issue' of a dead person would not be entitled to inherit where he had killed the person he would be inheriting from.

18.2.3 The mischief rule

This rule gives a judge more discretion than the other two rules. The definition of the mischief rule comes from *Heydon's case* (1584), where it was said that there were four points the court should consider. These, in the original language of that old case, were:

1   'What was the common law before the making of the Act?'

2   'What was the mischief and defect for which the common law did not provide?'

3   'What was the remedy the Parliament hath resolved and appointed to cure the disease of the commonwealth?'

4   'The true reason of the remedy. Then the office of all the judges is always to make such construction as shall suppress the mischief and advance the remedy.'

So, using this rule, the court should look to see what the law was before the Act was passed in order to discover what gap or 'mischief' the Act was intended to cover. The court should then interpret the Act in such a way that the gap is covered (so should provide a remedy). This is clearly a quite different approach to the literal rule.

Key term 🔑

Mischief rule – it looks back to the gap in the previous law and interprets the Act so as to cover the gap.

Cases using the mischief rule

The mischief rule was used in *Smith v Hughes* (1960) to interpret s 1(1) of the Street Offences Act 1959 which said 'it shall be an offence for a common prostitute to loiter or solicit in a street or public place for the purpose of prostitution'.

Key case

Smith v Hughes (1960)

The court considered appeals against the conviction under this section of six different women. In each case the women had not been 'in a street or public place'. One had been on a first-floor balcony of a house and the others had been at the windows of ground floor rooms, with the window either half open or closed. In each case the women were attracting the attention of men by calling to them or tapping on the window. It was argued for them that they were not guilty since they were not literally 'in a street or public place'. The court decided that they were guilty, with Lord Parker saying:

'For my part I approach the matter by considering what is the mischief aimed at by this Act. Everybody knows that this was an Act to clean up the streets, to enable people to walk along the streets without being molested or solicited by common prostitutes. Viewed in this way it can matter little whether the prostitute is soliciting while in the street or is standing in the doorway or on a balcony, or at a window, or whether the window is shut or open or half open.'

It can be seen that the judge was not looking at the exact meaning of the words 'in a street or public place' but he was looking at the mischief or problem that Parliament were attempting to deal with when passing the Act.

A similar point to *Smith v Hughes* arose in *Eastbourne Borough Council v Stirling* (2000).

Key case

Eastbourne Borough Council v Stirling (2000)

A taxi driver was charged with 'plying for hire in any street' without a licence to do so. His vehicle was parked on a taxi rank on the station forecourt, not on a street.

He was found guilty as, although the taxi was on private land, he was likely to get customers from the street. The court referred to *Smith v Hughes* and said that it was the same point.

Another case in which the House of Lords used the mischief rule was the *Royal College of Nursing v DHSS* (1981).

Key case

Royal College of Nursing v DHSS (1981)

In this case the wording of the Abortion Act 1967, which provided that a pregnancy should be 'terminated by a registered medical practitioner', was in issue.

When the Act was passed in 1967 the procedure to carry out an abortion was such that only a doctor (a registered medical practitioner) could do it. From 1972 onwards improvements in medical technique meant that the normal method of terminating a pregnancy was to induce premature labour with drugs. The first part of the procedure was carried out by a doctor, but the second part was performed by nurses without a doctor present. The court had to decide if this procedure was lawful under the Abortion Act. The case went to the House of Lords where the majority (three) of the judges held that it was lawful, while the other two said that it was not lawful.

The three judges in the majority based their decision on the mischief rule. They pointed out that the mischief Parliament was trying to remedy was the unsatisfactory state of the law before 1967 and the number of illegal abortions which put the lives of women at risk. They also said that the policy of the Act was to broaden the grounds for abortion and ensure that they were carried out with proper skill in hospital.

The decision in *Royal College of Nursing v DHSS* was a majority decision and the other two judges took the literal view. They said that the words of the Act were clear and that terminations could only be carried out by a registered medical practitioner. They said that the other judges were not interpreting the Act but 'redrafting it with a vengeance'.

It is clear that the three rules (literal, golden and mischief) can lead to different decisions on the meanings of words and phrases. See below for an activity based on a real case in which the different rules could result in different decisions.

Activity

Read the facts of the case set out below then apply the different rules of interpretation.

CASE: *Fisher v Bell* [1960] 1 QB 394

The Restriction of Offensive Weapons Act 1959, s 1(1):

> Any person who manufactures, sells or hires or offers for sale or hire or lends or gives to any other person – (a) any knife which has a blade which opens automatically by hand pressure applied to a button, spring or other device in or attached to the handle of the knife, sometimes known as a 'flick knife' ... shall be guilty of an offence.

FACTS: The defendant was a shop keeper, who had displayed a flick knife marked with a price in his shop window. He was charged under s 1(1) and the court had to decide whether he was guilty of offering the knife for sale. There is a technical legal meaning of 'offers for sale', under which putting an article in a shop window is not an offer to sell but an invitation to treat (students of contract law will learn this rule).

Consider the phrase 'offers for sale' and explain how you think the case would have been decided using:

a   the literal rule

b   the golden rule

c   the mischief rule.

Literal rule	Golden rule	Mischief rule
Words given their plain ordinary meaning	Can choose best interpretation of ambiguous words OR avoid an absurd or repugnant result	Looks at the gap on the law prior to the Act and interprets words to 'suppress the mischief'
Cases *Whiteley v Chappell* (1868) Not guilty of impersonating someone entitled to vote because a dead person was not entitled to vote *LNER v Berriman* (1946) Not literally 'relaying or repairing' track so widow could not claim compensation	**Cases** *Adler v George* (1964) The words 'in the vicinity' held to include being in the place *Re Sigsworth* (1935) A son who murdered his mother could not inherit her estate as it would be repugnant	**Cases** *Smith v Hughes* (1960) Prostitutes calling from doorways, windows or balconies were 'in a street or public place' *Royal College of Nursing v DHSS* (1981) Even though the second part of an abortion procedure was not carried out by a doctor, the procedure was lawful as it prevented the mischief of illegal abortions

Figure 18.1 The three rules of statutory interpretation

18.3 The purposive approach

The **purposive approach** goes beyond the mischief rule in that the court is not just looking to see what the gap was in the old law. The judges are deciding what they believe Parliament meant to achieve. They are looking to see what the purpose of the Act was.

Key term 🔑

Purposive approach – the courts look to see what is the purpose of the law passed by Parliament.

18.3.1 Cases using the purposive approach

The purposive approach was used in *R v Registrar-General, ex parte Smith* (1990).

Key case

R v Registrar-General, ex parte Smith (1990)

The court had to consider s 51 of the Adoption Act 1976 which stated:

> (1) Subject to subsections (4) and (6), the Registrar-General shall on an application made in the prescribed manner by an adopted person a record of whose birth is kept by the Registrar-General and who has attained the age of 18 years supply to that person ... such information as is necessary to enable that person to obtain a certified copy of the record of his birth.

Subsection 4 said that before supplying that information the Registrar-General had to inform the applicant about counselling services available. Subsection 6 stated that if the adoption was before 1975 the Registrar-General could not give the information unless the applicant had attended an interview with a counsellor.

An application was made by Charles Smith for information to enable him to obtain his birth certificate. Mr Smith had made his application in the correct manner and was prepared to see a counsellor. On a literal view of the Act the Registrar-General had to supply him with the information, since the Act uses the phrase 'shall ... supply'.

The problem was that Mr Smith had been convicted of two murders and was detained in Broadmoor as he suffered from recurring bouts of psychotic illness. A psychiatrist thought that it was possible he might be hostile towards his natural mother.

This posed a difficulty for the court; should they apply the clear meaning of the words in this situation? The judges in the Court of Appeal decided that the case called for the purposive approach. They said that, despite the plain language of the Act, Parliament could not have intended to promote serious crime. So, in view of the risk to the applicant's natural mother if he discovered her identity, they ruled that the Registrar-General did not have to supply any information.

The decision in *R v Registrar-General, ex parte Smith* is a very wide use of the purposive approach. Another case in which the purposive approach was used was *R (on the application of Quintavalle) v Human Fertilisation and Embryology Authority* (2003).

Key case

R (on the application of Quintavalle) v Human Fertilisation and Embryology Authority (2003)

The House of Lords had to decide whether organisms created by cell nuclear replacement (CNR) came within the definition of 'embryo' in the Human Fertilisation and Embryology Act 1990. Section 1(1)(a) of this Act states that 'embryo means a live human embryo where fertilisation is complete'.

When the Act was passed in 1990 there was only one way of creating an embryo outside the human body. This was by taking an egg from a woman and sperm from a man and fertilising the egg with the sperm. The fertilised egg could then be placed in a woman's uterus and, if it established itself, she would be pregnant. This is the normal method of helping those unable to conceive naturally to have children.

However, by 2003 another method of producing an embryo had become possible. This was through CNR. Fertilisation is not used in CNR. Instead, the nucleus from one cell of an unfertilised egg is removed. It is then replaced with the nucleus from an adult cell and, if the cell now divides, it is possible to produce an embryo. This technique is known as cloning.

Using the purposive approach, the House of Lords decided that embryos produced through CNR were covered by the 1990 Act. In his judgment in the case Lord Bingham said:

[T]he court's task, within permissible bounds of interpretation is to give effect to Parliament's purpose ... Parliament could not have intended to distinguish between embryos produced by, or without, fertilisation since it was unaware of the latter possibility.

Tip

When explaining a rule or approach, illustrate the description with a case to show how judges approached the interpretation. Also include the exact statutory words to show which words needed to be interpreted.

18.4 Advantages and disadvantages of the rules and approaches to statutory interpretation

18.4.1 The literal rule

Advantages

The main advantage of the literal rule is that the rule follows the words that the democratically elected Parliament has used. Parliament is our law-making body and it is right that judges should apply the law exactly as it is written. Using the literal rule to interpret Acts of Parliament prevents unelected judges from making law.

Another advantage is that using the literal rule should make the law more certain, as the law will be interpreted exactly as it is written. This makes it easier for lawyers to know what the law is and how judges will apply it.

Disadvantages

The literal rule assumes every Act is perfectly drafted. In fact it is not always possible to word an Act so that it covers every situation Parliament meant. This was seen in the case of *Whiteley v Chappell* (1868) where the defendant was not guilty of voting under another person's name.

Another problem is that words may have more than one meaning, so that the Act is unclear. Often in dictionaries words are defined with several different meanings. At section 18.1 we have already seen that there was difficulty in interpreting the word 'type' in the Dangerous Dogs Act 1991.

Following the words exactly can lead to unfair or unjust decisions. This was seen in *London & North Eastern Railway Co. v Berriman* (1946) where a workman's widow was unable to claim compensation when he was killed while maintaining the track.

Her claim failed because literally he was not 'relaying or repairing' it.

With decisions such as *Whiteley v Chappell* and the *Berriman case*, it is not surprising that Professor Michael Zander has denounced the literal rule as being mechanical and divorced from the realities of the use of language.

18.4.2 The golden rule

Advantages

The golden rule respects the exact words of Parliament except in limited situations. Its main advantage is that where there is a problem with using the literal rule, it provides an 'escape route'.

The fact that it is only used in limited situations means that it avoids the judges making law to any great extent. As it is based in the literal rule, it respects the words that Parliament has chosen except in very limited situations.

It allows the judge to choose the most sensible meaning where there is more than one meaning to the words in the Act. It avoids absurd outcomes. It can also provide sensible decisions in cases where the literal rule would lead to a repugnant situation. It would clearly have been unjust to allow the son in *Re Sigsworth* to benefit from his crime. In this case the use of the golden rule led to a just decision.

Effectively it avoids the worst problems of the literal rule.

Disadvantages

The main disadvantage is that it is very limited in its use. It is only used on rare occasions. Another problem is that it is not always possible to predict when courts will use the golden rule. Michael Zander has described it as a 'feeble parachute'. In other words, it is an escape route but it cannot do very much.

It can also be argued that it is not always possible to define what is 'absurd'. This is a subjective decision and use of the rule might give a judge too much discretion.

18.4.3 The mischief rule

Advantages

The mischief rule promotes the purpose of the law as it allows judges to look back at the gap in the law which the Act was designed to cover. The emphasis is on making sure that the gap on the law is filled. In *Smith v Hughes* the purpose of the law

was to stop men being propositioned in the street by prostitutes.

Another advantage is that this approach is more likely to produce a 'just' result. It also means that judges try to interpret the law in the way that Parliament meant it to work. The Law Commission prefers the mischief rule and, as long ago as 1969, recommended that it should be the only rule used in statutory interpretation.

Disadvantages

The main disadvantage is that using this rule there is the risk of judicial law making. This can be seen by the words of Lord Parker in *Smith v Hughes* when it could be said that it was his view of how Parliament was trying to deal with mischief.

The case of *Royal College of Nursing v DHSS*, where there was a majority 3–2 decision, shows that judges do not always agree on when to use the mischief rule.

Use of the mischief rule may lead to uncertainty in the law. It is impossible to know when judges will use the rule and also what result it might lead to. This makes it difficult for lawyers to advise clients on the law and the result of their case.

The mischief rule is not as wide as the purposive approach as it is limited to looking back at the gap in the old law. It cannot be used for a more general consideration of the purpose of the law.

18.4.4 The purposive approach

Advantages

The main advantage of the purposive approach is that it leads to justice in individual cases. It is a broad approach which allows the law to cover more situations than applying words literally.

The purposive approach is particularly useful where there is new technology which was unknown when the law was enacted. This is demonstrated by *R (Quintavalle) v Secretary of State*. If the literal rule had been used in that case, it would have been necessary for Parliament to make a new law to deal with the situation.

It also gives judges more discretion than using the literal meanings of words. This allows judges to avoid the literal meaning where it would create an absurd situation. If the purposive approach had been used in *Whiteley v Chappell* then it is probable that the judges would have decided that Parliament's intention was to prevent people voting in another person's name and found the defendant guilty.

Disadvantages

The main disadvantage of the purposive approach is that it may mean the judges refuse to follow the clear words of Parliament. How do the judges know what Parliament's intentions were? Opponents of the purposive approach say that it is impossible to discover Parliament's intentions; only the words of the statute can show what Parliament wanted. So, using the purposive approach allows unelected judges to 'make' law as they are deciding what they think the law should be rather than using the words that Parliament enacted.

Another problem with the purposive approach is that it is difficult to discover the intention of Parliament. There are reports of debates in Parliament in *Hansard*, but these give every detail of debates including those MPs who did not agree with the law that was under discussion. The final version of what Parliament agreed is the actual words used in the Act.

It also leads to uncertainty in the law. It is impossible to know when judges will use this approach or what result it might lead to. This makes it difficult for lawyers to advise clients on the law.

> **Tip**
>
> When evaluating a rule or approach to statutory interpretation, support each point with a case example or specific words in an Act.

18.5 Aids to interpretation: rules of language

Even the literal rule does not take words in complete isolation. It is common sense that the other words in the Act must be looked at to see if they affect the meaning of the word or phrase that has to be interpreted. In looking at the other words in the Act the courts have developed a number of minor rules which can help to make the meaning of words and phrases clear. These rules are:

- the *ejusdem generis* rule
- *expressio unius* – the express mention of one thing excludes others
- *noscitur a sociis* – a word is known by the company it keeps.

18.5.1 The *ejusdem generis* rule

This states that where there is a list of specific words followed by general words, then the general words are interpreted in line with the specific words. This is shown in the following case example.

Literal rule	Golden rule	Mischief rule	Purposive approach
Advantages • follows wording of Parliament • prevents unelected judge making law • makes the law more certain • easier to predict how the judges will interpret the law	**Advantages** • respects the words of Parliament • allows the judge to choose the most sensible meaning • avoids the worst problems of the literal rule	**Advantages** • deals with the mischief Parliament was trying to deal with • fills in the gap in the law • produces a 'just' result	**Advantages** • leads to justice in individual cases • allows for new developments in technology • avoids absurd decisions
Disadvantages • not all Acts are perfectly drafted • have more than one meaning • can lead to unfair or unjust decisions	**Disadvantages** • can only be used in limited situations • not possible to predict when the courts will use it • it is a 'feeble parachute' (Zander)	**Disadvantages** • risk of judicial law making • not as wide as the purposive approach • limited to looking back at the old law • can make the law uncertain	**Disadvantages** • difficult to find Parliament's intention • allows judges to make law • leads to uncertainty in the law

Figure 18.2 Advantages and disadvantages of the rules and approaches of statutory interpretation

Key case

Hobbs v CG Robertson Ltd (1970)

A workman injured his eye when brickwork that he was removing splintered. He claimed compensation under the Construction (General Provision) Regulations 1961. These regulations made it a duty for employers to provide goggles for workmen when 'breaking, cutting, dressing or carving of stone, concrete, slag or similar material'. The specific words were 'stone, concrete, slag' and the general words 'or similar material'. The court held that brick did not come within the term 'a similar material'. Brick was not *ejusdem generis* with stone, concrete, slag. The reason was that all the other materials were hard, so that bits would fly off them when struck with a tool, whereas brick was a soft material. This ruling meant that the workman's claim for compensation failed.

There must be at least two specific words in a list before the general word or phrase for this rule to operate. This is illustrated by *Allen v Emmerson* (1944).

Key case

Allen v Emmerson (1944)

The court had to interpret the phrase 'theatres and other places of amusement' and decide if it applied to a funfair. As there was only one specific word, 'theatres', it was decided that a funfair did come under the general term 'other places of amusement' even though it was not of the same kind as theatres.

18.5.2 *Expressio unius exclusio alterius*

This phrase means: the express mention of one thing excludes others.

Where there is a list of words which is not followed by general words, then the Act applies only to the items in the list. This is illustrated by the following case.

Key case

Tempest v Kilner (1846)

The court had to consider whether the Statute of Frauds 1677 (which required a contract for the sale of 'goods, wares and merchandise' of more than £10 to be evidenced in writing) applied to a contract for the sale of stocks and shares. The list 'goods, wares and merchandise' was not followed by any general words, so the court held that only contracts for those three types of things were affected by the statute; because stocks and shares were not mentioned they were not caught by the statute.

18.5.3 *Noscitur a sociis*

This phrase means: a word is known by the company it keeps.

This means that the words must be looked at in context and interpreted accordingly; it involves looking at other words in the same section or at other sections in the Act. Words in the same section were important in *Inland Revenue Commissioners v Frere* (1965).

Key case

Inland Revenue Commissioners v Frere (1965)

The case involved interpreting a section which set out rules for 'interest, annuities or other annual interest'. The first use of the word 'interest' on its own could have meant any interest paid, whether daily, monthly or annually. Because of the words 'other annual interest' in the section, the court decided that 'interest' only meant annual interest.

18.6 Aids to interpretation: intrinsic and extrinsic aids

There are some aids to help the judges with interpretation. These can be either intrinsic (internal) aids or extrinsic (external) aids.

18.6.1 Intrinsic aids

These are matters within the statute itself that may help to make its meaning clearer. The court can consider the long title, the short title and the preamble, if any. Older statutes usually have a preamble which sets out Parliament's purpose in enacting that statute. Modern statutes either do not have a preamble or contain a very brief one, for example the Theft Act 1968 states that it is an Act to modernise the law of theft. The long title may also explain briefly Parliament's intentions.

Some Acts will have an interpretation section in them. For example, s 4(1) of the Theft Act 1968 states that 'property' includes 'money and all other property real or personal, including things in action and other intangible property'.

Sometimes an interpretation section will just give an extended meaning to certain words. This is seen in s 9(3) of the Theft Act 1968 where it states that 'building' includes 'an inhabited vehicle or vessel'. So caravans and houseboats are included, although they are not literally 'buildings'.

The other useful internal aids are any headings before a group of sections, and any schedules attached to the Act. There are often also marginal notes explaining different sections but these are not generally regarded as giving parliament's intention as they will have been inserted after the parliamentary debates and are only helpful comments put in by the printer.

It is also possible to look at other sections in the Act as these may help. An example of this is shown by the case of *Harrow LBC v Shah and Shah* (1999).

Advantages of intrinsic aids

Some of these are placed in the statute by Parliament in order to make the law clearer. This means that the courts are more likely to come to the interpretation that Parliament intended.

In older statutes, the inclusion of a long preamble setting out the purpose of Parliament was particularly helpful.

In some statutes there may be a definition section which sets out what is meant by certain words or phrases. In the Theft Act 1968, definitions are given for a number of words. For example, in the offence of burglary, the word 'building' is used. There is a definition for this word which states that it applies to 'an inhabited vehicle or vessel'.

Disadvantages of intrinsic aids

They are not included in every statute. In particular, modern statutes do not have long preambles.

Some intrinsic aids such as headings may be placed there by printers and do not necessarily reflect Parliament's intention.

Definitions are not always included and this can lead to uncertainty. In the Theft Act 1968, the word 'dishonestly' is not defined, although there is a section setting out situations which are not to be regarded as dishonest. The lack of a definition for 'dishonestly' has meant that the judges have had to interpret it in case law.

18.6.2 Extrinsic aids

These are outside the Act, which can help explain the meaning of words in an Act. These undisputed sources are:

- Dictionaries of the time of the passing of the Act. It must be a dictionary published at the time when the Act was passed because the meanings of words change over time. A dictionary of 1847 was used in the case of *Cheeseman v DPP* because the Act in question was passed in 1847. See section 18.2.1 for the case of *Cheeseman v DPP*.
- *Hansard* – that is the official report of what was said in Parliament when the Act was debated. Until 1992 there was a firm rule that the courts could not look at what was said in the debates in Parliament. However, in *Pepper v Hart* (1993) the House of Lords relaxed the rule and accepted that *Hansard* could be used by judges in a limited way. *Hansard* may be considered but only where the words of the Act are ambiguous or obscure or lead to an absurdity. Even then *Hansard* should only be used if there was a clear statement by the minister introducing the legislation, which would resolve the ambiguity or absurdity.

Advantages of using *Hansard*

Hansard is available for everyone to consult. It gives the entire debate of Parliament on the statute in question. This means that not only can the minister or promoter's statements be found, but also the discussion and questions that led to the statement. This may make the words in the statute much clearer.

In some cases *Hansard* can be very helpful. This was shown in *AE Beckett & Sons (Lyndons) Ltd v Midland Electricity* (2001) where the meaning of s 21 of the Electricity Act 1989 was in issue. Lord Phillips in his judgment said that reference to *Hansard* had 'immediately made clear what had previously been obscure'.

Disadvantages of using *Hansard*

Referring to *Hansard* is not always helpful. The particular words at issue may not have been mentioned in the debate. Alternatively, what was said may not make the words any clearer.

In *R v Deegan* (1998) the Court of Appeal was concerned with the meaning of 'folding pocketknife'.

The court found that the statements made by the minister in the debate were not clear and they refused to take them into account.

Another disadvantage is the additional costs involved as lawyers feel obliged to spend expensive time reading through all the relevant debates in order to avoid being sued for negligence by their clients.

- Reports of law reform bodies such as the Law Commission which led to the passing of the Act. As with *Hansard*, the courts used to hold that reports by law reform agencies such as the Law Reform Agency should not be considered by the courts. However this rule was relaxed in the *Black-Clawson* case in 1975, when it was accepted that such a report should be looked at to discover the mischief or gap in the law which the legislation based on the report was designed to deal with.

With increased use of the purposive approach, the courts have become much more prepared to look at Law Commission reports. In the Law Commission's report for 2014–15 it was pointed out that the Law Commission's work had been cited in 404 cases in the United Kingdom and in three cases in other common law jurisdictions such as Canada. So today Law Commission reports are an important external aid to statutory interpretation.

See Chapter 20 for detail on the Law Commission.

Advantages of law reform reports as an aid to statutory interpretation

Reports by law reform bodies are issued after research, consultation and considerable preparation. Problems in the current law are usually identified and the report will set out the reasons for their proposed change to the law. All this will help the court understand the purpose for the new law.

In many cases the report will include a draft Bill. Where that Bill has become law without alteration, it is clear that Parliament agreed with the report. So it helps with finding the intention of Parliament.

Disadvantages of law reform reports as an aid to statutory interpretation

In some cases the proposals for reform and/or the draft Bill will not be wholly accepted by the government, and they will include different changes to the Bill. Or the Bill may start as the one drafted by the law reform body but be changed during the legislative process.

In these situations the report is not helpful, as Parliament's intention is not the same as in the report.

Law Commission reports are only available for limited areas of law. So there may not be any report on the particular point arising in court.

- International conventions, EU Regulations or EU Directives that have been implemented by English legislation. In the rare cases where the statute has been passed to bring an international convention into English law, it is possible to look back to the original convention.

In *Fothergill v Monarch Airlines Ltd* (1980) the House of Lords decided that the original convention should be considered as it was possible that in translating and adapting the convention to our legislative process, the true meaning of the original might have been lost.

The House of Lords also held that an English court could consider any preparatory materials or explanatory notes published with an international convention. The reasoning behind this was that other countries allowed the use of such material, known as *travaux préparatoires*, and it should therefore be allowed in this country in order to get uniformity in the interpretation of international rules.

18.7 The effect of EU law on statutory interpretation

The purposive approach is the one preferred by most European countries when interpreting their own legislation. It is also the approach which has been adopted by the European Court of Justice in interpreting European Union law.

From the time when the United Kingdom became a member of the European Union in 1973, the influence of the European preference for the purposive approach has affected the English courts in two ways. First, they have had to accept that for law which has been passed as a result of having to conform to a European Union law, the purposive approach is the correct one to use. Second, the fact that judges have had to use the purposive approach for European Union law for over 40 years has made them more accustomed to it and, therefore, more likely to apply it to English law.

Even though the UK voted to leave the EU, English judges are likely to continue to use the purposive approach.

18.7.1 Interpreting EU Law

Where the law to be interpreted is based on European Union law, the English courts have had to interpret it in the light of the wording and purpose of European

Union law. This is because the Treaty of Rome, which set out the duties of European Union Member States, required all Member States to 'take all appropriate measures ... to ensure fulfilment of the obligations'.

The European Court of Justice in the *Marleasing case* (1992) ruled that this included interpreting national law in the light and the aim of European Union law.

When the UK leaves the EU this strict requirement will no longer apply.

18.8 The effect of the Human Rights Act 1998 on statutory interpretation

Section 3 of the Human Rights Act says that, so far as it is possible to do so, legislation must be read and given effect in a way which is compatible with the rights in the European Convention on Human Rights. This applies to any case where one of the rights is concerned, but it does not apply where there is no involvement of human rights.

An example of the effect of the Human Rights Act on interpretation is *Mendoza v Ghaidan* (2002) which involved interpretation of the Rent Act 1977.

Key case

Mendoza v Ghaidan (2002)

The Rent Act applied where a person who had the tenancy of a property died. It allowed unmarried partners to succeed to the tenancy as it stated that 'a person who was living with the original tenant as his or her wife or husband shall be treated as the spouse of the original tenant'.

The question was whether same sex partners had the right to take over the tenancy. A previous House of Lords' decision, made before the Human Rights Act came into effect, had ruled that same sex partners did not have the right under the Rent Act to take over the tenancy.

In this case the Court of Appeal held that the Rent Act had to be interpreted to conform to the European Convention on Human Rights which forbids discrimination on the ground of gender. In order to make the Act compatible with human rights, the Court of Appeal read the words 'living with the original tenant as his or her wife or husband' to mean 'as if they were his or her wife or husband'. This allowed same sex partners to have the same rights as unmarried opposite sex couples.

	Brief definition	Case example
Literal approach	Words given plain, ordinary meaning	*London & North Eastern Railway Co. v Berriman* (1946)
Purposive approach	Looking at the reasons why the law was passed and interpreting it accordingly	*Royal College of Nursing v DHSS* (1981)
Rules of language	*Ejusdem generis* General words which follow a list are limited to the same kind *Expressio unius* The express mention of one thing excludes others	*Hobbs v CG Robertson Ltd* (1970) *Tempest v Kilner* (1846)
	Noscitur a sociis A thing is known by the company it keeps	*Inland Revenue Commissioners v Frere* (1965)
Internal aids	Within the Act	*Harrow LBC v Shah and Shah* (1999)
External aids	Outside the Act – includes: • Hansard • Law Commission reports • dictionaries of the time the Act was passed	*Pepper v Hart* (1993) *Black-Clawson case* (1975) *Cheeseman v DPP* (1990)
Impact of EU law	EU law uses the purposive approach • interpreting national law in the light and the aim of the European Union law • has made our judges more ready to use the purposive approach	*Marleasing case* (1992)
Impact of the Human Rights Act 1998	Legislation must be read and given effect in a way which is compatible with the rights in the European Convention on Human Rights	*Mendoza v Ghaidan* (2002)

Figure 18.3 Statutory interpretation

The Court of Appeal pointed out the importance of conforming to the Convention rights when they said:

> In order to remedy this breach of the Convention the court must, if it can, read the Schedule so that its provisions are rendered compatible with the Convention rights of the survivors of same-sex partnerships.

In 2004 the House of Lords confirmed the Court of Appeal's decision in this case.

Tip

When describing or evaluating a rule of language or the use of aids to interpretation, support your description or point with a case example or specific words in an Act.

Summary

- Interpretation is needed because of such problems as:
  - failure of legislation to cover a specific point
  - a broad term
  - ambiguity
  - drafting errors
  - new technological developments.

- The original three rules of statutory interpretation are:
  - the literal rule – the plain ordinary grammatical meaning
  - the golden rule – allows modification of words where the literal rule would lead to absurdity, repugnance or inconsistency
  - the mischief rule – considers the 'mischief' or gap in the old law and interprets the Act in such a way that the gap is covered.

- The purposive approach is more modern and looks for the intention of Parliament.

- The three rules of language are:
  - *Ejusdem generis* – general words which follow a list are limited to the same kind

- *Expressio unius* – the express mention of one thing excludes others
- *Noscitur a sociis* – a thing is known by the company it keeps.

- Intrinsic aids are those in the relevant Act and include:
  - the short title and preamble
  - interpretation sections
  - headings
  - schedules.

- Extrinsic aids to interpretation include:
  - previous Acts of Parliament
  - the historical setting
  - earlier case law
  - dictionaries
  - *Hansard*
  - Law Commission reports
  - international conventions.

- There are advantages and disadvantages to all the rules, aids and approaches of statutory interpretation.

Chapter 19

Judicial precedent

After reading this chapter you should be able to:
- Understand what is meant by the doctrine of precedent
- Understand the meaning of *stare decisis, ratio decidendi* and *obiter dicta*
- Understand the hierarchy of the courts (including the Supreme Court)
- Understand binding, persuasive and original precedent
- Understand overruling, reversing and distinguishing
- Discuss advantages and disadvantages of judicial precedent

19.1 The doctrine of precedent

Judicial precedent refers to the source of law where past decisions of the judges create law for future judges to follow. This source of law is also known as case law. It is a major source of law, both historically and today.

Judicial precedent is very important in common law legal systems. In the English legal system, the **doctrine of precedent** means that courts must follow decisions of the courts above. Also appeal courts will usually follow their own previous decisions.

In countries that operate a civil legal system, previous cases are used as a guide but they do not have to be followed.

> **Key term** 🔑
>
> **Doctrine of precedent** – judges following the decisions of previous cases.

19.2 Judgments: *stare decisis, ratio decidendi, obiter dicta*

19.2.1 *Stare decisis*

The doctrine of precedent is based on the Latin maxim *stare decisis et non quieta movere*, usually shortened to **stare decisis**. This means 'stand by what has been decided and do not unsettle the established'. So precedent is 'standing by' or following decisions in previous cases.

So, where the point of law in the previous case and the present case is the same, the court hearing the present case should follow the decision in the previous case. This concept of treating similar cases in the same way promotes the idea of fairness and provides certainty in the law.

It is particularly important in the English legal system as our laws developed from custom and the decisions of judges in cases.

> **Key term** 🔑
>
> **Stare decisis** – this means 'stand by what has been decided and do not unsettle the established'. It is the foundation of judicial precedent.

Example

In the English legal system, once there has been a decision on a point of law, that decision immediately becomes a precedent for later cases. This is illustrated by *Automatic Telephone and Electric Co. Ltd v Registrar of Restrictive Trading Agreements* (1965).

The Court of Appeal made a decision in *Schweppes Ltd Registrar of Restrictive Trading Agreements* (1965) on discovery of documents. One judge (Willmer LJ) disagreed with the other two. Later on the same day, the same point of law arose in *Automatic Telephone and Electric Co. Ltd v Registrar of Restrictive Trading Agreements*. This case was heard by the same three judges. This time Willmer LJ did not disagree. He pointed out:

I am now bound by the decision of the majority in the previous case. In these circumstances, I have no alternative but to concur in saying that the appeal in the present case should be allowed.

The decision in the *Schweppes case* had become a precedent that had to be followed in the next case.

19.2.2 *Ratio decidendi*

Precedent can only operate if the legal reasons for past decisions are known, so at the end of a case there will be a judgment. This is a speech made by the judge (or judges) hearing the case giving the decision and explaining the reasons for the decision. In a judgment the judge usually gives a summary of the facts of the case, reviews the arguments put to him by the advocates in the case, and then explains the principles of law he is using to come to the decision.

These principles are the important part of the judgment and are known as the *ratio decidendi* which means the reason for deciding (and is pronounced ray-she-o dess-i-dend-i). This is what creates a precedent for judges to follow in future cases.

It is also worth realising that there can be more than one speech at the end of a case depending on the number of judges hearing the case. In courts of first instance there will be only one judge and therefore one judgment. However, in the Divisional Courts and the Court of Appeal cases are heard by at least two judges and usually three. In the Supreme Court, the panel of judges must consist of an uneven number, so it could be three, five, seven, nine or even eleven. This means that there can be more than one judgment.

The fact that there are two or more judges does not mean that there will always be several judgments as it is quite common for one judge to give the judgment and the other judge/judges simply to say 'I agree'! However, in cases where there is a particularly important or complicated point of law, more than one judge may want to explain his legal reasoning on the point. This can cause problems in later cases as each judge may have had a different reason for his decision, so there will be more than one *ratio decidendi*.

> ### Key term 🔑
>
> *Ratio decidendi* – this is the reason for the decision. This forms a precedent for future cases.

A major problem when looking at a past judgment is to divide the *ratio decidendi* from the *obiter dicta* (see below). Older judgments are usually in a continuous form, without any headings specifiying what is meant to be part of the *ratio* and what is not. This means that the person reading the judgment (especially a judge in a later case) will have to decide what the *ratio* is.

Sir Rupert Cross defined the *ratio decidendi* as 'any rule expressly or impliedly treated by the judge as a necessary step in reaching his conclusion'. Michael Zander says that it is 'a proposition of law which decides the case, in the light or in the context of the material facts'.

It depends on the level of the court making the decision as to whether the *ratio* has to be followed by a later court (a binding precedent) or whether it merely has to be considered by that court.

19.2.3 *Obiter dicta*

The *ratio decidendi* is the only part of a judgment that forms a precedent. The rest of the judgment is known as *obiter dicta* (other things said). *Obiter dicta* are not binding on other courts.

Sometimes a judge will speculate on what his decision would have been if the facts of the case had been different. This hypothetical situation is part of the *obiter dicta* and the legal reasoning put forward in it may be considered in future cases, although as with all *obiter* statements it is not binding precedent.

> ### Key term 🔑
>
> *Obiter dicta* – this means 'other things said'. So it is all the rest of the judgment apart from the *ratio decidendi*. Judges in future cases do not have to follow it.

19.3 The hierarchy of the courts

In England and Wales the courts operate a very rigid doctrine of judicial precedent which has the effect that:
- every court is bound to follow any decision made by a court above it in the hierarchy and
- in general, appellate courts are bound by their own past decisions.

There are two exceptions where lower courts in our legal system are not bound to follow decisions by the English appellate courts. These are:

1 where there is a decision of the Court of Justice of the European Union when the English courts have to follow that decision (and will have to until the UK leaves the EU)

2 in cases involving human rights – for these, section 2 of the Human Rights Act 1998 requires courts to take into account judgments, decisions and opinions of the European Court of Human Rights, and it is unlawful for a domestic court, as a public authority, to act in a way that is incompatible with a Convention right.

So the hierarchy of the courts is the next important point to get clear. Which courts come where in the hierarchy? Figure 19.1 shows this in the form of a cascade model and Figure 19.2 gives each court and its position in respect of the other courts. The position of each court is considered in this section. Extra detail on the use of precedent in the Supreme Court (formerly the House of Lords) and Court of Appeal is given in sections 19.4 and 19.5.

19.3.1 Appellate courts

Appellate courts are those that hear appeals. In the English legal system these are:

- Court of Justice of the European Union
- Supreme Court
- Court of Appeal
- Divisional Courts.

The Court of Justice of the European Union

From 1973, and until the UK leaves the European Union, the highest court affecting the English legal system is the Court of Justice of the European Union. Points of EU law can be referred to it by courts in England and Wales. The Court of Justice of the European Union only decides the point of law; the case then comes back to the court in this country to apply that law to the case.

For points of EU law, decisions made by the Court of Justice of the European Union are binding on all courts in England and Wales. It does not affect other areas of law.

An important feature of the Court of Justice of the European Union is that it is prepared to overrule its own past decisions if it feels it is necessary. This flexible approach to past precedents is seen in other legal systems in Europe, and it is a contrast to the more rigid approach of our national courts.

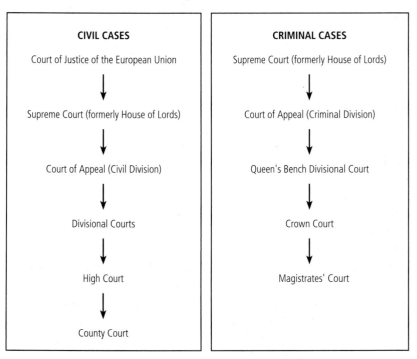

Figure 19.1 Cascade model of judicial precedent operating in the hierarchy of the courts

Supreme Court

The most senior national court is the Supreme Court and its decisions bind all other courts in the English legal system. It replaced the House of Lords in 2009. Decisions by the Supreme Court also bind all lower courts in the English legal system. The Supreme Court is not bound by its own past decisions, nor by decisions of the House of Lords, although it generally will follow them. This point is discussed in detail at section 19.4.

Court of Appeal

At the next level down in the hierarchy is the Court of Appeal; this has two divisions, Civil and Criminal. Both divisions of the Court of Appeal are bound to follow decisions of the Supreme Court. In addition they must usually follow past decisions of their own, although there are some limited exceptions to this rule. The Court of Appeal (Criminal Division) is more flexible where the point involves the liberty of the subject. The position of the two divisions is discussed in detail in section 19.5.

Divisional courts

The three divisional courts (Queen's Bench, Chancery and Family) are bound by decisions of the Supreme Court and the Court of Appeal. In addition the divisional courts are bound by their own past decisions. However, they operate similar exceptions to those operated by the Court of Appeal (see section 19.5.2).

19.3.2 Courts of first instance

The term 'courts of first instance' refers to any court where the original trial of a case is held. The appellate courts considered in the previous section do not hear any original trials. They only deal with appeals from decisions of other courts. Quite often an appeal will be about a point of law. This allows the appellate courts to decide the law. This is why appellate courts are much more important than courts of first instance when it comes to creating precedent.

The High Court

This is bound by decisions of all the courts above and in turn it binds the lower courts. High Court Judges do not have to follow each other's decisions but will usually do so. In *Colchester Estates (Cardiff) v Carlton Industries plc* (1984) it was held that where there were two earlier decisions which conflicted, then, provided the first decision had been fully considered in the later case, that later decision should be followed.

Inferior courts

These are the Crown Court, the County Court and the Magistrates' Court. They are bound to follow decisions by all higher courts and it is unlikely that a decision by an inferior court can create precedent. The one exception is that a ruling on a point of law by a judge in the Crown Court technically creates precedent for the Magistrates' Court. However, since such rulings are rarely recorded in the law reports, this is of little practical effect.

Court	Courts bound by it	Courts it must follow
European Court	All courts	None
Supreme Court	All other courts in the English legal system	European Court
Court of Appeal	Itself (with some exceptions) Divisional Courts All other lower courts	European Court Supreme Court
Divisional Courts	Itself (with some exceptions) High Court All other lower courts	European Court Supreme Court Court of Appeal
High Court	County Court Magistrates' Court	European Court Supreme Court Court of Appeal Divisional Courts
Crown Court	Possibly Magistrates' Court	All higher courts
County Court and Magistrates' Court do not create precedent and are bound by all higher courts		

Figure 19.2 The courts and precedent

19.4 The Supreme Court

The main debate about the former House of Lords and precedent was the extent to which it should follow its own past decisions and the ideas on this changed over the years.

Originally the view was that the House of Lords had the right to overrule past decisions, but gradually during the nineteenth century this more flexible approach disappeared. By the end of that century, in *London Street Tramways v London County Council* (1898), the House of Lords held that certainty in the law was more important than the possibility of individual hardship being caused through having to follow a past decision.

So, from 1898 to 1966 the House of Lords regarded itself as being completely bound by its own past decisions unless the decision had been made *per incuriam*, that is 'in error'. However, this idea of error referred only to situations where a decision had been made without considering the effect of a relevant statute.

This was not felt to be satisfactory. The law could not change to meet changing social conditions and opinions, nor could any possible 'wrong' decisions be changed by the courts. If there was an unsatisfactory decision by the House of Lords, then the only way it could be changed was by Parliament passing a new Act of Parliament.

This happened in the law on intention as an element of a criminal offence. The House of Lords in *DPP v Smith* (1961) had ruled that an accused could be guilty of murder if a reasonable person would have foreseen that death or very serious injury might result from the accused's actions. This decision was criticised as it meant that the defendant could be guilty even if he had not intended to cause death or serious injury, nor even realised that his actions might have that effect. Eventually Parliament changed the law by passing the Criminal Justice Act 1967.

19.4.1 The Practice Statement

It was agreed that the House of Lords should have more flexibility, so in 1966 the Lord Chancellor issued a Practice Statement announcing a change to the rule in *London Street Tramways v London County Council*. The Practice Statement said:

> Their Lordships regard the use of precedent as an indispensable foundation upon which to decide what is the law and its application to individual cases. It provides at least some degree of certainty upon which individuals can rely in the conduct of their affairs, as well as a basis for orderly development of legal rules.

> Their Lordships nevertheless recognise that the rigid adherence to precedent may lead to injustice in a particular case and also unduly restrict the proper development of the law. They, therefore, propose to modify their present practice and while treating former decisions of this House as normally binding, to depart from a previous decision when it appears right to do so.

> In this connection they will bear in mind the danger of disturbing retrospectively the basis on which contracts, settlement of property and fiscal arrangements have been entered into and also the especial need for certainty as to the criminal law.

> This announcement is not intended to affect the use of precedent elsewhere than in this House.

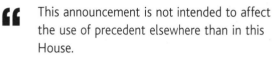

Activity

Read the following passage which comes from an extra explanatory note given to the press when the Practice Statement was issued, and answer the questions below.

The statement is one of great importance, although it should not be supposed that there will frequently be cases in which the House thinks it right not to follow their own precedent. An example of a case in which the House might think it right to depart from a precedent is where they consider that the earlier decision was influenced by the existence of conditions which no longer prevail, and that in modern conditions the law ought to be different.

One consequence of this change is of major importance. The relaxation of the rule of judicial precedent will enable the House of Lords to pay greater attention to judicial decisions reached in the superior courts of the Commonwealth, where they differ from earlier decisions of the House of Lords. That could be of great help in the development of our own law. The superior courts of many other countries are not rigidly bound by their own decisions and the change in the practice of the House of Lords will bring us more into line with them.

Questions

1. Why was the Practice Statement of great importance?
2. Did the note suggest that the Practice Statement was likely to be used often?
3. Do you agree that 'in modern conditions' (see the passage above) the law ought to be different from earlier law decided when social or other conditions in this country were different? Give reasons and examples to support your answer.
4. Why should the House of Lords (now the Supreme Court) want to consider decisions from Commonwealth countries? What authority do such decisions have in the English legal system?

19.4.2 Use of the Practice Statement

From 1966, this Practice Statement allowed the House of Lords to change the law if they believed that an earlier case was wrongly decided. They had the flexibility to refuse to follow an earlier case when 'it appears right to do so'. This phrase is, of course, very vague and gave little guidance as to when the House of Lords might overrule a previous decision. In fact the House of Lords was reluctant to use this power, especially in the first few years after 1966. The first case in which the Practice Statement was used was *Conway v Rimmer* (1968), but this only involved a technical point on discovery of documents.

The first major use did not occur until 1972 in *Herrington v British Railways Board* (1972), which involved the law on the duty of care owed to a child trespasser. The earlier case of *Addie v Dumbreck* (1929) had decided that an occupier of land would only owe a duty of care for injuries to a child trespasser if those injuries had been caused deliberately or recklessly. In *Herrington* the Lords held that social and physical conditions had changed since 1929, and the law should also change.

There was still great reluctance in the House of Lords to use the Practice Statement, as can be seen by the case of *Jones v Secretary of State for Social Services* (1972). This case involved the interpretation of the National Insurance (Industrial Injuries) Act 1946 and four out of the seven judges hearing the case regarded the earlier decision in *Re Dowling* (1967) as being wrong. Despite this the Lords refused to overrule that earlier case, preferring to keep to the idea that certainty was the most important feature of precedent. The same attitude was shown in *Knuller (Publishing, Printing and Promotions) Ltd v DPP* (1973) when Lord Reid said:

> " Our change of practice in no longer regarding previous decisions of this House as absolutely binding does not mean that whenever we think a previous precedent was wrong we should reverse it. In the general interest of certainty in the law we must be sure that there is some very good reason before we so act. "

From the mid-1970s onwards the House of Lords showed a little more willingness to make use of the Practice Statement. For example in *Miliangos v George Frank (Textiles) Ltd* (1976) the House of Lords used the Practice Statement to overrule a previous judgment that damages could only be awarded in sterling.

Another major case was *Pepper v Hart* (1993) where the previous ban on the use of *Hansard* in statutory interpretation was overruled.

19.4.3 The Practice Statement in criminal law

The Practice Statement stressed that criminal law needs to be certain, so it was not surprising that the House of Lords did not rush to overrule any judgments in criminal cases. The first use in a criminal case was in *R v Shivpuri* (1986) which overruled the decision in *Anderton v Ryan* (1985) on attempts to do the impossible. The interesting point was that the decision in *Anderton* had been made less than a year before, but it had been severely criticised by academic lawyers. In *Shivpuri* Lord Bridge said:

> " I am undeterred by the consideration that the decision in *Anderton v Ryan* was so recent. The Practice Statement is an effective abandonment of our pretention to infallibility. If a serious error embodied in a decision of this House has distorted the law, the sooner it is corrected the better. "

In other words, the House of Lords recognised that they might sometimes make errors and the most important thing then was to put the law right. Where the Practice Statement is used to overrule a previous decision, that past case is then effectively ignored. The law is now that set out in the new case.

A more recent major case on the use of the Practice Statement by the House of Lords in criminal law is *R v G* (2003). The House of Lords overruled their previous decision in the case of *Metropolitan Police Commissioner v Caldwell* (1982) on the law of criminal damage.

In *Caldwell* the House of Lords had ruled that recklessness included the situation where the defendant had not realised the risk of his action causing damage, but an ordinary careful adult would have realised there was a risk. In *R v G* it was held that this was the wrong test to use. The Law Lords overruled *Caldwell* and held that a defendant is only reckless if he realised there is risk and goes ahead and takes that risk.

19.4.4 The Supreme Court

When the Supreme Court replaced the House of Lords in 2009, the Constitutional Reform Act 2005 transferred the House of Lords' powers to the Supreme Court. It was initially not sure if this included the Practice Direction.

1898	*London Street Tramways v London County Council*	House of Lords decide they are bound by their own previous decisions
1966	Practice Statement	House of Lords will depart from their own previous decisions when 'it is right to do so'
1968	*Conway v Rimmer*	First use of Practice Statement Only involves technical law on discovery of documents
1972	*Herrington v British Railways Board*	First major use of Practice Statement on the duty of care owed to child trespassers
1973	*Knuller (Publishing, Printing and Promotions) Ltd v DPP*	Certainty in law was important and would not always use Practice Statement
1986	*R v Shivpuri*	First use of Practice Statement in a criminal case
1993	*Pepper v Hart*	Practice Statement used to allow courts to look at *Hansard* for the purpose of statutory interpretation
2003	*R v G and R*	Practice Statement used to overrule the decision in *Caldwell* on recklessness in criminal law
2010	*Austin v London Borough of Southwark*	Supreme Court state that the Practice Statement applies to it
2016	*Knauer v Ministry of Justice*	Supreme Court uses Practice Statement to overrule two previous decisions as to the amount of damages payable in tort cases or personal injury or death

Figure 19.3 The operation of judicial precedent in the House of Lords and Supreme Court

In *Austin v London Borough of Southwark* (2010), which was about tenancy law, the Supreme Court confirmed that the power to use the Practice Statement had been transferred to them. However, they did not use it in Austin to depart from an earlier decision as they took the view that certainty in tenancy law was important.

They quoted from the judgment in *Knuller (Publishing, Printing and Promotions) Ltd v DPP* (1973) where it was said that 'In the general interest of certainty in the law we must be sure that there is some very good reason [to depart from the previous law]'. (See section 19.4.2 for fuller quotation from *Knuller*.)

In 2016 in *Knauer v Ministry of Justice* the Supreme Court used the Practice Statement to overrule two previous decisions of the House of Lords regarding the date damages should be calculated in the law of tort.

19.5 The Court of Appeal

As already stated there are two divisions of this court, the Civil Division and the Criminal Division, and the rules for precedent are not quite the same in these two divisions.

19.5.1 Decisions of courts above the Court of Appeal

Both divisions of the Court of Appeal are bound by decisions of the Court of Justice of the European Union and the House of Lords (now the Supreme Court).

19.5.2 The Court of Appeal and its own decisions

The first rule is that decisions by one division of the Court of Appeal will not bind the other division. However, within each division, decisions are normally binding, especially for the Civil Division. This rule comes from the case of *Young v Bristol Aeroplane Co. Ltd* (1944) and the only exceptions allowed by that case are:
- where there are conflicting decisions in past Court of Appeal cases, the court can choose which one it will follow and which it will reject
- where there is a decision of the Supreme Court/House of Lords which effectively overrules a Court of Appeal decision, the Court of Appeal must follow the decision of the Supreme Court/House of Lords
- where the decision was made *per incuriam*, that is carelessly or by mistake because a relevant Act of Parliament or other regulation has not been considered by the court.

General rules for Court of Appeal	Comment
Bound by European Court of Justice	Since 1972 all courts in England and Wales are bound by the European Court of Justice
Bound by Supreme Court and the former House of Lords	This is because the Supreme Court is above the Court of Appeal in the court hierarchy. Also necessary for certainty in the law. The Court of Appeal tried to challenge this rule in *Broome v Cassell* (1971) and also in *Miliangos* (1976). The House of Lords rejected this challenge. The Court of Appeal must follow decisions of the Supreme Court/House of Lords
Bound by its own past decisions	Decided by the Court of Appeal in *Young's case* (1944), though there are minor exceptions (see below). In *Davis v Johnson* (1979) the Court of Appeal tried to challenge this rule but the House of Lords confirmed that the Court of Appeal had to follow its own previous decisions
Exceptions	Comment
Exceptions in *Young's case*	The Court of Appeal need not follow its own previous decisions where: • there are conflicting past decisions • there is a House of Lords/Supreme Court decision which effectively overrules the Court of Appeal decision • the decision was made *per incuriam* (in error)
Limitation of *per incuriam*	Only used in 'rare and exceptional cases' (*Rickards v Rickards* (1989))
Special exception for the Criminal Division	If the law has been 'misapplied or misunderstood' (*R v Gould* (1968))

Figure 19.4 The Court of Appeal and the doctrine of precedent

The rule in *Young's case* was confirmed in *Davis v Johnson* (1979). In this case the Court of Appeal refused to follow a decision made only days earlier regarding the interpretation of the Domestic Violence and Matrimonial Proceedings Act 1976. The case went to the House of Lords on appeal, where the Law Lords, despite agreeing with the actual interpretation of the law, ruled that the Court of Appeal had to follow its own previous decisions and said that they 'expressly, unequivocally and unanimously reaffirmed the rule in *Young v Bristol Aeroplane*'.

Since this case the Court of Appeal has not challenged the rule in *Young's case*, though it has made some use of the *per incuriam* exception allowed by *Young's case*. For example in *Williams v Fawcett* (1986) the Court refused to follow previous decisions because these had been based on a misunderstanding of the County Court rules dealing with procedure for committing to prison those who break court undertakings.

In *Rickards v Rickards* (1989) Lord Donaldson said that it would only be in 'rare and exceptional cases' that the Court of Appeal would be justified in refusing to follow a previous decision. *Rickards v Rickards* was considered a 'rare and exceptional case' because the mistake was over the critical point of whether the court had the power to hear that particular type of case. Also it was very unlikely that the case would be appealed to the House of Lords.

19.5.3 The Court of Appeal (Criminal Division)

The Criminal Division, as well as using the exceptions from *Young's case*, can also refuse to follow a past decision of its own if the law has been 'misapplied or misunderstood'. This extra exception arises because in criminal cases people's liberty is involved. This idea was recognised in *R v Taylor* (1950). The same point was made in *R v Gould* (1968).

Also in *R v Spencer* (1985) the judges said that there should not in general be any difference in the way that precedent was followed in the Criminal Division and in the Civil Division, 'save that we must remember that we may be dealing with the liberty of the subject and if a departure from authority is necessary in the interests of justice to an appellant, then this court should not shrink from so acting'.

19.6 Binding, persuasive and original precedent

19.6.1 Binding precedent

This is a precedent from an earlier case which must be followed even if the judge in the later case does not agree with the legal principle. A binding precedent is only created when the facts of the second case are sufficiently similar to the original case and the decision was made by a court which is senior to (or in some cases the same level as) the court hearing the later case.

> **Key term** 🔑
>
> **Binding precedent** – a decision in an earlier case which must be followed in later cases.

19.6.2 Persuasive precedent

This is a precedent that is not binding on the court but the judge may consider it and decide that it is a correct principle so he is persuaded that he should follow it. Persuasive precedent comes from a number of sources as explained below.

> **Key term** 🔑
>
> **Persuasive precedent** – a decision which does not have to be followed by later cases, but which a judge may decide to follow.

Courts lower in the hierarchy

An example can be seen in *R v R* (1991) where the House of Lords agreed with and followed the same reasoning as the Court of Appeal in deciding that a man could be guilty of raping his wife.

Decisions of the Judicial Committee of the Privy Council

This court is not part of the court hierarchy in England and Wales and so its decisions are not binding. However, as many of its judges are also members of the Supreme Court (formerly the House of Lords), the judgments of the Privy Council are treated with respect and may often be followed. An example of this can be seen in the law on remoteness of damage in the law of tort and the decision made by the Privy Council in the case of *The Wagon Mound (No. 1)* (1961).

In *A-G for Jersey v Holley* (2005) the Privy Council ruled that in the defence of provocation a defendant is to be judged by the standard of a person having ordinary powers of self-control. This was contrary to an earlier judgment by the House of Lords. In cases in 2005 and 2006 the Court of Appeal followed the Privy Council decision rather than the decision of the House of Lords.

Statements made *obiter dicta*

This is clearly seen in the law on duress as a defence to a criminal charge. The House of Lords in *R v Howe* (1987) ruled that duress could not be a defence to a charge of murder. In the judgment the Lords also commented, as an *obiter dicta* statement, that duress would not be available as a defence to someone charged with attempted murder. When, later, in *R v Gotts* (1992) a defendant charged with attempted murder tried to argue that he could use the defence of duress, the *obiter* statement from *Howe* was followed as persuasive precedent by the Court of Appeal.

A dissenting judgment

When a case has been decided by a majority of judges, for example 2:1 in the Court of Appeal, the judge who disagreed will have explained his reasons. This is a dissenting judgment. If that case goes on appeal to the Supreme Court, or if there is a later case on the same point which goes to the Supreme Court, it is possible that the Supreme Court may prefer the dissenting judgment and decide the case in the same way. The dissenting judgment has persuaded them to follow it.

This happened in the contract case of *Rose & Frank v Crompton Bros* (1974) where the House of Lords was persuaded to follow the reasoning of the dissenting judgment in the Court of Appeal on one point in the case.

> **Key term** 🔑
>
> **Dissenting judgment** – a judgment given by a judge who disagrees with the reasoning of the majority of judges in the case.

Decisions of courts in other countries

This is especially so where the other country uses the same ideas of common law as in our system. This applies to Commonwealth countries such as Canada, Australia and New Zealand. For example, in *R v Bentham* (2003) about possession of a firearm, the court was invited to follow the Canadian case of *R v Sloan* (1974). However, they decided against following that decision.

Decisions of the European Court of Human Rights

If there is a conflict between precedents in English courts and that of the ECtHR which is to prevail?

In the appeals of *Lambeth London Borough Council v Kay and Price v Leeds City Council 2006* the House of Lords ruled that the English courts had to follow their own rules of precedent. It was for English courts to decide how the principles set out by the ECtHR were to be applied. They commented that there had to be a degree of certainty in the interpretation of the law and that was best achieved by following English rules of precedent. If a judge felt that a decision was inconsistent with the ECtHR he had to follow the binding precedent, but could give leave to appeal.

19.6.3 Original precedent

If the point of law in a case has never been decided before, then whatever the judge decides will form a new precedent for future cases to follow. It is an **original precedent**. As there are no past cases for the judge to base his decision on he is likely to look at cases which are the closest in principle and he may decide to use similar rules. This way of arriving at a judgment is called reasoning by analogy.

> ### Key term 🔑
> **Original precedent** – a decision on a point of law that has never been decided before.

19.7 Overruling, reversing, distinguishing

When a new case is being decided the judges can follow a past decision. However, appellate courts can, instead of following, decide to overrule a past decision. Where a case goes to appeal, then the higher court can reverse the previous decision in that case. In addition, it is possible for any court to distinguish the present case from an earlier one and avoid having to follow it.

19.7.1 Overruling

This is where a court in a later case states that the legal rule decided in an earlier case is wrong. Overruling may occur when a higher court overrules a decision made in an earlier case by a lower court, for example the Supreme Court overruling a decision of the Court of Appeal. It can also occur where the Court of Justice of the European Union overrules a past decision it has made; or when the Supreme Court uses the Practice Statement to overrule a past decision of its own.

19.7.2 Reversing

This can only happen in the specific case being appealed. It is where the court hearing the appeal disagrees with the legal reasoning of the court below. For example, the Court of Appeal may disagree with the legal ruling of the High Court Judge and come to the opposite point of view. In this situation it reverses the decision made by the High Court.

19.7.3 Distinguishing

Distinguishing is a method which can be used by a judge to avoid following a past decision which he would otherwise have to follow. It means that the judge finds that the material facts of the case he is deciding are sufficiently different for him to draw a distinction between the present case and the previous precedent. He is not then bound by the previous case.

Two cases demonstrating this process are *Balfour v Balfour* (1919) and *Merritt v Merritt* (1971). Both cases involved a wife making a claim against her husband for breach of contract. In *Balfour* it was decided that the claim could not succeed because there was no intention to create legal relations; there was merely a domestic arrangement between a husband and wife and so there was no legally binding contract. The second case was successful because the court held that the facts of the two cases were sufficiently different in that, although the parties were husband and wife, the agreement was made after they had separated. Furthermore the agreement was made in writing. This distinguished the case from *Balfour*; the agreement in *Merritt* was not just a domestic arrangement but meant as a legally enforceable contract.

> ### Key term 🔑
> **Distinguishing** – a method by which a judge avoids having to follow what would otherwise be a binding precedent.

Concept	Definition	Comment
Stare decisis	Stand by what has been decided	Follow the law decided in previous cases for certainty and fairness
Ratio decidendi	Reason for deciding	The part of the judgment which creates the law
Obiter dicta	Other things said	The other parts of the judgment – these do not create law
Binding precedent	A previous decision which has to be followed	Decisions of higher courts bind lower courts
Persuasive precedent	A previous decision which does not have to be followed	The court may be 'persuaded' that the same legal decision should be made
Original precedent	A decision in a case where there is no previous legal decision or law for the judge to use	This leads to judges 'making' law
Distinguishing	A method of avoiding a previous decision because facts in the present case are different	e.g. *Balfour v Balfour* not followed in *Merritt v Merritt*
Overruling	A decision which states that a legal rule in an earlier case is wrong	e.g. in *Pepper v Hart* the House of Lords overruled *Davis v Johnson* on the use of *Hansard*
Reversing	Where a higher court in the same case overturns the decision of the lower court	This can only happen if there is an appeal in the case

Figure 19.5 The basic concepts of judicial precedent

19.8 Precedent and Acts of Parliament

Precedent is subordinate to statute law and delegated legislation. This means that, if an Act of Parliament is passed, and that Act contains a provision which contradicts a previously decided case, that case decision will cease to have effect. The Act of Parliament is now the law on that point.

An example is when Parliament passed the Law Reform (Year and a Day Rule) Act in 1996. Up to then judicial decisions meant that a person could only be charged with murder or manslaughter if the victim died within a year and a day of receiving his injuries. The Act enacted that there was no time limit, and a person could be guilty even if the victim died several years later, so cases after 1996 follow the Act and not the old judicial decisions.

19.9 Advantages and disadvantages of precedent

As can be seen from the previous sections, there are both advantages and disadvantages to the way in which judicial precedent operates in England and Wales. In fact it could be said that every advantage has a corresponding disadvantage.

19.9.1 Advantages

Certainty

Because the courts follow past decisions people know what the law is and how it is likely to be applied in their case. It allows lawyers to advise clients on the likely outcome of cases; it also allows people to operate their businesses knowing that financial and other arrangements they make are recognised by law. The House of Lords Practice Statement points out how important certainty is.

Consistency and fairness in the law

It is seen as just and fair that similar cases should be decided in a similar way, just as in any sport it is seen as fair that the rules of the game apply equally to each side. The law must be consistent if it is to be credible.

Precision

As the principles of law are set out in actual cases the law becomes very precise; it is well illustrated and gradually builds up through the different variations of facts in the cases that come before the courts.

Flexibility

There is room for the law to change as the Supreme Court can use the Practice Statement to overrule cases. The use of distinguishing also gives all courts some freedom to avoid decisions and develop the law.

Time-saving

Precedent can be considered a useful time-saving device. Where a principle has been established, cases with similar facts are unlikely to go through the lengthy process of litigation.

19.9.2 Disadvantages

Rigidity

The fact that lower courts have to follow decisions of higher courts together with the fact that the Court of Appeal has to follow its own past decisions can make the law too inflexible so that bad decisions made in the past may be perpetuated. There is the added problem that so few cases go to the Supreme Court. Change in the law will only take place if parties have the courage, the persistence and the money to appeal their case.

Complexity

Since there are nearly half a million reported cases it is not easy to find all the relevant case law even with computerised databases. Another problem is in the judgments themselves, which are often very long with no clear distinction between comments and the reasons for the decision. This makes it difficult in some cases to extract the *ratio decidendi*; indeed in *Central Asbestos Co. Ltd v Dodd* (1973) the judges in the Court of Appeal said they were unable to find the *ratio* in a decision of the House of Lords.

Illogical distinctions

The use of distinguishing to avoid past decisions can lead to 'hair-splitting' so that some areas of the law have become very complex. The differences between some cases may be very small and appear illogical.

Slowness of growth

Judges are well aware that some areas of the law are unclear or in need of reform; however, they cannot make a decision unless there is a case before the courts to be decided. This is one of the criticisms of the need for the Court of Appeal to follow its own previous decisions, as only about 50 cases go to the Supreme Court each year. There may be a long wait for a suitable case to be appealed as far as the Supreme Court.

Summary

- The doctrine of precedent is based on *stare decisis* (keep to the decision).
- *Ratio decidendi* is the reason for the decision and creates a precedent for future cases: the *ratio* is identified by judges in later cases.
- *Obiter dicta* is the rest of the judgment and does not create a binding precedent.
- Courts lower in the hierarchy must follow precedents set by higher courts.
- The Supreme Court is normally bound by its own previous decisions, but the Practice Statement allows the court to depart from a previous decision where it is right to do so.
- The Court of Appeal is bound by its own previous decisions: the only exceptions are those set out in *Young's case*.
- The Court of Appeal must follow the domestic rules of precedent when referred to a conflicting ECtHR decision.

- Section 2 of the Human Rights Act 1998 requires courts to take into account judgments, decisions and opinions of the European Court of Human Rights and it is unlawful for a domestic court, as a public authority, to act in a way that is incompatible with a Convention right.
- Courts higher in the hierarchy can overrule a previous precedent.
- An appeal court can reverse the decision made by the court below.
- Judges in later cases do not have to follow precedent if they can distinguish their case from the previous one.
- The advantages of judicial precedent are: certainty, consistency and fairness, precision, flexibility and time-saving.
- The disadvantages of judicial precedent are: rigidity, complexity, illogical distinctions and slowness of growth.

Chapter 20

Law reform

After reading this chapter you should be able to:
- Understand the need for a law reform body
- Understand the work of the Law Commission
- Understand the need to reform, codify, consolidate or repeal areas of law
- Discuss the advantages and disadvantages of reform through the Law Commission

20.1 The need for an independent law reform body

In Chapters 16, 17 and 18 we examined the different sources of law, and saw that the law of England and Wales comes from a variety of sources. This fact makes it important to keep the law under review, to ensure that it is reformed when necessary, and to try to keep it in an accessible and manageable state. There are many influences on the way our law is formed and the impetus for reform can come from a number of sources. Some of these will have more effect than others, while in some situations there may be competing interests in the way that the law should be reformed.

The government of the day effectively has the major say in what laws will be enacted, and the government will set out its agenda for law reform in each session of Parliament. However, much of this will be concerned with more politically motivated areas, rather than 'pure law' reform. In addition, we have already seen with the Dangerous Dogs Act 1991 in Chapter 16 that Acts of Parliament can actually lead to more confusion and complication of the law. This is especially true where one Act is used to amend another so that the law is contained in a series of Acts, all of which must be consulted before the law can be discovered.

Pressure groups can provide the impetus for law reform. Where a subject has a particularly high profile, Parliament may bow to public opinion and alter the law. The Law Commission (see section 20.2) in its consultation process will also receive the views of pressure groups with a special interest in the area of law under review.

As seen in Chapter 19, judges play a role in law reform by means of judicial precedent. In some instances they may actually create new law, as occurred in *R v R* (1991), when the courts ruled that a man could be guilty of raping his wife. In some cases the courts may feel unhappy with the decision they have to come to because of the clear wording of an existing Act of Parliament or because they are bound by a previous precedent. In this situation the judges may when giving judgment draw attention to the need for reform.

However, these influences do not lead to our law developing in an organised and controlled way. The law needs to be reformed so that it adapts to the changing needs of society. This may require new laws to be passed or, in some cases, old laws to be cancelled. Confused law also creates expense. Simpler law would save legal fees.

20.1.1 History of law reform bodies

The need to have a body supervising systematic reform has been recognised for centuries, with various Lord Chancellors (as far back as 1616) calling for the appointment of 'law commissioners' to revise the laws and keep them up to date. Prior to the nineteenth century, there were no organised efforts at law reform. In the nineteenth century there were piecemeal reforms, with some statutes which codified parts of the criminal law and others codifying the common law on specialised areas of contract law.

In the twentieth century calls for an institution to be set up with responsibility for law reform led to the creation in 1934 of the Law Revision Committee. This has been described as the 'source of the modern machinery of law reform', but it operated only until the outbreak of World War II in 1939. After the war, from 1945 to 1952, there was no permanent law reform body. It was not until 1965 that a full-time body with wide responsibility came into existence in the shape of the Law Commission.

20.2 The Law Commission

The Law Commission was set up in 1965 by the Law Commissions Act 1965. It is a full-time body and consists of a Chairman who is a High Court Judge, and four other Law Commissioners who are all highly qualified lawyers. There is also support staff to assist with research.

20.2.1 The work of the Law Commission

The role of the Law Commission is set out in s 3 of the Law Commissions Act which states:

> It shall be the duty of each of the Commissions to take and keep under review all the law with which they are respectively concerned with a view to its systematic development and reform, including in particular the codification of such law, the elimination of anomalies, the repeal of obsolete and unnecessary enactments, the reduction of the number of separate enactments and generally the simplification and modernisation of the law.

This is a very wide-ranging brief as it covers 'keep under review all the law'. It also specifically states that the Law Commission is to be concerned with:

● 'systematic development and reform'
● codification
● repeal.

20.2.2 Reform

The Law Commission considers areas of law which are believed to be in need of reform. The actual topics may be referred to it by the Lord Chancellor on behalf of the government, or the Law Commission may itself select areas in need of reform and seek governmental approval to draft a report on them. It concentrates on what is sometimes called 'lawyers' law' or 'pure law'. In other words it is concerned with substantive law, such as criminal law, contract law, law of tort, land law and family law.

The Law Commission works by researching the area of law that is thought to be in need of reform. It then publishes a consultation paper seeking views on possible reform. The consultation paper will describe the current law, set out the problems and look at options for reform (often including explanations of the law in other countries).

Following the response to the consultation paper, the Commission will then draw up positive proposals for reform. These will be presented in a report which will also set out the research that led to the conclusions. There will often be a draft Bill attached to the report with the intention that this is the exact way in which the new law should be formed. Such a draft Bill must, of course, go before Parliament and go through the necessary parliamentary stages if it is to become law.

See section 16.4.3 for more information on a Bill's journey through Parliament.

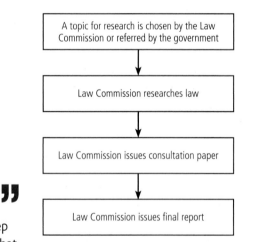

A topic for research is chosen by the Law Commission or referred by the government

↓

Law Commission researches law

↓

Law Commission issues consultation paper

↓

Law Commission issues final report

Figure 20.1 The way the Law Commission works

20.2.3 Codification

Codification involves bringing together all the law on one topic into one complete code of law. This makes the law simpler and easier to find.

Key term

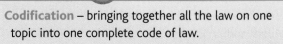

Codification – bringing together all the law on one topic into one complete code of law.

When the Law Commission was first formed in 1965, an ambitious programme of codification was announced, aimed at codifying family law, contract law, landlord and tenant laws and the law of evidence. However, the Law Commission has gradually abandoned these massive schemes of codification in favour of what might be termed the 'building-block' approach. Under this it has concentrated on codifying small sections of the law that can be added to later.

In particular, the Law Commission spent many years writing a draft criminal code which aimed to include the main general principles of criminal law. The draft Criminal Code was first published in 1985. However, no government has ever implemented it. In 2008, the Law Commission stated that it would be concentrating on smaller areas of the code, as there was more chance that the government would be prepared to make such reforms of the law.

In its 2015–16 Annual Report the Law Commission pointed out that 'the pattern in future is likely to be codification rather than a simple consolidation'. However, this would only happen in areas where 'statute law is incoherent or confusing and where codification would bring genuine practical benefits'.

20.2.4 Consolidation

The aim of consolidation is to draw all the existing provisions together in one Act. This is needed because in some areas of law there are a number of statutes, each of which sets out a small part of the total law. This is another way in which the law is being made more accessible.

Key term

Consolidation – combining the law from several Acts of Parliament into one Act of Parliament.

In some areas the law that was consolidated has been fragmented by further Acts of Parliament! This happened with the law on sentencing. The law was consolidated in the Powers of Criminal Courts (Sentencing) Act 2000. However, within a few months the law was changed again by the Criminal Justice and Courts Services Act 2000, which renamed some of the community penalties and also created new powers of sentencing. Then in 2003 the Criminal Justice Act 2003 changed much of the sentencing law again. Other reforms have since been put in place for young offenders and, in 2012, the Legal Aid, Sentencing and Punishment of Offenders (LAPSO) Act made further changes in the law on sentencing. It is not surprising

that it has now been suggested that there should be a new consolidated Bill for sentencing.

In its 2015–16 Annual Report the Law Commission stated that work was currently being undertaken by their criminal law team on important but technical provisions dealing with transitional arrangements in sentencing. This work is intended to pave the way for a consolidation Bill to introduce a new Sentencing Code.

20.2.5 Repeal

Another of the Law Commission's roles is to identify old Acts which are no longer used, so that Parliament can repeal these Acts. The Law Commission has been very successful in this. By 2015 there had been 19 Statute Law (Repeals) Acts. Over 3,000 out-of-date Acts of Parliament have been completely repealed. In addition, parts of thousands of other Acts have also been repealed.

Key term

Repeal of an Act of Parliament – this means that the Act ceases to be law. Only Parliament can repeal an Act of Parliament.

Look online

1 Look at the Law Commission's website (www. lawcom.gov.uk) and make a list of three areas of law which the Law Commission is currently researching.
2 Look for a Statute Law (Repeals) Act on the website www.legislation.gov.uk and find three old Acts that have been repealed. What is the oldest Act that you can find?

20.2.6 Implementation of the Law Commission's proposals for reform

The Law Commission has produced over 300 Reports proposing reform of the law in a wide variety of areas of law. However, in order to be effective, their proposals then have to be passed as law by Parliament.

In the first ten years of its existence the Law Commission had a high success rate with 85 per cent of its proposals being enacted by Parliament. During the next ten years, however, only 50 per cent of its suggested reforms became law. This lack of success was due to lack of parliamentary time, and an apparent disinterest by Parliament in technical law reform. The rate hit an all-time low in

1990 when not one of its reforms was enacted by Parliament.

Since then there has been an improvement and there have been some measures to ensure that more reforms are implemented. These measures include:

1 the Law Commission Act 2009 amending the 1965 Act, and which places a requirement on the Lord Chancellor to report to Parliament annually on the government's progress in implementing reports
2 a dedicated parliamentary procedure to implement Law Commission reports regarded as 'uncontroversial'. This has operated since 2010 and six Acts have been passed through this procedure.

Implementation rate

By March 2016 the Law Commission had published a total 217 law reform reports. Of these 143 (66 per cent) had been implemented in whole or in part and another eight had been accepted in whole or in part and were awaiting implementation. A response from the government was still being waited for in respect of 19 reports. Of the rest, the government had rejected 31 reports.

Examples of law implemented

Some important reforms have been passed in recent years. These include:

- Corporate Manslaughter and Corporate Homicide Act 2007, which made corporations and organisations criminally liable for deaths caused by their working practices

Set up	By the Law Commissions Act 1965
Personnel	Chairman and four other Commissioners Support staff
Function	To keep the law under review with a view to its systematic development and reform, including codification and repeal
Recent reforms following Law Commission reports	Coroners and Justice Act 2009 abolishing defence of provocation Criminal Justice and Courts Act 2015 creating offences of jury misconduct in using the internet Consumer Rights Act 2015 giving consumers the legal right to reject faulty goods
Success rate	First 10 years 85% Second 10 years 50% Since improved Overall (1965–2016) 66% of reform reports became law

Figure 20.2 The Law Commission

- Coroners and Justice Act 2009, which abolished the defence to murder of provocation and replaced it with the defence of loss of control
- Criminal Justice and Courts Act 2015, which includes reform of contempt of court by jurors and the creation of new offences of juror misconduct in relation to using the internet
- Consumer Rights Act 2015 which gives consumers the legal right to reject faulty goods and the right to a refund if they act within a reasonable time.

Key term 🔑

Contempt of court – disobeying a court's order; for example, where a juror uses a mobile phone in the court room when he has been told that it is not allowed.

20.3 Advantages and disadvantages of reform through the Law Commission

The Law Commission has made a large contribution to law reform in England and Wales. Before it was set up in 1965 there was no full-time law reform body. There were only part-time committees that considered small areas of law.

20.3.1 Advantages

The main advantages of having the Law Commission issue reports on areas of law are:

- areas of law are researched by legal experts
- it is non-political
- the Law Commission consults before finalising its proposals
- whole areas of law can be considered, not just small issues
- if Parliament enacts the reform of a whole area of law, then the law is in one Act, such as the Powers of Criminal Courts (Sentencing) Act 2000 (see above) and it is easier to find and to understand
- reform can simplify and modernise the law.

20.3.2 Disadvantages

Failure of Parliament to implement reforms

The main disadvantage is that the Law Commission has to wait for the government to bring in the reforms it proposes. The government is often slow to enact reforms and some Law Commission reports have not yet been made law.

A major area of criminal law that is still awaiting reform is non-fatal offences against the person.

This is an area of law you have to study for Unit 2 of both the AS and A Level; see Chapter 15.

In 1993 the Law Commission issued a report, 'Offences Against the Person' (Law Com No. 218) recommending reform to this area of law. Five years later, in 1998, the government issued a consultation paper which included a draft Bill on this area of law. However, the government did not proceed with the Bill and the reforms proposed by the Law Commission have never been made.

Clearly the Law Commission can only be effective if the government and Parliament are prepared to find time to enact reforms.

Lack of parliamentary time

There is a problem with the amount of time available in Parliament. A lot of time has to be given to financial matters such as the budget and taxation, health, education and foreign policy, especially at this time of our withdrawal from the European Union. So only a limited time is left for 'pure' law reform.

Other disadvantages

The government may accept the Law Commission's recommendations in principle. However, when reforming the law, the government may not follow all the recommendations. In addition, as a Bill goes through Parliament, changes to the wording may be made so that the final law is very different to that proposed by the Law Commission. This can cause the law to be less satisfactory than the original proposals.

The government does not have to consult the Law Commission on changes to the law. This can mean that major changes are made without the benefit of the Law Commission's legal knowledge and extensive research.

20.4 Royal Commissions

Apart from the full-time Law Commission, there are also temporary committees or Royal Commissions set up to investigate and report on one specific area of law. These are dissolved after they have completed their task. Such Royal Commissions were used frequently from 1945 to 1979, but from 1979 to 1990 when Margaret Thatcher was Prime Minister, none was set up. In the 1990s there was a return to the use of such commissions. However, since 2000, there have been no Royal Commissions.

Some Royal Commissions have led to important changes in the law; the Royal Commission on Police Procedure (the Phillips Commission) reported in 1981 and many of its recommendations were given effect by the Police and Criminal Evidence Act 1984. However, the government does not always act on recommendations, as was seen with the Pearson Commission on Personal Injury cases which reported in 1978.

20.4.1 Advantages and disadvantages of Royal Commissions

The main advantage is that a Royal Commission can take evidence from experts in the area concerned. Also the Commission concentrates on one area only, such as personal injury law.

The disadvantages are that they can only make recommendations and these are not always put into effect. This occurred with the Pearson Commission on Personal Injury cases where no change was made to the law.

In the twenty-first century the use of Royal Commissions has effectively been abandoned.

20.5 Reviews by judges

Another way that reform is considered is by asking a judge to lead an investigation into specific areas of law or the legal system. Examples of this have been the Woolf Committee on civil justice which led to major reforms of the civil court system in 1999 (see Chapter 3). A review on costs in civil cases was carried out by Lord Justice Jackson in 2010. A review of the civil court structure was carried out by Lord Briggs in 2015. This last review is likely to lead to the development of online courts by 2020.

Apart from judges, business people are occasionally asked to review some areas. This is illustrated by the Clementi Report (2004) into the legal profession which led to major changes in the organisation of the professions (see Chapter 9). Sir David Clementi, who did the review, was a business man, who had been Deputy Governor of the Bank of England and held other business positions.

20.5.1 Advantages and disadvantages of reviews into the law

Using judges to review the law or legal system means that they bring experience of the working of the law and legal system, which is an advantage. Where business people are used to lead a review, they bring expertise from a different walk of life. They are likely to take a different approach to people working in the legal system.

A disadvantage of using judges to review the law is that it takes them away from their work as a judge. The courts are very busy, and cutting the number of judges available for court work does not improve the efficiency of the courts.

A disadvantage of using a business person to lead a review is that he might not have an understanding of the current system and will therefore have to spend time researching this. He may not fully appreciate what will work in the legal system.

Summary

- Law comes from a variety of sources and it is necessary to the development of the law under review.
- The Law Commission was set up by the Law Commission Act 1965.
- Its role is to keep all the law under review. This is done by:
  - researching existing law
  - consulting
  - drawing up proposals for reform.
- It can make proposals for:
  - reforming the law
  - codifying the law
  - consolidating the law
  - repealing out-of-date law.
- Its proposals are put before Parliament who decides whether or not to implement them.
- Parliament does not always implement the Law Commission's law reform reports but the rate of implementation is improving.
- Advantages of reform through the Law Commission are:
  - law researched by legal experts
  - it is non-political
  - there is consultation before drawing up proposals
  - whole areas of law are considered
  - can bring the law on one topic together in one Act
  - reports suggest simplifying and modernising the law.
- Disadvantages are:
  - governments are slow to implement the reforms
  - some reforms may never be implemented
  - lack of parliamentary time to discuss the proposed reforms
  - Parliament may make changes to the proposed reforms without the benefit of legal expertise.
- In the past Royal Commissions, have been used to report on possible law reform.
- Judges or business people may be asked to review a specific area of law or legal system.

Chapter 21

European Union law

After reading this chapter you should be able to:
- Understand the role of the main institutions of the European Union
- Understand the different sources of European Union law
- Understand the impact of European Union law on the law of England and Wales

21.1 Formation of the European Union

On 1 January 1973 the United Kingdom joined what was then the European Economic Community, and another source of law came into being: European Union law. Since then it has had increasing significance as a source of law. The European Economic Community was originally set up by Germany, France, Italy, Belgium, the Netherlands and Luxembourg in 1957 by the Treaty of Rome. The name 'European Union' was introduced by the Treaty of European Union in 1993. Denmark and Ireland joined at the same time as the United Kingdom. In the 1980s and 1990s Greece, Spain, Portugal, Austria, Finland and Sweden joined. Then on 1 May 2004 another ten countries joined the EU. These were Cyprus, Czech Republic, Estonia, Hungary, Latvia, Lithuania, Malta, Poland, Slovak Republic and Slovenia. Bulgaria and Romania joined on 1 January 2007 and Croatia joined in 2013. There are now 28 Member States (see Figure 21.1).

In 2016 the UK voted to leave the European Union in an advisory referendum. The UK's exit will take effect under Article 50 of the Treaty of the European Union.

21.2 The institutions of the European Union

In 2009 the Treaty of Lisbon restructured the European Union. There are now two treaties setting out its rules. These are:
- the Treaty of European Union (TEU)

- the Treaty of the Functioning of the European Union (TFEU).

The European Union is an international organisation with institutions established originally by the Treaty of Rome. The main institutions which exercise the functions of the Union are:
- the Council of the European Union
- the European Commission
- the European Parliament
- the Court of Justice of the European Union.

21.2.1 The Council of the European Union

The government of each nation in the Union sends a representative to the Council. The Foreign Minister is usually a country's main representative, but a government is free to send any of its ministers to Council meetings. This means that usually the minister responsible for the topic under consideration will attend the meetings of the Council, so that the precise membership will vary with the subject being discussed. For example, the Minister for Agriculture will attend when the issue to be discussed involves agriculture. Usually, twice a year government heads meet in the European Council or 'Summit' to discuss broad matters of policy.

The Member States take it in turns to provide the President of the Council, each for a six-month period. To assist with the day-to-day work of the Council there is a committee of permanent representatives.

The Council is the principal law-making body of the Union. Voting in the Council is, in 80 per cent of decisions, by qualified majority which is reached if two conditions are met:

Date	Countries joining	Comment
1957	Belgium, France, Germany, Italy, Luxembourg, The Netherlands	These are the founder members Treaty of Rome signed
1973	Denmark, Ireland, United Kingdom	UK passes the European Communities Act 1972 on joining
1981	Greece	
1986	Portugal, Spain	
1995	Austria, Finland, Sweden	
2004	Cyprus, Czech Republic, Estonia, Hungary, Latvia, Lithuania, Malta, Poland, Slovak Republic and Slovenia	
2007	Bulgaria, Romania	
2013	Croatia	

Figure 21.1 The Member States of the European Union

- **55 per cent of Member States vote in favour** – meaning 16 out of 28 Member States, and
- the proposal is supported by Member States representing **at least 65 per cent of the total EU population**

This new procedure is also known as the 'double majority' rule.

21.2.2 The European Commission

This consists of 28 Commissioners who are supposed to act independently of their national origin. Each Member State has one Commissioner.

The Commissioners are appointed for a five-year term and can only be removed during this term of office by a vote of censure by the European Parliament. Each Commissioner heads a department with special responsibility for one area of Union policy, such as economic affairs, agriculture or the environment.

The Commission as a whole has several functions as follows:

- It puts forward proposals for new laws to be adopted by the Parliament and the Council.
- It is the 'guardian' of the treaties and ensures that treaty provisions and other measures adopted by the Union are properly implemented. If a Member State has failed to implement Union law within its own country, or has infringed a provision in some way, the Commission has a duty to intervene and, if necessary, refer the matter to the Court of Justice of the European Union. The Commission has

performed this duty very effectively, and as a result there have been judgments given by the Court against the UK and other Member States.

- It is responsible for the administration of the Union and has executive powers to implement the Union's budget and supervise how the money is spent.

Figure 21.2 Map showing countries of the European Union

21.2.3 The European Parliament

The members of the European Parliament (MEPs) are directly elected by the electorate of the Member States in elections which take place once every five years. The number of MEPs from each country is determined by the size of the population of the country. There are 751 MEPs at the moment.

Within the Parliament the members do not operate in national groups, but form political groups with those of the same political allegiance. The Parliament meets on average about once a month for sessions that can last up to a week. It has standing committees which discuss proposals made by the Commission and then report to the full Parliament for debate. Decisions are made by the Parliament and the Council.

The Parliament used to have only a consultative role, but it can now co-legislate on an equal footing with the Council in most areas. It can approve or reject a legislative proposal made by the Commission, or propose amendments to it. There are some areas, such as competition laws, where the Parliament cannot make law but only has the right to be consulted and put forward its opinion.

The Parliament also:

- decides on international agreements
- decides whether to admit new Member States
- reviews the Commission's work programme and asks it to propose legislation.

21.3 The Court of Justice of the European Union

Its function is set out in Article 19 TEU. This states that the Court must 'ensure that in the interpretation and application of the Treaty the law is observed'. The court sits in Luxembourg and has 28 judges, one from each Member State.

For a full court 11 judges will sit. The Court sits as a full court in the particular cases prescribed by the Statute of the Court (including proceedings to dismiss the European Ombudsman or a Member of the European Commission who has failed to fulfil his obligations) and where the Court considers that a case is of exceptional importance. For other cases the Court sits in chambers of five judges or three judges.

Judges are appointed under Article 253 TFEU from those who are eligible for appointment to the highest judicial posts in their own country or who are leading academic lawyers. Each judge is appointed for a term of six years, and can be reappointed for a further term of six years. The judges select one of themselves to be President of the Court.

The Court is assisted by eleven Advocates General who also hold office for six years. Each case is assigned to an Advocate General whose task under Article 253 is to research all the legal points involved and

> to present publicly, with complete impartiality and independence, reasoned conclusions on cases submitted to the Court of Justice with a view to assisting the latter in the performance of its duties.

21.3.1 Key functions

The court's task is to ensure that the law is applied uniformly in all Member States and it does this by performing two key functions.

The first is that it hears cases to decide whether Member States have failed to fulfil obligations under the Treaties. Such actions are usually initiated by the European Commission, although they can also be started by another Member State. An early example of such a case was *Re Tachographs: The Commission v United Kingdom* (1979) in which the court held that

Members of the European Parliament in Strasbourg, France, 2016

the United Kingdom had to implement a Council Regulation on the use of mechanical recording equipment (tachographs) in road vehicles used for the carriage of goods (see section 21.4.2 for further information on the effect of regulations).

The second function is that it hears references from national courts for preliminary rulings on points of European Union law.

21.3.2 Preliminary rulings

This function is a very important one, since rulings made by the Court of Justice of the European Union are then binding on courts in all Member States. This ensures that the law is indeed uniform throughout the European Union.

Article 267

A request for a preliminary ruling is made under Article 267 TFEU. This says that:

the Court of Justice shall have jurisdiction to give preliminary rulings concerning:

a   the interpretation of treaties;

b   the validity and interpretation of acts of the institutions of the Union;

c   the interpretation of the statutes of bodies established by an act of the Council, where those statutes so provide.

Article 267 goes on to state that where there is no appeal from the national court within the national system, then such a court must refer points of European Union Law to the Court of Justice of the European Union. Other national courts are allowed to make an Article 267 reference, but as there is still an appeal available within their own system, such courts do not have to do so. They have discretion (i.e. they can choose whether or not to refer the case).

Applied to the court structure in England and Wales, this means that, while the UK remains a member of the European Union, the Supreme Court must refer questions of European Union law, since it is the highest appeal court in our system. However, the Court of Appeal does not have to refer questions. It has a choice: it may refer if it wishes or it may decide the case without any referral. The same is true of all the lower courts in the English court hierarchy.

However, even courts at the bottom of the hierarchy can refer questions of law under Article 267 if they feel that a preliminary ruling is necessary to enable a judgment to be given.

Whenever a reference is made, the Court of Justice of the European Union only makes a preliminary ruling

on the point of law; it does not actually decide the case. The case then returns to the original court for it to apply the ruling to the facts in the case.

The first case to be referred to the Court of Justice of the European Union by an English court was *Van Duyn v Home Office* (1974).

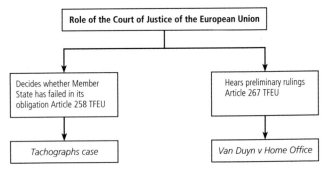

Figure 21.3 Role of the Court of Justice of the European Union

21.3.3 The operation of the Court of Justice of the European Union

When compared with English courts there are several major differences in the way the Court of Justice of the European Union operates. First the emphasis is on presenting cases 'on paper'. Lawyers are required to present their arguments in a written form and there is far less reliance on oral presentation of a case. This requirement is, of course, partly because of the wide range of languages involved, though French is the traditional language of the Court. It also represents the traditional method of case presentation in other European countries. An interesting point to note is that the English court system, in some areas, is now beginning to use this 'paper' submission.

A second major difference is the use of the Advocate General. This independent lawyer is not used in the English court system. However in the Court of Justice of the European Union the Advocate General who was assigned to the case will present his findings on the law after the parties have made their submissions. The court, therefore, has the advantage of having all aspects of the law presented to them.

The deliberations of the judges are secret and where necessary the decision will be made by a majority vote. However, when the judgment is delivered, again in a written form, it is signed by all the judges who formed part of the panel, so that it is not known if any judges disagreed with the majority. This contrasts strongly with the English court system, whereby a dissenting judge not only makes it known that he disagrees with the majority, but also usually delivers a judgment explaining his reasoning.

The Council of the European Union	• Consists of ministers from each Member State • Responsible for broad policy decisions
Commission	• 28 Commissioners whose duty it is to act in the Union's interest • Proposes legislation • Tries to ensure that the Treaties are implemented in each Member State
European Parliament	• Members elected by citizens in each Member State • Can co-legislate on an equal footing with the Council in most areas
Court of Justice of the European Union	• One judge from each Member State • Decides whether Member States have failed in obligations • Rules on points of European Union law when cases are referred to it under Article 267 TFEU

Figure 21.4 The institutions of the European Union

The other points to be noted are that the Court of Justice of the European Union is not bound by its own previous decisions and that it prefers the purposive approach to interpretation.

See section 18.3 for an explanation of the purposive approach.

The court has wide rights to study extrinsic material when deciding the meaning of provisions and may study preparatory documents. The Court of Justice of the European Union is important, not only because its decisions are binding on English courts, but also because its attitude to interpretation is increasingly being followed by English courts. The Court of Justice of the European Union pointed this out in *von Colson v Land Nordrhein-Westfalen* (1984) when it said 'national courts are required to interpret their national law in the light of the wording and the purpose of the directive'.

21.4 Sources of European Union law

There are primary and secondary sources of law. Primary sources are mainly the treaties, the most important of which was originally the Treaty of Rome itself and now is the Treaty of the European Union. Secondary sources are legislation passed by the institutions of the Union under Article 288 TFEU. This secondary legislation is of three types: Regulations, Directives and Decisions, all of which are considered below.

21.4.1 Treaties

While the UK is a member of the European Union, any Treaties made by the Union are automatically part of UK law. This is as a result of the European Communities Act 1972, s 2(1) which states that:

> " All such rights, powers, liabilities, obligations and restrictions from time to time created or arising by or under the Treaties and all such remedies and procedures from time to time provided for by or under the Treaties, as in accordance with the Treaties are without further enactment to be given legal effect or used in the United Kingdom, shall be recognised and available in law and be enforced, allowed and followed accordingly. "

As a reminder 'the Treaties' are the Treaty of Rome, also known as the Treaty of European Union (TEU), and the Treaty of Lisbon, also known as Treaty of the Functioning of the European Union (TFEU).

This means that law contained in the Treaties is directly applicable and does not need an Act of Parliament in the UK to make them into law. Therefore, once a treaty is signed, it instantly becomes applicable in the Member State.

This not only makes European Union law part of UK law but also allows individuals to rely on it. This is called direct effect.

Key terms 🔑

Direct applicability – EU law that automatically becomes part of UK law. There is no need for the UK to pass any Act of Parliament to bring it into force in the UK. Treaties are directly applicable.

Direct effect – allows a UK individual to rely on EU law in UK courts.

There are two types of direct effect – vertical and horizontal.

● Vertical direct effect means that an individual can use EU legislation to sue the UK or a public body.
● Horizontal direct effect means that an individual can use EU legislation against another individual.

Treaties have both vertical and horizontal direct effect. In contrast to direct effect, indirect effect is where national courts are required to interpret their own law in line with provisions of EU law.

In the case of *Van Duyn v Home Office* (1974) the Court of Justice of the European Union held that an individual was entitled to rely on Article 48 in the Treaty of Rome (now Article 48 TFEU) giving the right of freedom of movement. The Article had direct effect and conferred rights on individuals which could be enforced not only in the Court of Justice of the European Union, but also in national courts.

This means that while the UK is a member of the EU, citizens of the United Kingdom are entitled to rely on the rights in the Treaty of Rome and later treaties as they are directly applicable. They can be enforced in UK courts without having to argue any breach of UK law. This is clearly illustrated by the case of *Macarthys Ltd v Smith* (1980).

Key case

Macarthys Ltd v Smith (1980)

Wendy Smith's employers paid her less than her male predecessor for exactly the same job. As the two people were not employed at the same time by the employer there was no breach of English domestic law. However, Smith was able to claim that the company which employed her was in breach of Article 157 (TFEU) over equal pay for men and women and this claim was confirmed by the Court of Justice of the European Union.

UK courts can apply European Treaty law directly rather than wait for the Court of Justice of the European Union to make a ruling on the point. An example is *Diocese of Hallam Trustee v Connaughton* (1996).

Key case

Diocese of Hallam Trustee v Connaughton (1996)

The Employment Appeal Tribunal had to consider facts which had some similarity to the Smith case. Josephine Connaughton was employed as director of music by the Diocese of Hallam from 1990 to September 1994, at which time her salary was £11,138. When she left the position, the post was advertised at a salary of £13,434, but the successful applicant, a man, was actually appointed at a salary of £20,000. In other words, where in Smith's case she had discovered that her male predecessor was paid more than she was,

in the Connaughton case it was her immediate successor who was receiving considerably higher pay.

The Employment Appeal Tribunal considered Article 119 of the Treaty of Rome, now Article 157 TFEU and decided, as a preliminary point, that its provisions were wide enough to allow Miss Connaughton to make a claim, saying;

'We are sufficiently satisfied as to the scope of Article 141 so as to decide this appeal without further reference to the Court of Justice of the European Union.'

21.4.2 Regulations

Under Article 288 TFEU the European Union has the power to issue **Regulations** which are 'binding in every respect and directly applicable in each Member State'.

Key term

EU Regulations – laws issued by the Council of the European Union, which are binding on Member States and automatically apply in each member country.

Such regulations do not have to be adopted in any way by the individual states as Article 288 makes it clear that they automatically become law in each member country. This means that they are directly applicable.

This 'direct applicability' point was tested in *Re Tachographs: Commission v United Kingdom* (1979).

Key case

Re Tachographs: Commission v United Kingdom (1979)

A Regulation requiring mechanical recording equipment to be installed in lorries was issued. The UK government of the day decided not to implement the Regulation, but to leave it to lorry owners to decide whether or not to put in such equipment. When the matter was referred to the Court of Justice of the European Union it was held that Member States had no discretion in the case of Regulations. The wording of Article 288 was explicit and meant that Regulations were automatically law in all Member States.

Type of law	Effect	Source/Case
Treaties	Directly applicable	Section 2(1) of the European Communities Act 1972
	Have direct effect (both vertically and horizontally) if give individual rights and are clear	*Macarthys v Smith*
Regulations	Directly applicable	Article 288 TFEU
	Have direct effect (both vertically and horizontally) if give individual rights and are clear	*Tachograph case*
Directives	NOT directly applicable	Article 288 TFEU
	Have vertical direct effect if give individual rights and are clear	*Marshall case*
	NO horizontal direct effect	*Duke v GEC Reliance*
	BUT individual can claim against state for loss caused by failure to implement	*Francovitch v Italian Republic*

Figure 21.5 The effect of EU laws

This prevents Member States from picking and choosing which Regulations they implement. As a result laws are uniform across all the Member States.

21.4.3 Directives

Directives are the main way in which harmonisation of laws within Member States is reached. There have been Directives covering many topics including company laws, banking, insurance, health and safety of workers, equal rights, consumer law and social security.

> **Key term** 🔑
>
> EU Directives – these are issued by the Council of the European Union and direct all Member States to bring their own laws on a topic so that harmony is achieved throughout the EU.

As with Regulations, it is Article 288 TFEU that gives the power to the Union to issue Directives. There is, however, a difference from Regulations in that Article 288 says such Directives 'bind any Member State to which they are addressed as to the result to be achieved, while leaving to domestic agencies a competence as to form and means'.

This means that Member States will pass their own laws to bring Directives into effect (or implement them) and such laws have to be brought in within a time limit set by the European Commission.

The usual method of implementing Directives in the UK is by statutory instrument. An example is EU Directive 2011/65/EU (Restriction of the Use of Certain Hazardous Substances in Electronic and Electrical Equipment) which was given effect by The Restriction of the Use of Certain Hazardous Substances in Electrical and Electronic Equipment Regulations 2012.

Directives can, however, be implemented by other law-making methods such as Acts of Parliament. An example was the EU Directive on liability for defective products, which was issued in July 1985. The Directive had to be implemented by 30 July 1988. This was done in Britain by Parliament passing the Consumer Protection Act 1987, which came into force on 1 March 1988.

Directives can also be implemented by an Order in Council made by the Privy Council.

21.5 The impact of European Union law on the law of England and Wales

European Union law takes precedence over national law. This was first established in *Van Gend en Loos* (1963) which involved a conflict of Dutch law and European Union law on customs duty. The Dutch government argued that the Court of Justice of the European Union had no jurisdiction to decide whether European Union law should prevail over Dutch law; that was a matter for the Dutch courts to decide. However, the European Court of Justice rejected this argument.

In *Costa v ENEL* (1964) the Court of Justice held that even if there was a later national law it did not take precedence over the European Union law. This effect was seen clearly in *R v Secretary of State for Transport, ex parte Factortame* (1990) (usually referred to as the *Factortame case*) when the Court of Justice decided that Britain could not enforce the Merchant Shipping Act 1988. This Act had been passed to protect British fishermen by allowing vessels to register only if 75 per cent of directors and shareholders were British nationals. It was held that this contravened the Treaty of Rome. The Act could not be enforced against EU nationals.

A citizen in the UK can rely on directly applicable laws contained in Treaties and Regulations to enforce his rights as these automatically become part of UK law. As well as having to follow decisions of the Court of Justice of the European Union, EU law has affected our court decisions in another way. This is because the European Court uses the purposive approach to statutory interpretation. This has led to more use of the purposive approach in English courts when deciding questions of statutory interpretation.

For Directives the position is different. Where a Member State, such as the UK, has not implemented a Directive within the time laid down, the Court of Justice of the European Union has ruled that if the purpose of the Directive is to grant rights to individuals and that Directive is sufficiently clear, it may be directly enforceable by an individual against the Member State. This will be so even though that State has not implemented the Directive, or has implemented it in a defective way. The important point is that an individual who is adversely affected by the failure to implement only has rights against the State. This is because of the concepts of vertical direct effect and horizontal direct effect (see Figure 21.6).

Vertical direct effect

Vertical direct effect is where the individual can claim against the State even when a Directive has not been implemented. This happened in *Marshall v Southampton and South West Hampshire Area Health Authority* (1986).

Key terms

Vertical direct effect – an individual can claim against the Member State even when a directive has not been implemented by that state.

Horizontal direct effect – a concept under which individuals can rely on EU directives to bring a claim against their Member State even though the directive has not been implemented by that state.

Key case

***Marshall v Southampton and South West Hampshire Area Health Authority* (1986)**

Miss Marshall was required to retire at the age of 62 when men doing the same work did not have to retire until age 65. Under the Sex Discrimination Act 1975 in English law this was not discriminatory. However, she was able to succeed in an action for unfair dismissal by relying on the Equal Treatment Directive 76/207. This Directive had not been fully implemented in the UK but the Court of Justice of the European Union held that it was sufficiently clear and imposed obligations on the Member State. This ruling allowed Miss Marshall to succeed in her claim against her employers because her employers were 'an arm of the state', i.e. they were considered as being part of the State.

The Equal Treatment Directive had vertical effect allowing an individual, such as Miss Marshall, to rely on it and take action against the UK. This idea of vertical direct effect is shown in diagram form in Figure 21.6.

The concept of the State for these purposes is quite wide, as it was ruled by the Court of Justice of the European Union in *Foster v British Gas plc* (1990) that the State was:

> "a body, whatever its legal form, which has been made responsible, pursuant to a measure adopted by the State, for providing a public service under the control of the State and has for that purpose special powers beyond those which result from the normal rules applicable in relations between individuals."

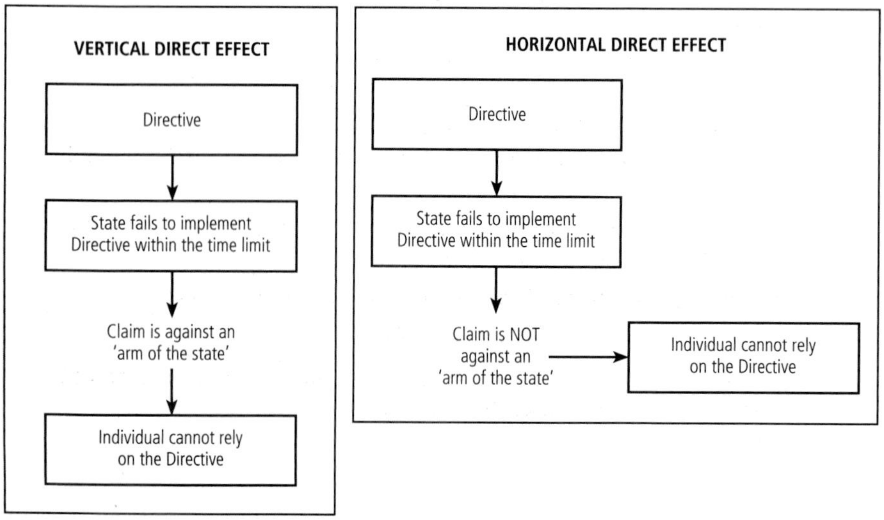

Figure 21.6 Diagram illustrating vertical and horizontal direct effect

In view of this wide definition the House of Lords decided that British Gas, which at the time was a nationalised industry, was part of the State, and *Foster* could rely on the Equal Treatment Directive.

The concept of vertical direct effect means that a Member State cannot take advantage of its own failure to comply with European Union law and implement a Directive. Individuals can rely on the Directive when bringing a claim against the State.

Horizontal direct effect

Directives which have not been implemented do not, however, give an individual any rights against other individuals. So in *Duke v GEC Reliance Ltd* (1988), Mrs Duke was unable to rely on the Equal Treatment Directive as her employer was a private company. This illustrates that Directives do not have horizontal direct effect and this was confirmed by an Italian case, *Paola Faccini Dori v Recreb Srl* (1995), in which the Italian government failed to implement Directive 85/447 in respect of consumer rights to cancel certain contracts. *Dori* could not rely on the Directive in order to claim a right of cancellation against a private trader. However, under the *Kücükdeveci* (2010) principle, Directives which give rise to fundamental human rights, such as non-discrimination, can give rise to horizontal direct effect.

Actions against the State for failure to implement a Directive

Clearly it is unfair that these conflicting doctrines of vertical and horizontal effect should give rights to individuals in some cases and not in others. The Court of Justice of the European Union has developed law under which it is possible to take an action to claim damages against the Member State that failed to implement the European Directive. This was decided in *Francovich v Italian Republic* (1991).

Key case

Francovich v Italian Republic (1991)

The Italian government failed to implement a Directive aimed at protecting wages of employees whose employer became insolvent. The firm for which *Francovich* worked went into liquidation owing him wages which he was unable to get from the firm. So, he sued the State for his financial loss. The Court of Justice held that he was entitled to compensation. The court said that:

Community law required the Member States to make good damage caused by a failure to transpose a directive, provided three conditions were fulfilled:

First, the purpose of the directive had to be to grant rights to individuals.

Second, it had to be possible to identify the content of those rights on the basis of the provisions of the Directive.

Finally, there had to be a causal link between the breach of the State's obligations and the damage suffered.

Case	Law
Van Duyn v Home Office (1974)	Individual entitled to rely on Treaty provision
Macarthys Ltd v Smith	Individual entitled to rely on Treaty provision even though national law is different
Re Tachographs: Commission v United Kingdom (1979)	Regulations are directly applicable in all Member States
Marshall v Southampton and South West Hampshire Area Health Authority (1986)	Directives have vertical direct effect In an action against the state, individuals can rely on a Directive which has not been implemented
Francovich v Italian Republic (1991)	Individuals can claim compensation from the State for losses caused by the State's failure to implement a Directive
Van Gend en Loos (1963)	ECJ has right to decide whether EU law or national law prevails
Costa v ENEL (1964)	EU law takes precedence over national law
Factortame case (1990)	EU law takes precedence over national law even where the Member State has enacted its own law to the contrary

Figure 21.7 Cases on the effect of EU law

1 Source A shows extracts from Articles 1 and 2 of the Equal Treatment Directive 76/207. Read these and then apply them, giving reasons for your decision, to the facts set out in Source B.

Source A

Council Directive 76/207

Article 1

1 The purpose of this Directive is to put into effect in the Member States the principle of equal treatment as regards access to employment, including promotion, and to vocational training and as regards working conditions ... This principle is hereinafter referred to as the 'principle of equal treatment'.

Article 2

1 For the purposes of the following provisions, the principle of equal treatment shall mean that there shall be no discrimination whatsoever on the grounds of sex either directly or indirectly by reference in particular to marital or family status.

2 This Directive shall be without prejudice to the right of Member States to exclude from its field of application those occupational activities and, where appropriate, the training leading thereto, for which, by reason of their nature or the context in which they are carried out, the sex of the worker constitutes a determining factor.

3 This Directive shall be without prejudice to provisions concerning the protection of women, particularly as regards pregnancy and maternity.

4 This Directive shall be without prejudice to measures to promote equal opportunity for men and women, in particular by removing existing inequalities which affect women's opportunities in the areas referred to in Article 1(1).

Source B

CASE FACTS: Amy Austin and Ben Bowen are employed by Green Gardens Ltd. There is a vacancy for a promotion to section manager, and both have applied for the post. Green Gardens have interviewed Amy and Ben and decided that both are equally qualified for the position. In this situation, if there are fewer women employed at the relevant level, Green Gardens have a policy of appointing the female applicant.

Ben complains that this is discriminatory and contrary to the Equal Treatment Directive.

21.5.1 The effect of European Union law on the sovereignty of Parliament

From the cases given above it can be seen that Member States, including Britain, have definitely transferred sovereign rights to the EU. None of the Member States can rely on its own law when it is in conflict with EU Law.

While Britain remains a member of the EU it is therefore true to say that the sovereignty of Parliament has been affected and that, in the areas it operates, European Union law has supremacy over national law.

However, each Member State has the ultimate right to withdraw from the Union.

- The institutions of the European Union are:
  - the Council – responsible for broad policy decisions
  - the Commission with one Commissioner from each Member State
  - the European Parliament with MEPs directly elected by citizens in each Member State
  - the Court of Justice of the European Union with a judge from each Member State and to which cases can be referred by national courts in Member States.

- The sources of law of the European Union are:
  - Treaties that become part of our law automatically under the European Communities Act 1972
  - Regulations that are directly applicable
  - Directives that have to be implemented by Member States – if not implemented they can be relied on against the Member State.
- European Union law takes precedence over national law even if a later Act is passed by Parliament to change the law.
- The sovereignty of Parliament is affected while the UK remains a member of the European Union.

SECTION B

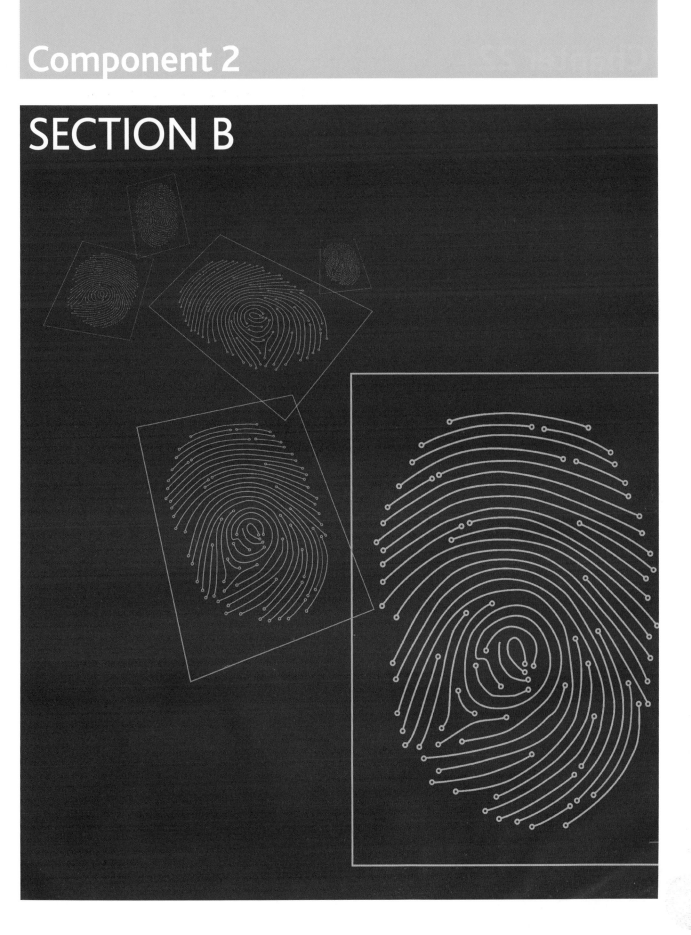

Chapter 22

The rules and theory of the law of tort

After reading this chapter you should be able to:
- Understand the rules of the law of tort in outline (for AS and A Level)
- Have an overview of the theory of the law of tort (for A Level)

22.1 The rules of the law of tort

Virtually everyone can identify and name some criminal offences. But how many civil actions can you identify and name?

There are many different types of civil action but they generally receive less publicity than criminal offences and the public generally are less aware of them. For AS, you have to learn about the actions of negligence and occupiers' liability. Both of these actions will come about when personal injury or damage to property has been caused. For A Level you also have to learn the rules of other civil tort actions related to land being actions of nuisance and *Rylands v Fletcher*. You will also learn about vicarious liability, where someone other than the person who committed the wrong can be liable. For both AS and A Level you need to understand the general principles involved in civil tort actions.

Key term 🔑

Liable – the judge's decision that the case against the defendant is proved and that the defendant should pay compensation or, in the case of Nuisance, may be subject to an injunction.

Civil law is concerned with settling disputes between individuals, between businesses, or between a business and an individual. The key difference between civil and criminal law is that civil law is mainly intended to settle disputes, not to punish wrongdoing. There are many different areas of civil law including:

- tort law, which allows a person to sue when he has suffered loss or injury, or his property has been damaged
- contract law, which operates when goods or services are bought and sold
- family law, which sets out rules governing family relationships
- employment law, which sets out rules operating between an employer and an employee.

Key terms 🔑

Civil law – the law concerned with the relationship between individuals.

Tort – a tort is a civil wrong and compensates a person who has suffered loss, been injured or whose property is damaged. The word 'tort' comes from the French word for 'wrong'.

In tort law, a civil case is started by the person who has suffered the loss or injury. The loss may be personal injury, damage to property, interference with other rights related to property or simply loss of money. Injury will often be some form of physical injury but could include mental injury. The injury may be minor or severe involving lifelong care. The person suffering the loss is called the claimant. The action will be taken against the individual or business that has caused the loss and they will be called the defendant.

The state is not usually concerned with tort law as the action is between the persons involved in the accident.

> ### Key terms 🔑
>
> **Claimant** – the person who has suffered loss or damage and is bringing a claim for compensation.
> **Defendant** – the person who has caused the loss or damage.

If the claimant is successful in proving his case he will be asking the court to award a remedy. Usually in a tort case this remedy will be **damages** but in some torts, such as nuisance, the claimant will be looking to the court to award an **injunction** to stop the action being complained of.

> ### Key terms 🔑
>
> **Damages** – the payment of money by way of compensation. The aim of damages in tort is to put the claimant back in the position he was in before the tort, so far as money can do so.
> **Injunction** – an order of the court to stop doing something, e.g. to stop making noise after 10 p.m. Failure to follow the court order can lead to further sanctions, including possibly imprisonment. An injunction can order a positive action, e.g. to move a muck heap to avoid causing a smell nuisance.

22.1.1 The courts

Civil and criminal laws operate separately from each other, and there are separate court systems to deal with civil and criminal cases. In a civil claim the claimant will have to prepare his claim and the initial evidence to show that he has a case. He will also have to suggest the amount of damages he is intending to claim, in order to issue the claim in the correct court and to follow the correct tracking procedure.

In civil trial courts a judge will sit alone to decide:

- the liability – whether the claimant or defendant has proved the case
- how much damages should be paid or to possibly consider another remedy if this is more appropriate
- if the winning party is entitled to the payment of his legal costs by the losing party.

In civil cases the general rule is that the loser pays the winner's legal costs in addition to his own costs.

One of the parties can appeal against the decision of the judge, either:

- against liability – this may be because it is suggested the judge misdirected himself on the relevant law or
- against the amount of damages awarded – that they were excessive or insufficient.

22.1.2 Burden of proof

The burden of proof is the obligation on a party in a court case to establish the evidence to a required degree. In civil cases, the burden of proving that the defendant is liable is on the claimant.

There are rules on the level to which the case has to be proved. This is referred to as the 'standard of proof'. The standard of proof in civil cases is 'the balance of probabilities'. This means that it is more likely than not that the claimant has produced sufficient evidence to suggest that on the balance of probabilities the law is on his side.

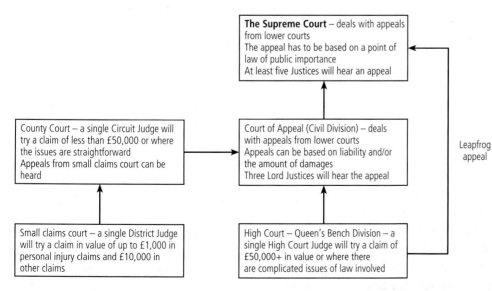

Figure 22.1 The system for dealing with tort claims

This is a lower standard than the one used in criminal cases. Civil cases have to be proved only 'on the balance of probabilities'. The reason that civil cases require a lower standard of proof is because the defendant is not being punished and is not at risk of losing his liberty if the case is proved. The claimant is merely proving that the defendant was at fault and responsible for the damage and injuries.

22.1.3 Defences

There are fewer defences available to a defendant in civil law than in criminal law, but the defendant can dispute the claimant's case and, in some cases, suggest that the claimant wholly or partly caused his own injury. These defences are called consent and contributory negligence and will be considered in Book 2.

22.1.4 Remedies in tort

If the claimant successfully proves his tort claim, he will be entitled to a **remedy**.

> **Key term** 🔑
>
> **Remedy** – the way in which a court will enforce or satisfy a claim when injury or damage has been suffered and proved. In tort law the remedy will usually be damages or occasionally an injunction.

Damages can place the claimant in the same position as if the tort had not been committed where the claim is for damage to property. However, if the claimant has suffered disabling personal injury, this is not possible.

Damages are divided into special and general damages:

- Special damages cover the period up to the trial and cover claims that can be specifically calculated. For a personal injury claim, these include the cost of treatment or loss of wages.
- General damages cover the period after trial and include the pain and suffering as a result of the accident, future loss of earnings, future medical costs and any loss of amenity.

In many personal injury claims where the injuries are severe and the amount of damages is large, the claimant will be hoping that the defendant was insured and will aim to recover compensation from the defendant's insurance company.

In a claim for damaged property, such as a *Rylands v Fletcher* claim, the amount of damages is likely to be smaller than a personal injury claim. The amount of compensation claimed will be what is required to replace or repair the damaged property.

In a claim for nuisance, the claimant will often be trying to stop the nuisance continuing and will be seeking an injunction from the court ordering the problem to stop. If the defendant does not observe the order then the court can impose further sanctions such as a fine or, at worst, imprisonment.

22.2 A brief overview of the law of tort

A Level students need to understand the theory of the law of tort.

22.2.1 Fault

Many civil torts, particularly those based on negligence, require the claimant to prove that the defendant was at fault. Fault in this sense means that there is some wrongdoing by the defendant. The claimant will have to prove this fault with evidence. In an accident claim based on negligence, this evidence will have to show how and why the accident happened and that it was due to the wrongdoing of the defendant. As will be seen later, this is known as a breach of duty by the defendant. This proving of fault is often difficult for the claimant as expert evidence may have to be paid for and produced. Torts that require fault to be proved in this specification are negligence and occupiers' liability.

If the claimant cannot present sufficient evidence to prove the fault he will be left without compensation, even if he is suffering physical injury or damage to his property.

22.2.2 Strict liability

Some torts do not require fault to be proved, and they are known as **strict liability** actions. They will usually be cheaper and simpler for the claimant to prove as they do not require evidence to be produced to show how and why the accident happened. In this specification strict liability torts are:

- nuisance – an action to stop unreasonable use of neighbouring land
- *Rylands v Fletcher* – an action for damage to land caused by material escaping from neighbouring land and
- vicarious liability – where an employee commits a tort in the course of his employment.

All these torts and actions will be covered in detail in Book 2.

> **Key term** 🔑
>
> **Strict liability** – a civil action where fault of the defendant does not need to be proved.

22.2.3 Balancing interests and tort

Legal scholar Rudolf von Jhering analysed law in the broad context of society. In his view the purpose of law is to secure the conditions of social life, and this determines the content of law. The conditions of social life include both physical existence and ideal values, but these are relative to the social order of the time and place. He developed the idea of a scheme of interests and designated them as individual, state and public, the last two of which he tended to treat as one. However, he did not develop a successful means of 'evaluation' of the interests as against each other. This theory was developed further by Roscoe Pound who identified public and private interests, claiming that a just result in every case could be achieved if interests could be balanced. However, in his view the interests could only be balanced if they were on the same level – public and public or private and private.

In the nuisance case of *Miller v Jackson* (1977), when Mr and Mrs Miller complained about cricket balls being hit into their garden, the public interest was represented by the local community and the cricket club using the cricket field for their matches and recreation generally. The private interest was that of Mr and Mrs Miller who were unable to use their garden because of cricket balls being hit into it during the course of games. The Court of Appeal decided in favour of the public interest and refused an injunction to the Millers to stop games being played. This illustrates Pound's theory that, as the interests were on different levels, the public interest would prevail.

22.2.4 Morality and tort

Morals are to do with thoughts and beliefs, and the moral values of a society lay down a framework as to how people should behave within that society. Morality can differ from person to person and between groups within society, but the law of a country will generally reflect the moral values of the majority within that country.

It is morally right that drivers in charge of a potentially dangerous machine should owe a duty of care to other road users, and that they should pay compensation to the other if they break that duty and injure another or cause damage to other property.

It can be said that it is morally right that a client relying on a professional's advice should be owed a duty of care if that advice turns out to be bad and the client loses money. It is morally right that doctors should owe a duty of care to their patients and if poor treatment is carried out causing injury, that the doctor should pay compensation. It is said that it is morally right that a doctor's employer, a hospital, should be responsible for the doctor's actions when they were carried out in the course of employment.

On the other hand, doctors have been able to justify what would otherwise be considered immoral actions. This includes the withdrawal of feeding and hydration leading to the patient's death. This was the case of a patient in a persistent vegetative state, and therefore incapacitated, in *Airedale NHS Trust v Bland* (1993). The sterilisation of a mentally incapacitated patient was justified in *Re F (mental patient: sterilisation)* (1990). Unwanted treatment was allowed in *Re S (adult: refusal of medical treatment)* (1992). Clearly these are cases that involve very complex and troubling moral issues.

22.2.5 Justice and tort

According to Lord Wright it is difficult to define exactly what justice is. He said:

> ❝ the guiding principle of a judge in deciding cases is to do justice; that is justice according to the law, but still justice. I have not found any satisfactory definition of justice … what is just in a particular case is what appears just to the just man, in the same way as what is reasonable appears to be reasonable to the reasonable man. ❞

People's ideas of what justice is may differ and depending on what is at stake, may differ widely. One approach to justice is the equal and consistent application of rules such as whether a duty of care exists. Justice can be seen by the then ground-breaking decision of Lord Atkin in *Donoghue v Stevenson* (1932) ruling that a manufacturer owed a duty of care to the ultimate consumer. However there may be situations, such as trying to sue the police, when justice is not seen to be done because public policy reasons may mean that they do not owe a duty of care. In other cases such as in *Wilsher v Essex Area Health Authority* (1988), justice was not seen to be done when the victim was injured in hospital but was unable to prove that the doctor was at fault.

One way in which tort is unable to provide justice is because of the remedies that are available. Damages may be thought of as an artificial remedy. The idea behind the award of damages in tort is to put the claimant back in the position he was in before the accident, so far as money can do so. However, it is impossible to achieve this for a victim of an accident who is permanently paralysed or has lost a limb.

22.2.6 Negligence and occupiers' liability

Both of these torts are covered in the AS course and they are similar to each other. In both cases the claimant will have suffered loss or injury due to the defendant's fault. In each case the defendant will owe a duty of care to the claimant, the duty will have been broken and the claimant will have suffered loss or injury from the breach of duty. In each case the claimant will be looking to claim compensation for his loss or injury.

Negligence	Occupiers' liability
Accident happens on road or other public place	Accident happens on defendant land
Defendant owes claimant a duty of care	Defendant owes claimant a duty of care
Defendant breaches duty of care causing accident	Defendant breaches duty of care causing accident
Claimant suffers loss or injury	Claimant suffers loss or injury
If defendant is liable he is ordered to pay compensation	If defendant is liable he is ordered to pay compensation

Figure 22.2 The difference between claims for negligence and occupiers' liability

Summary

- A tort is a civil wrong; the case will usually be between an individual and another individual or an individual and a business.
- The state is not usually involved in a tort claim.
- The aim of taking a tort action is usually to claim compensation.
- The standard of proof in a tort claim is 'the balance of probabilities'.
- The burden of proving the case is on the claimant.
- The aim of the award of damages in tort is to put the claimant back in the position he was in before the accident, so far as money can do so.
- Torts based on negligence require the claimant to prove the fault of the defendant.
- Some torts are strict liability which allows the claimant to succeed without having to prove the defendant's fault.
- Judges aim, where possible, to balance the interests of the parties in a case – provided the interests are on the same level. If they are on different levels, the public interest will usually prevail over the private interest.
- Morals are based on people's views and beliefs. It is morally right that if a duty of care is owed and broken, compensation should be paid to the injured victim.
- Judges attempt to provide justice – or what is fair – in every case. Justice can be seen in tort by requiring a person who breaks a duty of care to pay compensation to the victim. However this cannot be complete justice to a victim who is seriously injured.

Chapter 23

Liability in negligence

After reading this chapter you should be able to:
- Understand the concept of liability in negligence for injury to people and damage to property
- Understand the concept of duty of care and when it is owed: *Donoghue v Stevenson* (1932) and the neighbour principle, and the *Caparo* test
- Understand the need to prove breach of duty – the objective standard of care and the reasonable person; risk factors
- Understand the legal rules on remoteness of damage and causation – factual causation and the 'but for' test, and legal causation
- Understand defences available in this tort: contributory negligence and consent (*volenti non fit injuria*) (A Level)
- Critically evaluate liability in negligence, showing ideas for reform

23.1 What is negligence?

Negligence can apply in a wide variety of situations where a person is injured or his property is damaged as a result of an accident. One of the most common accidents is a car crash in which the vehicles are damaged and the drivers and passengers injured. When this happens the injured person will want to claim compensation for his injuries and for damage to his vehicle or other property. Other situations include people being injured at work or through medical negligence. In all of these situations the tort of negligence is used as the basis of the claim. Negligence needs proof of fault on the part of the person who caused the accident.

Negligence was defined in the case of *Blyth v Birmingham Waterworks Co.* (1856) by Baron Alderson as 'failing to do something which the reasonable person would do or doing something which the reasonable person would not do.' According to this definition, negligence can come from either an act or an omission.

Key term

Negligence – an act or a failure to act which causes injury or damage to another person or their property.

The newspaper article below shows how a claim arose in negligence for personal injuries suffered in an accident.

In the news

Man injured at theme park is to get pay-out

A man was badly injured on a theme park ride and is seeking up to £250,000 in compensation.

Mark Simpson was catapulted out of a boat on the water chute at Wicksteed Park, breaking his ankle and injuring his knee, shoulder and wrist. He later developed a clot on the lungs and has been unable to find work due to the long-term effects of his injuries.

The park has admitted liability, but the High Court will decide how much Mr Simpson is entitled to.

Mr Simpson was enjoying a family day out at the park when he decided to go on the water chute, an open-top boat which speeds down a ramp into a lake and then floats until it is stopped by a rope. As the boat was being winched back to the ramp, it became caught on a steel walkway.

Mr Simpson alleges that he was urged by park staff to climb out of the boat but was catapulted in the air as he tried to do so, as the boat moved violently towards the ramp.

The company is accused of negligence. Mr Simpson claims that the staff failed to slacken the tension on the rope while he got out, failed to inspect the winch mechanism and failed to notice the danger he was in.

He also claims the company negligently failed to warn him of the dangers of getting off in the circumstances, required him to get off when it was unsafe, and exposed him to a 'trap', it is alleged.

Source: Adapted from an article in the *Leicester Mercury*, 10 March 2012

Activity

1   Was there a negligent act or omission in this case?

2   The theme park has admitted blame (fault), and the amount of compensation has to be set by the court. Why does the court have to decide the compensation?

In any negligence claim the claimant will have to prove the defendant was at fault and to blame for the injuries or damage. The level of fault that has to be shown is on the balance of probabilities – it is more likely than not that the defendant's fault caused the injuries or damage. The burden of proving this fault is on the claimant. If the case goes to court, the claimant will have to provide evidence to show the fault. The evidence could be from experts, oral evidence of witnesses who saw the incident or medical reports of the injuries. If the claimant cannot present sufficient evidence to prove his case he will be left without compensation, even if he is suffering physical injury or damage to his property.

In negligence the person who caused the injury or damage is only liable if:

● he owes the claimant a duty of care
● he breaches this duty and
● the breach causes reasonably foreseeable injury or damage.

23.2 Duty of care

The idea of a duty of care in the tort of negligence is to establish a legal relationship between the parties. It has developed through judicial precedent – judges making decisions in cases. The start of the modern law of negligence was the famous case of *Donoghue v Stevenson* (1932).

23.2.1 *Donoghue v Stevenson* and the neighbour principle

Key case

Donoghue v Stevenson (1932)

Mrs Donoghue went to a cafe with a friend. The friend bought her a drink of ginger beer and ice cream. The bottle of ginger beer had dark glass so that its contents could not be seen. After drinking some of it, Mrs Donoghue poured the rest out and then saw that it contained a dead (and decomposing) snail. Because of the impurities in the drink she suffered both physical and mental injuries.

She wanted to claim compensation for her injuries. As she had not bought the drink she could not use the law of contract to sue the café or the manufacturer. Instead she sued the manufacturer in negligence claiming that they were at fault in the manufacturing process and that they owed her a duty of care.

In the House of Lords Lord Atkin set the test for when a person would be under a duty to another. He said: 'You must take reasonable care to avoid acts or omissions which you can reasonably foresee would be likely to injure your neighbour.'

He went on to explain this by saying:

Who then, in law, is my neighbour? Persons who are so closely and directly affected by my act that I ought reasonably to have them in my contemplation as being affected when I am directing my mind to the acts or omissions in question.

This established for the first time the broad principles of owing a duty of care and general liability in negligence, known as the **neighbour principle**.

Key term

Neighbour principle – the person who is owed a duty of care by the defendant. It is not the person living next door. According to Lord Atkin, it is anyone you ought to have in mind who might potentially be injured by your act or omission.

23.2.2 The *Caparo* test

This neighbour principle was used by judges until it was replaced by a **three-part test** in the case of *Caparo v Dickman* (1990):

● Was damage or harm reasonably foreseeable?
● Is there a sufficiently proximate (close) relationship between the claimant and the defendant?
● Is it fair, just and reasonable to impose a duty?

Key case

Caparo v Dickman (1990)

The claimant company wanted to take over another company – Fidelity Limited. They looked at the statutory accounts prepared for Fidelity by the defendant, which showed a profit. Based on these books they decided to take over Fidelity. After completing the purchase they looked at the detailed books, which showed a loss. They sued the defendant for their loss.

The House of Lords set the three-stage test for owing a duty of care. They decided that the defendant did not owe the claimants a duty of care as the accounts were prepared for Fidelity and for statutory reasons.

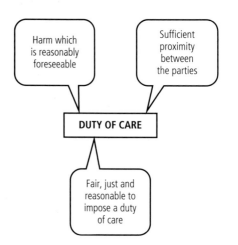

Figure 23.1 Duty of care tests

Key term 🔑

Three-part test – an update of the neighbour principle to show who is owed a duty of care in negligence. All three parts have to be satisfied in order that this test is satisfied.

Damage or reasonably foreseeableharm

Whether the injury or damage is reasonably foreseeable depends on the facts of the case. An example of this is the case of *Kent v Griffiths* (2000).

Key case

Kent v Griffiths (2000)

An ambulance was called to take the claimant who was suffering an asthma attack to hospital. Despite repeated assurances by the control centre, and for no obvious reason, the ambulance failed to arrive within a reasonable time. As a result the claimant suffered a respiratory arrest.

The court decided it was 'reasonably foreseeable' that the claimant would suffer further illness if the ambulance did not arrive promptly and no good reason was given why it failed to do so. A duty of care was owed by the ambulance service when they initially accepted the call and as they failed in this duty they were liable to pay compensation.

Proximity of relationship

Even if the harm is reasonably foreseeable, a duty of care will only exist if the relationship between the claimant and the defendant is sufficiently close or proximate. An example of this is the case of *Bourhill v Young* (1943).

Key case

Bourhill v Young (1943)

A pregnant woman heard the sound of an accident as she got off a tram. The accident was caused by a motor cyclist who died in the accident. After a short while she approached the scene of the accident and saw blood on the road. She suffered such shock that she later gave birth to a stillborn baby. She sued the relatives of the dead motor cyclist. Under the neighbour test at the time she had to prove that she was proximate, or close to, the motorcyclist so that he owed her a duty of care.

The House of Lords decided that he could not anticipate that if he was involved in an accident, it would cause mental injury to a bystander and so he did not owe Mrs Bourhill a duty of care.

One reason for the decision in this case could have been that Mrs Bourhill was not related to the victim and, if she was allowed to sue, it would open the floodgates to claims. A different result was achieved in *McLoughlin v O'Brien* (1982).

While she was at home, the claimant's husband and children were involved in a serious road accident. The accident was caused by the negligence of the defendant lorry driver. One of the children was killed at the scene and the other family members were taken to hospital. The claimant was told of the accident and went to the hospital. She saw her family before they had been treated. As a result she suffered severe shock, organic depression and a personality change. She claimed against the defendant for the psychiatric injury she suffered.

The House of Lords decided that the lorry driver owed her a duty of care and extended the class of persons who would be considered proximate to the event to those who came within the immediate aftermath of the event (in this case two hours after the accident).

A serial killer, known as the Yorkshire Ripper, had been attacking and murdering women in Yorkshire and across the north of England. The claimant's daughter was the killer's last victim before he was caught. By the time of her death the police already had enough information to arrest the killer, but had failed to do so. The mother claimed that the police owed a duty of care to her daughter.

It was decided by the House of Lords that the relationship between the victim and the police was not sufficiently close (proximate) for the police to be under a duty of care and that it was not fair, just or reasonable for the police to owe a duty of care to the general public. The police knew that the killer might strike again but they had no way of knowing who the victim might be.

The court may have accepted Mrs McLoughlin's claim because there could only be a limited number of people who could claim – they had to be related to the victim and suffer the injury within a limited time. These restrictions could not open the floodgates to unlimited numbers of claims.

Fair, just and reasonable to impose a duty

This third part of the duty of care test allows the courts to consider if, even though the harm was foreseeable and the parties were sufficiently close, there is no duty of care. The courts are often reluctant to find that it is 'fair, just and reasonable' to impose a duty of care on public authorities such as the police. In the case of *Hill v Chief Constable of West Yorkshire* (1990) it was pointed out that imposing a duty of care on police (and allowing them to be sued) could lead to policing being carried out in a defensive way which might divert their resources and attention away from the prevention and detection of crime. This could lead to lower standards of policing, not higher ones.

Tip

Make sure you can explain each of the three parts of the *Caparo* test. Use a case to support each point.

Look online

Should the police always be protected from being sued in negligence? Find case examples when the police do owe a duty of care and have been successfully sued.

Activity

It is well established law that certain categories of persons owe a duty of care to others. For example, drivers owe a duty of care to other road users, manufacturers owe a duty of care to consumers and doctors owe a duty of care to their patients.

Discuss in groups:
- Do teachers owe a duty of care to their students – when on a school trip, when teaching students in a practical lesson or in preparing them for an exam?
- How do the courts decide in novel situations whether a duty of care is owed?

Principle	Case	Judgment
Duty of care	*Donoghue v Stevenson* (1932)	You must take reasonable care not to injure your neighbour
General principles	*Caparo v Dickman* (1990)	Injury or damage has to be reasonably foreseeable There must be proximity of relationship It must be fair just and reasonable to owe a duty of care
Reasonably foreseeable	*Kent v Griffiths* (2000)	Ambulance took unreasonable time to arrive and take patient to hospital
Proximity of relationship	*Bourhill v Young* (1943)	Woman heard accident and suffered shock when saw blood on road
	McLoughlin v O'Brian (1982)	Mother suffered shock when saw injured family in hospital
Fair just and reasonable to owe a duty	*Hill v Chief Constable of West Yorkshire* (1990)	Not fair, just or reasonable for police to owe a duty to member of public not known to them

Figure 23.2 Duty of care

Extension activity ✔

What about other emergency services? Will they owe a duty of care? For example:

- Do coastguards owe a duty of care to a yachtsman whose boat is sinking?
- Do the fire brigade owe a duty of care to a house owner to put out a fire?
- Does a lifeguard owe a duty of care to a swimmer in difficulties in a supervised swimming pool?
- Does an off-duty lifeguard owe a duty of care to a swimmer in difficulties in the sea?

Activity ❓

Ryan collected his car from Sam's garage, where Sam had been working on the brakes. Sam told Ryan that the work was complete, but, in fact, Sam had forgotten to tighten the handbrake cable. Ryan parked his car on a hill, applied the handbrake and got out. The handbrake failed to hold the car which rolled down the hill and crushed Tanya, who was loading shopping into the back of her van. As a result of the collision, both Ryan's car and Tanya's van were slightly damaged.

Discuss whether Sam owed a duty of care to Tanya.

Tip 💬

When applying the three-stage *Caparo* test to a situation, say why each part is present or not using material from the scenario. Give reasons for your explanation, not just assertions.

23.3 Breach of duty

23.3.1 The objective standard of care and the reasonable person

Once it has been shown that a duty of care is owed, the claimant has to prove that the duty of care has been broken. The standard is objective – that of the **'reasonable person'** as set by Baron Alderson referred to above. This reasonable person is the ordinary person performing the task competently. It could be the reasonable driver, the reasonable doctor or the reasonable manufacturer.

There are a number of variations of the 'reasonable person' and the court may have to consider whether the defendant has a special characteristic. For example, is he an inexperienced learner, a professional or a child? If any of these apply, how should he be judged?

Key term 🔑

Reasonable person – this used to be said to be 'the man on the Clapham omnibus'. Now it is considered to be the ordinary person in the street or doing the same task.

Professionals are judged by the standard of the profession as a whole

This is illustrated by the case of *Bolam v Friern Barnet Hospital Management Committee* (1957).

Key case

Bolam v Friern Barnet Hospital Management Committee (1957).

The claimant was suffering from a mental illness and the treatment at the time was to receive a type of electric shock (ECT). He signed a consent form but was not told of the risk of broken bones while receiving the shocks and was not given relaxant drugs. He suffered a broken pelvis while receiving the treatment. There were two opinions within the medical profession while undertaking ECT. One opinion favoured the use of relaxant drugs in every case. The other was that drugs should only be used if there was a reason to do so, which was not present in Bolam's case.

The court decided that as the hospital had followed one of these courses of action, it had not breached its duty of care.

The principle from Bolam's case, and which applies to all professionals, is to ask the following questions:
- Does the defendant's conduct fall below the standard of the ordinary competent member of that profession?
- Is there a substantial body of opinion within the profession that would support the course of action taken by the defendant?

If the answer to the first question is 'No' and to the second 'Yes', then the defendant has not broken his duty of care.

This long established approach has been altered by the Supreme Court decision in *Montgomery v Lanarkshire Health Board* (2015).

Key case

Montgomery v Lanarkshire Health Board (2015)

The claimant gave birth but, due to complications during delivery, her son was born with cerebral palsy. She claimed damages against the doctor and hospital which were responsible for her care during pregnancy and labour. Her appeal to the Supreme Court focused on the doctor's failure to disclose the risks and obtain informed consent from Montgomery. The court was invited to depart from precedent and to reconsider the duty of a doctor towards a patient in relation to advice about treatment.

The court decided that the doctor was under a duty to disclose the risk of a major obstetric emergency which involves significant risks to the mother's health. The doctor would have been entitled to withhold information about the risk if it would have been harmful to the patient's health; however, this was not intended to enable doctors to prevent their patients from taking informed decisions. The doctor should have explained to the claimant why it was believed that a vaginal delivery was medically preferable to a caesarean, having taken care to ensure that the claimant understood the considerations for and against each option. As a result patients should be treated, so far as possible, as adults who are capable of understanding that medical treatment is uncertain of success and may involve risks, accepting responsibility for the taking of risks affecting their own lives, and living with the consequences of their choices.

Learners are judged at the standard of the competent, more experienced person

This principle was set by the case of *Nettleship v Weston* (1971).

Key case

Nettleship v Weston (1971)

Mrs Weston arranged with her neighbour, Mr Nettleship, for him to give her driving lessons. She was on her third lesson with him and failed to straighten up after turning a corner. She hit a lamppost which fell onto the car, injuring Mr Nettleship. The court decided that Mrs Weston should be judged at the standard of the competent driver, not at the standard of the inexperienced learner driver.

Although the decision does, on the face of it seem unfair to learners, it is logical as far as motorists are concerned as she was covered by an insurance policy. It would be unjust on an injured claimant if the defence was put forward that 'I am only on my third lesson and you cannot expect me to be as good a driver as someone who has been driving for some time'.

Children and young people

For this group the standard is that of a reasonable person of the defendant's age at the time of the accident. This is shown by the case of *Mullin v Richards* (1998).

Key case

Mullin v Richards (1998)

Two girls, aged 15, were play fighting with plastic rulers in class at school. One of the rulers snapped and fragments entered Teresa Mullin's eye, resulting in her losing all useful sight in that eye. The court decided that Heidi Richards had to meet the standard of a 15-year-old schoolgirl (and not that of a reasonable adult). As she had reached the required standard she had not breached her duty of care.

23.3.2 Risk factors

When the court considers whether there has been a breach of duty, it will take into account certain factors to decide whether the standard of care should be raised or lowered and ask the question: would the reasonable person take more or fewer risks in the same situation? The following risk factors may be considered.

Has the claimant any special characteristics which should be taken account of?

This is shown in the case of *Paris v Stepney Borough Council* (1951).

Key case

Paris v Stepney Borough Council (1951)

Mr Paris was known to be blind in one eye. He was given work to do by his employers which involved a small risk of injury to the eyes. He was not given any protective goggles. While doing this work, his good eye was damaged by a small piece of metal and he became totally blind. His employers were held to have broken their duty of care to him.

The employers knew that the consequences of an injury to his good eye would be very serious. They should have taken greater care because of this and provided him with goggles, even though, at that time, it was not thought necessary to provide goggles for other workers. Also, the cost and effort of providing goggles was very small compared with the consequences of the risk.

What is the size of the risk?

Where a risk is small, the defendants will not have to take as great a precaution. This is shown in *Bolton v Stone* (1951).

Key case

Bolton v Stone (1951)

A cricket ball hit a lady passer-by in the street outside a cricket ground. The evidence was that there was a 17-foot-high fence around the ground and the wicket was a long way from this fence. There was also evidence that cricket balls had only been hit out of the ground six times in the 30 years before the accident.

Because of the number of times balls had been hit out of the ground, it was found the cricket club had done everything it needed to do in view of the low risk and it had not breached its duty of care.

The principle that applies here is that the higher the risk of injury, the greater the precautions that need to be taken to prevent injury. As in this case, the lower the risk, the fewer precautions that need to be taken.

On the other hand, if there is a higher risk of injury then the standard of care is higher. This was shown by the case of *Haley v London Electricity Board* (1965).

Key case

Haley v London Electricity Board (1965)

The electricity board dug a trench for its cables and, following its standard practice, it only put out warning signs; it did not put any barriers around the trench. The claimant was blind and was injured when he fell into the trench. As it was known that that particular road was used by a number of blind people, greater precautions should have been taken, and the defendant had breached its duty of care.

Have all appropriate precautions been taken?

The courts will consider the balance of the risk involved against the cost and effort of taking adequate precautions to eliminate the risk. The case to illustrate this is *Latimer v AEC Ltd* (1953).

Key case

Latimer v AEC Ltd (1953)

A factory became flooded and, as the floor was very slippery with a mixture of the water and oil, the workers were evacuated. Sawdust was spread over the floor of the most-used areas to minimise the risk of slipping and the workers were required to go back in. Despite the spreading of sawdust, one worker slipped and was injured.

The court held that there was no breach of the duty of care. The factory owners had taken reasonable steps to reduce the risk of injury. There was no need to incur expense to eliminate every possible risk.

It is quite likely that if this situation occurred today, higher standards of health and safety would mean that the factory owners would have to do more than merely spread sawdust before allowing their workers back.

Also, if the risk had been much more serious, for example if there was a risk of an explosion, then there would have been a higher standard of care on the owners. It would have been reasonable to expect them to close the factory until the problem had been dealt with.

Were the risks known about at the time of the accident?

If the risk of harm is not known, there can be no breach. This is illustrated by the case of *Roe v Minister of Health* (1954).

Key case

Roe v Minister of Health (1954)

Anaesthetic was kept in glass tubes which were sterilised by cleaning solution after each use. At the time it was not known that invisible cracks could occur in the glass of the tubes which caused the anaesthetic to become contaminated by the cleaning solution. The claimant was paralysed by some contaminated anaesthetic.

As the risk of contamination was not known at the time, the court decided there was no breach and the claimant could not claim compensation.

Is there a public benefit to taking the risk?

If there is an emergency then greater risks can be taken and a lower standard of care can be accepted. This is consistent with the third part of establishing a duty of care (fair, just and reasonable). Also the courts take a realistic view of dealing with emergencies. They accept in hindsight the situation could have been dealt with differently but accept that speedy action was taken without the benefit of hindsight. This can be illustrated by the case of *Watt v Hertfordshire County Council* (1954).

Key case

Watt v Hertfordshire County Council (1954)

The claimant was a fire-fighter. There was a road accident a short distance from the fire station and the fire service was called to release a woman trapped underneath a lorry. A jack was needed to release the injured woman but the normal vehicle for carrying the jack was not available. A flatbed truck was found but there was no way of securing the jack. The claimant was injured when the jack slipped and fell on him on the way to the accident.

The court decided that the fire service had not breached its duty of care to the claimant because of the emergency situation and the fact that the utility of saving a life outweighed the need to take precautions.

Another more recent example is *Day v High Performance Sports* (2003).

Key case

Day v High Performance Sports (2003)

The claimant was an experienced climber but fell from an indoor climbing wall and suffered serious injuries. She had to be rescued by the duty manager from a height of 9 metres (30 feet) when she became 'frozen' in her position. The way the manager rescued her was inappropriate, causing her fall.

The court decided the manager and the centre had not breached their duty of care to the claimant in view of the emergency situation.

Person or risk factor	Case	Judgment
Professionals/experts	*Bolam v Friern Barnet Hospital Management* (1957)	Professionals judged according to standards in profession
Learners	*Nettleship v Weston* (1971)	Learners judged at the standard of the competent, more experienced person
Children and young persons	*Mullin v Richards* (1998)	Judged at standard of the defendant's age at the time of the accident
Vulnerable victim	*Paris v Stepney Borough Council* (1951)	Has claimant any special characteristics to be taken account of?
Size of risk	*Bolton v Stone* (1951)	Greater care to be taken if higher chance of injury
Cost of precautions	*Latimer v AEC* (1954)	Risk involved is balanced against the cost and effort of taking precautions
Knowledge of danger	*Roe v Minister of Health* (1954)	If risk not known at the time of accident, can be no breach
	Haley v LEB (1965)	If high risk of injury the standard of care is higher
Public benefit (utility)	*Watt v Hertfordshire* (1954)	Greater risks can be taken in emergency situations
	Day v High Performance Sports (2003)	Duty of care not breached in view of emergency

Figure 23.3 Cases for breach of duty

Activity

Assume that a duty of care is owed in each of the following situations. Has the duty been broken?

1 Harry is texting on his phone while driving his car at speed. He loses control and the car mounts the pavement, hitting Jamie who suffers a broken leg.
2 Katie, a childminder, is looking after Leo, a child aged six. She takes him to a park and while he plays she reads a magazine. She does not notice Leo leave the play area which is close to a busy road. Leo runs out into the road and is knocked down by a motorbike.
3 Peter fell off his bicycle and suffered a fractured skull. He needed an operation to remove a blood clot in his brain. During the operation the surgeon used an innovative procedure that had not been fully approved. Unfortunately, due to complications during the operation, Peter was paralysed.
4 Mavis, an 80-year-old partially sighted woman, was shopping in her local supermarket. She was injured when she slipped and fell on some yoghurt which had been spilt on the floor. She could not see the warning sign which had been placed by the spillage.

Extension activity

How do you think each of the cases referred to in the section on breach would be decided if they were brought to court now?

Tip

For breach of duty, start with the reasonable person test and then deal with any relevant risk factors. When discussing breach, you do not have to deal with the *Caparo* three-stage test first.

23.4 Damage

The third part of any negligence claim is for the claimant to prove that the damage suffered was caused by the breach of duty and that the loss or damage is not too remote. This is referred to as damage, and should be distinguished from damages which is the payment of compensation.

There are two parts to damage: causation and remoteness of damage. Causation is the idea that the breach of duty has caused the injury or damage being claimed. This is called factual causation. Causation in law decides if the injury or damage suffered was reasonably foreseeable. Both elements have to be proved for a negligence claim to succeed.

> ## Key term 🔑
>
> **Damage** – the legal test of a loss to the claimant from a breach of duty.
>
> **Damages** – compensation payable to the claimant who proves that the defendant is negligent.

23.4.1 Factual causation and the 'but for' test

Factual **causation** is the starting point – if factual causation cannot be proved there is no need to consider legal causation.

Factual causation is decided by the 'but for' test – but for the defendant's act or omission the injury or damage would not have occurred. This is illustrated by the case of *Barnett v Chelsea and Kensington Hospital Management Committee* (1969).

> ### Key case
>
> #### *Barnett v Chelsea and Kensington Hospital Management Committee* (1969)
>
> Three night watchmen went to a hospital A & E department complaining of sickness after drinking tea made by a fourth man. A nurse telephoned the duty doctor, who did not come to examine the men but, instead, recommended that they go home and see their own doctors. One of the men went home and died a few hours later from poisoning by arsenic. His widow sued the hospital claiming that the doctor was negligent in not examining her husband and had caused his death. She was able to prove that the doctor owed a duty of care to her husband and that by not examining him, the doctor had broken that duty of care. However, the evidence showed that by the time the husband had called at the hospital it was already too late to save his life. The arsenic was already in his system in such a quantity that he would have died whatever was done. This meant that his death was not caused by the doctor's breach of duty of care and so the claim failed.

> ## Key term 🔑
>
> **Causation** – a link between the defendant's act or omission and the injury, loss or damage caused to the claimant.

23.4.2 Legal causation

Intervening events

In the same way as in criminal law, an intervening event can break the chain of causation. For example, you fall down a badly repaired step at college, hurt your leg and are taken by car to hospital. On the way to the hospital the car is involved in an accident and you suffer head injuries. It could be said that 'but for' your fall you would not have been in the car and suffered the head injury. However the real cause of the head injury is the car accident, not the step. The car accident is a *novus actus interveniens* for the leg injury – an intervening act to break the chain of causation. The principle to be applied is whether the injury or damage was a foreseeable consequence of the original negligent act or omission.

> ## Key term 🔑
>
> *Novus actus interveniens* – an intervening act to break the chain of causation. It applies to causation in both negligence and criminal law.

23.4.3 Remoteness of damage

The damage must not be too remote from the negligence of the defendant. The rule comes from an Australian case decided by the Privy Council: *Overseas Tankship (UK) v Morts Dock and Engineering Co. Ltd,* more commonly known as *The Wagon Mound* (1961).

> ### Key case
>
> #### *The Wagon Mound* (1961)
>
> Fuel oil had been negligently spilled from the defendant's ship into water in Sydney harbour, which flowed towards the claimant's wharf where welders were carrying out repairs to another ship. Two days later the oil caught fire because of sparks from the welding. The fire spread to the claimant's wharf and burnt it down.
>
> It was decided that, although damage done to the wharf by oil being spilled was reasonably foreseeable, fire damage was not reasonably foreseeable. This type of damage was too remote from the original negligent act of spilling the oil.

The test for **remoteness of damage** that comes from this case is that the injury or damage must be reasonably foreseeable.

> ## Key term 🔑
>
> **Remoteness of damage** – the defendant is liable for the injury or damage that is reasonably foreseeable.

A large tanker in dry dock port of Gdansk

Type of injury to be foreseeable

The defendant will also be liable if the type of injury was **reasonably foreseeable**, even though the precise way in which it happened was not. This is illustrated by the cases of *Hughes v Lord Advocate* (1963) and *Bradford v Robinson Rentals* (1967).

Key term

Reasonably foreseeable – damage or injury, which a reasonable person should predict or expect from his actions.

Key case

Hughes v Lord Advocate (1963)

Post Office workmen left a manhole unattended, covered only with a tent and with paraffin lamps by the hole. The claimant, an eight-year-old boy, and a friend climbed into the hole. As they climbed out the boys knocked one of the paraffin lamps into the hole. This caused an explosion which badly burnt the claimant. The defendants denied liability, claiming that the injuries were too remote.

The court decided that the boy was able to claim for his injuries as it was foreseeable that a child might explore the site, break a lamp and be burnt. The type of injury he suffered was foreseeable, even though the explosion itself was not foreseeable.

Key case

Bradford v Robinson Rentals (1967)

The claimant was required by his employer to take an old van from Exeter to Bedford, collect a new van and drive it back to Exeter. It was an extremely cold winter and neither van had a heater. As the windscreen kept freezing over he had to drive the whole return journey with the window open. The claimant suffered frostbite and was unable to work.

The court decided that the employers were liable for his injuries, even though the injury he suffered was very unusual. Some injury from the cold was reasonably foreseeable.

An example of when the type of injury was not reasonably foreseeable is the case of *Doughty v Turner Asbestos* (1964).

Key case

Doughty v Turner Asbestos (1964)

The claimant was injured when an asbestos lid was knocked into a vat of molten metal. Shortly after, a chemical reaction caused an explosion of the metal which burnt the claimant. Scientific knowledge at the time could not have predicted the explosion and so the burn injuries were not reasonably foreseeable. It could be foreseen that knocking something into the molten metal might cause a splash but the claimant's injury was caused by something different.

Take your victim as you find him

This rule means that the defendant must take his victim as he finds him. If the type of injury or damage is reasonably foreseeable, but it is much more serious because the claimant had a pre-existing condition, then the defendant is liable for all the subsequent consequences. In negligence this is known as 'the eggshell skull' rule. A similar rule operates in criminal law where it is known as the 'thin skull' rule.

The operation of this rule is illustrated in the case of *Smith v Leech Brain and Co.* (1962).

Tip

'Take your victim as you find him' applies in both negligence and criminal law. In negligence it is known as 'the eggshell skull' rule.

Principle	Case	Judgment
Factual causation	*Barnett v Chelsea and Kensington Hospital Management Committee* (1969)	'But for' test – but for defendant's act or omission the injury would not have happened
Remoteness of damage	*The Wagon Mound* (1961)	Injury or damage can be claimed if reasonably foreseeable
Foreseeability	*Hughes v Lord Advocate* (1963)	Consequence foreseeable even if exact cause of injury not foreseeable
	Bradford v Robinson Rentals (1967)	Consequence foreseeable, even if more severe
	Doughty v Turner Asbestos (1964)	Consequence not known so injury not foreseeable
Eggshell skull/ take your victim as you find him	*Smith v Leech Brain and Co.* (1962)	Defendant liable for all consequences of negligence

Figure 23.4 Causation and remoteness of damage

Negligence has to be proved before the special rules of claims of psychiatric injury and negligent misstatement. These torts are covered in Book 2.

Activity

1 Because of his fault, Tariq's van and Rhona's car were involved in an accident which resulted in Rhona suffering injuries which have affected her mobility. She is no longer able to work as a cycle courier or play sport. Consider whether Tariq is liable for all of Rhona's injuries.

2 Polish Limited had developed a new floor polish that they were testing. Jade, a secretary of the company, did not know about the test and slipped and fell on the highly polished surface of the test area and fell down the stairs breaking her leg. She was admitted to hospital where she developed a rare medical condition that was missed by Dr Hari, an inexperienced junior doctor. As a result her leg had to be amputated. Consider whether Polish Limited would be liable for the injury caused to Jade.

3 William was sorting out some files which were on a high shelf next to the open window in his office. As he could not reach the files easily he used a pole to push them to the end of the shelf and then tried to catch them as they fell. William failed to catch a heavy file which fell out of the window onto Robyn who was sitting outside in her car. The car's sunroof shattered and Robyn suffered a broken collarbone. Because of the injury she was unable to work as a freelance hairdresser and had to cancel a planned skiing holiday. Consider whether William would be liable for all the injuries and damage suffered by Robyn.

Figure 23.5 What must be proved for negligence

23.5 *Res ipsa loquitur*

As has already been said, the burden of proving the negligence is on the claimant, on the balance of probabilities. In some situations it is difficult for the claimant to know exactly what happened, even though it seems obvious that the defendant must have been negligent. An example of this is where, after an operation in hospital, a patient is found to have a swab left inside him. The patient does not know exactly how the duty of care was breached as he would have been unconscious throughout the operation. He only knows that after the operation there is a swab inside him.

Key term

Res ipsa loquitur – the thing speaks for itself. The burden of proof shifts from the claimant to the defendant.

In such a situation the rule of *res ipsa loquitur* can be used. This means 'the thing speaks for itself'. The claimant has to show:

- the defendant was in control of the situation which caused the injury
- the accident would not have happened unless someone was negligent and
- there is no other explanation for the injury.

If the claimant can show these three points, then the burden of proof moves to the defendant who has to prove that he was not negligent.

An example of a case in which this was used is *Scott v London and St Katherine Docks* (1865).

Key case

Scott v London and St Katherine Docks (1865)

The claimant was hit and injured by six heavy bags of sugar which fell from the defendant's warehouse. The claimant did not know what had happened to make the bags fall. He could only show that he was injured by the falling bags.

The elements of *res ipsa loquitur* were present:

- The sacks fell from the warehouse which was under the defendant's control.
- Heavy sacks do not fall unless someone was negligent.
- There was no other explanation for the sacks to fall.

The court decided that the defendants were liable as they were unable to prove that they had not been negligent.

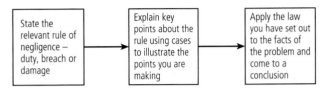

| State the relevant rule of negligence – duty, breach or damage | Explain key points about the rule using cases to illustrate the points you are making | Apply the law you have set out to the facts of the problem and come to a conclusion |

Figure 23.6 Content of an application answer

23.6 Evaluation of liability in negligence

23.6.1 The fault-based system

The main issue with the tort of negligence is that the claimant has to prove the fault of the defendant in order to be awarded compensation. Fault means the legal blameworthiness for causing the injuries or damage to the victim. This need to prove fault can result in problems of:

- cost
- delay
- the need to use lawyers and
- confrontation between the parties.

Cost

The proving of fault by the claimant/victim may be difficult or costly. Evidence will be required to show exactly how the injuries occurred and that they were caused by the defendant. This may be evidence of eye witnesses but it could also be of experts who will need to be paid. For example, if a road accident occurred to which there were no witnesses, or no reliable witnesses, the evidence of police or independent accident investigators would have to be obtained. The unsubstantiated evidence of the claimant driver would not be sufficient.

In addition, medical evidence may be required to show the extent of the injuries and the effect on the victim in the future. If property is lost or damaged, valuations will have to be obtained.

Having to cover all these costs to prove fault may act as a deterrent to a potential claimant to bring an action.

Delay

In many cases the person who caused the accident, or his employer, will be covered by insurance. In some cases insurance cover is compulsory, such as driving motor vehicles. In the event of an accident, where injury or damage is caused, a report will be passed by the driver to his insurance company, which is likely to take over the conduct of the case.

One benefit of the requirement of insurance cover is that the victim can be reassured that he will receive compensation, if he can prove the fault of the defendant and therefore his case.

On the other hand, insurance companies receive many claims against their insured parties so they become suspicious about dealing with claims. They will investigate thoroughly any potential claim to make sure that they only pay out in genuine cases. This need to investigate will often lead to delay in dealing with the case. If the evidence is complicated or extensive, it may be months or years before an insurance company is in a position to deal with a claim. This delay can place a strain, both emotionally and financially, on a claimant and eventually he may decide not to continue the claim.

Further, if it is necessary to take a case to court, this can lead to further delay in order to obtain all the evidence in a form that can be presented to the court. There is a three-year time limit from the date of the accident to issue a personal injury claim (six years in the case of damage to property). Except for fast-track cases in the County Court, there is no time limit when the case (including any appeal) has to be completed.

Need for lawyers

In a personal injury claim the injured claimant may need to employ a lawyer to help him with his claim. In the first place he may need the assistance of a lawyer in order to obtain enough evidence to convince the defendant or his insurance company that the claimant has a claim. A lawyer will in the first place try to negotiate a settlement in order to avoid a court action. However, a defendant or his insurance company will need convincing that the claimant has a case and could prove the defendant was at fault. So the claimant's lawyer will have to gather evidence to achieve a settlement.

If the defendant or his insurance company will not settle, it is more likely that a lawyer will be needed to take a case to court. Court documents are prepared for lawyers (a judge) by lawyers in order to clearly and concisely show their case. Lawyers will need to take witness statements and put them in a form that will be convincing in court.

All this procedure and the obtaining of evidence will be carried out by lawyers, but this does add to the cost and delay involved.

On the positive side, if a claimant engages a lawyer then the costs may be covered by a 'no win no fee' arrangement. This type of arrangement is only available from solicitors. It will mean that the lawyer will take the financial risk and cover the cost of the case, including paying for obtaining expert evidence until settlement or final conclusion in court.

In order to offer this arrangement the lawyer will require the claimant either to have a 'before the event' insurance policy in place, or to take out an 'after the event' insurance policy. A 'before the event' policy could be a house or car insurance policy where the claimant has already paid the premium. An 'after the event' policy is one where an insurance company will be approached to cover the costs of a claim. The premium will have to be paid by the claimant before the case can proceed, meaning more expense for the claimant.

However, a lawyer will only offer a 'no win no fee' arrangement if it is considered that the claimant has a good chance of succeeding. The lawyer will need to be satisfied that there is at least a 75 per cent chance of success. If the lawyer does not consider the case to be successful, the claimant will not be able to pursue his case. This may be even if the claimant is injured or his property has been damaged.

Confrontation

This need to prove fault, and the likely combative approaches of lawyers and insurance companies, could well lead to confrontation between the parties and their representatives. This may mean that a negotiated settlement is less likely. If the case has to then go to court, more confrontation is likely and entrenched positions will be taken. This approach can lead to more delay and greater cost.

Judicial law making

Tort law has been developed mainly from judicial precedent. Is this the right approach or should the law be developed by Parliament? On the one hand judges are unelected and, it is said, lack technical competence to deal with many issues of civil liability. Also, they are often neither informed or experienced enough to make the economic and social judgments which questions of policy in the field of torts so often involve. Many of the most important judicial decisions in the field of torts have involved issues of policy of which *Donoghue v Stevenson 1932* is the prime example as the decision produced a considerable extension of product liability.

On the other hand it can be said that the development of precedent in tort has come from centuries of judicial experience in dealing with a range of cases. The fact that judges have the right, and sometimes the duty, to develop rules of law means that their self-restraint is important as a judge should know when to leave policy-based developments in the law to Parliament.

The idea that Parliament will step in to make law is often little more than a pious hope, given the enormous pressure on legislative time and the limited political importance given to many, purely legal, issues. Also, when Parliament does intervene the consequences are by no means clear or well thought out as seen by the Compensation Act 2006.

Establishing the duty of care

The third part of establishing a duty of care allows the court to decide that, even though the harm is foreseeable and the parties are sufficiently close, whether it is fair, just and reasonable to do so. This *Caparo* test is used where there is a novel issue. The courts have used an incremental approach, rather than taking bold steps, to decide whether a duty of care is owed in a novel situation. The courts can be reluctant to find it fair, just and reasonable where the defendant is a public authority which may result in injustice and unfairness. As was shown in the decision in *Hill v Chief Constable of West Yorkshire*, imposing a duty of care on the police, when they did not know the victim, could lead to defensive policing. This was said to lead to resources being diverted away from reducing and investigating crime. This approach to excluding liability has been criticised, notably by the European Court of Human Rights, so the extent to which English courts will continue to follow this approach is in doubt.

Another more recent example was *ABC v St George's Healthcare NHS Trust and others* (2015) where the claimant was not told by doctors of the existence of Huntingdon's disease in her family when she was pregnant. Doctors knew the disease affected her parents but due to her father's refusal to give consent to disclosure she was not told. If

she had known she would not have continued with her pregnancy. She sued the hospital claiming that they owed her a duty of care due to their knowledge of the family history. The judge decided that this was not a case where a duty of care was owed. The claimant could not show any situation where a duty of care existed which was comparable, or close, to her case. It was also said that this was not an incremental development from a well-established duty. It was a radical departure to impose liability in these circumstances. And the judge was not prepared to take a 'giant step' to impose a duty as opposed to the proper development of the law of negligence by incremental steps.

Policy

Particularly in the higher courts, judges have been prepared to make policy decisions which go against established precedent. For example in *White v Jones* (1995), the House of Lords held by a majority that a disappointed beneficiary under a negligently drafted, and therefore ineffective, will was owed a duty of care and could sue the negligent solicitor. This result was inconsistent with established principles relating to the scope of a defendant's duty of care. Lord Goff stated what the court was doing was 'to fashion a remedy to fill a lacuna (gap) in the law and so prevent the injustice which would otherwise occur on the facts of cases such as the present'. This means that the court can and will, where it considers that policy or justice requires a departure from an established principle, depart from the principle. While this approach may be beneficial for the claimant in the case it provides confusion for future cases and injustice for those whose cases were decided on the 'old' principle. Judges owe it to lawyers and the public to provide clarity in the law. Certainty of outcome is important for anyone about to embark on an enterprise, and for anyone involved in a dispute. Clarity and predictability are vitally important ingredients of the rule of law. But if judges are developing policy principles this can confuse and mislead.

Changing the law

Judges in the appeal courts will sometimes make a new principle because they recognise that what was a well-established principle is wrong. For instance, in the *Bolam* case 1957 it was decided that 'a doctor's omission to warn a patient of inherent risks of proposed treatment constituted a breach of the duty of care that was normally to be determined by the application of the test ... whether the omission was accepted as proper by a responsible body of medical opinion'. That test was generally applied in medical negligence cases for over half a century. However in *Montgomery v Lanarkshire Health Board* (2015) this approach was said by the Supreme Court to be 'unsatisfactory'. They stated that the normal proper approach is now that a 'doctor is therefore under a duty to take reasonable care to ensure that the patient is aware of any material risks involved in any recommended treatment, and of any reasonable alternative or variant treatments'. In other words, a principle which judged doctors' professional competence was significantly changed. The change in approach could be attributable to the recognition of different professional and social standards. This could be said again to be a change of policy rather than using well-established and clear principles. Again this may provide justice in the particular case but confusion and lack of clarity in the general law.

23.6.2 Ideas for reform

One possible reform to the current system of compensating accident victims is a state-run benefit scheme which pays out compensation, either in lump sums or by regular payments, to all victims of accidents without the need to prove how or why the accident happened. This could be funded through general taxation or by a levy on motorists or employers.

The benefits of this scheme are as follows:

- There would be no need for insurance companies to be involved or to delay claims. Also, there would be no need for companies to make profits (paid for from premiums of their insured) or to pay the salaries of their employees. However there would be some expenses required to administer the scheme.
- There would be no need to pay lawyer's costs for either claimants or defendants. The scheme would therefore be cheaper, lead to quicker pay-outs and less confrontational.
- Perhaps the greatest benefit is that compensation would be paid to all those who were injured – not just those who can prove the fault of another.

Some countries already have this type of scheme in place. For example, Canada has had a state-run compensation scheme in place for many years. It covers accidents at work. Canadian employers are required to pay a contribution, based on the dangers in their workplace, to fund a compensation scheme which pays out to employees injured at work, without them having to prove that anyone was at fault.

Another possible reform is to follow New Zealand where they have gone further. There is in place a complete no fault accident compensation scheme which covers injuries suffered in all sorts of areas, not just the work place or on the roads. A claimant has no right to sue the person who caused the injury, except in exceptional cases. It is administered by the Accident Compensation Commission which raises levies from employers and self-employed persons, from general taxation, from government on behalf of non-earners and from sales of petrol and vehicle licences. A range of benefits are paid out to victims including the cost of medical treatment, payments in lieu of wages and, if appropriate, for alterations to property.

A version of this scheme was recommended by the Pearson Commission for the UK. It considered the issue of compensation for personal injury and reported in 1975. It recommended a no fault compensation scheme paid by a levy on the sale of petrol. However the scheme was not accepted by the Conservative Party and shelved completely when the Conservatives came into power in 1979. It has not been considered again since.

A rather different reform is to require every adult to have compulsory liability insurance which would pay out in the event of an accident. This scheme is used in the USA. There is no suggestion that this approach will be adopted in the UK.

An easier reform to consider dealing with issues of confrontation between the parties is to make greater use of out-of-court dispute resolving methods. Mediation is already used in family cases and there are suggestions that it could be used for personal injury claims. Online Dispute Resolution is a method of using modern technology to simplify and speed up the claims process, without the parties having to attend court. Another reform could be to speed up the court process by using online courts. There is already in existence an online court procedure to deal with debt claims and this could be extended to deal with personal injury claims up to a certain value.

The Compensation Act 2006 introduced steps to try to stop claims being brought into court and instead be settled by ADR. It provided that if the responsible individual offered an apology to the injured person this could end a claim. It also imposed greater regulation on claims management companies to attempt to reduce the compensation culture. In their 2012 Memorandum to the Justice Select Committee, The Ministry of Justice was unable to say whether the first two steps had produced any change to the number of claims. In relation to the regulation of claims management companies it concluded there had been some success in reducing cold calling and unauthorised marketing in hospitals and progress had been made in deal with fraudulent motor accident claims. It also concluded that the misleading use of the 'no win no fee' expression had been largely eliminated.

A recent proposal being considered by the government is to raise the lower limit of personal injury claims to a minimum of £5,000. The particular aim of this reform is to reduce the number of whiplash claims, but it could be introduced for all personal accident claims. All claims for lower amounts could then be dealt with either online or by an out-of-court method.

See Chapter 4 for more information on Online Dispute Resolution and online courts.

Look online

Research how Online Dispute Resolution and online courts work. What are their benefits for the parties? Are there any drawbacks?

Some areas of government are starting to realise the benefits of dealing with cases out of court in a less confrontational way. For example, in October 2016 the Health Secretary declared that he wanted to end the blame culture present in the NHS when things go wrong. He announced a consultation on a 'rapid resolution and redress' scheme for victims of clinical negligence during maternity care. He suggested that a voluntary compensation scheme could be introduced as an alternative to the 'costly' legal process.

23.7 Defences to a negligence claim

For the A Level course, you will need to understand the two main defences which can be raised by a defendant in a negligence claim:

- an allegation that the claimant has partly caused or contributed to his injuries and/or
- an allegation that the claimant consented or agreed to accept a risk of harm.

A defendant can allege either or both of these defences.

23.7.1 Contributory negligence

The Law Reform (Contributory Negligence) Act 1945 provides that any damages awarded to the claimant can be reduced according to the extent or level to which the claimant had contributed to his own harm. This means that both the defendant and the claimant are each partly to blame for the injury suffered by the claimant. The amount of blame will be decided by the judge. The judgment will firstly set the full amount of the damages as if there was no contributory negligence. The judge will then decide the percentage that the claimant is responsible for and then reduce the full amount by this percentage. It has to be appreciated that this is a partial defence and it will only result in a reduction in the amount of damages.

Key case

Sayers v Harlow Urban District Council (1958)

A woman was trapped in a public toilet when the door lock became jammed. After unsuccessfully calling for help, she tried to escape the cubicle by climbing through the gap between the door and the ceiling. She stood with one foot on the toilet seat and the other on the toilet roll holder. The holder gave way and she was injured. The court decided that the local council was liable for its negligent maintenance but the damages were reduced by 25 per cent because of the way she tried to escape.

It is possible for there to be a 100 per cent reduction in damages, as demonstrated in *Jayes v IMI (Kynoch) Ltd* (1985).

Key case

Jayes v IMI (Kynoch) Ltd (1985)

The claimant lost a finger at work while cleaning a machine with the guard off. The employers were liable for breach of health and safety rules for their failure to ensure that the guard was in place. However, the claimant was found to be 100 per cent contributorily negligent as he admitted his fault in taking the guard off.

The defence is commonly used in claims for injuries or damage suffered in road traffic accidents. Damages can be reduced where a motorcyclist fails to wear a crash helmet, or a driver or passenger in a vehicle is not wearing a seat belt.

O'Connell v Jackson (1972)

Damages were reduced by 15 per cent when the rider of a moped was injured and suffered greater injuries because he was not wearing a crash helmet.

Froom v Butcher (1976)

The driver of a car suffered greater injuries than would have been the case if wearing a seat belt. His damages were reduced by 20 per cent.

Stinton v Stinton (1993)

The damages were reduced by one-third for accepting a lift from a drunk driver.

The claimant knew the driver was over the limit. If the passenger does not know this, or it would not have been obvious to a reasonable person, the court may decide that an injured claimant was not contributorily negligent.

23.7.2 Consent (volenti non fit injuria)

For the A Level course, you will need to understand consent or *volenti* is a full defence when the claimant voluntarily accepts a risk of harm. Simply translated, it means that no injury is done to one who consents to the risk. If it successful, the claimant will receive no damages.

To succeed, the defendant has to show:

1   knowledge of the precise risk involved
2   exercise of free choice by the claimant
3   a voluntary acceptance of the risk.

One restriction on the use of the defence is s 149 of the Road Traffic Act 1988, which provides that the defence cannot be used for road traffic accidents. This is because of third party insurance.

The defence will not apply merely because the claimant knows of the existence of the risk; he must have a full understanding of the nature of the actual risk.

Key case

Stermer v Lawson (1977)

Consent was argued when the claimant had borrowed the defendant's motorbike. The defence failed because the claimant had not been properly shown how to use the motorbike and did not therefore appreciate the risks.

The defence will not succeed where the claimant has no choice but to accept the risk. An assumption of risk must be freely taken and the claimant must voluntarily undertake the risk of harm.

Key case

Smith v Baker (1891)

A worker was injured when a crane moved rocks over his head and some of them fell on him. The defence of consent failed. The workman had already done all that he could in complaining about the risks involved in the work taking place above his head. He had no choice but to continue work and did not give his consent to the danger.

Where a person has a duty to act and is then injured because of the defendant's negligence, *volenti* will not be available as a defence. The duty means that the claimant had no choice but to act. This is particularly relevant in rescue cases.

Key case

Haynes v Harwood (1935)

When the defendant failed to adequately tether his horse, the policeman who was injured trying to restrain the animal was not acting voluntarily. He was acting under a duty to protect the public. The defence of *volenti* could not be used against him.

Ogwo v Taylor (1987)

The defendant had set fire to his house when attempting to burn off paint. The claimant was a fireman who attended the blaze. He and a colleague had to access the roof space to deal with the fire, but, despite wearing breathing apparatus and protective clothing, he suffered burns from the intense heat. The defendant's argument that the claimant consented to the injuries was dismissed.

In the House of Lords, Lord Bridge pointed out:

> The duty of professional firemen is to use their best endeavours to extinguish fires and it is obvious that, even making full use of all their skills, training and specialist equipment, they will sometimes be exposed to unavoidable risks of injury, whether the fire is described as 'ordinary' or 'exceptional'. If they are not to be met by the doctrine of *volenti*, which would be utterly repugnant to our contemporary notions of justice, I can see no reason whatever why they should be held at a disadvantage as compared to the layman entitled to invoke the principle of the so-called 'rescue' cases.

The defence of *volenti* is likely to be relevant and important in medical negligence claims.

Key case

Sidaway v Governors of the Bethlem Royal and Maudsley Hospitals (1985)

The claimant suffered pain in the neck, shoulder and arms. Her surgeon obtained her consent for an operation but failed to explain that in less than 1 per cent of these operations paraplegia could be caused. Unfortunately she developed paraplegia as a result of the operation and she argued that she did not consent to this.

The House of Lords decided that consent in medical cases does not require a detailed explanation of remote side effects. As a result, there was no liability when the doctor had warned of the likelihood of the risk but not all the possible consequences.

If the claimant acts against the employer's orders or against statutory rules and is injured, the defence of *volenti* is likely to succeed.

Key case

ICI Ltd v Shatwell (1965)

The claimant and his brother were quarry workers. The claimant, following his brother's instructions, ignored his employer's instructions on the handling of detonators, and was injured when one exploded. He claimed in negligence and breach of statutory duty against his employer. The court decided that, by ignoring his employer's instructions and the statutory rules and by following his brother's unauthorised comments, he had assumed the risk of injury and the defence of *volenti* succeeded.

Before the defence can be applied successfully, it must be shown that the defendant did in fact commit a tort.

Key case

Wooldridge v Sumner (1963)

The claimant attended a horse show as a professional photographer. A rider who was riding too fast lost control of the horse, which then injured the claimant. The Court of Appeal confirmed that the rider owed spectators, including the claimant, a duty of care. However, they considered the rider had been guilty of an error of judgment in his riding of the horse but had not been negligent. There was no breach of duty, so *volenti* was not an issue.

The test of *volenti* is subjective rather than objective. It will not help the defendant to argue that the claimant ought to have been aware of the risk. The defence only applies where the claimant does actually know of the risk.

Tip

Remember that the defendant can argue both *volenti* and contributory negligence. If *volenti* fails, the defendant may still successfully claim contributory negligence and at least reduce the amount of damages that are payable.

Activity

Suggest which defence may be argued in each of the following situations. Is the defence likely to succeed?

1 Jed is sued for breaking Raj's collarbone during a kick-boxing contest.
2 Manjit accepts a lift from Steven, who already has a car full of passengers. Manjit sits in the open boot of the car, and is injured when another car hits Steven's car from behind when it fails to stop as the traffic lights change.
3 Mohammed is injured when he went for a flight in a light aeroplane with Pierre, who he knows does not have a pilot's licence.
4 Helga fell off her horse and was badly injured during a show-jumping contest when the horse pulled up at a large fence.

Principle	Case	Outcome
Contributory negligence is a part defence	*Sayers v Harlow UDC* (1957)	Damages reduced if claimant has partly caused her own injuries
Amount of contributory negligence decided by the judge	*O'Connell v Jackson* (1972)	No crash helmet – 15%
	Froom v Butcher (1976)	No seat belt – 20%
	Stinton v Stinton (1993)	Taking a lift from drunk driver 33⅓%
To consent, claimant must have a full understanding of the nature of the actual risk	*Stermer v Lawson* (1977)	No consent as the claimant had not been properly shown how to use the motorbike, and did not appreciate the risks
To consent, claimant must have had a free choice in accepting risk of injury	*Smith v Baker* (1891)	The claimant had complained about the risks and had no choice but to continue work
No consent if claimant is acting under a public duty	*Haynes v Harwood* (1935) *Ogwo v Taylor* (1987)	Police or fireman did not consent to injury when doing their public duty
Consent in medical treatment	*Sidaway v Governors of the Bethlem Royal and Maudsley Hospitals* (1985)	Not every possible risk has to be explained before valid consent can be given
Consent only available if following orders	*ICI Ltd v Shatwell* (1965)	A claimant ignoring his employer's instructions and not following statutory rules cannot use the defence of *volenti*
Consent only available if a tort has been committed	*Wooldridge v Sumner* (1963)	Although the rider owed a duty of care there was no negligence and *volenti* could not be argued

Figure 23.7 Cases on defences in tort

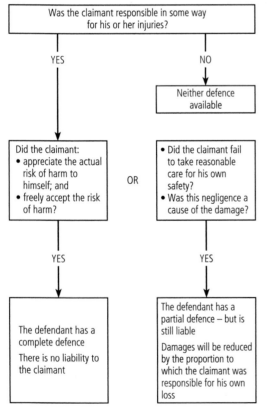

Figure 23.8 The availability of defences of *volenti non fit injuria* and contributory negligence and their contrasting effects

Summary

- Negligence can be caused by an act or omission which causes loss, injury or damage to another person.
- Negligence requires proof of a duty of care owed by the defendant to the claimant, a breach of that duty and loss or damage.
- A duty of care is a legal relationship between the claimant and the defendant.
- To establish a duty of care there is a three-stage test:
  - Is there proximity of a relationship?
  - Is the loss or damage reasonably foreseeable?
  - Is there a public policy reason not to owe a duty of care?
- Breach of duty means falling below the standard of the reasonable person.
- To judge whether a reasonable person would have acted in the same way as the defendant, matters such as the age of the defendant and whether he is a professional or experienced can be considered.
- Risk factors may be used to judge if there has been a breach of duty.
- The loss or damage must have been caused by the breach of duty.
- Causation is proved by the 'but for' test and if there has been an intervening event.
- The loss or damage must be reasonably foreseeable and not too remote. The type of injury has to be reasonably foreseeable, not the exact injury suffered. The defendant must take his victim as he finds him.
- *Res ipsa loquitur* (the thing speaks for itself) transfers the burden of proof from the claimant to the defendant.
- The most common remedy for negligence is the payment of damages.
- Obtaining compensation for injury, loss or damage caused by negligence requires proof of fault.
- The requirement to prove fault leads to greater cost for claimants, delay, the need for lawyers and greater confrontation.
- Alternative no fault compensation schemes exist in other countries.
- Other no fault schemes could be introduced as an alternative to court and fault-based resolution.
- Contributory negligence is a partial defence where the claimant is partly responsible for causing his injuries. If successful, the judge will reduce the amount of damages by the percentage of responsibility.
- Consent of the claimant is a complete defence. The consent has to be freely given and with the claimant's full knowledge of its effect.

Chapter 24

Occupiers' Liability

> After reading this chapter you should be able to:
> - Understand occupier's liability in respect of lawful visitors (Occupiers' Liability Act 1957)
> - Understand occupier's liability in respect of trespassers (Occupiers' Liability Act 1984)
> - Understand the application of relevant defences
> - Critically evaluate liability in occupiers' liability

24.1 What is occupiers' liability?

Occupiers' liability is a branch of negligence. While negligence is a common law tort created by judges, occupiers' liability has been created by statute. There are two separate actions:

- The Occupiers' Liability Act 1957 provides that an occupier of premises owes a duty of care to lawful visitors, and if that duty is breached and the visitor is injured he is entitled to receive compensation.
- The Occupiers' Liability Act 1984 sets out a similar rule for trespassers who are injured on the occupier's property.

The main remedy for a successful claim of occupiers' liability is compensation for the injuries or damage suffered.

24.2 Occupiers and premises

24.2.1 Occupiers

Potential defendants are the same under either Act – they will be occupiers of premises who may be, but do not have to be, the owner or tenant of the premises. There is in fact no statutory definition of 'occupier'.

The test for deciding whether a person is the occupier is found in case law.

Key case

Wheat v E. Lacon & Co. Ltd (1966)

In this case the manager of a pub was given the right to rent out rooms in his private quarters even though he had no ownership rights in the premises. A paying guest fell on an unlit staircase and died. The House of Lords decided that both the manager and his employers could be occupiers under the Act so there could be more than one occupier of the premises.

Harris v Birkenhead Corporation (1976)

A four-year-old child was injured in an empty house. The local council had served a compulsory purchase order on the house but they had not boarded it up or made it secure as they had not yet taken possession. It was decided they were in occupation as they were effectively in control of the premises.

In practice, a decision of who is in control of premises may be influenced by whose insurance policy covers the premises and is able to meet the claim. However, sometimes, the courts will find that no one is in control of the premises leaving the injured visitor with no claim.

Key case

Bailey v Armes (1999)

The defendants lived in a flat above a supermarket. They allowed their son to play on the flat roof above their flat but forbade him to take anyone else there. The supermarket knew nothing of the use of the roof. The boy took his friend onto the roof and he was injured when he fell from the roof. The Court of Appeal decided that neither the supermarket nor the defendants were occupiers as they did not have sufficient control over the roof.

24.2.2 Premises

There is no full statutory definition of premises except in s 1(3)(a) of the 1957 Act where there is reference to a person having occupation or control of any 'fixed or moveable structure, including any vessel, vehicle and aircraft'.

Besides the obvious such as houses, offices, buildings and land, premises has also been held to include:

● a ship in dry dock
● a vehicle
● a lift and even
● a ladder.

24.3 Lawful visitors and the Occupiers' Liability Act 1957

24.3.1 Adult visitors

Lawful adult **visitors** include:

● invitees – persons who have been invited to enter and who have express permission to be there
● licensees – persons who may have express or implied permission to be on the land for a particular period
● those with contractual permission – for example, a person who has bought an entry ticket for an event
● those given a statutory right of entry such as meter readers and a police constable exercising a warrant.

Key term

Visitor – in legal terms, lawful adult visitors are invitees, licensees, those with contractual permission and those with a statutory right of entry.

Activity

Consider which of the following potential claimants would be able to class themselves as lawful visitors for the purposes of the Occupiers Liability Act 1957, and why.

1 Trevor is a milkman delivering milk to Archie's door.
2 Kurt is a milkman who goes round the side of Archie's house, after delivering milk, and picks some flowers.
3 Craig is making door-to-door deliveries of flyers for a pizza restaurant.
4 Gordon has a season ticket for a Premier League football team and arrives at the ground on Sunday afternoon for a match.
5 Hannah regularly crosses farmer Giles' field, using a well-known public path.
6 Aaron, an electrician, arrives at Janet's house to fit some wall lights as agreed.
7 Ali is a police officer who has called at Brian's house to make routine enquiries about a recent break-in.

An adult visitor is owed a common duty of care. According to s 2(2) this means to:

> take such care as in all the circumstances … is reasonable to see that the visitor will be reasonably safe in using the premises for the purpose for which he is invited … to be there

The key point to be made is that the occupier does not have to make the visitor completely safe in the premises – only to do what is reasonable.

Key case

Laverton v Kiapasha Takeaway Supreme (2002)

The defendants owned a small takeaway shop. They had fitted slip resistant tiles and they used a mop and bucket to mop the floor if it had been raining. When the claimant went into the shop it was very busy and it had been raining. She slipped and broke her ankle. The Court of Appeal decided that the shop owners had taken reasonable care to ensure their customers were safe. They were not liable as they did not have to make the shop completely safe.

The court commented in this case that the safety of visitors to premises was not guaranteed and in this case that was not feasible as the shop had taken precautions and customers can be reasonably safe if they take reasonable care for their own safety.

Key case

Dean and Chapter of Rochester Cathedral v Debell (2016)

The claimant was injured when he tripped and fell over a small lump of concrete protruding about two inches from the base of a traffic bollard in the precincts of Rochester Cathedral. The bollard had previously been slightly damaged by a car.

The Court of Appeal decided that:

1 Tripping, slipping and falling are everyday occurrences. No occupier of premises like the cathedral could possibly ensure that the roads or the precincts around a building were maintained in a pristine state. Even if they were, accidents would still happen. The obligation on the occupier is to make the land reasonably safe for visitors, not to guarantee their safety. In order to impose liability, there must be something over and above the risk of injury from the minor blemishes and defects which are habitually found on any road or pathway.

2 The risk is reasonably foreseeable only where there is a real source of danger which a reasonable person would recognise as obliging the occupier to take remedial action. A visitor is reasonably safe even if there may be visible minor defects on the road which carry a foreseeable risk of causing an accident and injury.

The judgments in both these cases emphasised that the common duty of care imposes a duty on the occupier to keep the visitor *reasonably safe,* not necessarily to maintain completely safe premises. The state of premises must pose a *real source of danger* before foreseeability of the risk of damage can be found.

It is possible that if the case had been decided in favour of the visitor, it could have opened the floodgates to a tide of claims against occupiers and created a very high level of responsibility for the safety of visitors.

Rochester Cathedral

A visitor may be a lawful visitor for the purposes of the 1957 Act, but if he exceeds his permission and enters an unauthorised area he may become a trespasser and lose the protection of the 1957 Act. In this case the rules in the 1984 Act may apply.

The duty, however, does not extend to liability for pure accidents and a duty in respect of a specific risk cannot last indefinitely where there could be other causes of the damage.

Key case

Cole v Davis-Gilbert, The Royal British Legion and others (2007)

The claimant was injured when she trapped her foot in a hole in a village green where a maypole had been erected in the past. She argued that the owner of the village green had a duty to ensure that visitors were safe; that the British Legion had failed to properly fill the hole after a village fete; and that the local council had failed to adequately maintain the green. She won at first instance but failed in the Court of Appeal.

The court held that since her injury took place nearly two years after the maypole had been in place, the duty on the British Legion could not last that long. Although there was no specific evidence to support this view, the hole must have been opened again by a stranger, and the incident was a pure accident.

The village green featured in the above case

24.3.2 Occupiers' liability to children

The occupier will owe children coming onto the premises the common duty of care, but there is an additional special duty owed to child visitors. Under s 2(3) of the Occupiers' Liability Act 1957 the occupier 'must be prepared for children to be less careful than adults [and as a result] the premises must be reasonably safe for a child of that age'.

So, for children, the standard of care is measured subjectively, according to the age of the child. The reasoning is logical: what may not pose a threat to an adult may be very dangerous to a child. The occupier should guard against any kind of 'allurement' or attraction which places a child visitor at risk of harm.

Key case

Glasgow Corporation v Taylor (1922)

A seven-year-old child ate poisonous berries from a shrub in a public park and died. The shrub on which the berries grew was not fenced off in any way. The council were liable to the child's parents. They were aware of the danger and the berries amounted to an allurement to young children.

Where very young children are injured, the courts are reluctant to find the occupier liable as the child should be under the supervision of a parent or other adult.

Key case

Phipps v Rochester Corporation (1955)

A five-year-old child was playing on open ground owned by the council with his seven-year-old sister. He fell down a trench and was injured. The court decided that the council was not liable as the occupier is entitled to expect that parents should not allow their young children to go to places which are potentially unsafe.

A difficulty here is that there is no age limit set as to when this rule applies.

If an allurement exists, there will be no liability on the occupier if the damage or injury suffered is not foreseeable.

Key case

Jolley v London Borough of Sutton (2000)

The council had failed to move an abandoned boat situated on its land for two years. Children regularly played in the boat and it was clearly a potential danger. When two boys aged 14 years jacked the boat up to repair it, the boat fell on one, seriously injuring him. The claim for compensation succeeded in the High Court but failed in the Court of Appeal since it was decided that, while the boat was an obvious allurement, the course of action taken by the boys, and therefore the specific type of injury, was not foreseeable.

In an appeal to the House of Lords this view was reversed. In their view it was foreseeable that children would play on the abandoned boat. It was not necessary for the council to foresee exactly what they would do on it. They considered that children often find ways of putting themselves in danger which needed to be taken into account by an occupier when considering how to keep them safe.

24.3.3 Occupiers' liability to people carrying out a trade or calling

The occupier will owe a tradesman coming onto the premises the common duty of care. However, by s 2(3)(b) of the 1957 Act an occupier can expect that a person in the exercise of his calling will 'appreciate and guard against any special risks ordinarily incident to it so far as the occupier leaves him free to do so'.

The effect of this provision is that an occupier will not be liable where tradesmen fail to guard against risks which they should know about or be expected to know about.

Key case

Roles v Nathan (1963)

Two chimney sweeps died after inhaling carbon monoxide fumes while cleaning the chimney of a coke-fired boiler. The sweeps had been warned of the danger. The occupiers were not liable as they could have expected chimney sweeps to be aware of the particular danger.

This rule, which acts as a defence to an occupier, only applies where the tradesman visitor is injured by something related to his trade or calling. If the tradesman is injured by something different the occupier will still owe the common duty of care.

24.3.4 Occupiers' liability for the torts of independent contractors

As before, a lawful visitor will be owed the common duty of care while on the occupier's land. However if the visitor is injured by a workman's negligent work, the occupier may have a defence and be able to pass the claim to the workman. This is set out in s 2(4) of the 1957 Act, which provides that:

> Where damage is caused to a visitor by a danger due to the faulty execution of any work of construction, maintenance or repair

by an independent contractor employed by the occupier, the occupier is not to be treated without more as answerable for the danger if in all the circumstances he had acted reasonably in entrusting the work to the independent contractor and had taken such steps (if any) as he reasonably ought in order to satisfy himself that the contractor was competent and that the work had been properly done. "

From this, three requirements will apply and all have to be satisfied:

1   It must be reasonable for the occupier to have given the work to the independent contractor. The more complicated and specialist the work, the more likely it will be for the occupier to have given the work to a specialist.

Key case

Haseldine v Daw & Son Ltd (1941)

The claimant was killed when a lift plunged to the bottom of a shaft. The occupier was not liable for negligent repair or maintenance of the lift as this work is a highly specialist activity and it was reasonable to give the work to a specialist firm.

2   The contractor hired must be competent to carry out the task. Presumably the occupier should take up references or recommendations or check with a trade association, if any, to satisfy this requirement. The occupier should check that the contractor is properly insured. If the contractor fails to carry appropriate insurance cover this could be a fair indication that the contractor is not competent.

Key case

Bottomley v Todmorden Cricket Club (2003)

The cricket club hired a stunt team to carry out a 'firework display'. The team chose to use ordinary gunpowder, petrol and propane gas rather than more traditional fireworks. They also then used the claimant, who was an unpaid amateur with no experience of pyrotechnics, for the stunt. The claimant was burnt and broke an arm when the stunt went wrong. The stunt team had no insurance. The Court of Appeal decided that the club was liable as it had failed to exercise reasonable care to choose safe and competent contractors.

3   The occupier must check the work has been properly done. The more complicated and technical the work, and the less expert the occupier, the more likely that this condition will require the occupier to employ an expert such as an architect or surveyor.

Key case

Woodward v The Mayor of Hastings (1945)

A child was injured on school steps that were left icy after snow had been cleared off them. The occupiers were liable as they had failed to take reasonable steps to check that the work had been done properly and the danger should have been obvious to them.

As stated above, if all these conditions are satisfied then the occupier will have a defence to a claim and the injured claimant will have to claim directly against the contractor. It will be hoped that a reputable contractor will be covered by his own insurance, and so the claimant can still recover compensation.

24.3.5 Defences to a claim by a lawful visitor

A Level students will need to understand the following defences to a claim by a lawful visitor:
- contributory negligence
- consent (*volenti*).

Contributory negligence

This partial defence has been set out in Chapter 23. It applies to occupiers' liability in the same way as for negligence. The court will rule that the claimant is partly responsible for the injuries he has suffered. If it is successfully argued the amount of compensation will be reduced by such amount as the court thinks appropriate.

See Chapter 23 at section 23.7.1 for more information on contributory negligence.

Consent

This complete defence has been set out in Chapter 23. It applies to occupiers' liability in the same way as for negligence. If it is successfully argued, the defendant will not be liable to pay damages to the claimant.

See Chapter 23 at section 23.7.2 for more information on the defence of consent – *volenti*.

Warning notices

This is a complete defence to a claim of occupiers' liability. The warning can be oral or written. By s 2(4) of the 1957 Act a warning is ineffective unless 'in all the circumstances it was enough to enable the visitor to be reasonably safe'.

What amounts to a sufficient warning will be a question of fact in each case and will be decided by the judge on the evidence. If the premises have extreme danger or they are unusual, the occupier may be required to erect barriers or additional warnings to keep visitors safe.

Key case

Rae v Marrs (UK) Ltd (1990)

This case involved a deep pit inside a dark shed so a warning, by itself, was insufficient as it could not be seen.

However if the danger is obvious and the visitor is able to appreciate it, no additional warning is necessary.

Key case

Staples v West Dorset District Council (1995)

The danger of wet algae on a high wall should have been obvious and no further warning was required.

Exclusion clauses

By s 2(1) of the 1957 Act, an occupier is able 'to restrict, modify or exclude his duty by agreement or otherwise'. This means that the occupier will, in any warning, be able to limit or exclude completely his liability for any injury caused to the visitor. This is the case for residential occupiers, though whether an exclusion clause would work against a child visitor may depend on the child's age and ability to understand the effect of the exclusion.

In addition, s65 Consumer Rights Act 2015 provides that

> A trader cannot by ... a consumer notice exclude or restrict liability for death or personal injury resulting from negligence.

These provisions mean that if there are such clauses in a warning notice, they are ineffective and cannot operate as a defence to an occupier.

Activity

Look at the signs in Figure 24.1. Are either or both of these warning notices valid:
- if seen on a private house?
- if seen on a car park?

Figure 24.1 Warning notices

24.3.6 Remedies

If the occupier is liable for breach of his duty, the remedy to be claimed by the visitor is damages. The court can award damages for personal injury suffered and for any property damaged.

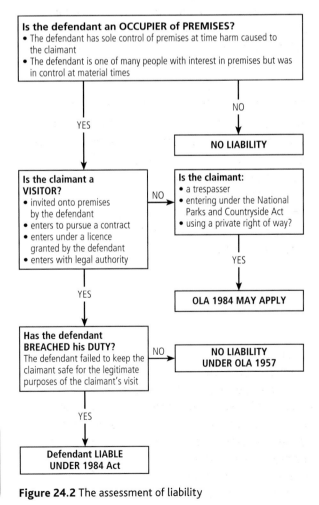

Figure 24.2 The assessment of liability

1. When a visitor comes to your home, how would you explain to a member of your family what the 'common duty of care' means?
2. Discuss why children are owed a different duty of care to adult visitors. Ask a parent or another adult for his views.
3. Do you think that the defence in *Phipps v Rochester Corporation* (1955) would/should apply today?

Case name	Facts	Legal principle
Wheat v Lacon (1966)	Visitor fell down stairs and died	Occupier is the person with control over the premises. There can be more than one occupier with control
Laverton v Kiapasha Takeaway Supreme (2002)	Customer injured in shop	The premises do not have to be completely safe. The occupier has to make the premises reasonably safe for visitors
Glasgow Corporation v Taylor (1922)	Child poisoned by berries growing on bush in park	Occupier has to protect child visitors from allurements
Phipps v Rochester Corporation (1955)	Young child injured when falling into a trench	Occupier can expect parents to supervise very young children
Jolley v Sutton LBC (2000)	Teenager injured when playing on boat on council's land	Occupier is liable for injuries suffered by children that are reasonably foreseeable
Roles v Nathan (1963)	Chimney sweeps killed when working in industrial chimney	Occupier can expect workmen to appreciate and guard against risks that are incidental to their work

Figure 24.3 The assessment of liability under the Occupiers' Liability Act 1957

Occupiers' liability	Case
Occupiers' liability is covered by two Acts: the Occupiers' Liability Act 1957 for lawful 'visitors' and the Occupiers' Liability Act 1984 for trespassers	
An 'occupier' is anybody in actual control of the land	*Wheat v Lacon* (1966)
Premises are widely defined and have included even a ladder	*Wheeler v Copas* (1981)
The duty and the standard of care in the 1957 Act	**Case**
A 'common duty of care' is owed to all lawful visitors	s 2(1)
The duty is to ensure that the visitor is safe for the purposes of the visit	s 2(2)
An occupier must take extra care for children, who are less careful than adults, and not put extra danger or 'allurements' in their path	s 2(3) *Glasgow Corporation v Taylor* (1922)
This applies to any foreseeable danger to the child regardless of what injury is actually caused	*Jolley v London Borough of Sutton* (1998)
Although it is assumed that parents should keep control of young children	*Phipps v Rochester Corporation* (1955)
A person carrying out a trade or calling on the occupier's premises must prepare for the risks associated with the trade	*Roles v Nathan* (1963)
The occupier will not be liable for damage which is the result of work done by independent contractors if: a it is reasonable to entrust the work b a reputable contractor is chosen c the occupier is not obliged to inspect the work	*Haseldine v Daw* (1941) *Woodward v Mayor of Hastings* (1945)
Avoiding the duty	**Case**
It is possible to avoid liability where: a adequate warnings are given b exclusion clauses can be relied on – subject to the Unfair Contract Terms Act 1977 c defences of consent or contributory negligence apply	*Rae v Mars* (1990)

Figure 24.4 Occupiers' liability to lawful visitors

24.4 Liability for trespassers: the Occupiers' Liability Act 1984

24.4.1 The background of the duty

Traditionally, at common law, an occupier owed a **trespasser** no duty at all, other than not to deliberately or recklessly inflict injury. This rule was harshly applied, particularly to child trespassers as in *Addie v Dumbreck* (1929). A four-year-old child was killed when he fell through the unprotected cover of a wheel on colliery land. No compensation could be claimed by the parents as the child was a trespasser.

Key term 🔑

Trespasser – a person who has no permission or authority to be on the occupier's premises or a visitor who has gone beyond their permission to be on the premises.

The House of Lords, making use of the 1966 Practice Statement, were able to change the law and introduced a duty of 'common humanity' owed by occupiers.

Key case

British Rail Board v Herrington (1972)

A six-year-old boy was badly burned when he trespassed onto an electrified railway line through vandalised fencing. British Rail was aware of gaps in the fencing and that children played in the area. The House of Lords established a duty of 'common humanity' which was a limited duty owed when the occupier knew of the danger and of the likelihood of the trespass.

The Law Commission investigated this area of law in its 1975 report entitled 'Report on Liability for Damage or Injury to Trespassers and Related Questions of Occupiers' Liability'. As a result of the report the 1984 Act was passed by Parliament.

24.4.2 The scope of the duty

By s 1(1)(a) of the 1984 Act a duty applies in respect of people other than lawful visitors (who are covered by the 1957 Act) for 'injury on the premises by reason of any danger due to the state of the premises or things done or omitted to be done on them'.

The 1984 Act provides compensation for personal injuries only. Damage to property is not covered, reflecting the view that trespassers are deserving of less protection than lawful visitors.

The occupier will only owe a duty under s 1(3) if:

a he is aware of the danger or has reasonable grounds to believe it exists;

b he knows or has reasonable grounds to believe that the other is in the vicinity of the danger concerned or that he may come into the vicinity of the danger (in either case, whether the other has lawful authority for being in the vicinity or not); and

c the risk is one against which, in all the circumstances of the case, he may be expected to offer the other some protection.

The duty owed under s 1(4) is to 'take such care as is reasonable in the circumstances to see that he [the trespasser] is not injured by reason of the danger'.

The danger referred to in these sections is the object or part of land on which the trespasser is injured. The standard of care is objective. What is required of the occupier depends on the circumstances of each case. The greater the degree of risk, the more precautions the occupier will have to take. Factors to be taken into account include the nature of the premises, the degree of danger, the practicality of taking precautions and the age of the trespasser.

These two provisions appear to have given trespassers a right to claim compensation when they have been injured while trespassing. However there have been a number of court decisions which appear to have restricted when a duty is owed to trespassers and, if a duty is owed, whether the occupier is liable.

Cases involving adult trespassers

When considering claims under the 1984 Act the courts have introduced the concept of obvious dangers, especially for adult trespassers. The occupier will not be liable if the trespasser is injured by an obvious danger.

Key case

Ratcliff v McConnell (1999)

A 19-year-old student climbed the fence of his open air college swimming pool at night and dived into the pool hitting his head on the bottom. He was seriously injured. The Court of Appeal decided that the occupier was not required to warn adult trespassers of the risk of injury arising from obvious dangers. In this case there was no hidden danger as it is well known that swimming pools vary in depth and diving without checking the depth is dangerous.

The time of day and the time of year when the accident happened will be relevant for whether the occupier owes a duty of care.

Key case

Donoghue v Folkestone Properties (2003)

The claimant was injured when he was trespassing on a slipway in a harbour and dived into the sea, hitting a grid pile used for mooring boats. The grid pile would have been visible at low tide. The injury happened in the middle of winter, at around midnight. The court held that the occupier did not owe the claimant a duty of care under the 1984 Act as they would not expect that a trespasser might be present or jump into the harbour at that time of day or year.

An occupier does not have to spend lots of money in making premises safe from obvious dangers.

Key case

Tomlinson v Congleton Borough Council (2003)

The council owned a park including a lake. Warning signs were posted prohibiting swimming and diving because the water was dangerous, but the council knew that these were generally ignored. The council decided to make the lake inaccessible to the public but delayed starting on this work because of lack of funds. The claimant, aged 18, went swimming in the lake, struck his head on the sandy bottom and suffered paralysis as a result of a severe spinal injury.

In the Court of Appeal his claim under the 1984 Act succeeded. The court felt that the seriousness of the risk of injury, the frequency with which people were exposed to the risk, and the fact that the lake acted as an allurement all meant that the scheme to make the lake inaccessible should have been completed with greater urgency. The House of Lords, however, accepted the council's appeal for three reasons:

1 In order to be liable under the 1984 Act there had to be a danger due to the state of the premises or things done or omitted to be done. In this case the danger was not due to the state of the premises but was due to the claimant diving into the water.

2 It was not the sort of risk that a defendant should have to guard against but one that the trespasser chose to run. So trespassers had to take some responsibility for their actions.

3 The council would not have breached its duty even if the claimant was a lawful visitor as it was not reasonable for it to spend a lot of money preventing visitors being injured by an obvious danger.

Warning sign at a lake in Weston-super-Mare

The occupier will not be liable if he had no reason to suspect the presence of a trespasser.

Key case

Higgs v Foster (2004)

A police officer investigating a crime entered the occupier's premises to carry out surveillance. He fell into an uncovered inspection pit suffering severe injuries, causing him to retire from the police force. The police officer was judged to be a trespasser on the premises. Although the occupiers knew the pit was a potential danger, they could not have anticipated his presence on the premises or in the vicinity, so they were not liable.

The occupier will not be liable if he was not aware of the danger or had no reason to suspect the danger existed.

Key case

Rhind v Astbury Water Park (2004)

The occupier did not know of a submerged fibreglass container resting on the bottom of a lake on its premises. The claimant ignored a notice stating 'Private Property. Strictly no Swimming' and jumped into the lake and was injured by objects below the surface of the water. Section 1(3)(c) requires the occupier to owe a duty if 'the risk is one against which, in all the circumstances of the case, he may be expected to offer the other some protection'. As the occupier did not know of the dangerous objects no duty was owed.

Cases involving child trespassers

The same statutory rules apply to child visitors as for adult visitors. The approach of judges towards claims by child trespassers is the same as for adults as can be seen by the following cases.

Key cases

Keown v Coventry Healthcare NHS Trust (2006)

An 11-year-old boy climbed a fire escape on the exterior of a hospital to show off to his friends and fell. The Court of Appeal held that, since the child appreciated the danger, it was not the state of the premises that was at fault, but what the boy was doing on it. There was no danger due to the state of the premises (the fire escape) and the hospital was not liable.

Baldaccino v West Wittering (2008)

On a summer's day a 14-year-old boy climbed a navigational beacon sited off a beach as the tide was ebbing. He dived off the beacon suffering neck injuries and tetraplegia. He was a lawful visitor to the beach but a trespasser to the beacon. It was decided that there was no duty on the part of the occupiers to warn against obvious dangers and the injuries did not result from the state of the premises. His claim failed.

24.4.3 Defences to a claim by a trespasser

A Level students need to know possible defences to claims by a trespasser:

- Contributory negligence – this defence can apply to reduce the damages payable to the claimant by such proportion as the judge thinks appropriate to reflect the claimant's responsibility for his injuries.
- Consent (also known as *volenti*) – this defence appears to be allowed by s 1(6) of the 1984 Act if the trespasser appreciates the nature and degree of the risk, more than just its existence.
- A warning can be an effective defence, especially to an adult visitor, if it warns of the danger in clear terms. Whether a warning will be sufficient for a child trespasser will depend on the age and understanding of the child.

Key case

Westwood v Post Office (1973)

The claimant was an employee of the Post Office and was injured when he entered, as a trespasser, an unlocked room which had the notice 'Only the authorised attendant is permitted to enter'. The door should have been locked. The defendants were not liable as the notice was a sufficient warning to an adult.

Warning sign on a construction site

Activity

See the warning notice on the left. Do you think this would be an effective warning notice to act as a defence against a trespasser?

The common law	Case/Statute
The law was originally not to deliberately cause harm	*Addie v Dumbreck* (1929)
Because of the harshness of this rule as it applied to children, a duty of common humanity to trespassers was introduced	*BR Board v Herrington* (1972)
Scope of the duty under the Occupiers' Liability Act 1984	Case/Statute
Duty is owed if: (a) [occupier] is aware of the danger or has reasonable grounds to believe it exists; (b) he knows or has reasonable grounds to believe that the other is in the vicinity of the danger concerned or that he may come into the vicinity of the danger (in either case, whether the other has lawful authority for being in the vicinity or not); (c) the risk is one against which, in all the circumstances of the case, he may be expected to offer the other some protection. The duty owed is to take such care as is reasonable in the circumstances to see that the trespasser is not injured by reason of the danger	s 1(3) s 1(4)
Occupier does not have to warn adult trespassers of risk of injury against obvious dangers	*Ratcliff v McConnell* (1999)
Occupier does not have to warn adult trespasser against obvious risks if trespasser enters at unforeseeable time of day or year	*Donoghue v Folkestone Properties* (2003)
Occupier does not have to spend lots of money in making premises safe from obvious dangers	*Tomlinson v Congleton Borough Council* (2003)
Occupier will not owe a duty to trespasser he does not expect to enter premises	*Higgs v Foster* (2004)
Occupier does not owe a duty for danger he is unaware of	*Rhind v Astbury Water Park* (2004)

Figure 24.5 Occupiers' liability to trespassers

24.4.4 Remedies

If the occupier is liable for breach of his duty, the remedy to be claimed by the trespasser is damages for personal injury only.

Activity

Discuss these points:

- How does the duty of 'common humanity' differ from the duty imposed by the 1984 Act?
- The approach taken by the courts towards claims by trespassers.

Tip

You must be able to recognise whether the visitor is a lawful visitor or a trespasser and apply the correct rules to consider a possible claim. Remember that a lawful visitor can become a trespasser if he exceeds his permission or enters a prohibited area.

24.5 Evaluating occupiers' liability

As a claim under this tort is based on negligence, most of the comments made in Chapter 24 apply equally to claims made in occupiers' liability. These are issues of cost, delay, need to use lawyers and confrontation.

See Chapter 23, section 23.6 for evaluation of the tort of negligence.

However, there are some specific comments that can be made about this topic.

24.5.1 Comparing the 1957 and 1984 Acts

The duty imposed on occupiers has been imposed by statute, whereas in negligence it is a common law duty. The statutes dealing with occupiers' duty were introduced at different times. The 1957 Act deals with liability to lawful visitors and the 1984 Act deals with liability to trespassers. There appear to be some differences between the two Acts and the duties imposed on occupiers.

1 The 1957 Act allows for claims for personal injury and for damage to property whereas the 1984 Act allows claims for personal injury only. This can be justified because, as Lord Hoffman said in *Tomlinson v Congleton DC* (2003):

> Parliament recognised that it would often be unduly burdensome to require landowners to take steps to protect the safety of people who came upon their land without invitation or permission. They should not ordinarily be able to force duties upon unwilling hosts.

As a result of this the compensation that can be awarded to trespassers is more limited.

2 The two Acts set two different approaches to the imposition of a duty. The 1957 Act requires an occupier to do everything that is reasonable to ensure the visitor will be reasonably safe – an objective test. This follows the standard approach to tort claims, where the defendant's actions are judged objectively. However, for a duty to exist under the 1984 Act, the occupier has to be aware of the danger and has to know, or have reasonable grounds to believe, that the trespasser is in the vicinity of the danger. This is a subjective test so that if the occupier does not have the required knowledge of the existence of the trespasser, he will not owe a duty. This subjective test is inconsistent with most torts, including negligence, which judges the defendant's actions objectively.

This means that each claim under the 1984 Act will depend on its own facts. For example, in *Donoghue v Folkestone Properties* (2003) the occupier had no knowledge of the presence or likely presence of the claimant and so owed no duty. This was because the accident happened at night in winter. A different result might have been achieved if the accident occurred during summer months. It seems unusual that liability depends on when the accident happened – the time of day or year.

3 For claims under both Acts it is 'necessary to identify the particular danger before one can see to what (if anything) the occupier's duty is', *per* LJ McCombe in *Edwards v Sutton LBC* (2016). The 1984 Act requires the occupier to have actual knowledge of the danger, whereas actual knowledge of the danger does not seem to be required by the 1957 Act. So, for a claim under the 1984 Act, if the occupier has no knowledge of the danger then he will not owe a duty. This was

the case in *Rhind v Astby* (2004) where the occupier had no knowledge of a submerged container on which the claimant trespasser was injured and was not liable. Also, under the 1984 Act, there does not seem to be an obligation on the occupier to check for any danger on the premises.

4 Except for child visitors, the 1957 Act does not require the court to consider whether the premises are safe for the particular visitor who is injured. However, under the 1984 Act a duty is owed if the occupier may reasonably be expected to offer the trespasser (who is injured) some protection. Whether the occupier may be judged to have acted reasonably may depend on the injured trespasser – what is reasonable for that particular person?

5 The 1984 Act gives trespassers the right to make claims, but judges seem to find reasons not to allow claims by trespassers. This reflects public opinion which does not support a person who should not be on premises from profiting from his actions. An example of this approach is where judges have introduced the concept of 'obvious dangers' into claims by trespassers.

6 No duty is owed by the occupier when the trespasser is injured due to an obvious danger. For example in *Ratcliff v McConnell* (1999) the claimant, as an adult, was not owed a duty due to the obvious danger in the swimming pool – he should have appreciated an obvious risk. Even though he was severely injured he was not able to claim compensation.

This concept of obvious dangers has also recently been introduced into claims under the 1957 Act. In *Edwards v Sutton LBC* (2016) when the claimant was badly injured when he fell off a bridge over a stream in a public park, McCombe LJ said:

> The approach to the bridge was clear and unobstructed. The width of the bridge and the height of the parapets were also obvious to the eye. Any user of the bridge would appreciate the need to take care and any user limiting the width of the bridge's track, by pushing a bicycle to his side, would see the need to take extra care. It is not necessary to give a warning against obvious dangers ... Not every accident (even if it has serious consequences) has to have been the fault of another ... [and] an occupier is not an insurer against injuries sustained on his premises ... occupiers of land are not under a duty to protect, or even to warn, against obvious dangers.

24.5.2 The current approach of the courts

It seems that the courts are trying to send a message that, despite publicity suggesting there is a compensation culture operating in the UK, visitors have to take personal responsibility for their safety and that sometimes pure accidents do happen. This was shown in *Laverton v Kiapasha Takeaway Supreme* (2002) and has been reinforced in the *Dean and Chapter of Rochester Cathedral v Debell* (2016). If these claims had been decided in favour of the claimants then it is likely that many other similar claims would follow and the cost of insurance would rise for all.

An illustration of public opinion not supporting trespassers benefiting from their actions is the case of *Revill v Newbery* (1996). Eighty-two-year-old Ted Newbery injured a trespasser who burgled his allotment shed. There was a media-led outcry when Mark Revill was granted legal aid to claim for personal injuries against Newbery. At the time he was in prison serving a sentence for burgling Newbery's property. His claim for civil damages was based on the 1984 Act and trespass to the person. Revill was subsequently awarded damages in the civil court but subject to a two-thirds deduction for his contributory negligence. The damages payable by Newbery were covered by public donations and the judge received a considerable amount of hate mail for finding Newbery liable.

Lord Phillips in *Donoghue v Folkestone Properties* (2003) summed up the judicial view of claims under the 1984 Act:

> There are, however, circumstances in which it may be foreseeable that a trespasser will appreciate that a dangerous feature of premises poses a risk of injury, but will nevertheless deliberately court the danger and risk the injury. It seems to me that, at least where the individual is an adult, it will be rare that those circumstances will be such that the occupier can reasonably be expected to offer some protection to the trespasser against the risk.

Generally, it is fair that an occupier is responsible for the reasonable safety of his lawful visitors.

This does not mean making premises completely safe but reasonably safe and judges will support this approach. However in some cases, such as *Edwards v Sutton LBC* (2016), they are also prepared to decide that lawful visitors should take some personal responsibility for their safety. Public opinion would support the view that an occupier does not deliberately injure a trespasser. However, there would be less support for allowing claims by trespassers. The approach of judges to make it difficult for trespassers to claim when injured by obvious dangers would have popular support. However it has to be borne in mind that if the visitor, whether lawful or trespasser, is severely injured and is unsuccessful in claiming, the burden of caring for him for the rest of his life is likely to be passed to the state.

24.5.3 Possible reforms

- To introduce no fault liability so that the injured visitor, whether lawful or trespasser, should be able to claim compensation. If the burden of paying for this liability is placed on the occupier, then compulsory insurance would have to be required for every occupier. This would not be popular and is unlikely to be introduced.

- A possible reform would be to have a state-run compensation scheme paid for by a levy, possibly on all property insurance policies. Currently the government is following an approach of imposing a general tax on all insurance policies and is not proposing to allocate any monies raised to set up such a compensation scheme.

- The main reform in this area seems to be the approach of personal responsibility imposed by judges. Initially, despite the rights given by the 1984 Act, judges imposed extra hurdles on claims by trespassers with the result that now very few such claims succeed. This approach appears to now apply to claims by lawful visitors as shown in the recent cases of *Edwards v Sutton LBC* (2016) and *Dean and Chapter of Rochester Cathedral v Debell* (2016).

Summary

- Lawful visitors are owed the common duty of care by an occupier of property.
- The common duty of care requires the occupier to keep the visitor reasonably safe.
- Greater care has to be taken by an occupier towards child visitors, especially if an allurement is present.
- Occupiers can expect very young children to be supervised by their parents but will be liable for injury that is reasonably foreseeable.
- Occupiers can expect workmen visitors to be aware of risks associated with their work.
- The occupier will not be liable for the work of independent contractors if:
  - it is reasonable to give the work to another
  - a reputable contractor is used and
  - if possible, the occupier checks the work has been properly done.
- Lawful visitors who are injured can claim damages for personal injury and damage to property.

- The occupier owes a duty to trespassers to ensure the trespasser is not injured by reason of the danger.
- The duty is owed when:
  - the occupier is aware of the danger or has reasonable grounds to believe it exists
  - he knows or believes the trespasser is in the vicinity of the danger and
  - the risk is one against which he is expected to offer the trespasser some protection.
- The occupier will not be liable if the trespasser is injured by an obvious risk or the injury occurs at an unusual time of day or year. The occupier is not required to spend considerable amounts of money in protecting the trespasser from obvious dangers.
- Trespassers who are injured can claim damages for personal injury only.

Chapter 25

Remedies

After reading this chapter you should be able to:
- Understand the principle of the award of compensatory damages in tort
- Understand the principle of mitigation of loss
- Understand the principle of awards of an injunction in tort (A Level)

25.1 Compensatory damages

In a tort claim the court can award a successful claimant compensation for the injuries he has suffered or damage to his property. This award is known as damages.

The aim of the award of damages is to place the claimant in the same position as if the tort had not been committed as far as money can do so. This is possible where the claim is for damage to property. However, if the claimant has suffered disabling personal injury, this is not possible.

25.1.1 Pecuniary and non-pecuniary loss

Pecuniary loss is a loss that can be easily calculated in money terms, for example the cost of hiring a car while the claimant's own car is being repaired.

Non-pecuniary loss is loss that is not wholly money-based. This can include:
- pain and suffering as a result of the accident
- loss of amenity or a change in lifestyle, such as not being able to play a sport.

25.1.2 Special and general damages

Special damages

These are amounts which can be calculated specifically up to the date of the trial or settlement. In other words they are the pecuniary loss. This could include the cost of repairing a vehicle and the hire costs of a replacement, replacing damaged clothes or bags. Any loss of earnings while recovering from the accident can also be claimed.

General damages

These are non-pecuniary losses and are looking forwards from the trial or settlement date. They can include:
- an amount for pain and suffering
- loss of amenity
- future loss of earnings and
- future medical expenses including adapting a house or car to be suitable for a severely injured person and paying for specialist care.

These amounts are, to an extent, speculative and evidence will have to be obtained to support the claim. This will include medical evidence of the effect of the accident on the victim and how long the suffering or injuries will take to heal, if at all. For future loss of earnings and future medical expenses there will have to be an annual calculation of the loss and this will be multiplied by the number of years of the loss. For example, five years' loss of earnings at £25,000 each year will lead to a total loss of earnings of £125,000. As stated above, the claimant will be expected to mitigate the loss, so if he can work part time or at a lower wage, he will be expected to do so and the amount of this wage this will be deducted from the award.

25.1.3 Lump sums and structured settlements

When the courts make an award for pain and suffering and loss of amenity, they can only award a lump sum. This also has to be a once only award. The claimant cannot come back to court to say that he has exhausted the damages.

This can be unfair to the claimant whose condition in the future might become worse. Also, where a large award is made for future medical expenses, there is the problem of inflation.

On the other hand an award of a lump sum might be unfair to the defendant if the claimant's condition improves considerably and there is no longer a need to pay for care.

To deal with these situations the Damages Act 1996 allows for structured settlements to be set. It allows parties who settle a claim to agree that all or part of the damages can be paid as periodical payments: that is so much a month or a year. This is arranged by the defendant (or more likely his insurer) who will purchase an annuity through a financial company, who then pay a set amount at regular intervals to the claimant.

The Damages Act also allows parties to agree that the payments may be made for life or for a specific period – for example, ten years – and the amount can be reassessed at intervals to ensure that its value in real terms is maintained. This type of settlement protects the claimant whose condition may become worse. At the same time it can also be fairer to the defendant who will only have to pay while the claimant's condition requires it. The courts have no power to order such structured settlements.

25.2 Mitigation of loss

The claimant is entitled to be compensated for his loss, but he is under a duty to keep the loss to a reasonable level. This is called mitigation of loss.

For example, the claimant cannot claim for private treatment for the injury if there is suitable treatment available under the NHS. On the other hand if treatment is only available privately, the cost of the private treatment can be claimed.

The same principles apply to property damage. If property has been damaged beyond repair, the cost of replacing that property can be claimed. Replacing the item with a more expensive replacement would not be allowed.

25.2.1 Examples of damages awards

The three case examples below show how damages can be awarded.

Activity

Read the three case examples carefully, then answer the following questions about each one:

1 Was this a fair award?
2 What award would you accept if this happened to a member of your family?
3 Can the principle of the award of damages in tort (to put the claimant back in the position he was in before the accident) apply to this case?

Case study 1:

Damage to hair and hair loss

The claimant was a regular client at her hair salon, attending every four weeks to have her hair bleached. Usually the salon used foils to apply bleach to her hair, but during one visit, a stylist recommended that, for the health of her hair, the bleach should be applied directly onto her roots. This was agreed, and the treatment was also carried out three times on subsequent visits to the salon.

After the fourth treatment, the claimant found that her hair broke and snapped when she was washing it. She raised this concern with the salon on her next visit, but was reassured that this was not connected to the treatment, and her hair was bleached in the usual way. However, clumps of her hair broke off during hair washing.

This caused serious distress to the claimant as her hair was much shorter than her preferred length. After different attempts to style her hair and cover the damage (which caused further hair loss), she left the salon and pursued a claim for the damage caused by the mistreatment. Reports from a consultant dermatologist and a clinical psychologist showed that the claimant had suffered from loss of hair over the crown and fringe, and an itchy and dry scalp with some scabbing that tended to weep when scratched. Further, the damage had caused the claimant to experience low moods, poor self-esteem, social avoidance and anxiety. The claimant received £5,750 from the salon in a full and final settlement.

Source: Adapted from www.jmw.co.uk/services-for-you/personal-injury/beauty-injuries/hair-injuries/success-stories/hairdressing-compensation/

Case study 2:

Delay in treatment results in brain damage

A 36-year-old woman suffered injuries caused by a delay in emergency treatment and has been awarded compensatory damages of £5 million in the High Court. The claimant collapsed at home and her partner phoned 999. However, the ambulance would not come within 100 metres of her home without a police escort, as the address was (wrongly) described as 'high risk'.

The delay to treatment lasted 100 minutes. By the time the ambulance and paramedics arrived at her home, the claimant had suffered brain damage caused by deprivation of oxygen and a cardiac arrest.

The claimant had previously worked as a genetic scientist, but now requires constant care in a specialist medical unit as a result of her injuries. She received a £1.4 million lump sum payment and annual payments thereafter.

Source: Adapted from www.worthingtonslaw.co.uk/articles-downloads/2014/june/5-million-damages-awarded-for-paramedic-delays

Case study 3:

Broken leg and loss of flesh in golf buggy accident

The claimant suffered injuries to his leg following an accident in a golf buggy. He was a passenger when the defendant drove the buggy downhill on a cliff-side golf course. The claimant feared that they were in danger of going over the cliff and claimed that he was thrown out of the buggy when the driver lost control of it. He broke his left leg, and lost some flesh when the broken bone stuck out of his leg. As a result, he suffered severe pain and received plastic surgery to repair the skin. However, the defendant denied responsibility for the accident, saying that the claimant jumped from the buggy while it was travelling at no more than walking pace down the hill.

The claimant was unable to work for over a year because of his injuries. He was self-employed, and claimed for loss of earnings as well as compensation for his injuries. Eventually, a settlement was negotiated out of court between the defendant and the claimant, with full and final payment of £27,987.50 made to the claimant.

Source: Adapted from www.jmw.co.uk/services-for-you/personal-injury/success-stories/broken-leg-and-loss-of-flesh/

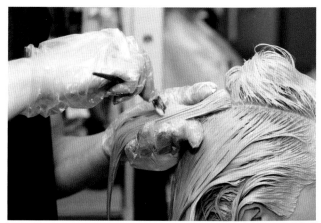

A hairdresser applying colour in a salon

25.3 Injunctions

For A Level, you need to understand the principle of the award of injunctions.

After damages, the most common remedy in tort is an injunction. This is generally an order of the court to stop doing something. If the person on whom the injunction is placed fails to follow the terms of the injunction he will be in contempt of court and can be punished with a fine or imprisonment for a maximum of two years.

Key term

Contempt of court – The failure to follow an order of the civil court. The court can order punishment if the failure is serious or continues for a period of time.

An injunction can be ordered during the case, for example to disclose documents or not to continue an action until a trial has taken place. Most commonly, an injunction can be ordered as a final order, known as a perpetual injunction. This can be ordered, for example, in a nuisance case to ensure a person does not continue to cause a nuisance to neighbours, perhaps by banning an activity outright or within certain hours.

A less common form of injunction could be a mandatory injunction which will order a party to carry out a certain action. This again could be used in a nuisance action; for example, to install sound proofing or an extractor fan to remove offending smells.

Injunctions will often be the main reason for a nuisance case to be brought, as the aim of taking the action is to stop the nuisance continuing.

However, following a ruling of the Supreme Court in *Coventry v Lawrence* (2014) fewer injunctions can be expected to be granted, especially in cases of nuisance. The court criticised the tendency to mechanically apply existing principles and award an injunction. Instead, the Supreme Court endorsed a more flexible approach when awarding a remedy. If the approach suggested by the Supreme Court is adopted in practice, it is likely that fewer injunctions will be granted and that damages will become a more common alternative remedy. This could include cases when the loss or inconvenience suffered is slight and the impact on the wrongdoer is severe.

See Book 2 for more information on the tort of nuisance.

Case study 4:

Injunction granted

A final injunction has been awarded against a Birmingham council tenant (PR) who has been responsible for causing nuisance and annoyance to local residents.

PR was handed a two-year Nuisance and Annoyance Injunction which means that he cannot:

1 use or threaten to use violence, harass or intimidate any person
2 enter his road in Birmingham
3 cause nuisance or annoyance in the road, including but not limited to fighting, shouting, verbal abuse, swearing, arguing or causing criminal damage.

If any of the conditions at 1 and 2 are breached during the next two years, the terms of the injunction allow his immediate arrest and return to the court within 24 hours.

Neighbours complained of his antisocial behaviour, which included verbal abuse to residents and visitors (particularly insulting people of ethnic origin or with a disability), drinking and taking drugs outside of the property and encouraging large groups of youths to congregate there. PR also encouraged retaliation, resulting in street fights and objects being thrown through his windows.

Source: Adapted from http://birminghamnewsroom.com/full-injunction-granted-against-antisocial-neighbour/

Summary

- *Actus reus* is the physical element of a crime and it can include conduct, circumstances or consequences.
- The aim of awarding damages is to put the claimant back in the position he was in before the tort, so far as money can do so.
- The claimant is under a duty to mitigate the loss.
- Special damages can be specifically calculated and cover losses up to the date of the court hearing.
- General damages are awarded for the future and cover loss of future earnings, future medical expenses, loss of amenity and pain and suffering.
- Damages can be paid as a lump sum or by structured settlement over a period of time.
- Injunctions can be awarded in specific types of cases, e.g. nuisance.
- An injunction can be awarded ordering a person to do something or not to do something.

Glossary

Act of Parliament – a law that has passed through all stages in Parliament and becomes part of the law of the land.

Actus reus – this is an act, an omission or a state of affairs that is the prohibited conduct in an offence.

Advocacy – the art of speaking in court on behalf of another; conducting a case in court as the legal representative of another person.

Assault – an act which causes the victim to apprehend the infliction of immediate, unlawful force with either an intention to cause another to fear immediate unlawful personal violence or recklessness as to whether such fear is caused.

Assault occasioning actual bodily harm – an assault which causes V actual bodily harm and D intends or is subjectively reckless as to whether the victim fears unlawful force or is actually subjected to unlawful force.

Battery – the application of unlawful force to another person intending either to apply unlawful physical force to another or recklessness as to whether unlawful force is applied.

Bill – the name for a draft law going through Parliament before it passes all the parliamentary stages to become an Act of Parliament.

Binding precedent – a decision in an earlier case which must be followed in later cases.

Causation – a link between the defendant's act or omission and the injury, loss or damage caused to the claimant.

Cause pressure group – a pressure group that exists to promote a particular cause.

Challenge to the array – a challenge to the whole jury on the basis it has been chosen in an unrepresentative way.

Civil claims – claims made in the civil courts when an individual or a business believes that their rights have been infringed in some way.

Civil law – the law concerned with the relationship between individuals.

Civil law system – this is based on a written code and aims to cover all possibilities with broad principles. Decisions of judges can be considered but are not binding.

Claimant – the legal term for a person who has suffered loss or damage and is bringing a civil claim for compensation.

Codification – bringing together all the law on one topic into one complete code of law.

Common law system – this is largely unwritten and relies on decisions of the judges. All lower courts are bound by decisions of judges in the higher courts.

Consolidation – combining the law from several Acts of Parliament into one Act of Parliament.

Contempt of court – disobeying a court's order; for example, where a juror uses a mobile phone in the court room when he has been told that he is not allowed to.

Corrective justice – the idea that liability rectifies the injustice inflicted by one person on another. This is also a major part of the theory of the law of tort.

Damage – the legal test of a loss to the claimant from a breach of duty.

Damages – the payment of money by way of compensation. The aim of damages in tort is to put the claimant back in the position he was in before the tort, so far as money can do so.

Defendant – the person who has caused the loss or damage.

Delegated legislation – law made by some person or body other than Parliament, but with the authority of Parliament.

Denunciation – expressing society's disapproval of an offender's behaviour.

Deterrence – giving a punishment aimed at putting off the defendant from reoffending because of fear of punishment or preventing other potential offenders from committing similar crimes.

Direct applicability – EU law that automatically becomes part of UK law. There is no need for the UK to pass any act of Parliament to bring it into force in the UK. Treaties are directly applicable.

Direct effect – allows a UK individual to can rely on EU law in UK courts.

Directed acquittal – where a judge decides there is insufficient prosecution evidence to allow the case to continue, the jury is directed to find the defendant not guilty.

Dissenting judgment – a judgment given by a judge who disagrees with the reasoning of the majority of judges in the case.

Distinguishing – a method by which a judge avoids having to follow what would otherwise be a binding precedent.

Doctrine of precedent – following the decisions of previous cases.

Due diligence – where the defendant has done all that was within his power not to commit an offence.

EU Directives – these are issued by the EU and direct all Member States to bring in the same laws throughout all the countries.

EU Regulations – laws issued by the EU which are binding on Member States and automatically apply in each member country.

Golden rule – a rule of statutory interpretation. It is a modification of the literal rule and avoids an interpretation that is absurd.

Green Paper – a consultative document issued by the government putting forward proposals for reform of the law.

Horizontal direct effect – a concept under which individuals can rely on EU Directives to bring a claim against their Member State even though the Directive has not been implemented by that State.

Indictable offence – an offence that has to be tried at the Crown Court.

Injunction – an order of the court to stop doing something, e.g. to stop making noise after 10 p.m. Failure to follow the court order can lead to further sanctions, including possibly imprisonment. An injunction can order a positive action, e.g. to move a muck heap to avoid causing a smell nuisance.

Lay magistrates – these are unpaid, part-time judges who have no legal qualifications.

Legal aid – government help in funding a case.

Liable – the judge's decision that the case against the defendant is proved and that the defendant should pay compensation.

Literal rule – a rule of statutory interpretation that gives the words their plain ordinary or literal meaning.

Mediation – using a neutral person in a dispute to help the parties come to a compromise solution.

Mens rea – this is the mental element (guilty mind) or the fault element in an offence.

Mischief rule – a rule of statutory interpretation that looks back to the gap in the previous law and interprets the Act so as to cover the gap.

Negligence – an act or a failure to act which causes injury or damage to another person or his property.

Negotiation – the process of trying to come to an agreement.

Neighbour principle – the person who is owed a duty of care by the defendant. It is not the person living next door. According to Lord Atkin, it is anyone you ought to have in mind who might potentially be injured by your act or omission.

Non-pecuniary loss – loss that is not wholly money-based. This can include pain and suffering as a result of the accident, loss of amenity or a change in lifestyle, such as not being able to play a sport.

Novus actus interveniens – an intervening act to break the chain of causation. It applies to causation in both negligence and criminal law.

Obiter dicta – this means 'other things said'. So it is all the rest of the judgment apart from the *ratio decidendi*. Judges in future cases do not have to follow it.

Original precedent – a decision on a point of law that has never been decided before.

Pecuniary loss – a loss that can be easily calculated in money terms, for example the cost of hiring a car while the claimant's own car is being repaired.

Persuasive precedent – a decision which does not have to be followed by later cases, but which a judge may decide to follow.

Prosecutor – the legal term for the person or organisation bringing a criminal charge against a defendant.

Purposive approach – an approach to statutory interpretation in which the courts look to see what is the purpose of the law.

Ratio decidendi – this is the reason for the decision. This forms a precedent for future cases.

Reasonable person – this used to be said to be 'the man on the Clapham omnibus'. Now it is considered to be the ordinary person in the street or doing a task.

Reasonably foreseeable – a danger which a reasonable person should predict or expect from his actions.

Reformation – trying to reform the offender's behaviour so that he will not offend in future.

Rehabilitate – trying to alter the offender's behaviour so that he will conform to community norms and not offend in future.

Remedy – the way in which a court will enforce or satisfy a claim when injury or damage has been suffered and proved. In tort law the remedy will usually be damages or occasionally an injunction.

Remoteness of damage – the defendant is liable for the injury or damage that is reasonably foreseeable.

Reparation – where an offender compensates the victim or society for the offending behaviour.

Repeal of an Act of Parliament – this means that the Act ceases to be law. Only Parliament can repeal an Act of Parliament.

Res ipsa loquitur – the thing speaks for itself. The burden of proof shifts from the claimant to the defendant.

Retribution – imposing a punishment because the offender deserves punishment.

Retributive justice – a system of criminal justice based on the punishment of offenders rather than on rehabilitation.

Rights of audience – the right to present a case in court on behalf of another person.

Sectional pressure group – a pressure group that represents the interests of a particular group of people.

Stare decisis – this means 'stand by what has been decided and do not unsettle the established'. It is the foundation of judicial precedent.

Statutory instruments – rules and regulations made by government ministers under the authority of an enabling Act.

Strict liability – a civil action where fault of the defendant does not need to be proved.

Strict liability offences – offences where *mens rea* is not required in respect of at least one aspect of the *actus reus*.

Subjective recklessness – where the defendant knows there is a risk of the consequence happening but takes that risk.

Summary offence – an offence that can only be tried in the Magistrates' Court.

Three-part test – an update of the neighbour principle to show who is owed a duty of care in negligence. All three parts have to be satisfied in order that this test is satisfied.

Tort – a tort is a civil wrong, and tort law compensates a person who has been injured or whose property is damaged. The word 'tort' comes from the French word for 'wrong'.

Trespasser – a person who has no permission or authority to be on the occupier's premises or a visitor who has gone beyond their permission to be on the premises.

Triable-either-way offence – an offence that can be tried in either the Magistrates' Court or the Crown Court.

Tribunals – forums used instead of a court for deciding certain types of disputes. They are less formal than courts.

Ultra vires – this means that it goes beyond the powers that Parliament granted in the enabling Act. Where any delegated legislation is *ultra vires*, then it is not valid law.

Vertical direct effect – an individual can claim against the Member State even when a directive has not been implemented by that state.

Visitor – in legal terms, lawful adult visitors are invitees, licensees, those with contractual permission and those with statutory right of entry.

White Paper – a document issued by the government stating its decisions as to how it is going to reform the law.

Practice questions

Component 1

Section A – The legal system (Chapters 1–11)

Civil courts and other forms of dispute resolution

1 Explain how the track system works in the civil courts.
2 Discuss the main problems that exist in civil cases.

Criminal courts and lay people

1 Describe the aims of sentencing and suggest a suitable sentence that meets each aim.
2 Discuss whether fines, as a sentence, prevent reoffending.

Legal personnel

1 Explain the system of appointment of judges.
2 Discuss why it is important for there to be judicial independence.

Access to justice

1 Explain how conditional fee agreements work.
2 Discuss the advantages and disadvantages of conditional fee agreements.

Section B – Criminal law (Chapters 12–15)

Aimee and Bryonie are hockey players. During a match, Aimee tries to win the ball from her but instead she hits Bryonie's leg causing bruising. Later in the match, Aimee is annoyed when Bryonie scores a goal, and shouts at her, 'I'll get you after the match.' Bryonie retaliates by hitting Aimee on the arm with her stick, breaking the arm.

1 Advise how the law relating to non-fatal offences against the person will apply to Aimee.
2 Advise how the law relating to non-fatal offences against the person will apply to Bryonie.

Josh comes up behind his friend Wesley in the street and playfully punches him in the back. Wesley is thrown off balance and falls against Padma, knocking her to the ground and breaking her wrist. Padma's friend, Nic who did not realise why Wesley had fallen against Padma, shouts at him 'You clumsy idiot! I'll get you for this later.' Wesley is scared.

1 Advise how the law relating to non-fatal offences against the person will apply to Josh.
2 Advise how the law relating to non-fatal offences against the person will apply to Nic.

A Level questions

Dev ran a call centre selling financial products. He wanted to improve his staff's sales performance so he introduced a new training programme with more aggressive techniques. One day Dev listened in while one of the call handlers tried to persuade a potential customer, Clara, to buy a product. After a few minutes Dev grew exasperated, and shouted into the phone: 'We've got your number, and we know where you live, so pay us your money!' Clara was so terrified that she suffered a nervous illness which required psychiatric treatment. After hearing this call Dev decided all his staff needed to be toughened up. One freezing day, he ordered them outside the building, where he had set up a tub of hot water, and told them that they must each strip to their underwear and get in the tub for one minute to demonstrate their commitment to the company. The oldest member of staff, 74-year-old Phil, removed his outer clothes but then refused to get in. Dev made him stand in the cold until he suffered frostbitten toes. Dev then ordered Selena to get in. She stood trembling on the edge of the tub until Dev her from behind. She was scalded all over her body by the hot water.

Advise whether Dev has committed any non-fatal offences against the person

Terry and Peter went to the cinema with Peter's new girlfriend, Nancy. They each bought hot dogs and fizzy drinks. As Peter wanted to be alone with Nancy he asked Terry to sit elsewhere. Terry found a seat a few rows back, but when the film started he crept forward again, until he was sitting directly behind the others. As a joke Terry removed the sausage from his hot dog and pushed it down the neck of Nancy's dress. Nancy screamed which caused one of the ushers, Steve, to come to her aid. Thinking that Peter had assaulted Nancy, Steve dragged Peter from his seat and started punching him in the face, breaking his nose. Seeing the scuffle Terry went to the aid of his friend, flung his arms around Steve's neck and tried to pull him off Peter. However, he applied more pressure than he intended and Steve suffered brain injuries as he was unable to breathe.

Advise whether Terry and Austin have committed any non-fatal offences against the person

Practice questions

Component 2

Section A – Law making (Chapters 16–21)

Parliamentary law making

1 Describe the stages of the law making process in the House of Commons.
2 Discuss the advantages of creating law using Acts of Parliament.

Statutory interpretation

1 Describe the intrinsic aids to statutory interpretation.
2 Discuss the impact of the Human Rights Act 1998 on statutory interpretation.

Judicial precedent

1 Describe the hierarchy of the courts, including the Supreme Court.
2 Discuss whether the exceptions in *Young's* case give the Court of Appeal sufficient freedom to depart from its own past decisions.

European Union Law

1 Describe the role of the Court of Justice of the European Union.
2 Discuss the impact of European Union law on the law in England and Wales.

Section B – The law of tort (Chapters 22–25)

Adrian was using a chainsaw to cut down a tree in his garden next to Sian's house. He was cutting a large branch when he lost control of it and the branch fell on Sian's conservatory, where her partner, Toby, was working on his computer. Toby was trapped in the conservatory. When Toby was freed he was taken to hospital for a check-up. He had very sensitive eyes. The inexperienced doctor did not notice some small splinters embedded in his eyes and which, because of his sensitivity, caused him to go blind.

Advise whether or not Adrian owes Toby a duty of care and whether he has breached the duty of care.

Kevin owned a gym. He had recently had new exercise machines fitted and checked by a specialist firm. Eva, a gym member, was using one of the machines when it broke, throwing her to the floor, causing her to break her leg.

Advise whether or not Kevin owes Eva a duty of care and whether that duty has been breached.

A Level questions

Richard and Jenny were celebrating their wedding anniversary and they went to Ken's Kitchen to celebrate with their young son David. Ken was aware that his restaurant had a mice infestation but he did nothing about it as he did not want to harm its reputation. While they were eating Jenny was bitten by a mouse on her leg and suffered an infection.

Richard saw the mouse and tried to stab it with his knife. He missed but the knife became embedded in some trailing electric wires and he was electrocuted. The restaurant was in the process of being rewired by Westbourne Electrical Co. and it is later found that they have failed to make the wires safe.

David is frightened by these events and runs from the table into the open plan kitchen area. David skidded on the kitchen floor, which was covered in cooking oil, breaking his leg and ruining his clothes. There was a sign by the entrance to the kitchen area which read 'Staff only – no admittance to customers'.

Advise whether or not Jenny, Richard and David have any claim in occupier's liability against Ken.

Lee worked as a scaffolder for Krazy Skaffolding. He asked for a protective hat and for the firm to take action against other scaffolders who play practical jokes on him at work but was told to 'just get on with the job'. One day another scaffolder, as a joke, threw a stone at Lee. It hit him on the head causing him to momentarily lose consciousness and fall off the scaffolding he was working on. He suffered a fractured skull.

He was taken to hospital where a junior doctor treated his injury but failed to order a brain scan. He was discharged and told to rest. A few days later he suffered a brain haemorrhage from which he died. Later tests showed that, if a scan had been taken, his condition could have been diagnosed and successfully treated.

Advise whether or not Lee's partner, Lucy, would be successful in an action for negligence against Krazy Skaffolding or the hospital. (You should ignore vicarious liability.)

Index